The
HOUDINI
CLUB

The
HOUDINI
CLUB

The EPIC JOURNEY *and* DARING ESCAPES
of the FIRST ARMY RANGERS *of* WWII

MIR BAHMANYAR

DIVERSION
BOOKS

Diversion Books
A division of Diversion Publishing Corp.
www.diversionbooks.com
Copyright © 2025 by Mir Bahmanyar

For more information, email info@diversionbooks.com

Hardcover ISBN: 978-1-63576-978-4
e-ISBN: 978-1-63576-970-8

Cover design by Jonathan Sainsbury
Design by Neuwirth & Associates, Inc.

Printed in the United States of America
1 3 5 7 9 10 8 6 4 2

Diversion books are available at special discounts for bulk purchases
in the US by corporations, institutions, and other organizations.

For more information, please contact admin@diversionbooks.com.
The publisher does not have any control over and does not assume any
responsibility for author or third-party websites or their content.

To

those politicians, statesmen and leaders of the world who either actively
brought on this war or passively failed to raise a finger to prevent it; to those
financiers, bankers and industrialists who armed Fascist Japan while she was in
the very act of crushing poor China, and who now, in the midst of war, are still
engaged in their slimy imperialist game of obtaining materials for the next war; to
those leaders and their henchmen who have twisted this war into what it should
not have been and who today are both consciously and unconsciously betraying
the democratic will of the enslaved people of Europe and Asia
—in hate—

and to the soldiers of all nations, who, as I write, are lying on the once good
but now mangled and bloody earth, striving to get at each other's throats, who
are staring up at the stars at night, recalling their lost youth and the forgotten
days of peace, who are consumed not so much with mutual hatred for each other,
as with their united hatred for war
—in love—
this book is dedicated

—JACK BELDEN
Still Time to Die

CONTENTS

Map The European Theater and
North African Theater of World War II ix

1 The First 1

**WHEN HE HAD TO KILL,
HE WOULD**
*Campo Prigionieri di Guerre 61,
Laterina, Italy
7 February 1944*

2 Volunteers 15

A DEAD GIVEAWAY
*Sesto, near Colonnata, North of
Florence, Italy
28 February 1944*

3 Commando Training 37

**LIKE A PYTHON
DOES ITS PREY**
*Train to Germany, Prato, Italy
28 February* 1944

4 Dieppe 51

"THE GERMANS ARE COMING"
*Florence, Italy
End of March 1944*

5 Spearheaders 105

PLAY IT COOL
*Rome, Italy
April 1944*

6 Italy's Boot 143

TOWARD THE MOUNTAINS
A Hamlet near Sansepolcro, Italy
9 April 1944

7 *Operation Avalanche—*
Salerno, Italy   207

A BROKEN WINDOWPANE
Stolpmünde, Germany
May 1944

8 The Winter Line at
Venafro   245

THEY TORE THE ANIMAL TO
PIECES
The Walter von Alton Farm,
Rachdammietz
Pomerania, Germany
Late July 1944

9 Anzio   271

10 The Houdini Club   319

Maps   361
Source Notes   375
Acknowledgments   377
About the Author   383

THE EUROPEAN THEATER AND
NORTH AFRICAN THEATER OF WORLD WAR II

• Dundee

NORTH SEA

DENMARK

BALTIC SEA

• Carrickfergus

IRISH
SEA

GREAT
BRITAIN

IRELAND

POLAND

HOLLAND

GERMANY

BELGIUM

CZECHOSLOVAKIA

• Dieppe

N

AUSTRIA

HUNGARY

ATLANTIC
OCEAN

SWITZERLAND

FRANCE

YUGOSLAVIA

ADRIATIC
SEA

ITALY

Cisterna di Latina

Anzio •

• Venafro

PORTUGAL

BALEARIC SEA

Sorrento Peninsula •• Chiunzi Pass
Maiori

SPAIN

TYRRHENIAN SEA

MEDITERRANEAN SEA

Porto Empedocle • • Butera
Licata Gela

• Arzew

• La Macta

ALGERIA

• Sened Station
El Guettar

MOROCCO

TUNISIA

The
HOUDINI
CLUB

1

THE FIRST

GELA, SICILY, D-DAY, 10 JULY 1943, 1030 HOURS. A BLUISH MORNING haze hung deceptively low, hiding the carnage but not the sounds of battle in the town. His eyes stung from sweat, dust, and lack of sleep. He blinked several times, clearing his vision, then readied the .30-caliber machine gun in the back of his peep, his jeep. His driver slammed into reverse, backing up quickly on the side street they had just entered. The driver stopped. The rear of the jeep stuck out just far enough to engage the small black Italian tank motoring down the main street toward the city square, firing at the exhausted Americans in the buildings and on the rooftops. Growing gunfire and explosions added to the desperate scene—the bluish haze now battled the dark gray of the raging inferno. He had lost men, taking this town.

Through the fog of war and uncertainty, one thing was clear to Lieutenant Colonel William Orlando Darby: If they didn't stop the tanks, all would be lost. All. And sure as hell, he wasn't going to get pushed out of this town, out of this beachhead back into the sea that had become the graveyard of men and ships already, slinking all the way back to North Africa. He knew that his men—the best combat soldiers in Africa—weren't going to give up the fight. And he was going to lead, like always, from the front. He cocked the machine gun with its 150 belt-fed rounds.

Handsome, with a high forehead, firm mouth and jaw, broad-shouldered and thick-chested, the 32-year-old West Point graduate of the class of 1933, from Fort Smith, Arkansas, seemed, despite the battle around him, calm and composed. Time slowed. He knew the mountains in the distance, the black-burned wheat fields beyond the town, the landing beaches behind him, the sandstone buildings of Gela they had just captured. He knew the disposition of his force and that his excellent battalion commander, Major Roy Murray, of the 4th Rangers, would handle anything the enemy threw at them. But he needed to be in the fight, to lead. His own 1st Battalion was to his left, the 4th in the right side of town, both battalions tied together by an understrength 1st Battalion of 39th Engineers reinforced with Charlie Company, 83rd Chemical Mortars. All were desperate to beat back the counterattack. Darby was right in the thick of things, right in the middle of Murray's battalion clinging on to the town with their fingernails. He knew all of this, but he did not see any of it.

He was too focused on stopping the tank right there, right now. His blue eyes squinted at the small, two-crewed black Renault R35 tank. He made out the crude white death-head symbol on its side. Along with his driver, Carlo Contrera; his bodyguard, Tommy Gunner Corporal Charles Riley; and a squad of hardened Rangers, he had just cleared a schoolhouse near the beach in close-quarter fighting, killing 22 Italian officers and capturing 30. His bodyguard remained at the hotel. And now here he was with his driver in his jeep, with a mounted .30-cal machine gun, and the tanks were rolling in, ready to throw the invaders back into the sea.

The tank came within rock-throwing distance. Darby pulled the trigger, unleashing hell, sending 150 rounds directly at the menacing machine. The rounds announced their arrival on target—metal hammering metal with an industrial clanging. Nothing. The bullets ricocheted off the tank like water hitting a wall. He watched it move away into a narrow side street, trying to avoid his machine-gun fire. Darby's ears rang with the high-pitched sounds of metallic screeching. The taste of combat floated in the air. He yelled at his driver to get going, to find Chuck.

Captain Charles "Chuck" Shunstrom, of Radburn–Fair Lawn, New Jersey, 22, was the bravest of the brave. A wild man, a killer of men, even a cold-blooded murderer. His reputation was two-sided, worshipped by some, seen as a psychopath and hated by a few. He had killed with a knife. He seemed reckless at times, endangering others—all to please his boss. Chuck moved from street to street, firing a 37mm anti-tank gun, the only one on the beachhead at the time, and originally set up near the cathedral in the main square in the early hours of the invasion, where it was needed now. Moving from spot to spot within the labyrinth of the multi-storied buildings bracketing the narrow streets, he was taking pot shots at the enemy whenever a target presented itself.

They found Shunstrom and his 37mm gun. It took no time to hook it to Darby's jeep. They raced toward the center of Gela, which was the enemy's objective. The fighting grew even hotter at the square when they pulled up. The peep backed up to wheel the gun into position. The two Ranger officers unhitched the gun quickly, readying it to fire.

The town was no longer awash in a bluish morning haze. Instead, combat had blackened the sky and exerted its dominance over everyone and everything. Darby and Shunstrom understood the gravity of the situation. Failure was not an option, or else it would be a repeat of the disastrous raid on Dieppe in France the previous year. Thousands of soldiers had died there. . . .

Even though their hearts beat violently within their chests, fear seemed absent: It lay suppressed within the recesses of their minds. Both loved the thrill of cheating death, loved being Rangers with a drive to accomplish their missions. Perspiration intermixed with dust, and cordite enveloped them. The artilleryman in Darby came to the forefront, the gun, like an old lover, handled with care and expertise.

Darby, bareheaded, with sleeves rolled up, and Shunstrom, helmeted, sprang into action, setting up the anti-tank gun for firing. "But before they could the Italian tank—bearing a death's head device— clanked around the corner and came charging down on them."

Swiftly, Darby positioned himself on the left side of the gun, looking barely through the optics, the tank but a hundred yards away. It took real guts to stay in a fight at that range. Traversing and elevating the gun took no time. Everything, though, seemed to move in slow motion for Darby. A shell snapped into place with a slow, stretched-out clank. Darby heard Shunstrom on his right. Breech shut. His mind's eye saw the desperate battle all around, Rangers firing and throwing everything at the approaching tanks in the streets. He saw his men toss their Sticky grenades from the rooftops. He saw Captain Jack Steele and Sergeant Shirley Jacobs move into a building, each carrying a pole charge with 15 pounds of TNT attached to the end, ready to throw them at the tanks. He saw another Ranger on top of a building firing a bazooka from his shoulder. Darby adjusted the traversing and elevation wheels without haste, smoothly, comfortably, like a pianist stroking his keys.

Darby and Chuck heard the clanking tank amidst the roar of combat. Now the moving black harbinger of death fired twice. Both rounds whooshed over their heads, pulverizing the wall behind them, filling the streets with rubble. With ordinary luck, they should have been ripped to shreds. Darby punched the trigger. The first round slammed into the turret, forcing the tank to stagger. The next round was loaded in a blink of an eye, Chuck loading without commands. Darby hit the trigger again. The second shot also hit the tank, but this time punching it back several feet from the recoil. Sheets of orange flames exploded, the orange hues bouncing off the blackness of the tank momentarily, before completely engulfing it in a fiery inferno, spewing black, angry tendrils into the sky. Darby heard his men cheer while the burning metal convulsed in its death, blocking the narrow street. But it was far from over. . . .

Leaving Chuck with the gun, Darby ran down another side street, where another black merchant of death was spewing hate and destruction at his men. He slipped to the side of the tank, climbed on top, riding the bucking and clanking tank like a rodeo cowboy. Unable to pry open the hatch, he calmly placed an incendiary grenade on its turret and jumped off. All of this to the chagrin of Fox Company's commanding officer, Lieutenant Stan Zaslaw, who couldn't fire his bazooka without killing his commander. Soon the tank's metal shone red hot, roasting the tankers inside as they desperately scrambled out of the death trap, screaming in surrender.

Bill Darby took a deep breath, surveying the carnage around him. The stench of war hung heavily, drenching him with its rottenness and glory: courage, cowardice, fiery infernos of melting metal and human alike, smoke, cordite, black powder, urine, feces, and the memorable, unforgettable stench of burned flesh. Darby blinked several times, the world returning to its normal speed. His eyes stung. He watched the tank burn in real time, shooting veins of black smoke all around him. A wind picked up the dark clouds and wrapped him in a cloak of smoky death: All he heard amidst the roar of war was "Why don't you give the job to Bill?"

"Why don't you give the job to Bill?" said Colonel Edmond H. Leavey, Chief of Staff to Major General Russell Hartle, Commanding General U.S. Forces, United Kingdom. Riding in a staff car from Wilmont House, home of the U.S. Army Northern Ireland Forces, to Belfast some seven miles northeast, for Sunday church services, aide-de-camp Captain Darby accompanied both. Hartle sat up front next to the driver, while Leavey and Darby were in back. The decision to create a unique strike force had only just been authorized, and Hartle knew he needed a good man to lead the small experimental unit. The ongoing discussion was about leadership. Hartle had said, "We can't get very far with this new job unless we have somebody good to put in charge of it—any ideas?" The response from Leavey was immediate. "Why don't you give the job to Bill?" He was suggesting Hartle's aide-de-camp, William Darby, born in 1911, a West Pointer despite the family's poor finances, and a regular artillery officer, who had been expressing his unhappiness at having to sit out the war on staff instead of leading a tactical unit. The junior officer had pleaded his case on several occasions. Hartle looked at Darby and asked: "Bill, what do you say to that?"

Darby couldn't believe his ears. In that instant, and in the time it took to answer with a resounding "Yes, sir," his military career played through his mind like a film. For eight years he had held various commands, attended schools, and participated in maneuvers in Louisiana, acquiring experience as a troop leader as well as gaining experience with amphibious landings in Puerto Rico. He had worked with mobile artillery units including horses, mules, and motor vehicles, things that were to prove valuable for the anticipated raids and invasions in the

coming years. He had married, but seemingly things had not gone as
well with whispers of a wife that was a little too fond of alcohol and a
little too fond of men. He would never write her throughout the war,
instead divorcing her upon his return stateside. Another officer, the
best man at the wedding, did not believe the rumors: To the contrary,
he thought her a wonderful person with a beautiful personality.

Preparing for an overseas move drastically changed with the
attacks on Pearl Harbor on December 7, 1941. In November 1941,
Darby had been initially assigned to Hawaii; but after the Japanese
destruction of the U.S. fleet, his orders were amended and he reported
as aide to Hartle on the 7th of January 1942. A 36-man advance
party of the V Army Corps, including Captain Darby, was organized
on 10 January 1942, and departed Brooklyn five days later, arriving
in Belfast, Northern Ireland, on 26 January. Scrambling to impose
the American footprint in Europe, by the 28th at 1000 hours, the
U.S. Army Northern Ireland Forces (USANIF), under Major General
Hartle, was officially established at Wilmont House, Dunmurry, in the
southern part of Belfast.

Those early days had been filled with excitement: The country
was at war. Darby was a professional soldier, and being an aide was
not to his liking. He, however, was well-liked. His boss, Major General
Hartle, on the other hand, lacked the charisma and charm that Darby
had in abundance. The aide was smoother and more personable than
the general. At the military academy, he had been in athletics, sung in
the choir, and attended services, but also liked to joke around. Darby's
first commendation came as a result of these early abilities as an aide.
On 18 July 1942, Darby received a citation of merit for his work during
the period of January to June 1942. The award "is given in recognition of tact and demeanour, which contributed much towards the
exceptionally pleasant relations existing between the American troops
and the citizenry of Northern Ireland." Performing his duty had been
drilled into him at West Point, where he graduated 177 out of 346, and
duty was important to him. Time moved slowly. He was ambitious; he
was itching to actually be in the war. Chafing at his inactivity, he had
asked the 34th Division's chief of staff, Colonel Edmond H. Leavey,

for a transfer. He knew Leavey liked him and was appreciative of his situation, but he would have to wait until the right time. Secret documents moved on and off Darby's desk. He may have kept an eye on opportunities. Things were to change quickly for him.

On 26 May 1942, Colonel Lucian King Truscott Jr. was promoted to brigadier general. He had arrived in London on 17 May, and by the 26th submitted proposals to General George Marshall Jr., Chief of Staff, U.S. Army, tasked with modernizing the Army, for the creation of an American unit along the lines of the British Commandos of highly trained volunteer shock troopers who could respond quickly to invasion or, as they did, carry the fight to enemy beaches with hit-and-run amphibious raids. The proposals had been discussed for a short while. One such letter, dated weeks earlier, on 15 April 1942, details the organization and numbers of personnel to be trained as Commandos: 12 officers, 20 non-commissioned officers, and 40 enlisted men were to form a nucleus. The small number was probably due to the limited personnel available. Truscott's new proposal, however, increased the number, using British terminology, to five or six Troops (of 400 to 500 in total) because more men had arrived in Northern Ireland. He also recommended Major Theodore Conway, who was attached to the Special Services Brigade, to assist him with this new organization.

The title *Commando* came from the Boer guerrillas in the war of Prime Minister Winston Churchill's youth. Commandos rekindled the belligerence of the desperate British Army after the humiliating defeat at Dunkirk in 1940 and gained the necessary experience for later, wider combat. Their raids drew increasing numbers of German divisions to the defense of the European coast. The original Table of Organization and Equipment (TO&E) for this unit was drafted by Major Conway after having visited British Commando units and having participated in training exercises. He decided, although there were differences, such as the British having small Bren gun carriers whereas the Americans had jeeps, that the way forward was a combination of British unit-strength figures and current American TO&Es, meaning the Americans were to be small like their Commando counterparts but with U.S. gear and equipment. The title *Ranger* was selected from several suggestions by General Truscott "because the name Commandos rightfully belonged to the British, and we sought a name more typically American." The War Department authorized Truscott and Major General Hartle to activate the U.S. Army's 1st Ranger Battalion. Unbeknownst to most, the Ranger unit was formed for the specific purpose of training soldiers in Commando skills and then reassigning them to other units, thus providing a well-trained and battle-experienced core for the newly forming American units at the beginning of American participation in World War II. The Ranger unit was therefore provisional by design and not to be a permanent unit. And the future commander William Orlando Darby knew about it but he never let his men know. It might have been a blow to their morale.

Truscott's proposal was approved on 31 May. "I delivered it in person on 1 June, and then spent the following two days in North Ireland discussing details with the Commanding General, Major General Russell P. Hartle, and his staff, as well as with various subordinate commanders and staffs of his command, particularly those of the 34th Infantry and 1st Armored Divisions." Undoubtedly, Darby was involved in these discussions.

The 1st Ranger Battalion communiqué dated 1 June 1942, written, and before returning to the U.S., by Major General James Chaney, Special Army Observer and Head of the Special Army Observers Group, stipulates:

> Since we are starting late in the organization of the unit which will be operating alongside similar British Units, with much experience, it is of the utmost importance that personnel selected for this unit be fully trained soldiers of the highest possible type. . . . It is especially desired that suitable personnel be encouraged to volunteer even though the resultant loss of key personnel may be a temporary inconvenience to some organizations.
>
> Officers and non-commissioned officers should possess qualities of leadership of a high order, with particular

emphasis upon initiative, judgment and common sense. All officers and men should possess natural athletic ability, physical stamina, and should be without physical defects . . . it is highly desirable that keen and intelligent personnel be selected. No age limit is prescribed, but it is noteworthy that British Commandos average about 25 years of age.

It was clearly understood by the organizers that "this outfit requires a high type of soldier with excellent character who is not averse to seeing dangerous action." The ideal volunteers were expert, or experienced, in the following fields or talents: demolitions, mechanics, heavy-vehicle drivers, martial artists, woodsmen, mountaineers, engineers, and weapons handlers, with an emphasis on maritime-experienced personnel anticipating amphibious raids and landings, and men with some knowledge of power plants, radio stations, etc. to facilitate demolitions. The unit was to be small and organized in Northern Ireland at a site of Hartle's choosing.

At the same time as the Ranger communiqué, the Headquarters, United States Army Northern Ireland Force, and Headquarters, V Corps, both commanded by Major General Hartle, moved from Wilmont House, Dunmurry, to Brownlow House in the town of Lurgan. Three days later, Brigadier General Truscott Jr., officially Chief of the American Section to the Combined Operations Headquarters, supervising raids, completed his visit to Northern Ireland, and had submitted additional reports on the plans to activate the 1st Ranger Battalion. An army cannot function without paperwork.

Colonel Edmond Leavey knew Captain William Orlando Darby to be an excellent choice for command when he recommended him to Major General Hartle. Darby had been a guide to then-Colonel Lucian Truscott during his visit to Northern Ireland; Truscott was favorably impressed by the aide. Darby's military credentials and his excellent demeanor made him the right choice and made sense to Leavey. Therefore, "the officer who was to be the first commander of the 1st Ranger Battalion, Major William O. Darby, General Hartle's aide (and my guide during my stay in North Ireland) was a young artillery officer from the Class of 1933 at West Point. He had had experience in both pack and motorized artillery, as well as with cavalry and infantry. He had had amphibious training with one of our divisions in the United States. He was outstanding in appearance, possessed of a most attractive personality, and he was keen, intelligent, and filled with enthusiasm." William Darby was an ideal candidate and would prove his supporters right.

Darby was swept up in the early days of the creation of the Rangers, appealing to his energetic demeanor and personal drive. Once things moved, they moved with a flurry of activities. On 7 June 1942, the original 1st Ranger Battalion communiqué from 1 June was elaborated on and reissued, with the 1st Ranger Battalion forming at Carrickfergus, Northern Ireland. The unit's core of some 500 men was to come from the 34th Infantry and 1st Armored divisions of V Corps, stationed in Northern Ireland with a total of 32,202 personnel. On 8 June 1942, General Hartle officially appointed Captain William Orlando Darby commander of the Rangers and promoted him to major, the orders for his promotion having been dated a week earlier.

Time was of the essence for the driven major. Darby had to build a top outfit from the top down, and to that end he hand-picked his Ranger officers. He was looking for unique men who were not afraid of action and could lead hard men typically attracted to dangerous challenges. He wanted young, athletic, and highly motivated officers who volunteered for action. The attitude he wanted was "the war's going on, let's get with it and get on with it." On the 8th of June, he interviewed the first officer volunteers at V Corp Headquarters at Lurgan and at 34th Division HQ at Omagh.

One of the young officers interviewed at the military barracks at Hollywood was James "Joe" J. Larkin. A typical interview started like this: "Why do you want to join the 1st Ranger Battalion?" asked Darby. "To fight, sir." Larkin couldn't think of a better answer. Larkin's opinion of Darby was high. The major was rather young, charismatic, and good-looking. His selected officers ranged from second lieutenants to experienced captains, representing all the services. The newly selected officers headed to Carrickfergus, which was across the bay from where he had then been stationed. On 9 June, orders for first officers were issued, with more interviews conducted at Wilmont House the following day. The next day, 29 officers were detailed to the new battalion. The width and breadth required of the men also translated to the officer corps of the Rangers. "There were only a few regulars, mostly citizen soldiers. Except for Darby, a West Pointer, the officers were all NG, reserve, and OCS." Eleven officers came from the infantry, five from the coastal artillery, four from field artillery, three combat engineers, two were cavalrymen, and one each from the Medical Corps, Signal Corps, Quartermaster Corps, and Ordnance. The enlisted selections began at Carrickfergus on 11 June, lasting 10 days, and were conducted by boards composed of Darby's new officers. On the 11th, the first group of 300 volunteers arrived from the 34th Infantry Division. Others were to come within the following days.

Darby's most significant pick was for executive officer (XO), the man responsible for the day-to-day operations of the battalion who needed a keen eye for detailed planning, and that was the blond-haired Captain Herman W. Dammer. Dammer was of German descent and had been born on 20 November 1910, in Staten Island, New York. Herm, as Darby called him, was tall and angular, with well-chiseled aristocratic features—and he was soft-spoken, the embodiment of a gentleman officer. He was a former enlisted man with the Headquarters Troop, 51st Cavalry Brigade of the New York National Guard, which he joined on 30 January 1934. Appointed to lieutenant on 6 December 1939, as a 2LT he was in the 7th Cavalry of the NYNG. By 10 February 1941, he was inducted into active military service with the HQ Battery, 102nd Coast Artillery Brigade (Anti-Aircraft). By the time Herm landed in Northern Ireland, he was an adjutant in the same unit, the 209th Coast Artillery Anti-Aircraft, as Joe Larkin had been. Dammer didn't wish to spend the war guarding a coastline as anti-aircraft units tended to do. He, too, had decided to answer Darby's call for officers.

These two influential officers molded the new-founded Ranger Battalion more than anyone else. They became legendary to the men.

Technician Fifth Grade Jim Altieri recalls Darby having a "magnetic quality that defied description. His expressions were lively, and he seemed to possess a dynamic energy. A stickler for discipline, but was a just man who knew the true psychology of leadership." Darby made quick decisions, relying on his analytical skills. "He was direct, forceful and sometimes explosive, and both officers and men when called down by him could probably remember the incident for the rest of their life, he was so cutting." Other Rangers noted his repeated use of the word *ass*, as in "it will be your ass" if you failed, but he never used profanity. Battalion Surgeon Sheldon C. Sommers wrote in 1990 that Darby was "cheerful, very energetic. He was strict, fair, and colorful dressing soldiers out of line. He would shout at one at once to straighten up and button up and look like a Ranger. He used no profanity." In contrast to Darby's "fissionable characteristics," the XO was a balancing influence. Herm was by nature reserved who rarely spoke—but when he did, it was to the point. They complemented one another "and each added to the other's stature." Years later, Herm's wife said that her husband had given Darby most of his tactical ideas. Dammer himself played down that assertion.

Sergeant Warren E. "Bing" Evans, born 29 December 1918, of Aberdeen, Brown County, South Dakota, with the 34th Division, who would receive a battlefield commission, shared those sentiments. He thought Darby had flair, and was more emotional and inspirational, whereas Dammer was not. "Dammer was a routine, think-it-through type." Darby's After-Action Reports were colorful; Herm's were the opposite: dry, to the point, and very sterile, representing the difference in them. "Darby followed the book on how to be a good leader, although he was somewhat carelessly flamboyant at times. [Dammer] was not demanding but we knew he meant what he said. We admired him even more because he was in on all the action with us."

WHEN HE HAD TO KILL, HE WOULD
Campo Prigionieri di Guerre 61, Laterina, Italy
7 FEBRUARY 1944

The warming rays of the sun had not yet fully kissed the wintry landscape, and Chuck Shunstrom should have felt the cold, but he didn't. He was too focused on his most pressing task. To escape, the young Ranger captain needed to tackle the two strands of barbed wire enclosing the prisoner-of-war camp. He sneaked into a deserted barn without arousing suspicion by moving in and out of prisoner work details and their accompanying German guards. Inside, he looked around the old building. No pliers, no tools, nothing but an old packing crate. He pried a board from it.

A quick glance out the window. Nobody. He climbed out. Crawling 30 feet on his stomach, he slid the board underneath the first strand of barbed wire, lifting the entanglement just enough to squeeze under without getting stuck. The second wire was four feet away. He was in no-man's-land until he breached it. Chuck took to a knee, only to see a German guard looking straight at him. A rifle was in his hands. A bullet could end everything quickly. He rose slowly, turning away to avoid the inquisitive eyes of the guard. Luck and quick thinking saw him pick up a nearby coil of wire while motioning to the strands. He was just another Italian laborer not worth a second look. Chuck listened to the footsteps disappear. He breached the wire with his plank, crawled into a gully, and hid. Now what?

War had taught Chuck many things he would need if he were to survive and make good his escape. Thirty yards away, he spotted a typical small Italian farmhouse. He moved toward it, keeping a sharp eye out. He was wired tight, a loaded spring ready to pounce. When he had to kill, he would; he had done it plenty of times. Tension crackled in the air. He strained to hear: He was partially deaf from combat. An enemy could be in the house, ready to kill him. He hesitated, then stepped to the front door, making a fist, ready for anything. . . .

2

VOLUNTEERS

A CRUCIAL PICK TO JOIN THE RANGERS WAS CAPTAIN ROY A. MURRAY JR.,
of Walnut Creek, California, born on 9 March 1909. He was a reserve
officer graduate [ROTC] of the University of California at Berkeley.
At 33 years old, Murray was older than Darby. Murray stood at five foot
nine, of medium build, good-looking, with dark hair and blue eyes.
His ears stuck out a fair bit, making him instantly recognizable. He
was a true athlete, playing University and Olympic club basketball and
running cross-country "as fast as a deer," and he was an outdoorsman.
"He had the agility of a nineteen-year-old and was tough as nails."
Murray had experience in navigation and boat-handling as a civilian. He was a deacon for his church, the St. John's Presbyterian in
Berkeley: A newspaper once described him as the "fighting deacon."
He was charming, a womanizer, noted for it during his early time
in Northern Ireland. Murray was called to active duty commanding
a Civilian Conservation Corps (CCC) camp near Chicago. He had
also participated in the Louisiana Maneuvers and was ready to join
the 100th Provisional Airborne Ranger Battalion to test parachutes
and training techniques when orders were rescinded, and he shipped
overseas with the 34th Infantry Division. "His air of daring befitted a
man who had flown one of the first air mail routes along the coast of
California." Murray's personality shines through with his recollections
of his early adventures in Northern Ireland:

We were stationed at Castlerock, a very nice sea coast resort town, with the 133 Infantry. I met the pastor's daughter, she wanted to know if I played golf, and I stupidly said "Yes." We went out on the links one day, and she beat me. I thought, "Okay." So we went out again, and she beat me again. Of course, I blame it all on the wind there, coming in from the sea, and I had a hook to begin with, or a slice, and the slice really developed with that wind. So I wasn't sure of the hospitality of Castlerock at that time. We also went into Coleraine. We were always looking for good watering places and to see if there were any girls in town. Somehow, we always ended up at Mary's Bar, where we had something called Coleraine whiskey [moonshine whiskey made from potato mash]. I'm sure they made it the night before so the revenuers would never get it. And I managed to lose my voice twice in that bar—and I'm not that talkative. The bar was right around the town hall. That was the main part of town, where they had the dances the whole time. We were doing intelligence work at Mary's Bar.

But Murray had left the days of entertainment behind. Now as a Ranger Company Commander, he was leading barely trained men over rough terrain in the hills around Carrickfergus, and the pace he set was purposely punishing. He was well-liked by the enlisted men for his forgiving nature, but on the second infringement he became strict. Darby, on the other hand, was always a disciplinarian, nearly fanatical. Murray, too, like Dammer, would prove to be the foil to blunt Darby's edge: Otherwise there would have been few Rangers left as Murray once said. Captain Murray had a keen analytical skill and communicated effectively. His recommendations were sound, and he was a strong commander, leading his men in battles to come. Murray had a profound influence on all subsequent Ranger activities.

Another pick for company command was Captain Alvah Morgan Miller. Born on 14 October 1914, in Highland Park, Michigan, he moved to Saginaw in 1930, where he graduated from Saginaw High School. He was a large, broad-shouldered man. He was a talented, driven, and dedicated officer. Miller was a student at Michigan State College [University] from 1933 to 1937, where he majored in economics. During his college days he was president of the Men's Glee Club, singing baritone and second bass. He was a member of the prestigious Mortar and Ball of the Coast Artillery, an advanced ROTC unit. The Mortar and Ball was a Coast Artillery fraternity that had as its purpose the better preparation of advanced artillery cadets for the ROTC camps through cooperation with the military department. It was one of the three chapters in the country. The local chapter, Battery E, 1st Regiment, was organized in 1930. Membership was limited to advanced students in the Coast Artillery Corps who had proved themselves outstanding both in military science and in college activities. The organization stressed the social side of ROTC work as well as the strictly military phases, with the aim of making the coast-artillery men better acquainted. Mortar and Ball received its new members with a formal initiation held throughout an entire week. A banquet, two formal parties, and business meetings were scheduled during the academic year. It was quite an honor for Miller to have been accepted into this fraternity. After graduating, he worked for General Motors. Miller married in 1937 and had a young son before deploying overseas five years later. He served in the 209th Coast Artillery (AA) headquartered in Rochester, New York, the same unit then-1st Lieutenant Herm Dammer was in. The 209th was inducted into federal service on 10 February 1941, where Miller served with HQ Battery, 1st Battalion, Battery A, as a 1st Lieutenant. The battery had a TO&E of five officers and 207 men. Alvah Miller was not just musically gifted; he would go on to write a poem about the men under his command, just a few days before their final battle.

Captain William E. Martin was also an artillery officer who joined Darby, serving with the newly arrived Headquarters Battery, 34th Division Artillery. Martin was born on 13 September 1914 in Minneapolis, Minnesota, and was married. The National Guard turned federal with Martin promoted to 1st Lieutenant in February

1941, serving with the 58th Field Artillery. After spending nearly one year at the artillery and basic training center of Camp Claiborne, Louisiana, where the Louisiana Maneuvers involved 400,000–500,000 men, he was promoted to captain in May 1942, and his division deployed to Northern Ireland the same month. He was one of the five captains selected by Major Darby and would rise subsequently to Intelligence Officer.

Deafness and a silver plate in his forehead did not keep First Lieutenant Max Schneider, of Shenandoah, Iowa, from volunteering for the Rangers. Born on 8 September 1912, and deaf in one ear since childhood, he was a champion swimmer and diver. Max was a Boy Scout, an ROTC college student at Iowa State College in Ames, Iowa, for one quarter, and later a pilot who barely survived an airplane crash. The crash, on 10 June 1933, fractured his skull, resulting in emergency surgery, where he was not only revived on the operating table, but also had a small piece of silver implanted into his forehead. He continued flying for American Airways as a transport pilot. Max rejoined the Iowa National Guard on 27 April 1936, having previously enlisted at 18. The National Guard was federalized to the 168th Infantry of the 34th Division, where he rose to sergeant with E Company. He was commissioned 2LT in September 1939. On 2 January 1940, the 34th Infantry Division was placed on active duty. Schneider, like nearly all soldiers, participated in the Louisiana Maneuvers. On 16 July 1941, he was promoted to 1LT, becoming the company commander of E Company until he joined Darby's Rangers. He was interviewed by Darby on 8 June 1942. His later action during the landings at Normandy, France, on 6 June 1944 proved crucial during the amphibious assault. Demons of war or perhaps his silver implant would haunt him for the rest of his life.

A highly influential and controversial officer was Second Lieutenant Charles Merton "Chuck" Shunstrom, born 20 November 1920, who had previously enlisted on 11 September 1939, and was stationed at the 19th Infantry Regiment Field Artillery in Schofield Barracks, Hawaii. He rose to the rank of sergeant with Company G, 19th Infantry. Chuck was handsome with Hollywood-movie-star good looks and was a supreme champion athlete in weight lifting. After his enlistment, he was accepted in the Officer Candidate School at Fort Benning, Georgia, on 12 December 1941, and two months later, in February 1942, newly commissioned 2LT Shunstrom arrived in Northern Ireland. He volunteered for the 1st Ranger Battalion at Carrickfergus. He had been unhappy and dissatisfied in his enlisted service, far away from home; but as a newly commissioned officer, he saw, like others, the opportunities presented for a unit composed of dangerous men for dangerous missions. He was the youngest officer in the 1st Ranger Battalion. He would fight every campaign and earn a harsh reputation as a killer of men, even a murderer, and a wild man. In a just world, and according to some Rangers, Shunstrom would have received the Medal of Honor for his exceptional battlefield conduct. Civilian life, however, would prove too much for the "bravest of the brave."

A colorful and tough Ranger officer was Captain Stephen J. Meade, of Fort Thomas, Kentucky. He had joined the National Guard in 1929 at 16. He went on to serve in the 123rd Kentucky Cavalry Squadron, which was converted to the 103rd Coastal Battery, and was based out of Fort Sheridan, Illinois. The 103rd posted to Northern Ireland after the United States entered the war. Meade was married to Hazel Hale. He was close friends with fellow officer Earl Carran Jr., of Fort Mitchell. His letter addressed to his wife details not only his experience of volunteering but says a lot about his personality:

Dear Hair Trigger

Well, anyhow, about a year ago they decided they needed some American Dead End Kids to work with British Commandoes. Since I hadn't had my picture in the paper at home for quite a while my press agent having been caught in a hell of a draft, I timidly raised my hand. Since you have gone out of my life, I've taken Earl Carran to raise and guide along the straight and narrow paths of virtue and safety, so when he didn't show too much enthusiasm about my proposal for Hara-kiri, I just up and volunteered for him. Remember the system? While he didn't know whether to save his face or lose his ass or vice versa, so I gave him a quick drink of Irish whiskey, and pat on the back, a kick in the pratt and sales talk #3 and bingo we were Rangers. Men and officers, all volunteers underwent a two-week period of organization and physical training at Carrickfergus prior to reporting to the Commando Depot located in the Scottish Highlands at Achnacarry on 2 July, 1942.

Captain Meade succinctly put things into perspective. "After three weeks of getting organized and eliminating some of the weaker souls, and conducting what we thought was pretty rigorous training, we were attached to British Combined Operations and sent to the Commando Training Depot in the Scottish Highlands. You wouldn't believe how happy those battle-seasoned Commando instructors were to have a go at their first over-fed, overpaid, and oversexed American cousins."

Multi-lingual with French, Spanish, German, Portuguese, and Russian, later adding Farsi and Chinese, Meade would become America's overseas troubleshooter after the war, working with the Office of Strategic Services and the Central Intelligence Agency for covert missions. After the war, he served as a military attaché in Beirut, Lebanon, and later was as a liaison to the Shah of Iran.

Dozens of first and second lieutenants were accepted, and only one was relieved, First Lieutenant James W. Jensen, who returned to his parent unit within a few short days as recruits from the 1st Armored Division arrived. There was no shame in rejection, or desiring to leave, or in failing to meet the new exacting standards set by Major Darby. These were just a few of the Ranger officers who were to lead the American war effort. A number of them would die leading their men on the battlefields of North Africa, Sicily, and Italy.

SUNNYLANDS, CARRICKFERGUS

Enlisted volunteers were selected by senior officers in Carrickfergus, some 11 miles northeast of Belfast. The town features a magnificent Norman castle founded in 1178 by Anglo-Norman knight John de Courcy. The new battalion was getting organized, and drew uniforms and gear, at a small British military installation called Sunnylands Camp, one mile from the center of town, featuring a narrow macadam [crushed stone bound by tar] road between neatly spaced rows of large Nissen huts. The dirty huts were cleaned by the new occupants while others made do with large tents. The weather was foul, rain and fog, but not terribly cold. The camp filled quickly with new recruits whose profanity-laced vocabulary mirrored the weather.

You couldn't help but notice one of the early recruits. Sergeant Alex John Szima of Dayton, Ohio, born on 24 May 1920, arrived with the 13th Armor Regiment of the 1st Armored Division, on 11 June 1942. Since youth, the sergeant had carried a six-inch scar from his left cheek to the eye. Because of it, he was in the process of getting dismissed from the service while stateside. He previously had secured a waiver to get into the Army in the first place because some doctors thought the scar could get infected, leading to the loss of the eye—by falling out. But before that could happen, and before his early trial period was over, Szima was accidentally shot in the upper left thigh in September 1940 on a training range by a West Point officer. Coming out of the hospital during the investigation of the shooting incident, and while at Armored Force School at Fort Knox, he was given the choice to stay on as a clerk or to be discharged from the Army with a disability certificate based on his injury. Szima, desperate to experience the looming war, chose the clerical job, rising in rank. He tossed away his cane, removed any implicating medical paperwork from his own file, and deployed to Northern Ireland. All Sergeant Szima wanted to do now was to go to war.

He chronicled his and other Rangers' experiences in a series of long letters, full of details and opinions. His first encounter with

Major Darby showed his confidence, perhaps even arrogance. Or perhaps Szima was a man driven to accomplish things he had set his mind on. Inside a Nissen hut at Carrickfergus, Sergeant Szima reported to Darby, who was seated behind a rickety card table holding a dozen or two files. A couple of clerks with thousands of files filled the rest of the hut. It was clear "who was in charge and he acted like a man who knew it too." Without wasting time, Darby said, "I want you to be my Sergeant Major." It was nothing Szima was interested in. He disliked paperwork, wanting to avoid paper shuffling as he had been forced to do so far in his previous posting. He also understood the politics of the new Army. The majority of volunteers would be from the National Guard, with a small number comprised of professional soldiers who had time in service, as well as draftees from Selective Service. Unifying them all under one command was a challenge, and one he personally wasn't interested in. He respectfully declined and explained that ultimately the commanding officer would need to have a sergeant major from one of the National Guard units, as they represented the majority of the volunteers. Darby listened as the sergeant clearly stated his intentions. "Also, sir, I desire to be in combat and not a caretaker of typewriters and service records. If you don't get a National Guard Sergeant Major now, you'll get one eventually." Darby was clear about who was in charge. "I'll be the judge of that, Sergeant." And that was that: The interview was over. There must have been some sympathies for the senior enlisted man, as Darby had been disgruntled when he was on staff, so he must have understood Szima's reluctance. Nonetheless, he needed organization and capable men to handle building the new unit.

A couple of days later, recalls Szima, he was called back. Fretful that he was to get his walking papers, back to his old unit or another one, he stood in front of the man in charge. In typical Darby fashion, he simply ordered Szima to take the job until another Sergeant Major from a National Guard unit in London was going to report. A temporary assignment, much to Szima's relief. Darby ordered him to organize the men into platoons of 36 men each and train them with forced marches. "Those that fall out will be returned to the area with a truck that follows the platoon and these men will be returned to their organizations without exception. Here, sign for your watch and here's your whistle, that is all and, oh yes, congratulations." That was that, Szima couldn't help but add. "I'll take this on a temporary basis with the promise I'll get to go on the first [combat] job." His wish for combat was to come soon enough. In the meanwhile, he had plenty of things to do.

Technician Fifth Grade James J. Altieri was born in Philadelphia, Pennsylvania, on 4 March 1920. A former steelworker at Lukens Steel Company near Philadelphia, he enlisted on 8 October 1941 and joined the 68th Field Artillery of the 1st Armored Division. While serving with the 1st Armored Division in Northern Ireland, he volunteered for the Rangers. He wrote numerous books, published and unpublished, and several articles on the Rangers. His writings capture what thousands of volunteers went through when they met the Ranger officers.

The officer interviewing him and some of the others looked over the men as though appraising cattle, and the things that stood out were how well-built they were, but also, importantly, a sureness rarely seen before. They walked into the castle where each officer was given a room for the interviews. Altieri reported and saluted.

"I'm Captain [Alvah] Miller. Why do you want to join this outfit? Do you realize the dangers of being in such an outfit? All training will be with live ammunition, and a certain percentage of men are wounded or hurt during training."

"I fully realize the dangerous possibilities of training and that the rough training should fully condition a man for real warfare," he answered.

"Are you of Italian descent?" Miller asked. A question asked of a number of European Americans who were to return to their homelands to fight.

"Yes, sir, both my mother and father were born in Italy, but they've lived in the States for over 40 years."

"What would your attitude be about fighting hand to hand with Italians? There's every possibility that our actions might bring us into contact with them. Do you feel you would give your best against your own blood?"

"Well, Captain, naturally I would much prefer to fight the Germans or the Japs. I would feel bad about fighting the same people my father came from—but I feel that when the time comes, that factor won't interfere with my duty as an American soldier."

"Do you think you would have guts enough to stick a knife in a man's back and twist it?"

"I guess a fella can do anything in the heat of battle," Altieri replied. "Sure, if it had to be done, I think I could do it." He lied. The mere thought of using a knife on someone repelled him. He even hated to see chickens killed. "But if knife-twisting was what these people specialized in, then I would be a knife-twister. What's the difference if you kill someone with a bullet or a knife? A dead man is a dead man regardless of how he is killed." Words that would subsequently come to haunt Altieri on the battlefields of North Africa and Italy.

Wayne Archibald Solomon Ruona, of Hector, Minnesota, born 7 November 1914, was a member of the National Guard's 135th Regiment, 34th Infantry Division. He joined the Civilian Conservation Corps (CCC) for one year from April 1934 to February 1935. "In the Second World War one of the biggest factors that helped a whole bunch of infantry people was the CCC's," the same organization Captain Murray had served in. "Those guys learned how to live with a canteen and mess training and how to live off the land, really. That was the best training that anybody ever had. And people forget that. They learn to be soldiers." He enlisted on 22 April 1941, at the age of 26 at Fort Snelling, Minnesota, because he was drafted, having registered for it in October of 1940. Ruona did not care for the draft, since it was unfair in many ways as some people were able to defer because of favoritism. His basic infantry training, like that of most recruits, took place at Camp Claiborne, Louisiana. Ruona felt the training he had received in the Army was terribly inadequate to keep him alive in anticipated combat. He wanted better, needed better if he were to survive the cauldron of war. It was as simple as that. He volunteered for the Rangers and, along with it, far superior training to what most soldiers destined for combat received. His desire came true, for the training that he so desperately wanted and received would ultimately save his life.

Sergeant Warren E. "Bing" Evans graduated from Central High School in Aberdeen, South Dakota, in 1938 ("Bing" because of his singing voice). A short-lived attendance at South Dakota State University, on an athletic scholarship, eventually led him to enlist in the National Guard (NG) on 10 February 1941 in Brookings, South Dakota, earning a dollar per drill. In 13 weeks, he made $13 he used for spending money while in school. The NG federalized on 19 February 1941, and he shipped out to Camp Claiborne where he was a private with Company B, 109th Engineers, 34th Division. He traveled overseas to Northern Ireland in the first week of January 1942, anticipating a year of service. Sergeant Evans saw a posting that caught his interest. It was a call for volunteers for a British Commando–type outfit—the Rangers. They said it would be very difficult; very few would make it because of how hard it would be.

> "Well, that's a challenge." And I was *Gung Ho!* I was never one to resist a good challenge. So, I volunteered for the Rangers along with several hundred others. Yes, [Darby] was impressive. He was very military and all seriousness—a West Point man. I knew he wanted to get the best men he could and so I did my best to impress him. He was one guy that we all wanted to impress. Darby asked me about my educational background and questions about my athletics background. I think he was trying to determine what kind of soldier I would be. While Darby was interviewing me, I could see Colonel [Captain] Dammer interviewing someone else in another corner of the room. Some of the other officers—Max Schneider and Roy Murray, also helped. Five hundred men were chosen from those that volunteered as the top specimens. They posted those that made it, and the rest went back to their units. I was lucky. I made the cut.

Staff Sergeant Gino Mercuriali, born 19 September 1920, of Cedar Rapids, joined the Iowa National Guard on 4 June 1937, at the age of 17, while still in high school. In October 1938, he was promoted to corporal and, rising in rank, served with Company L, 133rd Infantry, 34th Division. He and another sergeant often talked about wishing they had a unit such as the British Commandos. When the call for volunteers was announced at reverie, he raised his hand. The other sergeant didn't. Then they called the names to step aside to go for the interview. Surprisingly, his name wasn't called. Mercuriali went to the company commander to ask about his exclusion. The answer was swift and not to his liking. He was to be sent back to the States for officer training, probably like the other sergeant who hadn't volunteered. He was adamant to his CO (commanding officer) that he would not return stateside. In fact, if he were to become an officer, it would be in the field. In fact, Mercurialis would receive a battlefield commission. He told his commander that he'd go to battalion headquarters to get a different answer. The interesting thing was he had no idea that Captain Murray, his acting battalion commander, was also intending to go to the Rangers. Murray simply said for Mercuriali to get his belongings and he'd see to it that he'd be interviewed. The Ranger officers who interviewed him asked why he'd wanted to join this kind of a unit. His interview was short and to the point. "Do you think you can take the punishment, kill a person, and endure the hardships and more?" Of course he could. Why else join an outfit like the Commandos? Staff Sergeant Gino Mercuriali thought they were looking for more independent types. Perhaps even a bit on the wild side. Many of his comrades wanted out of their units just like he did. Although many volunteers were dismissed, to Mercuriali it seemed that the Ranger officers did not turn away too many, that they were subsequently culled during training with the British Commando instructors. But it wasn't so. The selection process did weed out a great number of volunteers. SSG Gino Mercuriali was assigned to Company D, commanded by Captain Alvah Miller. He would witness and experience great carnage throughout his service.

Merritt M. (Bert) Bertholf, of Marion, Ohio, was serving in the field artillery when he saw a notice for volunteers for American Commandos. He was a 28-year-old staff sergeant, older than many men, but he didn't let that stop him from signing up for the program. Things moved quickly, and he was called in along with another seven or eight men from his battery within a couple of days. "Volunteering for the Rangers was the only volunteering I ever did. Darby asked me what my qualifications were, and I told him four years in the Navy. He studied me for a minute and said, 'I think you're a little too old,' but I said, 'I'm the same age you are.'" It wasn't long before Bertholf was accepted. Training at Carrickfergus began immediately: speed marches with pack and weapon were set at a standard of six miles per hour. Later, in Commando training, Bertholf would have his collarbone broken when he was thrown down during hand-to-hand fighting practice. He completed training with his injury in a cast. He would join No. 3 Commando at Dieppe, recommended by Captain Murray.

Charles F. Leighton was born in a small town in South Dakota, where he worked in the small grocery store, slowly earning enough money to pay for his first year of college. He went to Eastern Normal State Teacher's College, where he was told that he could earn a little bit of money by joining the National Guard—much like Evans had done. He lied about his age, being three months shy of 18, and enlisted while attending college, where he received his teacher's certificate after one year in order to be able to teach at country schools in South Dakota. In the summer of 1940, he had a 30-day training course at Camp Riley in Minnesota. Although he had a contract to teach, the war was approaching, and everyone knew they'd be called to active duty. He was asked to give up his contract, which he did, and, finally, in December, received his call-up for active duty with a deployment to Camp Claiborne, Louisiana, in February 1941. They trained and expanded the training areas, the rifle and the artillery ranges. He also participated in the Louisiana Maneuvers. While on leave in December, Pearl Harbor was bombed by the Japanese.

"We had a division ceremony, and the general said that he would not be afraid to send the 34th Red Bull Division into combat any time, and two days later we were packing. We were shipped out on New Year's Eve in 1941. We landed in Fort Dix and took our shots and everything, and then my company drew the long straw with the 109th Engineers, and we were on the first boat." They landed in Carrickfergus, and his company was the first one to walk down the gangplank and among the first to land in Northern Ireland. The 109th Engineer Battalion Regiment was reorganized into a battalion, and a lot of promotions were made in the States. His company was already in Carrickfergus with the advanced party, and he did not receive a promotion. Around 1 June, a buddy of his signed him up to volunteer. Five men from his engineer company were about to leave for Carrickfergus, but, "Our commanding officer saw the names of some of the guys who volunteered; 'No,' he said to one of them, 'you're married.'" The CO only allowed single men to join the American Commandos. "Milt Session, the Indian from the Black Hills, tried to join, but no dice. He was married and had a kid." He recalled 3,000 volunteers from which about 400 were picked; a number of them passed out during the blistering road marches. "Those 400 had to be pretty qualified guys. The training was discipline."

A key witness to all things Ranger was Thomas S. Sullivan, nicknamed Sully, an intelligent college student who duly filled out his draft card on 16 October 1940, and within a few short months after graduating *cum laude* from Saint Michael's College, in Colchester, Vermont, entered the Army on 5 September 1941. Despite orders banning such things, Sully maintained a diary throughout his military career. Every intimate detail and thought were preserved. Sullivan was born in Newport, Rhode Island, on 5 August 1919. He was well-read, loved movies, was studious and religious, attending Mass when he could, and although small he was fit and possessed a strong will. He was "genial, enthusiastic and much-liked and admired" by his comrades. Basic training was at Camp Wheeler, Georgia. Although interested in the Air Corps, he spent time waiting for an answer with guard and kitchen duties. He and his new friends would go to the nearby town to enjoy all its benefits. Sully knew Captain Meade from his time in the National Guard.

Sullivan joined the 34th Division at Fort Dix, New Jersey, serving in Company G, 168th Regiment. A sour entry of his new comrades with few exceptions reads, "All the rest can't drill worth a tinker's dam." The 34th's convoy comprised 10 destroyers, the USS *New York,* and 20 transport ships. It departed from New York harbor on 19 February with Navy blimps floating overhead. The voyage sounds familiar to the military men and women who made their way to Europe during the war. "Lifeboat drills, alerts, and what have you. The food is fair, good, often terrible. Our quarters are jammed. We are sleeping in hammocks. The voyage is getting on our nerves. The air is sickening down here. We circle the decks. Officers have beautiful dining salon—and we? The cockroaches are even on our tables."

On 2 March 1942, Sullivan's convoy reached Belfast, Northern Ireland, where, in addition to getting to know the enthusiastic Irish, the soldiers continued to train. Challenging road marches of 22 miles in seven hours in the never-ending winds and rain added to the misery. Sullivan trained as a radio operator until he heard a new outfit was looking for some tough volunteers. He passed the interview.

From 8 June through 3 July, he, along with hundreds of other volunteers, took physical exams at Carrickfergus. Sully noted its beautiful waterfront and medieval castle. A location, he writes, that John Paul Jones had shelled in 1778—in fact, it was a successful naval engagement with another vessel Jones captured. A few days later, Sully went before a board of officers for additional questioning and was selected for a 10-day trial. Lieutenant Dean Knudson led him on his first speed march, which gave him troublesome blisters. Knudson would suffer a foot injury in North Africa and subsequently train new Rangers in the United States. The weeding-out process was conducted six and a half days a week. By mid-June, Sullivan had been assigned to the iconic Captain Stephen Meade in command of Able Company. Day-to-day training started with early-morning speed marches, calisthenics, tumbling exercises, jiujitsu, and sport. Training ended at 1700 hours.

The slight, genial Sullivan would save Bing Evans's life during combat in North Africa.

Altieri, too, recounts the grueling speed marches that became a Ranger hallmark. Captain Murray and a small, wiry lieutenant from Louisiana named Loustalot, who would lead an attack on Dieppe, were at the head of the double column, with full pack and equipment, leading briskly down the narrow road, past the camp gate. and up a steep road through green fields. The march turned into a quick run for 300 yards or more before returning to the speed march. "I was breathless. We were now beginning to sweat heavily, and I was thankful that I had cut down my leggings to half their usual size so they fitted snugly below the calf." The speed march lasted a circular five-mile and was completed in one hour. Five men failed to finish.

The next weeks increased in difficulties, driving the men even harder, increasing in distance and speed, up to 12 miles in two hours. Like many soldiers looking for something better, Altieri was not to be disappointed. "I could sense the difference in spirit between this outfit and the one I had just left." A memorable moment for Altieri came when Loustalot gave them a short speech afterwards. "He spoke slowly and deliberately with a faint suggestion of a drawl:"

> Men, I want to welcome you all to Company F. We are all here for the same purpose—to prove ourselves qualified for the new American Commando outfit. We may be here for two or three weeks before leaving for Scotland, and during that time our training will be stepped up each day. Any man who can't keep up with us will be sent back to his old outfit immediately. Discipline in this outfit rests with the individual himself—it's up to you, as we don't intend to waste any time on foul-ups. And remember, you are free to request to return to your old outfit at any time.

Sergeant Szima recalls the volunteers having been trimmed to around 550 men of all ranks, allowing for a 10 percent overage for anticipated losses during the upcoming Commando training with many soldiers arriving and not liking the program, leaving on their own accord. "There were also those who were like myself with their bridges burned behind them, and when these men failed the forced marches it was heartbreaking. The end result was that the rejects composed the largest convoy of trucks ever seen in Ireland."

The accepted ones represented a cross section of America. The youngest was 17 and the oldest 35. Their average age was 25, similar to that of the Commandos. They were not bible-thumping, good old boys. Evans gave a breakdown of the kind of men who joined:

> Let me tell you that in my company, I had a man who was beating several federal indictments for moonshining in Kentucky. I had a man in my outfit who was in from the seminary, a Presbyterian seminary in Louisville, Kentucky. I had another man who ran a house of prostitution in New Orleans. Then I had a lot of farm boys from the prairies of South Dakota and Iowa that had grown up hunting, grown up in the harvest fields. So I can't tell you physically what set them apart. I think it was more of a feeling of *gung-ho*, of *esprit de corps*, of a certain confidence in themselves, a certain spirit of "I can do it."

Sixty percent came from the 34th Division, 30 percent from the 1st Armored Division, and 10 percent from the medical, quartermaster, and signal troops of V Corps. The original battalion had a uniquely British-American look about it, as conceived by Conway and Chaney. It consisted of a headquarters company of 8 officers and 69 enlisted men, as well as 6 rifle companies (A, B, C, D, E, F) of 3 officers and 63 enlisted men each. Each company in turn had 2 platoons, a headquarters section comprised of the CO, a runner, a supply sergeant, and a sniper. Each of the platoons consisted of 2 assault sections composed of 12 men and a mortar section with 5 men. The size of these companies was determined by the small British Commando landing craft used for raids. A Ranger battalion was therefore significantly smaller than the traditional infantry battalions, and this was something often forgotten by American commanders.

By 15 June, 104 of the 575 volunteers had been returned to their units, forcing Darby to send out six boards of Ranger officers on recruitment drives. On 18 June, seven officers and 12 non-commissioned officers were selected from United States Army Northern Ireland Forces and received orders to report to the 2nd Canadian Division on the Isle of Wight for Commando training. They were awaiting favorable weather to be part of the first Americans committed in the war but rejoined the battalion while it had been at the Commando Training Depot in Scotland on 11 July. The weather turned against the raid code-named *Rutter*, and if they had been committed it would have been senseless slaughter because none of the men had training beyond what was received in basic training, wrote Szima years later.

On 19 June 1942, the 1st Ranger Battalion was composed of 26 officers, 447 enlisted with a 10 percent over-strength to compensate for training losses: 20 percent would fail. Finally, on 22 June, 488 enlisted men transferred to the new organization, much to the relief of the Ranger officers busy recruiting men. Almost immediately thereafter, on 25 June, Brigadier R. E. Laycock, GOC (General Officer Commanding) Special Service Brigade of the Commandos, along with Major Darby, reviewed the troops and gave speeches to the men at Carrickfergus before moving to Commando training in Scotland. Brigadier Laycock would do so again with two more reviews by 19 July 1942. Major General Russell P. Hartle, Commanding V Army Corps, conducted an inspection on that day as well. The interest in the 1st Ranger Battalion under its first commander, Major William O. Darby, was high. Until 28 June, the battalion spent most of its time drawing equipment, getting organized, and training.

By 3 July, the battalion had arrived in Scotland, where they trained from 4 July until 31 July under the commandant of the Commando Depot, Colonel Charles E. Vaughn. It was a momentous day, given the excitement within parts of the allied force of the new Rangers. It was a unique experience for the Americans when they met their new instructors at the junction leading to the estate—accompanied by pipes. They speed-marched from Spean Bridge to Achnacarry near

Loch Lochy. From the railroad station at Spean Bridge to Achnacarry was seven miles.

Whereas Carrickfergus was the birthplace of the U.S. Rangers, the Achnacarry Commando Depot—and subsequent amphibious training—raised them, and combat would mature them. The officers and the men would become known as the best soldiers of North Africa and would lead the way in liberating Europe from the National Socialist and Fascist scourge.

A DEAD GIVEAWAY

Sesto, near Colonnata, North of Florence, Italy

28 FEBRUARY 1944

The knuckles of his fist hit the wooden door—nonstop. Feigenbaum kept at it. It was dark. He and Duffy had been moving at night. They needed food and clothing. Their uniforms were a dead giveaway that they were escaped prisoners. He kept knocking. They were lucky to have found the house away from the village. Duffy kept an eye out on the house and the surrounding area. Italians or Germans might very well be right on their heels. Feigenbaum kept at it. Finally, the door creaked an inch, and that inch was enough. The two Rangers from Dog/3 barged in. The older man inside held a shotgun in his hand, but there was nothing he could do as the Rangers overwhelmed and disarmed him immediately, violently. Duffy closed the door. They cleaned, cleared, the house—the man was its only occupant. What a relief.

Inside, they stripped off their uniforms and swapped them with the Italian, who was now forced to wear their dirty, stinking clothing. Not that his was much better, but at least it didn't stink of piss, shit, blood, and sweat. Both Rangers now dressed like locals. They had hit the mother lode. Everything they needed, they got. Bread, cheese, wine, and tobacco leaves were dumped into cloth sacks. There was no time to linger. Patrols might already be sweeping the areas around the rail tracks, and maybe they had been spotted as they made their way through the night.

South—they needed to go south: That's where the friendlies were. Back the way they had been transported. At gunpoint, they forced the man along, toward a hill rising in the south. It was going to get light soon, and Rangers moved better and safer at night: That is what they had been trained to do, and that's what they had done since Sicily. Moments later on the hill, and without much discussion, they knew what they had to do: Feigenbaum killed the Italian. And it wasn't with the shotgun, for that might have alerted any nearby enemy, civilian or otherwise. Capture would mean death, one way or another, and the two young privates weren't going to lie down without a fight. He and Duffy covered the corpse with brush. It took a few minutes, not longer. They listened for sounds penetrating the disappearing night. Had they been discovered?

3

━━━┿━━━

COMMANDO TRAINING

THE RANGERS ARRIVED WITH PIPE MAJOR MACLAUCHLAN PLAYING AS he had never played before—to his biggest-ever audience. With Commandant Charles Vaughn—who had a wonderful understanding of men—and Major Darby at its head, and flanked by the other Achnacarry instructors, the columns set off on the historic march to Achnacarry, which was the ancestral home of the Camerons of Lochiel.

For the Rangers, training at the Achnacarry Commando Training Depot was a two-part affair. The first week or two proved disastrous, with men failing the standards set by their Commando trainers, be that on speed marches, tackling the assault courses, or weapons handling. Near the midpoint of the course, the Americans somehow, and finally, got a hold of themselves and hit the training with a renewed confidence and capability that made everyone proud.

The man tasked with guiding the training of the Rangers was six-foot-two Lieutenant Colonel Charles Edward Vaughan, a ruddy-cheeked, husky British officer of about 50, who radiated enthusiasm and goodwill. Vaughan was a former drill sergeant, serving as an officer in the First World War including the early British retreat at the Battle of Mons in 1914 during the opening stages of the Great War. In the early period of the current war, he, as well as many instructors at the depot, conducted raids against Vaagso and the Lofoten Islands in Norway. He was second-in-command of No. 4 Commando, with 28 years in the Coldstream Guards and

the Buffs. Some 25,000 men would go through his training, including Americans, Belgians, Dutch, French, Norwegians, Poles, and
police officers. Some of the instructors had escaped from Singapore
when it fell to the Japanese, and others had evaded the Italians in
Somaliland.

What the Rangers didn't know was the impact they had on
Vaughan before their arrival. When he first heard of the Rangers coming, he was scared that the Americans would find it too easy. He was
determined to make it as hard as hell. "Gentlemen," he concluded,
"we must make it hard for them, very hard indeed." This despite having had American Marines train recently. Darby recalls Vaughan's
impact on the Rangers:

> The tremendous personality of Colonel Vaughan pervaded
> the atmosphere of the Commando Depot. He was in excel-
> lent physical condition and was remarkably agile. He was
> constantly in the field, participating in, observing, and
> criticizing the training of the men. During it all, he was
> highly enthusiastic. Observing a mistake, he would jump in
> and personally demonstrate how to correct it. He insisted
> on rigid discipline, and officers and men alike respected
> him. He was quick to think up means of harassing the poor
> weary Rangers, and, as he put it, "to give all members the
> full benefit of the course. The British Commandos did all
> in their power to test us to find out what sort of men we
> were. I told the Ranger officers that they would receive the
> same training as their men. Furthermore, the ranking offi-
> cer present was to be the first to tackle every new obstacle,
> no matter what its difficulty. I included myself in this rule,
> believing deeply that no American soldier will refuse to go
> as far forward in combat as his officer."

The depot was built on the grounds of Clan Cameron of Lochiel's
Achnacarry castle between Loch Lochy to the east and westerly Loch
Arkaig. These lochs were connected by the River Arkaig, roughly 50

feet wide. It featured rock faces for climbing and abseiling (the tallest mountain range, Ben Nevis, was nearby). The entire area seemed mountainous to the Americans. Small-boat operations and opposed landings were conducted in Loch Lochy, where it housed its own Achnacarry fleet used in training. The fleet was a collection of miscellaneous small boats and landing craft used to develop boat-handling skills. On the grounds of the castle stood a variety of Nissen huts for accommodations, cooking, and training. The bell tents afforded housing for the Rangers, who were spread out like the spokes of a wheel around the center post, wigwam-style. A large hut served as a lecture hall, cinema, and indoor arena where unarmed combat instruction was given. The all-action one-minute boxing bouts, the famous "milling," were part of the Commando Depot's lore. Captain Meade calls the event "A Bucket of Blood."

> I remember our first evening; a beautiful place—so we thought—as it stayed light until about midnight at that time of the year. Some of the Commando officers asked a couple of us if we'd like to go to the Bucket of Blood. Thinking this was a local pub in the vicinity, we said sure. They walked us through the area and stopped at a clearing where a boxing ring had been set up. There were two groups of about 30 Commandos at opposite corners outside the ring, wearing sneakers and stripped to the waist. Before long, an officer climbed into the ring, blew a blast on the whistle, and one man from each side jumped into the ring and started to beat the hell out of each other with their bare fists. No boxing, slugging only. After exactly 1 minute, another blast on the whistle, the first two climbed out—if they were able—and two others jumped in and went at each other in the same fashion. The first two went over to a bucket of water on the ground and washed off the blood in the bucket. After about 10 minutes, it was apparent why this little happening was called the "Bucket of Blood."

Fake wooden crosses had been built near the castle, reminding newly arriving recruits that failure to adhere to training or instructions could lead to death. "He failed to keep his rifle clean, He showed himself on the skyline, He was too slow to take cover, This man advanced over top of cover," were some of the legends on the crosses. Achnacarry Castle itself was used as the headquarters and officers' mess for the training centre. In front of the castle was the barrack square where the Commandos drilled. Basic weapon-firing ranges were close to Loch Lochy, while assault courses and live firing ranges were below Loch Arkaig. The ranges included training for snap-shooting (from the hip), house-clearing, and pop-up targets. Other tasks included hand-to-hand combat, ambushes, and infiltration missions.

The Dark Mile, a five-mile road circuit, was used for the trainees' first speed march, to be completed in less than 50 minutes. The standards for speed marches were as follows: 7 miles under 70 minutes, followed by digging a defensive position; 9 miles under 90 minutes, followed by firing practice; 12 miles under 130 minutes, followed by a drill parade on the square; 15 miles under 170 minutes, followed by assault course and firing. There were cross-country marches, which included times of living rough, fieldcraft, rock-climbing, and mountain marches, and the assault course, and close combat using bayonets and knives. The Tarzan Course consisted of the Toggle Bridge and the Death Ride. The Death Ride, also called the Death Slide, was the idea of instructor Lieutenant Alick Cowieson, nicknamed Alick Mor (Alick the Mighty), and covered a distance of about 50 feet across the river, the descent being from a height of about 30 or 40 feet above the river. The Course consisted of ropes and grappling nets where recruits would swing from a rope and let go to fall onto the grappling net.

Training for the Rangers was threefold: physical fitness, weapons familiarity, and small-unit tactics. Many remembered not only the speed marches but the log drills, borrowed from ancient Scottish games, and hand-to-hand combat. Obstacle courses required stamina, shooting ability, and finally, when completely exhausted, ferocious bayonet drills that further honed the Rangers in the

Commando trade. The days started at 0645 and ended with supper at 1900.

The important two-man buddy system (Me and My Pal) was learned here. The two-man training meant that when one Ranger advanced, the other supported him with covering fire, including the use of Tommy (Thompson) submachine guns. Live fire exercises with "enemy rounds" striking around the Rangers, sometimes shooting the paddles out of their hands, provided realistic training that had not been part of their previous experience. Innovative equipment included bullets made of soap. Knife fighting, using the Fairbairn-Sykes Commando blade, was primarily intended for sentry removal by either cutting through the side of the throat, then pushing the blade straight out, cutting through everything—a bloody affair—or by driving it into the kidney. One of the weaknesses of the famed Commando dagger was its blade: It could snap when it hit bone. Eventually it would be redesigned as the Applegate-Fairbairn knife. The Commando knife was intended for killing people, nothing else. No doubt many Rangers did not expect to be using these techniques in combat, but some did, and Ranger Altieri surely must have recalled his interview with Captain Alvah Miller when he lied about his ability of killing men up close. Brass knuckles were also issued, and men had to learn how to kill an enemy quickly. One Ranger passed out after a Commando used a stranglehold. Physical training instructors were very good and rugged. To many Rangers, including Staff Sergeant Mercuriali, the training was rough. The wet weather, tents, uniforms, and gear also challenged them mentally, not just physically. However, this kind of misery would be encountered in future combat operations.

Vaughan was quite merciless. Training simulated battle conditions because good training meant a higher ability to survive combat. The Death Slide and rope bridge were challenging under normal conditions, but he made it far more frightening with bullets fired by skilled Commando marksmen whizzing all around the Rangers. Hand grenades were hurled into the river below the men fighting the ropes. To add to the realistic scenario, Vaughan also deployed machine-gun fire, bigger rounds, and demolition charges more powerful than hand grenades. "As far as the Rangers were concerned, the order of the day was bigger and better bangs." The impact on the Rangers early on was clear. Exhausted, pushed to their limits, it seemed the Rangers just couldn't cope. They were found wanting on the assault course, fell off the ropes and the Death Slide, failed the speed marches.

Captain Meade recalls those days: "Off your knees. Ye're bloody bone-idle, lad," still rings in many ears. The approach was basic. They took the body, made it tough and enduring, at the same time instilling in the mind and heart a degree of self-confidence in that body that had not existed before. By constant harassing with live fire during practically all phases of training, and through the use of training devices designed to overcome the inherent fear of bodily injury, they prepared them psychologically for combat.

Early in the training, on 6 July, the program temporarily halted to make preparations for a visit of inspection by Scottish Command. The next day, Lieutenant General Thorn, General Officer Commanding (GOC) Scottish Command, came for a review of the Rangers. The 1st Ranger Battalion conducted training exercises divided by companies. HQ Company executed reconnaissance techniques; Company A the infamous toggle ropes and Death Slide; CO B hit the shore in an opposed landing using Goatley Folding Boats (wood and canvas) with a follow-on attack on an objective and withdrawal. Company C's men hit an assault course, while CO D attacked a pillbox. Company E conducted rope climbs; while, last but not least, CO F demonstrated firing from the hip, bayonet fighting, and obstacle climbing. How well they did is up for debate. The training only got tougher, as Sullivan notes, "Fastest speed march yet—thought I was out on my feet but made it. Rope bridges, two ropes over river. I got almost across when *palomp* and an icy splash! Scaled down—abseiling—castle sheer drop of forty feet. Most of us burn or blister hands and thighs. Captain first as always." During the early stages of training, on 11 July, seven officers and twelve enlisted men who had been on temporary duty with the 2nd Canadian Division returned.

Perhaps part of the reason the Rangers finally improved and threw themselves into their training after a disastrous start was an event that had unfolded in training on 12 July 1942, some eight days after they started at the Depot. Private Lamont Durward Hoctel, of Lakeville, Indiana, born on 18 October 1916, like many others volunteered for the exciting new outfit. He had enlisted on 17 October 1941 at Fort Benjamin Harris in Indiana, and by the time he was 25 he made it into Easy Company (Company E), 1st Ranger Battalion. The Commandos were instructing Company E in river-crossing techniques. Fully kitted out, the Rangers began their movement across the river when several of the men were washed away. Either one or several of them might have collided with one another, losing their footing and handholds. Either way, two Rangers nearly drowned, while Hoctel went missing despite best efforts to locate him. It took some time to scour the river's banks going toward Lake Lochy, where Hoctel's body was finally discovered at 1930 hours. He was seen by 1st LT William A. Jarrett, Medical Officer 1st Ranger Battalion. Cause of death was "asphyxia due to drowning incurred in line of duty while undergoing instruction in new River Crossing." There were no handouts given. "That particular company had to return to go over it again." Undoubtedly, this loss affected Vaughan and his cadre as well as the Rangers.

Within a couple of days, according to Commando Donald Gilchrist, an amazing thing happened. The Rangers were back in business. They charged over the assault course and met the standards on the challenging speed marches. "Even Vaughan couldn't fail to be impressed by their newfound spirit, and in the end he mellowed towards them."

The training continued unabated. Vaughan did submit progress reports to Darby, who in turn forwarded some of the information to Brigadier General Truscott, the founder of the Rangers. Darby's report, *Progress Report on USA Rangers*, dated 17 July, mentions teething troubles, that Darby must make the best of this time in the Commando Depot to weed out all his duds by 31 July when the program ended. Other recommendations by Vaughan were also taken, such as removing unnecessary kit in order to be 100 percent mobile, and to consolidate the mortars away from the sections and to the company commander's headquarters. Additionally, the U.S. .30-cal machine guns were too heavy for the speed with which the Rangers needed to move and should be replaced with the lighter British Bren guns or the highly rated BAR with bipod—the Browning Automatic Rifle. Regarding weapons proficiency, the Rangers were behind, but Darby was confident they would soon be up to standards by the end of the course. He and his men, Vaughan notes, "are a very fine physique and are getting down to the hardening part of the course most cheerfully and willingly. There is a good feeling between the Depot instructors and the Rangers."

Vaughan was a man who maintained and demanded the highest standards. He kept a close eye on all his students and shared his thoughts with Major Darby, as both men thought alike, wanting the very best for the upcoming battles they were certain to face. The Depot Commandant, however, singled out five officers:

FIRST LIEUTENANT L. F. DIRKS: A very efficient officer who thinks that he has nothing to learn and in consequence gets very casual. The sooner he tries to teach and instill into the men under his command all that he knows, the better for him and his company.

CAPTAIN W. E. MARTIN: Lacks the personal character, enthusiasm, and keenness of a Commando leader. He is a very nice fellow but will have to improve his power of leadership if he's going to be a successful commander.

SECOND LIEUTENANT C. M. SHUNSTROM: Very capable officer who works hard and is 100 percent fit but requires more instruction in Men Management.

FIRST LIEUTENANT M. F. SCHNEIDER: Experienced and resourceful. An exceptionally good leader but must try and tighten up the discipline in this company.

FIRST LIEUTENANT A. H. NELSON: Very good officer who has not yet got the full cooperation and confidence of his men. He must try and improve his discipline.

Vaughan was prophetic in his analyses, as the future would bear out. The rest of the officers were doing very well, he writes. His last paragraph pointed out something very important, which was the significance of the non-commissioned officers. That now was the time to weed out the duds and replace them with the best material at hand. The Army relied on its NCOs—they were the backbone of success.

In the report to Truscott, Darby mentions the return of one officer and 17 enlisted men to their original organizations. The weeding-out process had already begun. Keeping track, Darby notes injuries, wounds, casualties, and sicknesses of the men. Again, it demonstrates the extremely realistic training Vaughan had designed and that he and his cadre had implemented. John Galbraith "suffered a gunshot wound of his left heel during night training, missing the tendon, it is considered a superficial wound and not a permanent disability and will probably be out of duty until end of July and is currently at a military hospital." Robert Merryman "suffered a severe strain of the lumbar spine, and it is suggested he transfer back to his own organization." Donald Hayes "accidentally shot himself causing a long superficial wound, return to duty." Private Robert B. Loman was "hit in right thigh by flying fragment of a grenade. Lacerated wound. Cleaned, sutured, dressed. Returned to duty." "Additionally, there have been numerous cases of sprained ankles, sprains, sneeze, etc. with varying severity. Seven men suffered from sickness, most from jaundice," but, Darby notes, no cases of venereal disease!

Darby's former boss, Major General Russell P. Hartle, conducted a review on 19 July, similar to that of Brigadier Thorn. The same exercises were performed, but the companies were switched around. Toward the end of their training cycle in late July, the Rangers were tasked with problems, some of which involved seizing the local town or the inn, blending in with the local populace as best as possible, while other war games pitted them against one another. Sullivan and some of his comrades were fifth columnists disguised as sheepherd-ers at Spean Bridge, where they met a Mister Camerun, ten sheep, and one sheepdog, who was a marvel to behold. The next day, they were captured because Camerun had noticed their GI [Government Issue] boots. The smallest details could prove fatal, a lesson that was drummed into the Rangers repeatedly. Others included rescuing a female hostage. One Ranger dressed as a woman, infiltrated the ene-my's headquarters, hiding his Tommy gun underneath his dress and successfully capturing the commander of the opposing force.

These problems required map and compass reading, amphib-ious operations, climbing, rough living, and guerrilla warfare, including attacking and defending key areas. These skills were vital and would be used by many Rangers escaping Italian and German prisoner-of-war camps.

There was an additional moment toward the end of training that could have been terrible but instead led to amusement among the Americans. It was on 26 July, when tragedy nearly struck down the first sergeant of Roy Murray's F Company. "A first sergeant was hit by a bullet in the rump not that serious, in fact, it amused nearly everyone." No doubt exhaustion played a part in this, or perhaps arrogance befit-ting a soldier who may have thought himself special. Exhaustion, how-ever, was real. "There followed a period in our lives," recalls Captain Meade in his letter to his wife,

> that is now a blur of shouting Sergeant Majors, sore feet, aching back, tea and dried herring for breakfast, unceas-ing drizzle, stormy nights in open boats on the high seas, and I do mean high seas, where puking to windward is a fatal mistake, mountains where you find marches on the very top after struggling through them all the way up, trace bullets enough and so close you could light a cigarette off them, while splashing around in a tiny little canvas assault boat [Goatly Folding Boat], smashing your pad, and one time creasing your first sergeant [Sergeant Donald "Butt"

Torbett] across his humpus while leering instructors lob
hand grenades at you for the shore.

The mission was completed successfully, and the men found the
butt-shot amusing—except for Vaughan, who viewed the incident
as disobedience by the American. One Commando said that the
Americans were fat chaps and presented excellent targets. There was
nothing funny in that. It was to fester within the Commandant while
the Rangers completed their remaining days. "The incident was forgotten by everyone except Vaughan," writes Gilchrist. "He was giving the
Rangers his famous farewell address in the big hut. After a few general-
ities, he got down to what had been preying on his mind. His huge Yank
audience was electrified when he suddenly said in confidential tones:

> Now I don't want to cause an international incident. What
> I'm going to say to you must remain here in this hut. . . . A
> few nights ago, on the night assault landing, a man was
> hurt. He had been told to kneel in the assault craft. But
> what does he do? He disobeyed orders. He sits on his back-
> side on the gunwale. And the silly bloody fool gets himself
> shot just as he deserves. We are at war, gentlemen. We must
> expect casualties. But not needless casualties like this one.
> Men who disobey orders and aren't disciplined can jeop-
> ardize the whole force. This man could've been responsi-
> ble for getting you all killed or maimed for life. That man
> is here with us today. Gentlemen, that man is of no use
> to you. There he is! Why don't you take them outside and
> shoot the bloody fool now before he gets you all killed?

But Vaughan had taught the Rangers a lesson, and had done it in
such a manner that it was a lesson they would not forget. Torbett must
have been embarrassed.

The outcome of the training under Vaughan and his instructors
was enormous. After a total of 4 weeks under Commando tutelage, a

Ranger was able to march 5 miles in 45 minutes, 7 miles in 72 minutes, 10 miles in 112 minutes, all with combat equipment. He had fired 1,200 rounds of caliber .30, 400 rounds of caliber .45, 4 rounds of 60mm or 81mm mortar ammunition, and had thrown at least 6 hand grenades. For, as Colonel Vaughan said, "If you swim half a mile from the landing craft, scale a 200-foot cliff, run 3 miles cross-country, vault 5 feet of barbed wire, it's all to no avail if you take a shot at the enemy and miss him."

These truisms would come to full force for some Rangers shortly. In a final report on 2 August to the Special Service Brigade, Combined Operations HQ, Vaughan reviewed the performances of the officers. Vaughan had high praise for a number of officers, validating Darby's selections: Darby, Dammer, Meade, Miller, Murray, Karbal, Saam, Loustalot, Carran, and Schneider were singled out, implying the others to not be of the same quality. The company commanders of Baker and Charlie were found wanting and were relieved and returned to their original organizations. First Sergeant "Butt" Torbett received excellent marks. Vaughan acknowledged the great improvement of the Rangers, noting their high morale even during difficult times. In particular, he recalled their mission of covering 30 miles, to a point where the Rangers discovered a canal's locks and bridges blown, and without hesitation they proceeded to cross the canal by going into the water. The final days included a 12-mile speed march around Loch Lochy involving a cross-canal movement using ropes, and an all-night march followed by a dawn attack across the river, which was swift and bitterly cold, on the castle. "During this month of basic Commando training," Meade writes, "we learned for the first time what the human body could endure, a lesson we never forgot. I'm sure no more grueling course was ever devised." But they had graduated, entitled to wear the famous Commando Green Beret and the tartan of the Clan Cameron, which the U.S. Army did not authorize, chests out, feeling proud, marching onward to their next training course.

LIKE A PYTHON DOES ITS PREY
Train to Germany, Prato, Italy
28 FEBRUARY 1944

The guards at the end of the train were oblivious to the dangerous men held in the boxcars. The train chugged along north, en route to Germany, and the cold darkening afternoon kept the guards focused on staying warm. Each boxcar was crammed with 50 men, some defeated, some weeping, and others determined to escape. There were several men hard at work with a small pocketknife they had smuggled in. The doors were locked, and they had to be creative to get out.

The Rangers took turns digging away at the floorboards, but the small knife wasn't up to snuff for that kind of work. Yet, all the hard work paid off when a piece of metal from the boards was pried loose. Metal tool in hands, the Rangers went to work on the small wooden window, a ventilator. It had been nailed shut, and barbed wire had been nailed on the outside. By 1600 hours, they had gone to work on it. And it definitely wasn't an easy task, made more complex by the train stopping every 15 to 20 minutes with guards checking the boxcars for any fools attempting to escape. Flashlights had come out as the hours went by, the guards marched up and down the train, only then, after the Rangers had replaced the wire and window and after the check, did it motor along again. The Rangers dug away for six hours. It was night. It was bitterly cold now, but the men working away hardly noticed. Finally . . .

Gustave Schunemann helped tie strips of a blanket together to form a rope, with one end tied to the biggest man inside the car, the other end thrown out the very small window. One, two, three, four Rangers made it out the window, then Schunemann climbed up, squeezed through the tiny opening, and dropped to the outside while desperately clinging onto the blanket rope with all his might. He was now strung along the outside of the boxcar, in the middle of the night, with his life depending on a blanket rope.

Schunemann got scared shitless. He couldn't believe his bad luck as the train slowed. First Cisterna, and now this. . . . "This" was the arrival of a dimly lit train station filled with civilians and German soldiers. Things slowed down for him as he scanned the crowded platform, people not noticing him, soldiers with rifles slung over their shoulders . . . the train sped up again. Schunemann watched as one or two civilians just stood there with their mouths agape, they in as much shock as he. Past the marshaling yard, the train got faster. He hung on tighter. Finally, he pushed off and jumped into the darkness that swallowed him, like a python does its prey.

4

DIEPPE

ON 1 AUGUST 1942, THE RANGER BATTALION MOVED TO DORLIN House, near Argyle, Scotland, for combined operations training with the British Royal Navy. Companies Able and Baker located at Roshven, Companies Charlie and Dog at Glenborrodale, Companies Easy and Fox at Glencripesdale, and Headquarters Company at Salen and Shielbridge. Whereas Achnacarry taught and honed the individual skills of the Rangers and forced them to work as a team, the training here coalesced them into sections, platoons, and companies, incorporating everything for future amphibious operations. Time had come for everything amphibious: After all, that was the bread and butter of Commandos. Much to their displeasure, the place was a desolate wasteland. The West Coast of Scotland, in a region so isolated and foreboding in nature, was immediately dubbed "Dracula's Birthplace." Sullivan considered it a beautiful spot, wild, rugged, while Meade thought it "a spot so isolated that your connection with the outside world is by mail boat and your only delicate feminine atmosphere is a passing doe, sheep, or goat; and in Christ how they can run all that white slavery they call Commando training. A hardening course, in more ways than one. If anyone ever suggests taking a walk to me when I get home or even getting on the *Island Queen,* I'll kick seven different colors of business right out of him."

Physical conditioning, weapons firing, night operations, and small problems under fire were carried out along with amphibious training. From 3 to 31 August, amphibious landing operations used wooden boats, lightly armored with a thin sheet of metal and without a ramp, known as R-boats, and made by the Higgins Corporation of New Orleans, and fishing boats such as drifters and cobles, and cutters. These missions were conducted often in rough surf, landing on rocky shores, and as always were accompanied by Bren gun fire by qualified marksmen. Rangers worked with young naval officers from the Commonwealth and three young women from the WRNS [Women's Royal Naval Service]. Darby was promoted to Lieutenant Colonel on 6 August 1942.

It was during this interim that a portion of the Rangers received its first baptism of fire, when six officers and 44 enlisted men participated in the Dieppe raid on 19 August 1942. Meade's thoughts on Dieppe were simple: "Christ, how we wish we could have been along." Sergeant Szima, on the other hand, got his wish. Although initially not on the roster to deploy, he found his replacement sergeant major, formerly from the National Guard, and discovered that one of the 50 men to deploy had come down with a cold the morning of their departure. Receiving permission to speak with Major Darby, Szima made his pitch yet again to be one of the first to see combat. Dismissed by Darby, who offered no encouragement, Szima was not hopeful. During the formation, Darby was to give the Rangers a departure speech, when he turned to Szima and said, "How long for you to pack your bag?" He said, "They've been packed ever since I came here." His wish had come true. The raid would not be what he had been expecting.

For the rest of the battalion, training continued. Meade notes in his diary the arrival of mail with a short entry, "2 letters from Hazel— 'bout time, the hussy!" One night, during a field training exercise in the never-ending rain, Dammer was tasked with a raid on a town and a mock radio tower. Leading four companies, A through D, he was to defeat the opposing forces under Lieutenant Schneider, comprised of the remaining two companies, E and F, and supported by elements of the Scottish Police and Home Guard. The opposition commander, Schneider, launched his patrol boats and intercepted several of the attacking forces' boats. Nonetheless, the attack raged using soap bullets, finally surrounding Schneider's defenders and successfully blowing up the tower. Unfortunately for some of the locals, the excessive use of explosives shattered windows and knocked plaster off homes a mile away. The mission was a success. The Rangers improved with each day.

At the end of their training, the Rangers were permitted to take a boat to Oban where they enjoyed drinks, shopping, and more. Several Rangers dressed in Scottish attire, including kilts, and posed for images at the local studio. Meade notes that Carran got drunk and was sad. Meade went to a dance and stopped 20 fights. And almost got into one himself. On the way back, the Rangers, minus six men AWOL, did not do themselves proud, brawling with the crew, vomiting a lot, all amidst civilian passengers sharing the boat ride with them. Getting back to Dorlin House, and past the Naval HQ, required some kind of order, which was hard to come by; and two Rangers, clearly not recovered, nearly drowned in mud puddles. Meade writes, "The holiday over, thank Gawd! Everyone was bitter as hell about not being at Dieppe." Meanwhile at Dieppe . . .

GREEN BEACH, POURVILLE, *OPERATION JUBILEE*, 19 AUGUST 1942, 0450 HOURS

The cold night, the rhythm of the boat, and the seawater spray didn't bother Sergeant Marcel Swank as he slept in the tiny, cramped wooden landing craft crossing the channel toward France. No, what startled him awake was the distant thunder, a murderous roar. His tired eyes saw the tense faces of the Canadians beneath their steel helmets. The Queen's Own Cameron Highlanders packed the vessel, gripping their weapons tightly. He rose unsteadily, shaking the cobwebs from his mind. There. In the distance he saw bright flashes dotting the horizon and the sky, illuminating the dark with its pinpricks, followed by slow rolling thunder. It took a second to put together the roar and the flashes . . . war, to his front.

Close to him was fellow Ranger Sergeant Lloyd Church from Able Company. A man who'd play a significant role in the rest of his life—Marcel Swank just didn't know it yet. Next to Church stood the figure of a professional Canadian sergeant they had been assigned to for the past two days. The two Rangers shared the same terrifying voyage as their fellow Canadians. The 67-mile ride from Newhaven was full of uncertainty. The French coastline seemed to move slowly yet quickly toward them. Some 35 minutes later, Swank noticed the movement of his landing craft. The flotilla of assault boats formed into a single line, like a snake slithering across the water, some 500 yards in length. He was but a thousand yards away from the war. The column moved toward its intended target. He cursed not knowing the details of the mission at hand. They were just there to accompany the Canadians, to observe, to participate at a distance. He had to ask for details; few had been forthcoming. He remembered something about having to pass through the other Canadian unit, the South Saskatchewan Regiment, that had just landed to secure the beachhead and to reduce German defenses. The two Rangers were going to follow the Canadian sergeant and the Cameron Highlanders as they were to seize the headlands at Pourville, securing the beachhead, and then push farther inland to neutralize other targets including an inland airfield.

The closer they got to the beach, the angrier the German defense sounded, seemingly sending all hell at them. Shells and tracers grew in volume and light—a celebration of impending death. The heavy voices of shore batteries, intermixed with the middling crumps of mortars and the staccato of machine-gun fire, were war's choir. They overwhelmed the sound of his small landing craft's engine . . . the fury of war was close, mortars slammed into the waters all around. Swank looked incredulously at the destruction ahead when suddenly a strange sound tore him away from contemplating his own fate . . . a bagpipe. On the right small forward landing deck, and next to him, stood the most triumphant figure he had ever seen. A defiant piper—Corporal Alex Graham, he would learn later—announced the arrival of the Camerons by playing a "Hundred Pipers," ready to kick the enemy's ass. Impervious to fear and the dangers all around, the bagpiper announced the arrival of the fucking hardcore Camerons. A glorious moment, a surreal moment, a sight that remained the most significant in Swank's life, one that inspired not just him but all the soldiers aboard the wooden landing craft. With a great, inspired shout, they leaped out and hit the beaches at 0535, as light broke through the night and mortars exploded in the water, automatic weapons fire showering everything—all at once, it seemed. He and Church scrambled after their Canadian sergeant, struggling, rushing across the rocky beach toward the seawall some 50 yards away. They needed to clear it, get on top of the promenade. Swank took hurried steps onto the shale beach. He could only focus on the Canadian NCO barely a few steps away. . . . Fuck, the man went down, crumpled, hit the beach hard. Swank kept running. The lump of former life littered the beach with his dead body, one among many Canadians mowed down mercilessly, savagely. Swank hunched forward as though that would help him avoid angry lead, and he ran like hell.

The raid on the sleepy coastal town of Dieppe in France on 19 August 1942 was in all likelihood designed to snatch or pinch valuable intelligence from the German Navy—to capture any material found onboard vessels anchored in the harbor and in the naval headquarters building, identified to be in one or two buildings a couple of blocks away from the beach. The material was related to the new naval 4-rotor electromechanical cipher machine ("Enigma") if not the machine itself. In addition to this operation, British sergeant Jack Nissenthal was attached to seize intelligence from a radar station on the high cliffs near Green Beach. His bodyguards had orders to kill him in the event of capture, because he knew too much of Allied intelligence and technology. Importantly, though, the planners wanted to obscure the true nature of the raid as it was not a smaller, more precise raid into Dieppe. A slightly bigger operation would disguise the true intent of a small group of Marine Commandos and others who were to seize the vital intelligence. Dieppe was the only port big enough to have this or other cypher aides to help crack the codes. But it wasn't so large a town as to make the attack nearly impossible.

Dieppe, located at the Arzues River, was a relatively small town of 25,000 inhabitants. The beaches were for the most part fist-sized chert rocks (shale, shingle, pebble, flint rock), making it less than ideal for beachgoers. The contours of the beach also changed, depending on the time of day, tide, and weather. The town's main attraction was its casinos, making it the "poor man's Monte Carlo." The town and surroundings looked similar to the layout of half an amphitheater: high chalky cliffs on either side, penetrated occasionally by the mouths of rivers, setting the town as the central stage. The terrain overall was foreboding and harsh. The elevation ranged from 16 to 300 feet. As such, the key to the attack was in securing the headlands on either side of Dieppe and eliminating its strong German defenses that dominated the coast and shoreline below. These strong points consisted of bunkers, pillboxes, and machine gun nests. And, of course, gun batteries. The plan called for their seizure before the main attack into the center of Dieppe, thereby allowing for unencumbered access to the channel leading to the harbor itself. Once in the harbor, certain units were to execute the vital pinch-raid. Some 800 fighters and fighter-bombers, including cannon-firing Hurricane fighters and Boston bombers, the latter of which were to lay smoke, were part of the operation. The naval contingent provided some 250 vessels for the raid. Bombardment from the ships was not favored, since the true intent was to steal sensitive material and not to accidentally destroy it or to create massive piles of rubble in the streets, preventing tanks and infantry from seizing their key objectives—the harbor and headquarters building. Casualties were taken into account for the successful grab of cyber assets.

The original operation had been dubbed *Rudder* (and *Rudder II*), but was canceled in the first week of July, on the 5th, because of poor weather. This led to the return of the 19 Rangers, on 11 July, previously assigned to the operation. *Rudder* included U.S. Marines to join the attack into the harbor alongside Marine Commandos. The rebranding of *Rudder* to *Jubilee* led to the inclusion of 50 Rangers, in lieu of the Marines. But the Rangers were now spread throughout the attacking forces, not just to one boat as the U.S. Marines previously had been. The selected Rangers were picked to represent each company of the 1st Ranger Battalion. The Rangers were distributed in "penny packets" throughout the various Troops of the Commando.

Forty of them were attached to No. 3 Commando, four with No. 4 Commando, and the remaining six were spread throughout the 2nd Canadian Division, which was tasked with the central attack into Dieppe. Their experiences and treatment by the Allies varied, from being equals to being left in the dark. Additionally, they were not supposed to take an active part in the missions; however, since most had participated in the rehearsals, it seems clear that they were, for the most part, to be involved in the assaults.

For the Rangers, the "special demolition training" began with Captain Roy Murray of F Company who, along with 3 officers and 36 enlisted men, left Scotland on 1 August by rail to London, connecting to Seaford where they joined No. 3 Commando under Lieutenant Colonel Dunford-Slater. Why Murray was picked to lead the detachment, he didn't know. "I have the foggiest idea. I guess I'm the oldest living Ranger [32 and 6 months older than Darby], so I guess it chose me for my great maturity." A small detachment of 4 Rangers under Staff Sergeant Stempson, who had just turned 23 and was from Minnesota, traveled to Portland to join 4 Commando under Lieutenant Col. Simon "Shimi" Lovat. Lovat was officially Simon Fraser, the 24th Chief of Clan Fraser of Lovat, but known universally to the men as "Shimi," which stems from the traditional medieval Gaelic title he inherited in 1933 of "Mac Shimidh"—the Son of Simon, after Simon Fraser, the founder of the clan. Two weeks later, on 15 August, 5 Rangers under 1st Lieutenant Robert Flanagan traveled also by rail to London, then on to Farnham, East Bridge House, where they arrived on 17 August. He reported to Major G. M. Stockley, who was involved in planning for the 2nd Canadian Division, the next day. One of the Rangers, Sergeant Marcel Swank, felt like a tourist intruding on the Canadians. These last Rangers received no information whatsoever and were split between various Canadian units. Flanagan believed East Bridge House, disguised as a Royal Navy Rest Center, to be the release point for special troops such as French Commandos, Sudeten Germans, a Russian, and other "phantom" soldiers—all non-English, and disguised as Canadians. He could only guess their missions. Once on board and en route, Flanagan was told that the target of the intended raid was Dieppe, and his transport, along with Canadian troops, was going to Green Beach. Sixty LCAs (Landing Craft Assault) were employed to carry the assault infantry of the 2nd Canadian Infantry Division, A Commando Royal Marines, and No. 4 Commando.

The Rangers who were attached to 3 Commando were completely embraced by their counterparts, recalled 1st Lieutenant Leonard Dirks, who was attached to 3 Troop, 3 Commando. Maps, aerial photographs, and a relief map made out of plaster of Paris and colored, were studied first by the officers and NCOs, then by the men. Finally, on 18 August, the entire troop assembled, and in typical fashion were checked by their NCOs to make sure that everything was in order. By 1700, they were transported to the harbor and loaded onto LCPs (Landing Craft [Personnel]). "At the last moment, I was placed in boat 17, boat 16 carrying troop HQ. I was the only Ranger in 17," writes Dirk in his After-Action Report. The Rangers dressed like the Commandos, who wore denim trousers. The Americans didn't wear their traditional Ranger short-cut leggings.

On 18 August 1942, on a moonlit night, some 237 vessels departed England from various ports with the intent to land just before dawn on the 19th at 0431 hours, with the sun rising at 0550 and high tide occurring at 0405. The landings were timed under the cover of darkness and then to exploit the early light for their advances. The raid took place along five major points, divided into eight beaches, covering a front roughly 24 kilometers long from the far east at Petit Berneval to the far western flank at Sainte-Marguerite-sur-Mer, near Varengenville-sur-Mer. These far-flank attacks were carried out by Commandos and Rangers with the mission of destroying the batteries on high ground and allowing for the staggered central assault into Dieppe to occur unmolested. It was vital to disable the gun batteries on each flank, a point driven home to the men before the raid, including the expected high casualties, to the point that a handful of Rangers thought about quitting.

The eight beaches were from left (east) to right (west), looking south toward Dieppe:

Yellow Beach I and II at Petit Berneval and Grand Berneval—eliminate gun battery Goebbels on high ground to protect main attacking force, dubbed *Operation Flodden*.

Blue Beach at Puys—capture eastern headlands to protect naval penetration into channel and harbor of Dieppe to seize intelligence assets.

Red Beach—Dieppe, west of channel and harbor—to seize town and vessels in harbor, which may have intelligence assets in boats.

White Beach—Dieppe, seize and hold town.

Green Beach at Pourville—seize western headlands and gun battery Göring to protect main assault on Dieppe.

Orange Beach I and II at Vasterival-sur-Mer and Sainte-Marguerite-sur-Mer—to destroy gun battery Hess dominating the coastline and beaches of Dieppe, dubbed *Operation Cauldron*.

Both flanks were composed of veteran pinch Commandos who had conducted previous raids, who would start the landings. The plan then called for the assault on Blue and Green; then a frontal assault on Red and White to commence some 30 minutes after the flank attacks had begun; followed by a subsequent wave led by the Royal Marine Commandos, in two strike groups, to execute the core mission of the raid—to get into Dieppe harbor after the frontal assault had cleared the way. The Marine Commando was to navigate in the up-armored and up-armed HMS *Locust*, through the channel, a gauntlet with German strong points along the cliffs and in the town, into the harbor to search and seize Enigma assets in German boats and naval headquarters. In order for all this to work, the gun batteries at Yellow and Orange had to be silenced, and Green and Blue needed to drive the Germans off the beaches and headlands that were flanking the town. The latter beach objectives and tasks were twofold—the first, to allow the Royal Marines into the channel unmolested; and secondly, to make the attacks into Dieppe on Red and White far less deadly. *Jubilee* had many interdependent parts; in fact, it would prove to be a house of cards . . . falling on top of the men.

YELLOW I AND II—*OPERATION FLODDEN*, BERNEVAL, 13 KILOMETERS EAST OF DIEPPE, GOEBBELS BATTERY

The far-left flank assault at Berneval took place on two beaches some 8–9 kilometers east of Dieppe. The farthest to the left [east] was Yellow I; the one closer to the central attack was dubbed Yellow II. Here, No. 3 Commando under Lieutenant Col. Dunford-Slater and his 325 men; 40 Rangers under Captain Roy Murray; five Free French Commandos of No. 10 Inter-Allied Commandos; and four signals unit members, all part of Group 5, were to take the high ground and eliminate the four-gun battery code-named Goebbels next to Berneval-le-Grand about half a mile inland. The Goebbels battery, with its three 170mm and four 105mm guns, had a range of over 20 kilometers, placing them within range of the assault on Dieppe. The Rangers had conducted rehearsals with the Commando for a two-week period and knew the details of the mission. The groups were to converge on Goebbels in a pincer move.

No. 3 left New Haven with 20–24 CP/R[aid]-Boats with 20 men per vessel at 2030 hours. This early version of the landing-craft assault craft had no ramp in front. Instead, the troops just jumped over the side. Of plywood construction with armored bulkhead, the 34-foot boats at very shallow draft could normally carry about 25 men. Twelve men would be under the gunwale, with the rest in the stern. They were crewed by four sailors, an officer, and three ratings, and armed with 7.62mm Lewis light machine guns. Each craft carried added two-gallon fuel cans for the 67-mile voyage. Some concerns were raised about the fuel cans in case of an attack. Four boats returned during the voyage, unable to continue after experiencing engine trouble. Half the force was under Dunford-Slater, intended for the eastern part of the attack on Yellow Beach I. The other half, led by

Second-in-Command Major Peter Young, was to hit Yellow II, the western beach. The flotilla had crossed the large maritime minefield that the Germans had laid without incident. Their anticipated landing at 0450 was good to go, despite having lost the four aforementioned boats to engine trouble.

A cloth-covered British steel helmet protected his head; dark paint covered his face. Ranger Staff Sergeant Gino Mercuriali pondered the mission. They were still miles offshore. It was for the most part dark, lit by the moon, the landing craft churning through the dark waters. He observed the details of the men. Same steel helmets, denim and olive-drab shirts. Like him, they had smeared dark brown color on their faces to kill the shine, to break up their otherwise bright white faces. His thoughts were interrupted: A flare popped in the sky, exploding the assault boats from darkness into light. Gunfire hit the landing craft and all around. Gino gripped his weapon tightly, unable to avoid watching the developing naval action. Small German boats fired on them. The landing crafts took evasive actions. Gino saw something that looked like a flaming onion, coming straight for his head—shells from the German boat. They missed him. It was a beautiful sight; lost in thought, he was mesmerized. Beautiful, except for the men in damaged craft, perhaps wounded, perhaps killed. He saw landing craft get hit, desperate men swimming to other vessels, laden with heavy gear. Just before panic set in, the engagement ended as quickly as it had begun. He thought he spotted a tanker and a boat get sunk by a British destroyer. There wasn't much time for him and his section, though: His landing craft had been hit. They had to evacuate to another one as best as possible. This was his first time under fire. Years later, he recalled this action and other amphibious assaults. "On this occasion, as with later ones, my composure, I would say, was very good. I always seemed to be engaged enough that things weren't so scary when it was happening but at some time later, when recalled to mind, you are scared out of your pants. I had nightmares after returning to home." The time of the engagement was 0347 hours, 19 August 1942. He did not land.

Lieutenant Dirks, with 3 Troop, 3 Commando, also didn't land. His craft was also engaged by the German boats at the time. Trying to dodge the incoming fire, the boat officer took evasive actions, resulting in a delay, as the landing-craft convoy dispersed while under attack. By the time things were sorted out and the attempt was made to head toward an unknown beach in daylight, they were under constant fire. By six in the morning, Dirks and many others had made their way to Dieppe proper, joining the central flotilla.

Sergeant Ed Thompson, section leader in Lieutenant Loustalot's second platoon, which was headed toward Yellow I, had a brutal experience, thinking, "It was pure murder. They were waiting for us. They had us zeroed in with motors and artillery fire. Then this armed trawler came in and raked our deck with high explosives. Twenty Commandos and sailors were killed. The boat commander had his leg shot off right next to me."

Chaotic scenes abounded, with many believing small and fast German E[nemy] boats to be the attacking force. None of the R-boats used by 3 Commando were sunk. Many were damaged, however, and many people had to climb aboard other vessels. The German coastal convoy, alerted around 0347 of enemy vessels, was composed of five coastal freighters and two armed trawlers, UJ (U-Jäger) 1404 and UJ 1411, and a Motor Launch 4014. The Germans were not spared confusion either.

UJ 1411, who was ahead of the convoy, engaged a British force and UJ 1404 followed suit a moment later. Survivors said they sank two or three MGBs [motor gun boats] with their 88mm gun at a range of about one mile, but they were not consistent on this point. Several rounds of star shell were fired during this stage of the action. The Captain was killed soon after the engagement opened, and the senior CPO [Chief Petty Officer] took over from him. Shortly afterwards, however, she [naval craft are typically assigned the female gender] was attacked by five more MGBs, and

was hit in her engines. She continued on her course until
her engines were hit again, and she caught fire.

The raiding force, however, suffered, ripping to shreds the
planned attack on Yellow beaches. This despite the fact that the
Germans had been detected by British radar earlier at night.
Seemingly, though, this channel clash did not alert the Germans of
the impending raid. Dunford-Slater transferred to an R-boat from
Steam Gunboat (SGB) 5, the *Grey Owl*, as the boat turned and limped
away. Captain Shunstrom, who was on board with Dunford-Slater
on SGB5, never made it ashore, and neither did Dunford-Slater.
Supposedly, Shunstrom was so frustrated that he later fired a machine
gun from the rail of the ship at attacking German airplanes, implying his crazed state of mind, at least from the perspective of a few
Rangers, a reputation that followed him over time. Ranger Sweazey
recalls in his diary that he and others wired machine guns to the rail
when they knew they were not going to land, subsequently firing at
aircraft. This was common practice during the operation, especially
during the massive air battle that was to come: Many small arms were
fired at the Luftwaffe, strafing the men and vessels. The Allied forces
suffered casualties at sea including five wounded Ranger casualties;
Sergeant John J. Knapp, with 3 Commando, was wounded on board
the SGB5 by German naval gunfire off Berneval-sur-Mer (Yellow
Beach), along with PFC Stanley Bush and PFC Charles Reilly. Other
casualties included PFC James Edwards and PVT Edwin Moger. Only
a dozen out of 50 Rangers landed at their objectives.

YELLOW I AND II

This accidental naval encounter and clash rendered No. 3 Commando
ineffective as the raiding force suffered an immediate setback with
a loss of personnel. Only five or seven craft landed with either 80
or 96 men, including four Rangers, making an effective landing at
Yellow I at 0510/15 hours under Commando Captain Richard Wills.

Ranger Bertholf's landing craft sunk, and he lost his weapon and held on to rocks near a cliff until he was picked up much later by a small Commando boat. He didn't make it ashore. Later on, he asked Darby for survivor's leave like Commandos received after raids. It was rejected with a simple "You can have it 'after the war.'" Once landed, they faced a 300-foot cliff with a gully leading to the top, where a small church and white house were situated. German troops looked down on them. This was not going well, to say the least.

At Yellow II, the second group landed successfully at 0445, five minutes ahead of schedule. That was great; the problem was that only one boat landed. Twenty Commandos, and no Rangers, under Major Peter Young had to do the job of moving forward with their crucial mission. They landed some 50 yards to the right of the gully, hoping to avoid a potential machine-gun (MG) nest guarding it. They breached wire obstacles and attempted to move to the top of the high, chalky cliff. Failing, they caught a lucky break. Germans had hammered iron stakes, pitons, into the face of the cliff. Grabbing ahold of them and using toggle ropes, which the Commandos had used in all their training and experience, they climbed the cliff. Reaching the top by 0510, some 25 minutes later, they observed the delayed arrival of five landing craft under Captain Wills on Yellow Beach I. The craft were under heavy small-arms fire. Seeing his comrades in trouble, Young had to make a decision. Considering that they were heavily understrength, and some of his men were realizing the near impossibility of accomplishing their mission, he argued for moving toward Wills and his beleaguered Commandos on the other beach unless the Goebbels gun battery opened fire. That barrage would endanger the whole operation. If and when it fired, they would have to silence it as best as possible under the circumstances with or without Wills's Commandos stuck on the other beach.

En route to the east and toward Yellow I, they reached a small wood some 20 minutes later. Here, Young encouraged his men. Having decided to join the fight at the other beach unless the battery started to fire, they advanced in a cornfield, along a cart track that ran from Berneval to Dieppe. A young French boy was detained and questioned. They released him, being told that roughly 200 Germans were in the vicinity. The Commandos moved forward cautiously, entering the town of Berneval where they cut the wires on a telephone pole. Near a small church they were shot at while pushing forward. Suddenly the German battery opened fire. That was that. They now had no choice but to try to silence those guns, no matter whether they had five or five hundred Commandos. Every time the battery fired, it emitted large clouds of smoke, most likely obscuring the gunners' views. Fortunately for Young and his handful of men, the Germans could not depress their barrels low enough to pose any threat to them, even though they tried. The greatest threat came from German small-arms fire.

The Commandos, now exposed and under fire, suppressed the battery with their own weapons. The tactic worked very well, forcing the German crews to seek cover. For 90 minutes, the few No. 3 Commandos suppressed the battery and the supporting Germans. Finally, running low on ammunition, and with an increase in German return fire, Young decided to retreat from the beach. He ordered his men to do so at 0745 hours, covering their retreat down the cliff. Under fire the entire time, they accidentally triggered a mine, but safely evacuated all men. They got back on the boat, which had waited offshore, and had departed for New Haven by 0820 hours. The effective use of sniper fire prevented the battery from engaging Allied troops and ships.

YELLOW I—SURRENDER

The small, wiry lieutenant, Edward Loustalot, was born on 17 March 1919 in Franklin, St. Mary Parish, Louisiana. His slight drawl clearly identified him as being from Louisiana. He had graduated from Louisiana State University with a degree in engineering in 1939 and, having graduated from ROTC, received his commission as Second Lieutenant. Friends thought him a fun-loving extrovert—which seemingly changed once he joined the Rangers, where he mostly kept to himself although he was well-liked. "Edward was the kind of guy to volunteer for something like that," William Maurin, a college friend of Loustalot, said. "He was fearless about almost anything." Following graduation, Edward spent a year working for Louisiana Power and Light before being called to active duty.

Unlike Yellow II, at Yellow I the situation proved disastrous for the Commandos and Rangers. Captain Richard L. Wills, with his ragtag group of over 80 men from Troops 2, 5, and 6; four Rangers of LT Edward Loustalot with 6 Troop; Sergeant Albert Jacobsen; PFC Walter Bresnahan; and PFC Edwin Furru, along with four French Inter-Allied Commandos, attempted to break out of the beachhead with daylight fast approaching. It was around 0510–0515 and they were 20 to 25 minutes behind schedule. The shale beach had three distinct gullies leading to the top of the high, chalky cliff. The landing was unopposed—although ineffective shots rang out from the gully on the right, despite Peter Young from Yellow II claiming heavy fire. The ragtag group didn't worry about mines on the rocky beach, knowing it was a near impossibility to lay any under the rocks. Shortly into their climb, they hit far more barbed wire than earlier briefs had led them to expect. It took them a slow-going 10 to 15 minutes to cut through the obstacles. Wills led his group through a deep bank of wires and thrust inland with vigor, wrote Major Young years later.

Moving in column, the men advanced 150 yards along the right ravine, where they passed two unmanned automatic-weapons positions. When they made it to the heights, some Commandos encountered nests of machine gunners and pill boxes, which they silenced. They then launched a disjointed attack through a built-up area, Petit Berneval, to the gun battery to their west. In effect, if things had gone well, the groups would have converged and destroyed the guns. But this was not to be the case.

Advancing up a narrow road, bordered by villas and hedges, the group made slow progress. This was probably no farther inland than 500 to 600 yards. Some of the men, including Ranger Edwin Furru, moved cautiously through a garden behind a small cottage. They stopped when they saw a large building or hotel ahead; they hunkered down, waiting for the scout to return to their position. The scout gave the all-clear, and they advanced toward the building, and then along a trail. They became engaged in a heavy firefight and realized they'd not be able to push through to their objective. Wills, whose eyesight was not remarkable, wrote Young, accounted for one German— probably the best shot of his life—but soon afterward was shot through the neck (or hit by fragments of a grenade). With his fall, the momentum was out of the attack. It was clear to everyone that to continue the attack would amount to a forlorn hope, and the order was given to retreat to the beach.

During the withdrawal, the group had to fight its way back through enemy positions. They had landed a couple of hours before. The group was slowly making its way when a machine-gun nest blocked their movement. It was here, toward the end of the action, that Lieutenant Loustalot took charge and moved forward to destroy the machine gun, and was cut down, seemingly hit by a burst of automatic-weapons fire. Ranger Private First Class Bresnahan, who was near his officer when both had just been pinned down by the enemy's fire, took a few seconds and stared at the crumpled body of the well-liked lieutenant. He had been shot in the stomach, and his field glasses were shattered by the bullets. The machine-gun nest must have been silenced by someone, unless, of course, Bresnahan looked at Loustalot while under cover. Ranger Furru, too, saw the body of Lieutenant Loustalot as he made his way down the beach. He came across two Commandos, who warned him not to linger near Loustalot's body or else he'd get hit by the small-arms fire in the area. One assumes that the Commandos were wounded around the time Loustalot was killed. Nonetheless, Furru and others made their way down the ravine to the beach, with Furru almost getting his head torn off by a 75mm shell from a captured French gun well above him. It was so close that he felt something go by his neck. Ranger Furru bumped into Sergeant Jacobsen, and they shared cigarettes and waited on the beach.

By the time the men had reached the beach, they were in a hopeless situation, as they came under fire from a bunker at the top of the western end of the cliffs. Although the Commandos silenced it with rifle fire, many of them were low on ammunition, and the terrain was unforgiving. The cliffs provided minimal cover, as small arms and grenades showered them from above. Some of them thought of swimming into the sea, hoping to get picked up by one of the many boats in the area. Others thought maybe they could outlast the day, hoping some brave naval personnel would return with the assault vessels to pick them up off the beach. It was when German troops climbed down to sweep the area and called on them to surrender that "Lieutenant William Wright, a veteran of earlier raids and Norway, wounded and the only officer still on his feet, saw little point in continuing the fight and he surrendered the remnants of 3 Commando on Yellow Beach One." Furru was subsequently wounded by Allied aircraft when he was transported to the rear of the German lines. All of the Americans captured in the raid—Jacobsen, Bresnahan, Furru, and later Church from Green Beach—were sent to Stalag VII in Germany.

Although the loss of the men was regrettable, were it not for the actions of No. 3 Commando under Major Peter Young suppressing the battery for nearly two hours, more men would have been killed on the beaches of Dieppe and more ships sunk in the graveyard of the sea.

As to 2nd Lieutenant Edward Loustalot, he was posthumously awarded the Distinguished Service Cross by King George VI. Beforehand, he received a Posthumous Mention in Despatches by Lieutenant Colonel J. F. Dunford-Slater, which was a prerequisite for the DSC, a higher award. Lord Mountbatten issued a Letter of Certification dated 29 March 1943 to Edward's father.

> Second Lieut. Loustalot was attached to the party of No 3 Commando which landed on Berneval, Dieppe, on August 19th 1942. This party consisted of only three boat loads out of fifteen which had been engaged and dispersed by the enemy before reaching shore. They immediately went into the attack against greatly superior forces. Throughout

the action, in which he lost his life, Second Lieut. Loustalot displayed the greatest coolness and gallantry under heavy fire and by his example and leadership contributed greatly to the attack, which successfully engaged large numbers for a long time and enabled another party, a mile distant, to approach their objective with only minor opposition.

Captain Wills, who had been imprisoned until the end of the war, wrote a letter to the Loustalots, stating that the group and Edward Loustalot had fought for several hours and that he had been killed at the end of the action. Edward's younger brother Albert would be devastated by the news. It haunted him throughout his life. But there was more to the story. One could simply write that Edward Loustalot was one of the first American servicemen killed in Europe, and, subsequently, buried at the Ardennes American Cemetery in Belgium. But that reduces history to a mere cold footnote.

In the immediate aftermath of the disaster, the remains of the Rangers were not immediately recovered by American forces, and therefore considered missing in action. Years passed and the men officially remained in MIA [Missing in Action] status. In 1948, a high school friend of Loustalot was determined to find his friend's burial location. After many letters to the War Department and visits to the American Graves Registration Service (AGRS) with facts and evidence, three remains were exhumed from the Canadian cemetery in Dieppe and sent to an identification lab at Ardennes American Cemetery in Belgium. The AGRS confirmed that the exhumations were the remains of Loustalot, Henry, and Randall.

Loustalot's death was well documented. In the ensuing confusion of the raid, Rangers Henry and Randall would die that day surrounded by strangers, barely noticed, and alone.

ORANGE I AND II—*OPERATION CAULDRON,*
9.7 KM WEST OF DIEPPE, HESS BATTERY

Things had not gone well on objectives Yellow Beaches I and II. Events unfolding simultaneously on the other far end differed greatly. The far-right flank, the western assault, also featured two beaches designated for No. 4 Commando and four Rangers to assault. These beaches were code-named Orange I at Vesterival-sur-Mer, with Orange II representing the farthest extent of the Allied attack at Sainte-Marguerite-sur-Mer. The intended target was a German battery just inland of Vesterival called the Hess Battery 813. The plan also called for a pincer attack from the two beaches.

Orange I, under Major Derek Mills-Roberts and just C Troop, 4 Commando, saw Sergeant Szima, who had been itching for combat since the war began, and had told Darby he wanted to be in the first fight, along with Corporal Franklin Koons of Iowa. Mills-Roberts was to strike directly at the battery. The outer beach, farther west, was Orange II; it included Minnesotans Staff Sergeant Stempson and CPL Bill Brady, who were seconded to No. 4 Commando's Troops A, B, F, and HQ under LT Col. Lord Simon "Shimi." This larger group was going to move in a semicircle toward the battery from the side and rear. In total, No. 4 had 250–252 Commandos and 4 Rangers.

Both assault groups landed on time: 0450 for Orange I, and 0453 for Orange II. Their target was Battery 813, which was composed of six 150mm guns roughly three-quarters of a mile from the chalky cliffs. The battery had camouflage netting and was protected by a concrete-and-sandbag berm. It was not a fortified bunker complex. Just behind the battery facility stood a radar station and an anti-aircraft gun emplacement. The perimeter was fortified with barbed wire and machine-gun emplacements.

Prior to the mission, two teams of two Rangers each trained with the Commandos for a two-week period. They knew all the details of their operation and could trace it on maps. One item of note during training for the mission came from Szima, of course. He was unimpressed with the Commandos' shooting ability, calling it pathetic, doubting 10 percent would have made it through U.S. basic training. Szima's marksmanship destroyed their morale. Five shots in an 8-inch group at 200 yards with his brand-new M1 rifle had Major Mills-Roberts accuse him of being part of the U.S. Army rifle team. "My response that I'm a bartender from Dayton Ohio was unconvincing." Ironic, given that the Rangers had been poor with their weapons training at Achnacarry. Later on, his skills made him part of the rear guard covering the withdrawal. He was equally unimpressed with the outdated weapons of the Commandos, especially the 50-round drums of the Thompson submachine gun used by gangsters in Al Capone days. However, where the Commandos did impress was with their bayonet drill: "It was their meat." The bayonet charge proved valuable during the upcoming battle when "hate took command."

Before the attack, "Boss" Lord Mountbatten, aboard the HMS *Prince* (*Prins*) *Albert*, gave a speech to the men, saying, "Tomorrow we deal the Hun a bloody blow. We expect 60 percent casualties, and, those of you that will die, may God have mercy on your souls." This infuriated Szima and the other Rangers, because they were to be sent to their deaths on a suicide mission. Hardly an inspiring speech, even though in a subsequent interview with the BBC, Koons said it was a fine speech—probably tongue in cheek. There was talk among the Rangers of not joining the raid. Koons went bananas and cried "that Captain [Alvah] Miller never did like me and just wants to get rid of me." Trying to calm things down and because of who he was, Szima told the other three Rangers that they would be in the surviving 40 percent. In fact, he was going to go but not wear the British uniforms, which they had just received. No, he was going to wear his American-issued uniform, rank and all. If he were to die, the Heinies (Germans) would know he was an American. The only item he accepted was the British wool cap. "If they get one, they'll know it's an American sergeant," he told them. He was going to combat. And so were the other three.

ORANGE BEACH I—SZIMA AND KOONS

Major Mills-Roberts and Group One landed unopposed. For Ranger Sergeant Szima, attached to 1st Section, 2nd Platoon, and Corporal Koons with the 2nd Section of 2nd Platoon of Major Derek Mills-Roberts's Troop C, they headed into their objective at Orange I with the purpose of driving south toward the coastal battery dubbed the Hess Battery.

The landing went well, although the Commandos and Rangers landed in two feet of water around 0450. There were two eight-foot-wide gullys that were to be used to climb up the chalky cliffs that featured a pronounced overhang. The gully to the left, the eastern one, was impassable because of heavy falls of chalk and masses of wire.

The beach itself was suitable for bathers, noted Szima in his censored After-Action Report. Years later, he'd corrected the report in a series of long letters. A long set of 10-foot-wide concrete steps led to the top but was heavily fortified by the Germans with barbed wire 25 feet tall and signs in German that read "Attention: Mines." The obstacle meant they either had to cut through the massive entanglement, potentially hiding mines, or they had to climb the sheer cliff face some 75 to 100 feet high. Unable to scale the eastern cliffs, they breached wire obstacles with two Bangalore torpedoes, creating a gap just big enough for one man, and moved up on the western cliff. Szima and his Commando buddy followed sections of C Troop, which had blasted its way through the entanglement. They used enough explosives to blow it to smithereens. Mortars were used subsequently to suppress the battery.

Following C Troop straight up for about 800 yards, he found his first dead German on a road crossing, killed by his own potato masher, "stretching his steaming 5-foot-8 body to 8 feet," obviously killed in the fight with the section ahead of him. C Troop covered their movement until his section found good cover under some ferns. They met no opposition, despite the breach explosion at the beach. They hit another road and advanced toward their intended target, the Hess Battery. The road led directly inland, and the section skirted left of a small village, all the while watchful for German snipers. The second dead German he saw was in a bed, and he fired at him reflexively, when he entered the room. His Commando buddy came rushing downstairs, but Szima told him everything was all right. Suddenly, two German Messerschmitt fighter planes flew overhead at barely 300 feet looking for targets, as Szima and his section deployed to assault the gun battery. Strangely, the German fighter planes did not open fire. This was perhaps due to the challenges of identifying enemy targets near German positions, but perhaps also to avoid friendly fire. The pilots may not have noticed the Allied forces creeping around.

The gun position they were about to attack and destroy consisted of "6-inch guns and one Anti-aircraft gun. The Anti-aircraft gun had no cover being entirely exposed, but the 6-inch guns were armored," noted Szima. Sniper fire erupted suddenly. Cautiously they moved ahead. They were near a series of buildings when Szima heard a German whistling inside a building, unaware of the doom he was about to meet. The Ranger sergeant motioned to his Commando counterpart, Haggerty, who was just behind him carrying the 50-drum Thompson. In near-perfect Me and My Pal training each knew, the German walked out the door into the archway and was met by Haggerty's 20 rounds hitting him with speed and lethality. The Yank, as Americans were known to the British, was worried that the natural rise of the Thompson's barrel as it fired on Automatic might end up near him or hitting him; but Haggerty was in control of the weapon. So far, so good. Simultaneously, the Allied air forces engaged the battery.

They continued patrolling forward toward more farm buildings, clearing houses—or "house cleaning," as Szima called it—when a German hand grenade, a "potato masher," flew out of the upper window. Haggerty shouted, "Look out, Yank," as he dove behind a tree. Szima instinctively ducked away from the potato masher behind the corner of the building where the hand grenade exploded, showering the corner with shrapnel. Haggerty once again hammered the Heinie in the window, emptying his 50-round drum. He didn't get the German, but Szima threw a hand grenade through the window, eliminating the threat. If it hadn't been for Haggerty, Szima would have been killed.

Everyone now threw hand grenades into all the stable enclosures and the tack room. Once in the courtyard, the gun battery was exposed and the targets, the crew, stood out in their white T-shirts (the Germans wore the *Drillichanzug*, an off-white denim fatigue uniform of a plain drill jacket with no pockets and trousers with two pockets) and shiny black bucket helmets. The range was about 150 to 200 yards, and they heard the commands given in German. Had it not been for German counter-snipers, at this point the crews of the guns would've been wiped out, lamented Szima years later. The German shooters started scoring, and the courtyard was now strewn with Commando casualties. Sergeant Szima took a bullet through his stocking cap—for the record, he wrote years later, the hat got shot off right at the Orchard, before the snipers did some of them in. Again, another time while lying prone, they put three of them very near him: one into the hat; concrete got into his eyes from another miss; and lastly one that was so close that it sucked the air out of his ear cavity. Szima realized his precarious, exposed location and changed positions three times, with the last landing him in a manure pile. During this exchange, he lost his Commando stocking cap twice and later found two holes through its crown. Those guys, the German snipers, were all going for head shots, he thought. It became apparent that snipers were zeroed in when they killed a Commando, then hit the men who went to his aid, and then the Troop sergeant major. Sergeant Szima scanned the courtyard he had been fighting around, looking for Koons. Instead, he saw Haggerty and the sergeant major wounded but patched up. Haggerty and the troop SGTMAJ were billeted together at Weymouth, and they had been assigned to make reports on the Americans before, during, and after the raid—or at least that's what Szima thought. Koons, in the meanwhile, who was part of C Troop but not with Sergeant Szima, had found himself in a stable to fire from and had a clear field of fire onto the gun pits, and so was spared the sniper exchanges. With his continued firing at the pits, the coastal guns never fired another round.

Szima and his section fired onto the gun battery and Germans as best as possible, given the situation. During the sniper/counter-sniper activity, Platoon Leader LT Coalson ordered half the men firing on the guns to "about face" and fire in the direction of the incoming sniper fire. This back-to-back tactic saved some lives, as it provided needed time to spot the sniper fire coming from the dense foliage that makes up the typical French hedgerow and countryside. At long last, the sun rose, exposing the Germans by the rays highlighting their shiny black helmets. That proved their downfall, as the helmets presented easily identifiable targets. The sun gave away the positions of two of them, one on the other side of the road to the right; and the other on top of a roof about 150 to 200 yards, also to the right. The Yank demonstrated his excellent marksmanship, using the rest of a belt full of AP (armor-piercing) clip where the Germans just sat like puppets. The AA battery, just behind the gun battery, was without cover, and the crew was killed. "It was BANG when you fired and CLANK when you hit their helmets. One round hit the chinstrap and sent the helmet spiraling at least 25 feet into the air." AP was all Szima carried in his belt, with regular ball ammo in the eight reserve bandoleers on him, and by the time Lovat's group made the assault his belt was empty. And he had a problem: He could not retrieve clips from his bandoleers. Szima had to hang it on the brick and fence facing the guns, "and think if you can the impossibility of getting a clip out of an exclusively designed bandoleer compartment which has an overlapping cloth opening; and, to add to your dismay, there is a paper covering surrounding the clip, making it altogether impossible to track to extract a clip from the pouch with one hand." He was not happy.

Finally, the group under Shimi Lovat with Stempson and Brady, from Orange Beach II, launched their assault from the west to C Troop's right flank. Everyone aimed at the gun pits again, hitting the Germans, allowing for Lovat to issue the bayonet charge to kill the Germans and force the survivors out, thereby buying time for his demolition team to blow up the gun battery. "You couldn't tell the scream of the doomed from the attackers. And we didn't lift fire until contact." The Commandos of F Troop made the assault on the gun position: Packing everything with explosives, they blew up the guns.

When Lovat made the assault and C Troop was ordered to hold its fire, Szima immediately took all the paper shields out of two bandoleers. He prepared for withdrawal, if he survived. He had been assigned as number two to Commando MacDonough's .55 Boys Anti-Tank rifle gun. The number two man was solely the muscle to help move the gun by means of "a handle affixed to the bipod at the muzzle of the 8-foot-long monstrosity. I inherited this task because, with hangover and all, I got an 8-inch grouping of five shots." It had been the first time the Ranger sergeant had fired his new M1 rifle at the rifle range at Portland. Because of this, one of his assignments was to be part of the rear guard and the M1 rifle became classified as an automatic weapon for this job, along with the Boys AT rifle.

After the assault, the guns were blown, the wounded were rounded up, and the withdrawal proceeded down the road back to the beach. MacDonough was on one side of the road and Szima on the other. They had been told to hold the position until the main body reached the curve in the road and then he was to double over, grab the handle, and, with the rifle between the two of them, to make it to the next curve of the road and repeat until the last section had cleared to the beach. The order of withdrawal saw first Lovat's sections, who had charged the battery, then the Mills-Roberts group. Four German prisoners carried some of the wounded to Orange I's beach.

It seemed forever before the Commandos reached the first curve; before then, Szima listened and watched for Germans. He heard cautious footsteps on the other side of a stonewalled fence. Germans, he thought, and quietly let Mac know to be silent. Szima waited at the gate of the fence, the natural point of entry, and "who came walking through but Koons, who had forgotten the timing and was still waiting to be called in from the flank when he noticed everything had gotten quiet." When Koons surfaced through the gate, Szima had taken up all the slack of the trigger, holding his breath, ready to shoot. Koons was never closer to death in his life. "Needless to say, I ordered him to catch up with the main body which by now had cleared the first curve." This near-fatal incident led to Sergeant Szima forgetting about a smoke canister he had been carrying. He was to have set the six-inch canister up during their retreat to create concealment with its smoke.

Mac and Szima stayed behind, some half a mile's distance to the newly formed beach perimeter. As the rear guard, there would be no support if they encountered any probing Germans. This time it wasn't Koons; instead, their worst fears were confirmed. The two-man Boys AT team was at the second turn in the road when the German truck arrived, right at the spot they had just vacated, and moved to the next curve. The two men quickly decided not to engage unless they had to—and, of course, they had to when the Germans, after having checked the German and Commando dead strewn about the area, got back into the truck and headed toward them. Mac fired the heavy-caliber anti-tank weapon, creating an enormous cloud of dust from its recoil, while Szima laid a full clip into the Germans. Without reloading, Szima hustled over to Mac, and both ran side by side down the road. Mac, being faster, started to pass the American, forcing him to run sideways, holding onto his rifle in one hand and the much heavier .55 in the other, until they tumbled and hit the dirt, all the while under heavy return fire. Staying low, they managed to keep going and reached the beach perimeter.

In all the excitement, first with Koons and then the Germans, Sergeant Szima forgot the password. "It was something easy like Worcestershire," he recalled, "and had it not been for Mac remembering, I'd probably have ended up as one of the statistics of the raid." He reported to Lieutenant Coalson and Lieutenant Styles as to what had happened; Styles just said coolly, "That's all right. We have plenty of time. It'll take them 15 minutes to form a line [of skirmishers], but then we'll all be at the beach." However, while on the beach, a German sniper sent a round between Mills-Roberts and Szima. The Commando captain immediately "turned around with the best of off-stage Charles Laughton mannerisms I ever heard: He shouted, 'get that bloody sniper.' With that, I whirled around and fired what was to be my last full clip of the Dieppe Raid."

The exfiltration was a truly charming affair, as the men had to wait and then run through the ferns, drawing fire from unchallenged German shooters. "Knowing what's in the back of me gave me all the courage to volunteer running, the sooner the better." What made their escape easier was the smoke laid down by the Spitfires, obstructing the view of the Germans. Fortune favored the bold, because the smoke screen was so thick and the offshore breeze just right that visibility for the retreating men was barely 20 yards. The Commandos carried the wounded into the neck-high water and waited until they could spot the vessels through the smoke clouds. The boats had to wait to identify the men as friendlies before they were permitted to approach the landing site. Szima carried his M1 on one shoulder and the Boys AT on the other and was neck-deep in the water waiting for the smoke to lift for the boat to approach. It was an experience in itself, he would write years later. "I finally ended up being towed out to the PT-type naval vessel, where we deposited all the wounded and yours truly made it up the scramble net." And he was still intact and on the *Prins Albert*. The great air battle littered the skies, with many planes going down. On their way to England, they picked up the downed Captain (1st LT) Sam Junkin, the first American to shoot down a German plane.

Corporal Koons was originally attached to SSG Stempson and the other beach at Orange II, but then was reassigned to Orange I with Sergeant Szima. His section was at a distance and to the left of Szima's. Koons's group waded to shore for about 30 to 40 yards, where they consolidated on the beach before moving out. There was little resistance in the beginning, climbing unchallenged over wire obstacles up the gully of the cliff. He recalls in his censored report that "sniper fire started on us from our right." They took no casualties, although enemy fire increased. The section moved forward to a little farm built around a yard some 200 yards away from the German battery. Eventually, he situated himself nearby, in a barn, after clearing it, while the sniper fire started to inflict casualties on the Commandos inching forward. They placed their wounded in a stable.

Once done, Koons looked for a way to engage the enemy, some at close range near 25 yards. "I kind of lost my head then and surged in front of the barn, but I soon realized that was foolish and got back into the stable. There I found a splendid spot for sniping through a slit in a brick wall." He fired through it at the Germans around the battery. He killed at least two Germans, perhaps as many as or more than 20, but in the confusion and heat of battle things were not always clear. The mortars of the Commando group hammered the battery throughout, while Koons shot at stray German shooters who had caused them serious trouble. "Other troops, the ones attacking the batteries directly, were luckier. They rushed in and blew up the batteries and ammunition dumps. The noise was terrific and I saw them go into the air a few hundred yards from me." Koons remained in place, firing, killing, until he heard the massive explosion destroying gun battery Hess, which happened after a bayonet charge of the British, who were under enfilade fire and mortar fire as they had advanced. Shortly thereafter, Koons and his section withdrew across open ground, where they bumped into a French civilian family. The accompanying Free French Commando told the family that Koons was American. En route to the exfiltration point, they seized any and all papers, wallets, and other items for Intelligence to analyze. Koons and Stempson, along with a Commando, formed the rear guard using a Boys AT rifle. The destruction of the battery occurred around 0650 hours, and by 0730 the extraction had begun. Corporal Koons, along with others, retreated to the beach for pickup, bringing along their wounded but not their dead. He was impressed by his counterparts. "They were calm and quiet," he is quoted, adding, "They've got plenty of guts." The fact that he was unaccounted for, forgotten, until he retreated and bumped into Szima is part of the story.

Corporal Franklin Koons would receive his British Military Medal award in Casablanca eight months later during the African campaign in the presence of President Roosevelt, Prime Minister Churchill, General de Gaulle, and General George Patton. Lord Mountbatten pinned the medal on Koons, who was wearing Bill Darby's personal Sam Browne belt. Sam Browne belts were only authorized to be worn by officers and not by the enlisted. Darby gave Koons a personal mark of distinction with this act. Orange I was a success.

ORANGE II

Orange II was assigned to the larger attacking force under Lord "Shimi" Lovat. Things went a bit differently at this landing site. The Germans became aware of the raiders' approach by 0445 when messages were sent from the battery. Within a few short minutes, the battery opened fire on the approaching flotilla traveling in V-formation toward Orange Beach II. Lieutenant A. F. S. Veasey was in the lead, with Stempson and Brady attached to 1st Section, 1st Platoon, A Troop.

The briefing Stempson received, after they left Southampton on the afternoon of 18 August, included detailed plans of their attack on Orange Beach near Dieppe using a large-scale model made from an air mosaic of the ground they were to cover, which included the beach landing spot, two pillboxes, and their routes. Preparing for the mission, they had cleaned their weapons, drawn ammunition and grenades, and then loaded into the squadron of Assault Landing Craft, which were lowered into the water at 0300. This entire force was in eight ALCs with one support craft in the lead that was armed with an anti-aircraft gun, two .50 cal machine guns, one 4-inch smoke mortar, and two .303 rifles.

Fortunately for him and his comrades, the boat landed without drawing any fire at 0455 hours. For them, it was a dry landing; and during their movement they took two unoccupied pillboxes. Suddenly, there came long-range machine-gun fire. The sections headed inland for about 500 yards with the intention of swinging left to Orange Beach I and the battery. En route to the battery, they were caught out in a gully that was roughly 15 feet deep where two German machine guns fired on them. Just before, at the head of the gully, they had been sniped at, wounding one. The German machine-gun fire killed seven Commandos, leaving only three in Stempson's section. It turned out that the MG nest was only 30 feet from the bunker. Undeterred, the three, under cover of the ferns, tried to eliminate the machine guns. "You just had to wait for them to run with the ammo and when you hit them, they rolled over like a jackrabbit, and this went on until a Commando, name forgotten, but he was an immense redhead and section leader, took advantage and worked his way alongside the sandbagged machine gun emplacement and lobbed the Mills bomb [hand] grenade into it." The other machine-gun nest was not located.

Meanwhile, Lovat's larger group double-timed along the river Saane for about 1,600 yards, where they turned inland and headed east toward the wood behind the Hess Battery. Near the wood, B and F Troops divided. Lovat's HQ moved forward to the edge of an orchard near the battery's perimeter wire, while F Troop advanced through the orchard, where they surprised a large group of Germans in the village of Le Haut, who were preparing to counterattack. They were quickly killed. C Troop laid down supporting fire on the defensive positions to their front.

Finally, Staff Sergeant Stempson reports, "We then made our way to the jetty on Orange Beach II where we met an English officer. We were then ordered to take up positions on the cliff, reinforcing the beach arty [artillery], G Troop." Here they stayed covering the withdrawal of the demolition team until ordered by the Battalion Executive Officer to withdraw to the boats at around 0810 hours. They hurriedly made their way down to the beach, only to discover a single ALC that they had to swim to, some 100 yards, where they embarked. The return voyage was mercifully uneventful. "Dieppe was hotter than hell. My group of twelve was assigned to knock out a coastal battery. The battery was knocked out. Five of our men returned," recalled Stempson after the raid.

Corporal William Robert Brady of Brooten, Minnesota, born on 21 August 1919, was a semipro basketball player and guide on the Northern Forest Section of Minnesota, and he was drafted into the Army. An Original, he became part of the First Special Service Force, serving in Rome and Pisa, Italy. Injured badly in his face with Darby's Rangers in December of 1943, he retired out of the Air Force as a lieutenant colonel. His awards included the Bronze Star with Oak Leaf Cluster for the North African Campaign and the Anzio landing; the Presidential Unit Citation with two clusters; the unauthorized Canadian Dieppe Raid Award; the Combat Infantryman Badge; the

Purple Heart, the American Theater Ribbon; and the European Theater of Operations Ribbon with six stars. In his censored After-Action Report, Corporal Brady explained the landing procedure for the first section coming ashore: "The 1st man that landed on shore had the Scaling Ladder (all three sections), the 2nd man had Bangalore torpedoes, the 3rd man was a scout, the 4th man was a Platoon Sergeant, and I was the fifth man with 6 grenades." Under fire they climbed up the tubular ladders, only to discover a double apron of barbed wire, about 1m by 20 wide. They scaled the cliffs with the aid of tubular ladders. Just beyond was a concrete pillbox, fortunately unoccupied. Moving past it, Brady and a Commando cut a telephone wire. The Commando was helped up by Brady's 6-foot-6 frame. The pole itself protected them from sporadic sniper fire.

They located a second pillbox. Moving between the two German defenses, they drew more occasional sniper fire from a nearby house, but otherwise encountered no resistance. Some 20 men continued up the ravine to the second objective. Here they formed a perimeter on crossroads and waited for the demolition of the gun battery. Right after the explosion, a German patrol moved down the road toward them with five men on each side. Not knowing that the Commandos lay in wait, they marched straight up the road with two Commandos and Corporal Brady opening fire at close range, about 15 yards, dropping three or four German soldiers. The Germans took off, allowing Brady and the others to secure the perimeter. The mission was completed with the destruction of the battery, and Brady, along with the Commandos, headed inland and then swung back toward the beach. The movement led them to the high cliff a half mile west of the beach, where they remained until ordered to withdraw and to embark.

Out of 100 Germans, an estimated 30 were killed, and 30 wounded in action. The Commandos captured 4 POWs. Losses by the Allies were 12 KIA, 20 WIA, and 13 missing. This raid at Orange I and II was the only successful one at Dieppe.

BLUE AND GREEN BEACHES—DISASTER

Whereas operations on Yellow and Orange Beaches proved for the most part successful, although with some costs to the Commandos and Rangers, the operations of equal importance were at Blue and Green beaches. These beaches flanked the main assault into Dieppe proper taking place on White and Red beaches. Blue and Green were tasked with the seizure of the headlands on either side of the town and destroying the German defenses on them. Controlling the heights would allow for far safer and easier landings on the two groups tasked with taking Dieppe and the pinch-mission. Blue Beach at Puys was tasked to the Royal Regiment of Canada, plus three platoons from the Black Watch of Canada and an artillery detachment, and were to neutralize machine-gun and artillery batteries protecting this Dieppe beach. But unfortunately for them, the nearby Channel Clash with Yellow Group and an alert local German unit proved disastrous. Blue landed at 0507 just as light broke open the night, some 30 minutes late. Ranger Sergeant Kenneth G. Kenyon luckily never made it onto the beach despite his craft attempting to do so on three occasions, each time driven off by heavy enemy fire. Finally off-loaded onto the destroyer *Calpe*, he did not escape unscathed, for he was wounded in the subsequent battle at sea during the retreat when German aircraft strafed the Allies around Dieppe. The Royal Regiment of Canada never even made it off the beach. The casualties were enormous. There was one staircase leading up from the beach, but the German defenses were alert and had the beaches sighted in from several bunkers and machine-gun positions near the cliff and stairs. The fact that they landed late, during daylight hours, deprived them of concealment. Three waves hit the shale beach, and each was mercilessly cut down, unable to secure the eastern headlands. For the rest of the invasion force, disaster loomed ahead for the Canadian-British forces. On Blue Beach, the Royal Regiment of Canada saw absolute destruction with only 3 men returning, 227 dead, all mercilessly cut down on the beaches, with 260 Canadians captured. The regiment suffered a

94 percent casualty rate, the Black Watch 66 percent. It was a shocking bloodbath.

On the other (outer) side of White and Red Beaches, tasked with seizing the western headlands was Green group, targeting the cliffs near Pourville and the Hindenburg Battery east of that village. Some of the men landed west of the river Scie in the confusion. This task was assigned to the South Saskatchewan Regiment and the Cameron Highlanders of Canada. This, too, turned into a bloodbath during the landing and with the arrival of German reinforcements. Rangers' 1st LT Robert Flanagan was assigned to the Saskatchewans, and SGT Lloyd N. Church and SGT Marcel G. Swank were with the Cameron Highlanders. The South Saskatchewan Regiment landed on time at 0450 hours. Ranger Lieutenant Flanagan, like many others, did not manage to land. There was a local success by taking the bridge over the River Scie, but the Winnipeg regiment took massive casualties, rendering them combat-ineffective. Some 66 percent of the men became casualties.

Right on schedule, at 0550, the second wave of Canadians arrived along with Swank and Church, and the Queen's Own Cameron Highlanders led by their bagpiper. The Saskatchewans were to capture the headlands and the battery near Quatre Vents Farm. The Highlanders were to pass through the lines of the first wave to move inland and capture the airfield at St. Aubin. But no such thing happened.

Swank and Church had departed from New Haven with the Canadians. Midway through, they went to a Canadian lieutenant to find out what the hell was going on. The Canadian officer did his best to give them a fragmented brief using a strip photo of the beach area lit by a hooded flashlight. His last words to them were to follow the unknown Canadian sergeant. "Hell, I can't even see him," thought Swank at the time.

Swank and Church had found and followed their Canadian sergeant, who was killed within a few steps off the landing craft as the whole area, some 800 to 900 yards of beach, was covered by machine guns and mortars. Both Rangers made it up to the promenade through a hole in the seawall, where its barbed-wire entanglement had been blown up by someone in the first wave. Bullets whizzed by as the two made it into the town's nearby buildings. The Saskatchewans had not managed to clear the defenses in general. The assault stalled. Pillboxes on hillsides and machine guns hammered them at a choke point leading to a radar station and defenses. There were heavy casualties.

They joined a company out of town on a road but received incoming sniper fire and mortars, which forced them into concealment and the cover of the nearby woods. The woods ended abruptly, and they were hit from entrenched positions above them. Swank, Church, and the Canadians took out a strong point with bayonets, jumping into trenches, killing seven of the enemy. But it was clear that the attack was going nowhere, suffering monstrous casualties. By 0945 or 1015 hours they were ordered to retreat to Pourville for exfiltration by landing craft. Somewhere during the confusion of the battle, Swank and Church got separated. Church moved to the western headlands, while Swank went east and reentered the small village, where he took up a defensive position with other surviving Canadians. Suddenly, a Bren gun right next to him opened fire like a madman possessed. All Swank could think of was that the man had lost it, until . . . until he heard and saw a bunch of leaves and branches right next to him rattling and getting mowed down by a German MG, missing him by the smallest of margins due to the Bren gunner's action. He became paralyzed with fear and lay there unable to move for a while. Soon he withdrew and thought of Church. Hoping to locate him and thinking Church might possibly have been wounded, Swank made his way to an aid station, bumping into Church and an irate medical officer recruiting them as litter bearers while under withering heavy-weapons and mortar fire, moving some 75 yards to the actual beach.

Time had come for the withdrawal to the landing craft. The men ran under constant fire toward the shore and waters, when Swank looked back and saw that Church had been shot. Swank turned around and saw him with a nasty head wound. He dragged Church back to the seawall. He took a long look at Church, possibly remembering that the wounded were to be left in place . . . perhaps Church was able to speak, but whatever happened, a decision needed to be made, and whatever thoughts he had or were said, they prompted Marcel Swank to take off and swim to a landing craft. While swimming, he was shot and wounded. Arriving at the *Calpe*, Kenyon, who had never landed, helped him on board, where a short time later Ranger Kenyon was hit by a strafing German airplane.

Having left Church behind hit Marcel Swank hard. Years later he reunited with Lloyd Church, who had been operated on by a German doctor, implanting a silver plate into his skull. He remained a prisoner until the conclusion of the war. Iowan Sergeant Lloyd N. Church never really recovered from the surgery but held no grudge against Swank, saying he had done the right thing that day on the beach, much to Swank's relief. Lloyd died of his injuries on Armistice Day, 11 November 1950, at the age of 27. Swank would feature in a print advertisement for Coca-Cola. The fortunes of war.

The Highlanders made the deepest penetration of anyone on the raid, but didn't reach their objectives. Three hundred forty-six Canadian soldiers of the Winnipeg-based Saskatchewan Regiment were killed out of 503 total, some 65 percent. Their actions, however, allowed for No. 4 Commando to withdraw later without undue attention from the Germans in the area. The Queen's Own Cameron Highlander suffered near-identical casualties of 69 percent. By 1145 hours, the attack had ended. Ranger Swank was off-loaded to the *Calpe* 30 minutes later, where he found SGT Kenyon, who was wounded around 1230 hours. Twenty-two-year-old Ranger LT J. H. Randall, of Washington, D.C., was killed in action, believed to have been with the South Saskatchewans at Pourville (Green Beach), although it seems more likely that he was at White Beach, in front of the casino near the shore, just steps away from the edge of the water, while landing with the Royal Hamilton Light Infantry.

The devastation witnessed and experienced by many left indelible marks on the participants. First Lieutenant Flanagan, who did not land, witnessed the horror unfolding along the beaches of Dieppe. He was so "visibly disturbed by the events of August 19," the mass slaughter, that, shortly after returning to the U.K. with several Rangers, he requested a transfer out of the 1st Ranger Battalion. Who could blame him? The lieutenant, however, never left. Seemingly, Szima was wrong, or it was idle talk and never went beyond that.

Success on the outer flanks by the Commandos and Rangers did help prevent some of the carnage, but the destruction of the task forces assigned to Blue and Green Beaches left the central attack into Dieppe exposed. The raid-in-force sent its men into the slaughterhouse.

RED BEACH AND WHITE BEACH—A HOLOCAUST

Next to Blue Beach, this landing site, Red Beach, was directly in front of the town, landing on the pebble beaches. The Essex Scottish Regiment landed on time at 0510 hours but later than the flank attacks as planned. Those were intended to sweep off the Germans from the high grounds and clear the way forward for the main assault. Its failure let the Germans sweep the beaches with everything on hand. The Canadians threw themselves forward but could not breach the seawall but for one small group, which led to a false interpretation of impending success, launching more waves into the attack. Believing that victory was close at hand, the reserve battalion of *Les Fusiliers Mont-Royal* was sent in. The fusiliers landed as the tide was falling and immediately received fire from the German positions on the cliffs near Blue Beach. They had no cover. They met the same fate as their comrades—exposed to withering fire, sweeping up and down the beachhead, suffering 513 casualties out of 584 men—96 percent.

White Beach saw the Royal Hamilton Light Infantry land on time at 0520 hours. The smoke screens laid by aircraft proved ineffective. The Germans had time to regroup after the attacks by the Allied air force and some accompanying naval gunfire. The Canadians took massive casualties almost immediately, even though they succeeded in seizing a large casino and several strongpoints, including a pillbox along the promenade. "Some of the men of the battalion got across the bullet-swept Boulevard and into the town where they engaged in vicious street fighting." The unit lost 81 percent of its men. The Calgary Regiment and its new 30 Churchill tanks arrived in 2 waves, after a delay of 15 minutes due to intense air and naval bombardments. Part of the beaches dropped off almost without bottoms, forcing some tanks to gun their engines. Of the tanks that landed, only 15 out of 27 managed to cross the seawall, but they were prevented from penetrating into the town by roadblocks in the narrow streets. Arriving late and discovering that attached engineers, many killed within minutes, could not get far enough to breach roadblocks at key points, the tanks were also exposed to enormous enemy fire. The tanks rolled back and forth on the promenade, many forced back to the beaches where they acted as pillboxes for the remaining infantry. Ranger T/4 Howard M. Henry, 23 years old from Kentucky, was killed in the World War I–style carnage. He was believed to have been part of a Canadian demolition team, the Royal Canadian Engineers Beach Assault Party, supporting the Calgary Tanks. He may have been on board Tank Landing Craft 7, Flight 3. According to Swank, who researched Dieppe in great detail, "Edwin Bennett, 10 Troops Leader, B Squadron, 14 Calgary Tank Regiment, Technician Fourth Grade (T/4) Howard M. Henry, was believed to have been attached to the RCE Beach Assault Party." Bennett states T/4 Henry was on LCT-7 with him and saw him killed on landing on White Beach at the water's edge near the Casino. A post-raid German photograph shows a dead American, identified by the Ranger-style leggings, near the tank Blossom, in front of the Casino. The tank regiment took 42 percent casualties and lost all their tanks. The poor bloodied infantry was unable to dig into the hard beaches, leaving them exposed.

On White Beach, the last desperate gamble played out when the Royal Marines A Commando was ordered into the action at 0825 hours. They were there to execute the mission—the seizure of German naval crypto intelligence. Most did not land. The channel they were to penetrate along the high, chalky cliffs was full of German defensive positions. At 1100, the withdrawal order was issued, and by 1400 the last landing craft pulled away; some men were picked up at sea, swimming toward England.

The raid, lasting 8 to 10 hours, was over. A great air battle had been fought throughout, resulting in enormous losses for the Allies with some 119 planes lost to the German air force, the *Luftwaffe*, which had committed 945 planes and only lost 48 of them. The 2nd Canadian Division and the 4,963 Canadians who had embarked for the operation, saw only 2,210 return to England, and many of these were wounded. There were 3,367 casualties, including 1,946 prisoners of war; 916 Canadians lost their lives, as well as all 30 tanks and other vehicles. The Royal Navy suffered 550 casualties, lost 33 landing craft, and the destroyer HMS *Berkley* was torpedoed after she had been severely bomb-damaged. British killed numbered 247 men. Americans lost 3, 4 if we include Lloyd Church who died of his wounds a few years later. Lord Mountbatten's speech had been prophetic, but Sergeant Szima's proved correct as well.

There was some bitterness in the aftermath of the raid-in-force and subsequent holocaust of men. Captain Roy Murray, the commanding Ranger on the raid, who like most did not land, stated:

> The problem was that in all of our activities, we've always been used to night raids and surprise. There was no preparation before this attack on Dieppe. And the cliffs on either side of Dieppe had many German machine-gun emplacements, and they had mortars in the center of town. And since we were supposedly going in quietly, we found at the last minute it had been decided that aircraft would go in with just using their machine guns five minutes before we attacked. The net result was that we awakened all the Germans and had them ready for us when we came in. The Canadians did a great job—very courageous. But they were enfiladed by the fire and by the mortars. And the only cover they had on this beach at low tide was the tanks that came in with them. The unfortunate part of having the tanks coming on that beach was that the exits from the beach were three stairways from the beach up, about twenty feet to the esplanade at the top. The stairways were

not really suitable for tank efforts. So the tanks stayed on
the beach, and they got knocked out.

The broad strokes were correct—the minutiae of examining failure was not that significant. Whatever the flaws and the outcome, men
died in the slaughter, to retrieve German intelligence. Any recrimina-
tion would not bring them back.

Rangers Lieutenant Joseph H. Randall and T/4 Howard M. Henry
died that day, barely noticed, and alone.

Forty years later, 19 August 1982, Marcel G. Swank (1 & 4 HQ)
remembered these men in a memorial dedication at Dieppe.

Ladies and Gentlemen,

I want to tell you of the men whose names are inscribed on
the memorial we are dedicating here today. It is important you know they were something much more than simply
names on a bronze plaque. They were magnificent young
men who knew full well the risks but nonetheless came to
this place.

Lieutenant Edward Loustalot was killed while with the
3 Commando, on the outskirts of Berneval Sur Mer. He
died in a small field of poppies while leading an assault
on a machine-gun position, an act of gallantry for which
he was mentioned in British Army dispatches. He was an
engineer officer, remembered for his youth and aggressive-
ness. He came from Franklin, Louisiana, was a graduate of
Louisiana State University and an architect by profession.
He was twenty-three years old at the time of his death. He
is interred in the Ardennes American Cemetery at Neupre,
Belgium.

Lieutenant Joseph Randall was killed close-by where we
now stand while with the Royal Hamilton Light Infantry
Regiment. He died on landing, a few short steps from the
water's edge, charging head-on into the holocaust. He was

a big, fine-appearing man, an excellent and respected officer of the do-or-die tradition. He was twenty-three years old, from Washington, D.C., and the only child of a military family. He is interred side by side with his mother and father in Arlington National Cemetery, Arlington, Virginia.

Tech 4 Howard Henry died while with the Essex Scottish Regiment and, like Joseph Randall, he landed here on the main Dieppe Beach. He was one of the very few men who succeeded in fighting his way into Dieppe, where he was killed. He was a big, well liked, impressive-looking mountain man from Science Hill, Kentucky. He wanted to be an electrical engineer and had worked his way through one year of college. He was twenty-two years old and is interred in the Normandy American Cemetery at St. Laurent, France.

These three men of the 1st United States Ranger Battalion were the first United States soldiers to die for the liberation of France in World War II. They were of that breed of men who make nations great, the kind who, of their own accord, move to the sound of the guns. They were volunteers whose sense of honor and duty gave them the will to carry the fight to this place forty years ago today. I doubt if it occurred to them to conduct themselves in any other manner. Also, I don't suppose they thought of themselves as heroes or even particularly brave men, but of course they were. They were uncommon men who willingly led the way for the millions of Americans who would follow. They have been long and well remembered. God rest their souls.

HOW AMERICA LED THE WAY AT DIEPPE

After Dieppe, four Rangers would become the men associated with the raid as they were the only ones immediately interviewed by the press. Photos were taken of Rangers with the returning Commandos, standing out in the American uniforms. Interviews were given. Szima poses in one with another Commando, staged in such a manner to not show his scar—it was Szima who insisted on it. Brady, Koons, Stempson, and Szima became celebrities. LT Flanagan went to London to report to General Truscott, while the others had a 14-day leave and a few pounds in their pocket. Szima's letter in 1978 recalls the immediate aftermath of the raid.

> It was an awesome feeling to go to London the next day and see yourself staring from every newsstand and front page of every newspaper. And when the American Headquarters Forces finally caught up with us at a bar, they had to ration us out to the press. So four Rangers spent seven days being squired by no less than Lieutenant Comd. Douglas Fairbanks Jr., Edward R. Murrow, Quentin Reynolds, Robt. St. Johns, John McVane, Chas. Collinwood, Ralph Ingersoll, and other American reporters. Maj. Leslie Howard (The Actor) demanded from me one of my men for the pending BBC broadcast. Koons was tagged for this and the other 3 of us went on The Army Hour on NBC the following Sunday.

Eventually Lieutenant Flanagan and the other four traveled back to Scotland—there was a war to be fought. According to war correspondent Quentin Reynolds, "now they were men. They'd killed their Germans and had seen men die." Of course, with the press reports, nearly every soldier suddenly became a Ranger overnight. Sergeant Anthony Rada, HQ Company and a native of Michigan, designed the famous black, white, and red Ranger scroll. Although not officially approved until 1983, the men started to wear the insignia.

Back in the U.K., Darby gave the dope to some of the men back at training, not knowing the full casualty list or who had been killed, captured, or whatnot. At the meeting, the mood was depressed. Meade reflected on having sent one of his best, Sergeant Church, to what he thought was billets but was now missing in action. Yet when Lieutenant Dirks returned from Dieppe, Meade could only think what a lucky bastard he was. "Our boys arrived this afternoon. They seem quite changed, older, some still upset. Got the real dope from them. Must have been pretty rough, with the Jerries waiting for them for 3 days. What few of our boys did manage to land had a hell of a time, and few returned."

SSG Gino Mecuriali, who did not land, had a different experience:

After returning to our base in England, Sergeant Kavanaugh and myself went to a place much like our USO, I guess, and were asked the question, "What do you think of the Raid, Yank?" They didn't realize we were part of it. We never let on that we were there and wouldn't intrude on their elation for anything. It was pretty hard to understand the celebration when approximate of 5,000 Canadians, only 2,200 returned to England. Also there were 3,367 Casualties, including 1,946 POWs, including 907 Canadians lost their lives. In contrast, we later learned of the news about the Raid in the U.S. newspapers, you would think it was a U.S. operation! The British and Canadians didn't much appreciate this. Quite understandable! The fact that many of us that were assigned to this raid did not have the opportunity to actually land is frustrating for us. In truth, we are fortunate to come out of it unscathed. My Platoon LT. Randall was killed in the raid but he wasn't with us. Hardly knew him as we were only together, maybe two months. Dieppe was "memorable," PFC Jacques Nixson of Iowa said in a phone interview. "The first time you are shot at is always memorable. There wasn't any panic, but to say that we were awed would be putting it mildly. When you see tracers coming at you and you know between those tracers there are five more bullets flying toward you. It's an extremely eerie experience." He really was a tuff guy. Nixson said he changed boats five times before he got back to England. When I look back, even being on the sea 24 hours wasn't too bad compared with some of the other landings we have made. I was never hurt. Somehow I was very lucky.

West Point Cadet William Orlando Darby, 1911-1945.
(USMA LIBRARY)

Lieutenant Colonel Charles Vaughn and Major William Darby at Achnacarry, Scotland in July 1942.
(US ARMY SIGNAL CORPS)

The town of Carrickfergus and surrounding area.
(THE CARRICKFERGUS MUSEUM & CIVIC CENTER)

2nd Lieutenant Edward Vincent Loustalot was among three Americans killed at Dieppe on August 19, 1942. He died while fighting alongside Rangers and British Commandos. The other two, who died amongst Canadian strangers, were T/4 Howard M. Henry and Second Lieutenant Joseph H. Randall.
(EDWARD BROUSSARD)

A skull session enroute to Arzew. Every Ranger knew his job. The map depicts the high ground and defensive positions north of the harbor. (US ARMY SIGNAL CORPS)

1st Platoon Leader Lieutenant Walt Nye, 2nd Platoon Lieutenant Leilyn Young, and Company Commander Captain Roy Murray on board of the *Queen Emma* for an aborted raid in December 1942. (US ARMY SIGNAL CORPS)

Rangers offload from their transport ship into the smaller assault landing craft which then dropped into the sea. (US ARMY SIGNAL CORPS)

Captured Vichy French and colonial soldiers at the Arzew train station. (US ARMY SIGNAL CORPS)

Fox Company of the 1st Ranger Battalion at Arzew. The front three officers are Young, Murray, and Nye. One can see the small size of a Ranger company.
(US ARMY SIGNAL CORPS)

Darby on his motorbike with the tall figure of Herman Dammer walking to his bike. Darby was known to travel by foot, camel, mule, bike, or car. He was always at the front.
(US ARMY SIGNAL CORPS)

Captain Stephen J. Meade would leave the Rangers in North Africa because of complications following surgery. He'd join the staff of General Ernest Dawley of VI Corps. After the war he became instrumental in the expansion of the American footprint across the globe. (US ARMY SIGNAL CORPS)

The carts were used to transport heavy weapons and in this case Corporal Bob Lowell who would get killed on November 10, 1943, in Venafro during the bitter months on the Winter Line. (US ARMY SIGNAL CORPS)

Two Ranger riflemen. Note the small blocks of TNT that would be used throughout their campaigns. The Ranger on the right carries a commando toggle rope. (US ARMY SIGNAL CORPS)

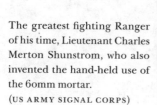

The greatest fighting Ranger of his time, Lieutenant Charles Merton Shunstrom, who also invented the hand-held use of the 6omm mortar.

(US ARMY SIGNAL CORPS)

General Theodore Roosevelt with Lieutenant Colonel Darby awarding the Silver Star to Captain Frederick Saam, who was a demolition expert. Saam would become a dentist in California after the war.
(US ARMY SIGNAL CORPS)

Darby, Murray, and fighting General Terry Allen of the First Infantry Division celebrating the one year anniversary of the Rangers. These officers represented the epitome of training and fighting at night. Hard men who led from the front.
(US ARMY SIGNAL CORPS)

"THE GERMANS ARE COMING"
Florence, Italy
END OF MARCH 1944

Markham and Lyons had done well. They were living inside an apartment house in Florence. Both men looked suspiciously non-Italian, with Markham having blond hair while Lyons was a redhead. Certainly no way to integrate into Italian society. Plus, of course, they were Americans and spoke no Italian whatsoever. Nor did they have any interest in learning it. But they did wear civilian clothing and still wore their dog tags. But their ambition was not to wait out the war: No, they wanted to get back to Allied lines as soon as possible. The problem for them and many other prisoners was that the mountain passes in February and March were not just bitterly cold, but also buried under snow. And that could be a killer.

There was no help forthcoming any time soon. Two months ago, they had been captured at Cisterna, fighting with F/1. Now they were stuck. But Ranger planning was in effect. Markham and Lyons decided to wait it out, but not for too long. At first chance, they'd head toward Venice, then Friuli, by going across the mountains and up the coast, with the Balkans the intended target. In Yugoslavia, they hoped, they'd find some kind of intelligence operative from the OSS to help them make their way back to the American lines—somehow. For them, the departure date on their continued escape was coming in mid-April.

A huge problem to the Rangers were their flatmates who'd leave to go to bars or restaurants in the city. The British spoke Italian, but it made the Americans uncomfortable for them to take such risks. Risks that could endanger Markham and Lyons, but not just them: also the old Italian couple that was part of the Rome Escape Line, helping escapees as much as possible.

One day, while killing time, Markham had looked out the window, as was his habit, when he noticed the absence of the usual lunch crowd. He immediately knew there was a problem. He called for Lyons, and they spied out their window onto the empty streets around the block. They strained looking through the window, looking for any signs of trouble. Time passed, and then the silence was broken, startling both men: Someone rapped their knuckles on the downstairs door. Fuck. "The Germans are coming," they were told. Both Rangers looked out the window again, and the Nazis were everywhere— surrounding the apartment house with machine-gun positions at every junction around the block. The jig was up. The Brits had been followed home from one of their nighttime bar hops.

Markham and Lyons, quickly but quietly, made their way up to the attic of the house and from there onto the roof, where they lay low on their bellies, squeezing and willing themselves so far down as to be part of the structure. Their shit was weak, and they knew it. They saw the old Italian couple on the front of the roof slowly get up, struggling with their aching bones, trembling with fear, slowly raising their hands as they shuffled to the front of the building . . . machine-gun fire ripped them apart.

5

✦

SPEARHEADERS

BY 3 SEPTEMBER 1942, THE RANGERS MOVED TO DUNDEE AND STAYED with civilians who were curious about the Yanks coming to billet in their homes. Dundee was on the East Coast of Scotland, where it joined No. 1 Commando under Lieutenant Colonel T. Trevor of the Welsh Guard for proposed joint operations. This phase of training, from 4–23 September, included attacking pillboxes; seacoast defense batteries; securing and destroying dock areas; street fighting, which was done in an abandoned building project; and other special training for future definite operations. The battalion was at 450, having lost the 10 percent in training predicted at the onset by Special Service Brigade. Ever the chronicler, Sully notes his hostess was a "Misses McClaren, 39 N. Court St.—younger sister about fifty—haughty, domineering—other about sixty, rather deaf, likeable. Well-furnished modern apartments." At Able Company's assembly point, Baxter Park, he writes, "The whole city cheers us and gapes from windows as we march down flagstone streets."

It was during this time where Father Albert E. Basil, a chaplain captain, who was attached to the British Special Service Brigade, first met the Rangers. His task was not a pleasant one. He had been in Dundee when the Rangers entered their final phase of training before leaving for Corker Hill. At Arbroath, a coastal town near Dundee, the Rangers had concluded a training session and were dismissed to return individually to their billets. Unfortunately, but known to many, various areas had been protected with strands of barbed wire and mined against possible German raids. Ranger James Ruschkewicz, born 19 March 1920, of C Company, was torn to pieces when he jumped from a platform over a section of concertina wire and straight onto an anti-tank mine. This happened on 11 September 1942. The Ranger behind him, one Aaron M. Salkin, from the same company, was horrifically mutilated and blinded. A team of hardworking surgeons struggled to save Aaron's life while Father Basil attended. One of them said out loud what others may have been thinking, that even if they were successful in saving his life, it might not be worth living. It was then when Father Basil said: "If that boy dies, I shall repeat your words to the proper authority." That Jewish boy still lives in Baltimore, Maryland. Darby was so impressed by the Green Beret–wearing man that he requested Brigadier Laycock to allow Father Basil to accompany the 1st Ranger Battalion.

By 24 September, the 1st Ranger Battalion had moved yet again by rail to Corker Hill Camp in the vicinity of Glasgow. The planning for the North African invasion at this time envisaged the use of the 1st Ranger Battalion for that operation, and they were assigned to II Army Corps and attached to the 1st Division in the Glasgow area after three weeks at Dundee. Combat cameras Phil Stern and Henry Paluch arrived; ultimately only Phil Stern stayed with them. Training was conducted with the operational objective in mind. Darby, ever the artilleryman, sought heavier support weapons for his lightly armed Ranger Battalion, and to that end he included the heavier 81mm mortars—Darby had a fetish for heavier firepower, according to Dammer. To move them around the battlefield, he needed transport. Former blacksmith Sergeant Robert E. Ehalt, born 10 August 1915, converted the lightweight cart used for transporting heavy water-cooled machine guns to fit their needs, in effect creating a mobile heavy-mortar platform for their future campaigns. Things were now becoming more serious, as clearly an operation was in the near future. The men knew it. Sullivan went to Mass and Communion with Father Basil present on 13 October 1942. The next day, they took trains to Gourock, east of Glasgow, and arrived to board the *Royal Scotsman*. A and B Companies of the 1st Ranger Battalion along with some Marines and

Quartermaster were attached to the ship. From the 14th to the 16th, they stayed in the Clyde area in preparation for the amphibious landing exercise *Mosstrooper* with the 1st Infantry Division and 1st Engineer Amphibian Brigade. The next day, they left Clyde for Loch Linnhe, north of Oban, where they spent the next two days executing their tasks as part of *Mosstrooper.* "The *Mosstrooper* force was largely made up of units that would form the Centre Task Force for *Torch* [the impending allied invasion of North Africa]. The 18th Regimental Combat Team and a battalion of U.S. Rangers was to land at Duror and march south to Oban, seizing a coastal battery at Port Appin on the way."

Back in Clyde, they spent 20–25 October preparing for their next movement. Everyone knew something was coming, but where and when was a secret known to a few. The anticipation of war was reaching its zenith. Captain Meade put it succinctly: "We finally loaded on transport and set off, destination unknown."

TLEMCEN, ALGERIA, 1943

The square of the large town, known for its beautiful grand mosque, held the trucks needed to transport the Rangers back to their base at Nemours. Drunken, tired, filthy Rangers filtered in alongside more sober men oblivious to the now-approaching column of fantastic-looking Free French cavalry prancing into the square on their beautiful horses. Immaculately dressed with a light dusting on their uniforms, the horsemen slowed their mounts looking at the disheveled Americans who had no doubt spent their time in whorehouses consuming vast quantities of dubious alcohol—literally looking down on *les americains.* The captain of the French troop rode a horse so white, it looked out of this world. It was magnificent. He and his horse made a beautiful sight. The nobility of the French military and colonial tradition . . . separating the two worlds, old and new, by its sheer magnificence . . . until a drunk Ranger sergeant, one Sergeant Albert Jacobsen of B/CO, weaved through the crowd and kicked the animal's rear. Stunned, perhaps frightened, the glorious creature reared, its mane flowing in the wind, the front hooves high into the air, throwing the captain off the saddle, tossing him hard onto the ground, as it charged forward, through the parading cavalry ranks, shattering them into disarray . . . to the amusement of the Americans.

SIX MONTHS EARLIER, *OPERATION TORCH*, PORT OF ARZEW—8 NOVEMBER 1942

Within a year of America's entry into the war, a second front was to be opened to release the near-total pressure of the Germans on the Soviet Union, which had suffered enormously. The front, however, was not to be opened directly across the English Channel as American strategists had favored, but in French-held North Africa, comprised of Algeria, Morocco, and Tunisia. So far, the German forces had been successful in driving Allied forces into Egypt, but it was not German forces controlling French North Africa. The French Vichy forces were responsible for its defense. Part of the decision to make this a primarily American-led invasion was based on the belief that the French Vichy Navy harbored a grudge against the British, who had attacked the French fleet, killing 1,300 sailors and sinking nearly all the ships, at Mers-el-Kebir, on 3 July 1940 near Oran, therefore the need for Americans, and not the British, to lead the way. Perhaps the Vichy French would fight less hard against the Americans—that's what the planners hoped for, in any event.

Operation Torch was the first combat for the untested American military. *Torch* had three main points of attack. The Western Task Force, leaving from the U.S., centered around Casablanca; the Center Task Force, which included the 1st Ranger Battalion, leaving from the U.K., focused on Oran; and lastly, the Eastern Task Force, mostly composed of British troops but under American command, targeted Algiers. Arzew was some 30 miles east and slightly north of the large French naval base at Oran and part of the Western Task Force's objective. Its location was vital to the success for the Allies at Oran.

As part of *Operation Torch* and rehearsed under *Mosstrooper* in the U.K., the Rangers were tasked with a typical Commando-style mission:

a daring night raid on two main defensive strongpoints, each with a gun battery overlooking the port and approach to Arzew, Algeria. The town itself, situated on the western side, overlooked the beach. The northern portion was dedicated to the industrial sector, filled with warehouses and refineries. Running along the coastline was a railroad that separated the nearby northern heights overlooking Arzew Bay and the port. The port featured two jetties stretching a quarter of a mile out, converging on each other at right angles, forming a narrow entry into the harbor. Across the narrow entrance stretched a retractable boom, comprised of buoys connected by a cable with anti-torpedo netting attached, allowing for the closure of the harbor. To offset this, the LCAs featured steel skids or runners underneath to ride over the obstacle without damaging the propellers. The mission required the seizure and destruction of two gun batteries dominating Arzew's port, the capture of a Foreign Legion Fort on the heights above Arzew, all part of the eastern sector of the assault; and to occupy the town before the 1st Division's Combat Teams 16 and 18, under Major General Terry Allen, and Task Force Red of Combat Command B, 1st Armored Division, were to land.

The two batteries in question were the Fort de la Pointe with two 75mm artillery pieces, just a stone's throw away in the base of the hill, north of the Grand Quay intersecting with the Jetty Abril, the outermost part of the port. On its seaside was a rather steep bank of some 30 feet in height and covered in wire. To the northeast, and on higher ground, was the larger of the two batteries near the Blockhaus du Fort du Nord (Fort Superieur) with a battery of four 105mm guns. The port held a small French flotilla in its southern part as well as some military seaplanes. The area was garrisoned by colonial troops, housed in nearby barracks in the western part of the harbor.

The Rangers had been briefed on their mission, but only found out the names of their objectives once en route. Meticulous planning had gone into the operation, and every Ranger from Darby to the lowest rank reviewed and studied the photographs, sand tables, and other intelligence during the sea voyage.

The assault had two elements. The first and smaller group was under Herm Dammer and featured A and B Companies for the capture and destruction of the smaller strongpoint, Fort de la Pointe, just near the harbor. To infiltrate, the two companies, plus HQ and naval artillery liaisons, were transported to eight landing craft with quiet-running motors from the *Royal Scotsman* and expected to arrive on target by 0130 hours on a cloudy and moonless night. But things proved a bit more challenging because of the darkness. The small flotilla made a successful run, loading and launching the LCAs by 1215, despite Boat #1 carrying Major Dammer, naval crew, and Rangers for a total of 45 people. Space was nonexistent. The lighthouse on the shore was clear, and they made it into the port; but they were unable to find its exact location, the darkness and numerous vessels causing confusion, and the flotilla went around in circles, bumping into two docks. Twenty minutes later, they made it. The three-foot-high climb from the water onto the street was easily handled by the men. The platoons deployed unchallenged.

The plan called for A Company under Captain Meade to assault the fort, while B Company, reinforced with machine guns and 60mm mortars, blocked the roads to the west leading into town. Some alcohol-related minor looting already had begun. To that end, 2nd Platoon, B Company, under Lieutenant Larkin moved across the railroad tracks and street intersections, setting up defensive positions. Larkin checked on the positions and was satisfied, as the sand tables they had studied were spot-on, and each Ranger was able to take up his precise position.

By 0330, eight French marines had sneaked under a flatcar but were discovered by Corporal Anders Arnbal, who would write a fine memoir in later years, and PFC Hayes. Along with Lieutenant Carran and three other Rangers, they routed the enemy and captured them. Another large group of Marines attempted to pierce the defensive blocking position and were driven away by the Rangers, including Larkin and his runner. The marines retreated but were captured. Defensive positions were reinforced with nearby rocks, while other men were sent to bring up deckloads from the LCA, including four light machine guns, making their positions even stronger. They would eventually suffer one killed in action, PFC George W. Grisamer, in a firefight. Grisamer, who had been ill with pneumonia in the U.K., had made his way back to the battalion even though he had been hospitalized. He served as assistant gunner to Corporal Arnbal and was hit by incoming sniper fire while in a blocking position, showering the corporal with blood. "Agonizing, piercing cries and convulsive movements." They had been fired on from their front right near a cemetery wall. Seeing three legionnaires running, Arnbal killed them with several bursts of his .30 machine gun, sending the French tumbling down the slope, coming to rest against shrubs and rocks. He fired three more bursts into them. It took a little while for Grisamer to die despite efforts to save him. Arnbal recounts: "Then here at the corner of the dock-front warehouse at 0630 hours, November 8, 1942, under a heavy-duty trailer, he had given of himself all there is ever possible to give of oneself."

It was also in the western blocking area that 19-year-old Ranger Murray A. Katzen, Lieutenant Larkin's runner, with Tommy gun and grenades captured some 42 French marines and civilians. Receiving sniper fire from the rear of 2nd Platoon and from a row of warehouses near the waterline, Katzen moved toward it with PVT Jospeh. Both rounded the corner, throwing hand grenades and stunning the occupants. The two Rangers charged into the building firing submachine guns and capturing five snipers. This was the same Katzen who once had been busted for talking back to a British officer, another time while guarding a whorehouse, some of the hookers he frequented regularly in his off-time, and went AWOL later to go back to the Rangers after he had been reclassified to limited service because of battle fatigue, and was to rejoin the 105 Anti-Aircraft Artillery (Automatic Weapons), Louisiana National Guard. Katzen thought highly of draftees as soldiers and valued them more than the guardsmen. Katzen was Jewish and hated having to go to church, and a Baptist chaplain in the 105 AAA tried to convert him. He was called "Jew bastard" and worse by a few guys throughout his time in the military. After his heroics in Arzew, he was busted for another transgression. He received a

Silver Star in 1952, well after the conclusion of the war. Katzen seemed unaware of it.

Meanwhile, 1st Platoon, B Company, under LT Knudson, moved onto the slight embankment just north of the fort, from the eastern shoreline to a cemetery, thereby containing the fort and blocking any reinforcements from the town's garrison to the west, establishing the mortar position in the center of their line, and seizing the nearby refineries north of the fort. In the morning, B Company Lieutenant Carran, who had been volunteered for the Rangers by his friend Meade, was shot in the shoulder when taking on sporadic fire from the east, while containing the situation. After the action, Carran had thought he'd be on his way back to the United States, but his best friend, Captain Meade, advised the doctors that the injury was only slight and to leave him with the Rangers. What are friends for?

Meade's A Company moved through their sister company, a passage of lines, and advanced on to the fort within 10 minutes. It was a smoothly executed maneuver. 1st PLT, A Company, under Lieutenant Manning Jacob, launched from the HMS *Scotsman*, had a short delay because of difficulties lowering the landing craft. They moved up the quayside past several warehouses in an easterly direction, then onto the grassy embankment just northwest of the French fortification, which turned inward to the entrance. Along the way, they thought they had arrived at the gun position, but it turned out to be a foundation and cellar of a small building that had been torn down. The scouts encountered a French sentry who was fooled into believing them to be French, Jacob notes, as they responded with "*nous sommes vos amis*" ("we are friends"), and they were passed on. What happened to the sentry is not recorded, although Sullivan notes "one Arab was killed at entrance." At the embankment, and after having placed the BAR for supporting fire if needed, they encountered the first of three stands of a barbed-wire defensive perimeter. The first breach led to the garrison being alerted, since a siren was sounded. The alarm distracted the enemy forces to focus on the location of the smaller fort, drawing attention away from Darby's group. Lieutenant Dirks, who had received a stern report from Vaughan while at Achnacarry and

who had not landed at Dieppe, led his 2nd Platoon to the front gate.
As Jacob's men cut the last wire, a clear shout of "Hi-Ho, Silver" was
heard coming from the 2nd Platoon at the front gate. The countersign was "Away" (the finishing word to the Lone Ranger's call to his
horse Silver). They advanced, forcing the action to commence. The
assault was on, with both platoons in sections moving to the objective.
Jacob's Rangers charged over the embankment to climb the walls.
Sixty prisoners were taken and the guns set to be destroyed.

By 0215, Major Dammer, commanding the assault, signaled with
red flares that they had been successful. A small American and British
naval unit, along with 12 U.S. Marines, waited for the signal and proceeded to seize four vessels in the southern part of the port. Captain
Meade also had tasked Lieutenant Jacob with 1st Platoon to seize and
hold the nearby refinery.

The second part of the night raid was led by Darby, who commanded four companies from the *Royal Ulsterman* and *Ulster Monarch*
up the cliffs from a landing point southeast of Cap Carbon. His
time on target was set for some 30 minutes later with C, D, E, and F
and HQ elements. For this mission, Darby converted Captain Alvah
Miller's D Company into the 81mm mortar company for support,
using walkie-talkies for control. As the LCAs were lowered, one did
not lower correctly, spilling Rangers and radio equipment into the sea.
One of the men was Army Signal Corps Sergeant Phil Stern. No doubt
some terrifying moments, as Darby mentions in his later briefing in
Washington, D.C.: "It created a little bit of consternation because we
were terribly crowded and we had to fish these people out of the water.
This being our first landing, it was quite nerve-racking."

The *Ulster Monarch* led the remaining LCAs to the correct spot, but
one of the landing craft got stuck on rocks some 30 yards out from the
landing spot. The craft carried LT Leilyn Young. He and five others
swam to a beach, and then, 100 yards on, they encountered a 100-foot
cliff they could not climb at night so they missed part of the action.
The others on the stuck LCA waited to be rescued. The Darby force
landed late, whereupon they tackled a 15-foot cliff and subdued a
sentry. After a three-plus-mile march on the coastal highway, Darby's

group cut southwest, making its way slowly up a ravine to the rear of the position. By this time, Dammer Force had already captured the other fort.

The Rangers set up the 81mm mortars for indirect fire support at the base of a ravine some 500 yards north of the fort. Darby deployed his companies from left to right, facing the battery, with Klefman's C, Murray's F, Schneider's E, and the scouts in front, all anxious for Darby to launch the attack. By 0300 they encountered a double-apron 14-foot-tall wire perimeter. The scouts began to cut through the obstacle, triggering two French machine guns that opened up with searching tracer fire. At this point, Darby conferred with Murray. After that, Darby ordered Klefman's Charlie Company to pull his unit back and to direct D Company's mortar barrage. The first 81mm round landed spot-on in the middle of the battery. Klefman did not need to adjust fire, instead letting Captain Miller know to "pour it on." The thundering barrage of the heavy mortars shook the earth beneath the Rangers and certainly shook the French defenders. Klefman's company opened up with its small-arms arsenal, while Easy and Fox Companies blasted through the wire with Bangalore torpedoes, then charged the battery's crew with the bayonet—"the meat" of the English-trained Americans. Dog Company had fired 50 rounds onto the battery, enabling the successful assault. "Acrid smoke from the mortar barrage was still swirling around the gun emplacements as the Rangers moved in, meeting no resistance. The gun crews had taken cover in their sandbagged positions; and one by one, thirty dazed Frenchmen came out with their hands over their heads." Another group of some 40 French soldiers barricaded themselves inside a powder magazine until a Bangalore torpedo was thrust into the ventilating duct, along with a few concussion grenades. They, too, surrendered.

At the battery, Bangalore torpedoes were placed inside the battery's barrels. Once the guns had been destroyed, Darby moved his Rangers toward the Fort du Nord proper, which was used as a convalescence home for Legion veterans, spearheaded by E Company's Edwin Dean. His 50-round drum magazine to the Thompson fell out as he aimed it at the French, much to their amusement, but they were ready to surrender anyway. At 0400, Darby, unable to use shore-to-ship communications, ordered green flares fired into the air. A white flare was to follow; but not having one, it took a little while for the Navy to send a patrol to confirm capture of the larger battery. This was done one hour later. The two raids had been successful, with only sporadic firefights, resulting in 300 prisoners and the destruction of two gun batteries.

It was at a fort in Arzew that First Sergeant Scotty Munro penned a Ranger Song sung to the tunes of "Ivan Sakvinski Skavar":

They were gathered from near, they were gathered from far,
They were picked from the best in the land.
A Hell raising crew that sailed the blue,
Was Darby's Ranger Band.
Now they will tell of the Marine and Sailor, I know,
And tell of the deeds that were done,
But Darby's Rangers will sing for themselves,
And tell how Arzew was won.
How they fought all that night where the old Med flows,
Under a moonless sky;
Fighting and sniping till came the dawn,
Well knowing that some must die.
But Darby's Rangers still carry on,
To revenge their buddies that fell,
And this be our motto and we will fulfill:
To stand our last post in Hell.

Follow-on operations resulted in several more Ranger casualties near Saint Cloud and La Macta. Easy Company under LT Max Schneider supported the 1st Battalion of the 16th Infantry Regiment by moving by rail to Port-aux-Poules. Here they took two 75mm half-tracks from the 16th toward La Macta, some four miles southeast along the coast. Throughout the latter movement, they came under sporadic fire. 2nd Platoon of E Company flanked the enemy position while under fire, and the French fled, leaving behind some killed and prisoners. Thereafter, the company provided protection of the town until 10 November, when it took the train to Arzew to rejoin the battalion.

On the road toward Oran lies St. Cloud, a small town, which held out against the American advance. Originally Company C was assigned to the defense of the command post of the 1st Division at Tourville, a village on the outskirts of Arzew, but then was ordered to Saint Cloud, although the exact military situation was unknown. Not wanting to inflict casualties on the civilian population with artillery, an infantry attack was launched by one battalion while the other two bypassed and moved toward Oran.

Charlie Company under Lieutenant Gordon Klefman was attached to 1st Battalion, 18th Infantry Regiment. A night march saw the Rangers move around and south of the town to set up blocking positions. At dawn they spotted a motor convoy stopped on a road roughly a quarter mile away, where it had set up an artillery position. Lieutenant Chuck Shunstrom took 2nd Platoon minus one section to the left, while Klefman moved the other platoon straight ahead. The Rangers encountered mortar fire, 75mm artillery fire, and machine-gun fire about a quarter of a mile to the convoy. Shunstrom's flanking movement got pinned down and they dug in, exchanging fire. Once Major General Allen captured Oran, the French at St. Cloud were ordered to surrender, netting 400 prisoners. First Lieutenant Gordon L Klefman, Private Elmer T. Eskola, and PFC Alder L. Nystrom were killed in the firefight. Sullivan considered them fine fellows. Father Basil was called upon for burial services. The hard-charging Charlie Company returned on the 10th of November. Sergeant Warren "Bing" Evans received a battlefield commission to 2nd Lieutenant.

Major Darby became the mayor of Arzew with the local dubious brothels overflowing with sex-starved Rangers and venereal disease. Visits to Oran's whorehouses and sex with some of the old whores didn't help either. Darby bore down on the men under the hot African sun and cold nights. For nearly three months, the Ranger Battalion at Arzew would train day and night in exceptional mountaineering, night operations, and amphibious assaults using live ammunition throughout, sometimes reviewed by the watchful eyes of the brass. Other duties included typical garrison jobs such as security and guarding prisoners, nothing exciting for men who wanted action. The Morning Reports of all Ranger companies of the 1st Battalion are filled with the daily minutiae of garrison-type soldiering.

By 30 November, total losses for the Ranger Battalion were nine officers and 82 enlisted men, of which four had been killed with eight wounded, the rest suffering from a variety of ailments—some were probably dismissed from the Rangers because of ill-discipline. Awards were handed out on 16 December by Major General Lloyd Fredendall, Commanding General, II Army Corps after a training exercise near Cap Carbon to several Rangers for their participation in Dieppe. A potential raid on a small island called Galita, code name *Peashooter*, was called off after a period of training, adding to the frustration of the men. Their continued use as a demonstration and training unit for amphibious assaults, while assigned to the Fifth Army Invasion Training Center, further drove the men nuts, probably increasing their use of profanity and incessant complaining.

Their anger was also vented toward the local Arabs, and not just for driving up market prices, but because for some reason some believed them to be selling information not only to the Allies but to the Germans and Italians as well. Lieutenant Charles Shunstrom saw an Arab looking down from a window observing the Rangers marching by when Chuck pulled out his .45, with clear plastic handles, having replaced the standard-issue ones, with one side featuring a picture of his daughter, the other one of his wife, and murdered the onlooker. It was also in North Africa where Shunstrom threw grenades from the tops of boxcars on Arab huts near the track. The death of Klefman probably didn't help. Nonetheless, Ranger Ruona of B Company wrote many years later how, in his company, some Rangers used ethnic slurs toward Blacks, Hispanics, and Jews. He also points out that he set the record straight on several occasions in supporting the Jews, since they were loyal. One can easily see how the Rangers thought of the locals, given the state of society back in the States. Sullivan commented on the filth he saw throughout North Africa. Animal abuse was also rife. General Patton noted in his memoir how similar the Arabs were in the cruel mistreatment of their animals to the Mexicans. This and other kinds of issues broke down the discipline of many Rangers. Even Darby got tired of some of the men who believed they were super soldiers now, while others were AWOL (Absent Without Leave), drunk, or just ill-disciplined. First Lieutenant Alfred H. Nelson, commanding officer of B Company, who annoyed some Rangers with his pretentious swagger stick and gloves, which he had used ever since the early days at Achnacarry, would eventually get "shot up in Africa." But importantly, he shot a drunken Ranger between the legs, although he had threatened to shoot the drunk when he challenged Nelson.

Many Rangers did not care for the endless training, and discipline broke down, resulting in the replacement of over 20 percent of the force by 31 January 1943: 108 new officers, enlisted under Captain Jack Street, arrived. These had been trained in the States and were established as Company G for training under several lieutenants from the 1st Ranger Battalion. A short week later, the battalion moved by plane to Tébessa, Algeria, near the Tunisian border, where it was trucked five miles east of the town to HQ II Corps. By February, the Rangers had moved by truck, driven by "negroes" to Gafsa. Their mission to harass, raid, and recon enemy forces would occur within a couple of days, with a daring night raid on Italian positions northwest of Sened Station, Tunisia. Three officers were relieved of duty for injuries: Captain Jacob, Lieutenant Knudson, and Lieutenant Lanning.

SENED STATION

The oasis of Gafsa, home to the great Numidian king Jugurtha, and captured by Romans in 106 BC, had changed hands several times already in the back-and-forth of mobile desert warfare. It became the base of operations for the Rangers. "It was a very nice town and it had a beautiful swimming pool," recalled Roy Murray. During this time of the war, the front "lines" were scattered outposts with distances as much as 20 miles between them. These outposts were manned by

Italians, as the Germans kept the experienced Afrika Korps in the rear at strategic points, wanting to avoid attrition of its elite troops. The Americans wanted to raid enemy outposts to destroy their morale and hoodwink the Germans and Italians into believing there were far more U.S. troops in the area than there were, forcing them to deploy their highly vaunted Afrika Korps, thereby reducing the German reserves. Another point was to force the Axis to abandon their mountainous fortified position and move westward into the desert to fight out in the open. The unit to force this move was, of course, none other than the men who had trained for these types of daring night raids: Darby's Rangers. The impending raids lifted the men's morale as they finally again felt these missions to be following proper Ranger doctrine. Sneaking behind enemy lines in the dark with painted faces, silencing sentries, and killing everything in sight: true Ranger operations.

On 9 February 1943, the 1st Ranger Battalion received its first combat order in Tunisia. The target: Sened Station. Sened Station was a small Arab town made significant by its road and rail lines near the mountains. Five miles north of Sened, on a series of rocky hills, and guarding the approach to Sened Station, was a fortified emplacement manned by Italian *Bersaglieri* straight from Italy wearing their bluish-gray uniforms. It was a mountain gateway into the Tunisian plains to the west of nearby Maknassy, which also had changed hands repeatedly, recently back to the American 1st Armored Division. Allied intelligence believed that one key mountain cutting through the Sened that led to the plains of Maknassy was the area from which a German attack was anticipated. In early afternoon, Darby and Dammer, along with the commanders of the three companies to be used for the night raid, conducted a visual reconnaissance, looking for suitable hiding places and routes for the fewer than 200 Rangers. Returning to Gafsa, in a nearby olive grove, the Ranger Headquarters Company prepared for movement for the raid to depart in a few hours.

The companies tasked with this daring night raid were Able under Lieutenant Dirks, who grew into leadership, Easy under the much-respected Lieutenant Max Schneider, and Fox under Captain

Roy Murray, who told the Rangers, "We've got to leave our mark on these people with grenades, bayonets, and knives—the works. They've got to know they've been worked over by Rangers. And remember this: We're only bringing back ten prisoners—no more and no less." Fox Company, for example, carried one ground sheet, two rations, one water canteen, bandoleers with 72 rounds, knit caps, no helmets, flashlights with 63 men and five Rangers with an 81mm mortar, a medic, and headquarters. Weapons were M1 Garand rifles and Tommy guns. Murray's company was to capture three prisoners, and no shooting was to occur until ordered to do so.

On 10 February, the Ranger companies traveled in trucks northeast from Gafsa 24 miles along the road from Gafsa to Sidi-bou-Zid to an isolated French outpost some 16 miles west of the enemy positions. The drive took two hours under blackout conditions, as during daylight the road was under constant observation and shelling. Getting organized with last-minute checks, the Rangers marched in columns of two silently through the night across rugged terrain for 12 miles, from 0400 to 0600 hours, to the predetermined hiding place over varied terrain, coming to a stop on a high jebel (Djebel: hill, mountain) with many depressions and cacti. No enemy was the wiser for their presence. Stopping short of the Italians, the Rangers settled in high on a saddle of a towering ridge between three peaks in a mountain valley overlooking the enemy positions protecting the Maknassy Valley. Mountaineering had paid off. They were some four miles away at this point. The men concealed themselves from the naked eye with camouflaged shelter halves, useless against the biting mountain cold, and brush from the immediate area without disturbing anything. Eating cold rations, they rested while sharp Ranger eyes monitored the scenes below them, paying particular attention to the actual positions and movements of the Italians, along with the terrain they'd cover in the darkness of the coming night. This was accomplished during the day as commanders took the officers and sergeants and section leaders to vantage points. Counting enemy troops, the Rangers believed some 100 were occupying the defensive emplacements. The actual strength turned out to be around 130 or more. In the late afternoon, they proceeded to their second hideout and the Observation Post, just three miles away from their target in a high mountain ravine, shielding them from the enemy.

By noon, Lieutenant Colonel Bill Darby and Herm Dammer, as always leading from the front, made their way through a small creekbed to within one mile of the Italian outposts. They remained unobserved. Using field glasses, they identified the exact locations of machine guns and larger-caliber weapons. Satisfied about their leaders' reconnaissance, they returned to Ranger lines and, as the sun slipped behind the mountain range to the west, plans were made and passed down. Here they made an on-the-spot plan of attack. Intel was shared among the officers and senior noncoms, of emplacements and MG nests and actions on the objective. The leadership then passed word to the Rangers themselves, who each knew of their specific objectives, terrain features, and the overall plans. On the back of each Ranger's backpack was a "distinguishing mark," a white tape for identification purposes, always part of night operations. Final prep for the nighttime raid was made: faces perhaps re-darkened or simply just dirty; equipment tightened to avoid any noise that metal or wood or anything could possibly make; and wool caps placed on their heads, as the noise-making helmets had been left behind before the mission. Weeks before, knowing of the series of raids they were to conduct, all equipment had already been carefully checked to maintain noise discipline as per Ranger Standard Operating Procedure, vital for nighttime raids. Azimuths (compass bearings) were shot to their individual companies' objectives. Officers and NCOs checked their men's gear and weapons one final time, as did the men in any event. The raiders settled in and tried to catch some sleep waiting for the crescent moon to slip below the mountain heights, darkening the desert plain they needed to cross.

At 2240, "on your feet" commands were whispered, bayonets fixed, and within a few short minutes the Ranger columns moved down the rock-strewn slope until they hit the plain. The three companies moved cautiously forward. All those many months of training and training and training now paid off. In the near-silent night, with the moon rising, the Rangers made their ways through ravines, ever cautious to keep the terrain between them and the Italians. The companies slithered to a slow halt just shy of their objective at the edge of a pebbled plain that needed to be crossed to attack the enemy positions, a flat desert some two and a half miles long, broken by numerous dry wadis and djebels, from 500 to 1,800 feet in elevation, with sparse vegetation and patches of cacti. Ensuring formation and avoiding a break in the column, the front came to a stop, waiting for the "all present" before moving on. The companies, Able in the lead followed by Easy and Fox, moved in a single column across the pebbled plain, coming to a stop 500 yards short of the enemy for final reorganization and deployment.

At 350 yards, dogs barked, and the Rangers sank into the hard ground, waiting patiently for the go-ahead. Reaching their final checkpoint, the line of departure, some 75 yards away from the Italians, they deployed along their line of attack with Able on the left, Easy in the middle, and then Fox. This movement and deployment had been rehearsed for seemingly ever, and it had paid dividends so far. Using pinpoint multi-colored flashlights, the companies signaled to the rear for Darby to control their advances, making final adjustments, and when necessary, using handheld walkie-talkies. Boundaries between the companies had been planned to avoid friendly fire, using terrain features and allowing platoon leaders who'd be at the front to make changes when required without asking permission. Dogs barked in the distance, but the Italian outpost was quiet. Finally, between 0100 and 0130 hours, it was time.

It was a dark, inky night, hiding the black-faced killers advancing slowly toward the unseen enemy. The darkness and quiet of the mountains exploded as the flanking companies were still 30 yards out. The center company's target was closer than the recon had revealed by some 25 yards, meaning the middle of the attack began sooner than the flanks. There was not to be a simultaneous assault. A long machine gun burst on Able's front lit up the area, followed almost immediately by more than "a dozen machine guns joined in a deadly chorus, spewing out blue, green and white tracers" above the black-faced devils. The Italian defenders on the flanks had 20 more seconds to man their positions.

The Rangers ran toward the enemy: The faster they covered the ground, the sooner they'd get to killin', and that was why they were here. Low-crawling underneath the machine-gun fire, they closed. Rifles and cannon fired at them at point-blank range as the Rangers crawled up the gradual slopes toward the positions and then Darby's boys got up and rushed forward, shooting, hollering, screaming. Grenades flew through the air, followed by Tommy submachine gun fire and the "meat" of the infantry, the bayonet and the knife. Three companies of well-trained, frustrated Rangers moved like a wave across the Italians without remorse or mercy, while the Rangers' 60mm mortars pummeled the rear, believed to be a vehicle park, and then their aim was adjusted with calls for fire onto defensive positions with quick communications between each company and their boundaries. At least two stubborn positions were annihilated this way. The mortar section leapfrogged forward, supporting the assault.

The center of the *Bersaglieri* was crushed within five minutes, but the flank companies took a bit longer because of the earlier error in terrain recon allowing the enemy to man their guns. Defenders indiscriminately threw grenades everywhere. Larger shells landed behind the Ranger force. But by firing, the Italians also gave away their positions. It was on the left flank where now-Lieutenant "Bing" Evans, with pistol and knife in hand, moved into the attack with his runner, Tommy Sullivan, behind him when suddenly a dark shadow of an Italian popped out in front of him. Evans froze.

> The next thing we knew, we were in amongst them engaged in hand-to-hand combat and very fierce fighting. But we had the advantage. With the complete surprise, we had created a real havoc. We were using Tommy guns, bayonets, knives, and hand grenades. That's something that most infantry soldiers have never experienced—hand-to-hand combat. They usually never see the man they are about to kill. Very few of us did. On this particular night, I had my

knife in one hand and my .45 in the other, and I was using both of them. We were fighting Germans along with some Italians. Then the sky became as bright as day. Our opponents began to throw up flares so they could see what was happening. At that point, they could see us and we could see them. All of a sudden, out of the dark came an enemy soldier. He was running toward me with a gun in his hand. He got very close. His eyes were big as saucers, frightened and wild. Looking into his eyes, I became paralyzed and found that I couldn't pull the trigger on my .45 piece. I couldn't do it! I knew he was ready to kill me, but I couldn't do it. Up until then I hadn't looked into the eyes of the one that I was about to kill. But now I did. Little Tommy Sullivan, my runner, was probably five steps from me to my right and a little to the rear. Being my runner, he was to stay with me at all times unless I sent him on a mission. The runner is used as the main means of communication in case the walkie-talkies didn't work. A lot of times they didn't. Tommy sized up the situation and, without hesitating, shot my attacker in the chest and killed him for me. If he hadn't, I wouldn't be here today. Tommy Sullivan saved my life. I think Tommy wondered what in the world was wrong with me. I told him my gun jammed. But I think he knew better. I think he knew I froze on the trigger. That incident is imbedded in my mind. All of a sudden, I looked into a man's eyes, a man about my age, and I was a softie. I couldn't pull the trigger. That's one of those times that I am not particularly proud of. I was not the hero. Tommy Sullivan was.

PFC Elmer Garrison had low-crawled toward the Italian lines. He looked up, some seven or eight feet away from a gun muzzle, stood up, and had his head blown off by a 47mm cannon. In return, the spirit of the bayonet and, at times, the dagger asked for their pound of flesh. Darby harangued Murray on the radio to get to the top and Murray sure did, destroying a .50 cal heavy machine-gun nest in a daring charge, allowing for more Ranger assault sections to close with the enemy, while PFC Ferrier and SGT Rensick destroyed a 37mm cannon almost immediately thereafter with grenades and bayonets, while mortars blocked and hammered the Italian retreat.

Twenty minutes of killin' without mercy by crazed black-faced, death-dealing devils, destroying defensive dugouts and two cannons, killed all but 10 Italians—no mercy. It was perhaps this night that Captain Murray's Commando dagger broke its blade when it hit bone. The raid had come to its natural conclusion once men returned to reason, hate no longer in command. PFC Biro and Corporal Ladd were wounded, as were many others. Ladd would lose his leg. The moans and cries of the wounded, occasionally interrupted by shouts for the medic, settled into the otherwise return of the quiet and dark night. The Rangers mopped up until the whistles and yells had them move back. Fox Company under Murray withdrew and assembled 100 yards to the rear near their medic station.

The tally of the raid was 1 Ranger killed, with 14 to 18 wounded, the majority of whom were wounded by grenade fragments. Eighty-five Italians of the 10th *Bersaglieri* Regiment were butchered, 25 severely wounded and left as dying, and 10 to 13 prisoners, with 4 or 5 Italian escapees. Captain Max Schneider shot 2 prisoners while speaking with Darby about POW status and numbers—they were to not have more than 10. Six automatic cannons, perhaps 37mm or 47mm in size, were destroyed, along with 1 50mm anti-tank gun, and 5 heavy machine guns.

Darby decided that his command needed to get back to safety, some 20 miles away. To that end, he took the wounded, the slow column, under his command and made Dammer take the other Ranger group to move on as fast as possible. The new battalion medical officer, Captain Joseph Goldstein, did a remarkable job caring for the wounded during and after the battle. Barely into the march, the Rangers divided into four smaller groups of 50 men each to move quickly and to have greater concealment from the enemy than a larger force would have. Dammer reached the French outpost at dawn with a forced speed march, from where they were trucked back to Gafsa. Darby and his wounded group arrived at noon but hid in nearby hills when enemy half-tracks and tanks were spotted. They returned at night by trucks. One memorable moment occurred during the slow column withdrawal. The Rangers had to use their shelter halves or ground cover as litters, and it required shifts of four to six men to carry a wounded man. In this case, it was Corporal Garland S. Ladd being carried and one of his litter bearers was Sergeant Donald W. VanArtsdalen. Ladd started to slide off the makeshift litter, leading VanArtsdalen to pound the back of the man in front of him, cursing him to slow the fuck down. The man ahead turned out to be Darby, who whispered quietly, "I'm sorry, but we have to keep going." Back at Gafsa and, "Over cups of steaming coffee and warm chow, the men, visibly tired from the exacting sortie, rehashed their vivid experiences with one another. Men of other Ranger companies who had not been on the raid listened intently, as they were scheduled for similar action the next night."

This first Ranger night raid was a smashing success, with 12 Silver Stars, including one for 1st LT Dirks and others including Darby and Murray, awarded by Major General Fredendall, while two enlisted men were promoted to commissioned officers.

Within two days, the Axis launched an attack on Sidi-bou-Zid, forcing the Allies to withdraw from Gafsa. The Ranger Battalion moved out, leaving D and C Companies as a rear guard. The problem for the lightly armed Rangers was that they were on foot; if caught out in the open by motorized enemy units, they'd be done for. It was during this crucial moment that Lieutenant Colonel William Darby gave his famous speech encouraging his men: "If we get caught by the tanks, God help the tanks." The extended version of Darby's speech, given near the destroyed American airfield outside of Feriana, was written by Jim Altieri: "Behind us and on our flanks are enemy armored columns looking for stragglers to cut up. We have no transport except our legs, no artillery, and no tanks. We have only a few rocket guns and bazooka grenades to fight against armor. Onward we stagger— and if the tanks come, God help the tanks." Some of the men were not that uplifted by his speech. Although they encountered some tanks, the Rangers were unseen and arrived the next day on the high ground east of Feriana. On 16 February 1943, they were ordered south of Bou Chebka and occupied the defensive positions some four miles wide astride the Feriana-Tébessa road, where they remained until 1 March.

The Axis forces launched a series of attacks during the end of February known as the Battle of the Kasserine Pass, hammering the 1st Infantry Division and 1st Armored Division. The attacks occurred northwest of the 1st Ranger Battalion but while the fighting was going on, one company was required to help the hard-pressed Americans, and Charlie Company did so and then returned by 24 February to the battalion. Each night, Ranger patrols went out. One night, two Rangers from A Company scouted well beyond their normal area during a night filled with light rainfall, when they bumped into a German motorized infantry unit that was halted for the evening and in the process of getting fed from their field kitchen. Our heroic two self-assured Rangers rolled up their collars, hunched over, and got hot chocolates, hot sausages, and bread.

Another evening, Lieutenant-Colonel Darby made the rounds as he usually was prone to do and found three men asleep at a 37mm gun position. He cussed so loudly, although some thought he never used profanity, that others heard him berate the men, threatening them with execution by firing squad the next morning. Needless to say, Darby was prevailed upon to stand down for the battalion's morale.

During this time, Darby's boys, notably the recently promoted Captain Shunstrom and Charlie Company, participated in several smaller clashes, killing six Italians, capturing eight Italians and eight German Military Police, whose photos were taken by Sergeant Phil Stern. The Rangers destroyed three wheeled scout vehicles while capturing three others. The price for this was one missing Ranger. It was also during this time that Father Basil set up Mass for all faiths even once while an artillery shell exploded nearby, no doubt sending some cussing Rangers into the rocks, but not impacting the Commando priest whatsoever. The Swear Jar no doubt overflowed.

One day, around 13 March 1943, a section under Lieutenant Larkin was sent to pick up barracks bags that had arrived at a rail station. Disheveled and wearing knit caps, the men encountered a notorious stickler for discipline. Leading the approaching convoy were two motorbikes and a half-track, followed by two more motorbikes. The convoy came to a screeching halt with the general standing up and hollering at the men, asking who was in charge. A meek Lieutenant Larkin responded and was told that he was a disgrace—they were out of uniform and filthy. The general ordered them to line up. All were immediately court-martialed and fined one-third of their pay for three months. "This was our introduction to General Patton." Orders came into Ranger HQ demanding that all personnel wear helmets, be clean-shaven, and have haircuts. These orders did not help morale; some officers, more inclined to be the garrison type, ordered inspections and more details for the offenders. Any operation would be welcome relief. And that, they'd get.

EL GUETTAR

The Allied push commenced once they had regrouped from the Kasserine debacle. Lieutenant General George S. Patton took command of II Corps, and a major offensive was in the works. Orders were given by Patton's staff to Darby, on 13 and 16 March, to have his battalion be in reserve, approximately six miles north of their intended target, which was the American push to recapture Gafsa. The Rangers tagged along and encountered limited resistance during the attack on the town. On 18 March 1943, General Terry Allen of the 1st Infantry Division, who very much liked Darby as both men shared a love for tough night training and night operations, ordered Darby and his excellent unit toward El Guettar to ascertain the enemy's strength, dispositions, and unit identification, and, importantly, to remain in the area. The reconnaissance in force was vital for the Allied plan to attack El Guettar. There was, of course, a caveat. The area seemed to be crawling with some 2,000 enemy troops, and Darby was cautioned not to get into a fight he could not get out of by himself.

Moving at night over several mountains, they advanced down the slopes behind the town; scouts informed Darby that it was deserted. South of the town were two roads that came to a fork. The right, southern one led to the open plain while the left, the northern one, and the key in controlling both, was just south of the mountain, where it entered into a towering and narrow pass shaped like a funnel—Djebel el Ank. Both areas near the roads had been mined by the Americans. Aggressive combat patrols moved east, looking for enemy forces, when they finally located an Italian force astride the Gafsa-Gabes road at the Jebel (Djebel) el Ank pass. This was four miles southwest of El Guettar. The plan was simple but challenging: The Rangers needed to punch open the towering pass, break out onto the plains, and link up with the British Army advancing from the southeast. To do so, the Rangers were to assault the defensive position from the rear while the 26th Infantry attacked frontally in preparation to move south. The latter really needed the Rangers to succeed, or else they would be exposed to interdicting and intersecting gunfire. At the mouth of the pass were minefields, several perimeters or tiers of barbed-wire entanglements with anti-tank and machine guns on either side of the pass, which was rather narrow, a funnel—and in the flats beyond, the highly dangerous German 88mm guns were prepared to pour hell onto advancing troops.

Major Darby conducted a daylight leader's reconnaissance and, together with a two-night recon led by newly commissioned 2nd Lieutenant Walter Wojcik, a Minneapolis weight lifter with the physique of Charles Atlas, who discovered the possible approach to the rear of the pass, it seemed feasible to Darby and Dammer. Wojcik's scout had found a difficult route over gorges, saddles, crevices, and slopes to their target. Local Arab shepherds provided more knowledge of the area. It was an improbable, challenging task for the Rangers. But the route led to a small plateau directly above the objective. Making it up the precarious route with weapons and gear would require excellent discipline and mountaineering experience. Darby was confident enough. This nighttime march over harsh terrain to strike at the enemy at night, well, that was what Rangers had trained to do.

The 1st Ranger Battalion, minus Murray's Fox Company tasked with protecting headquarters where Generals Eisenhower and Patton held a meeting, moved out at night around 2345 hours, bringing along, with their own 60mm mortars, an engineer mortar company and its heavy 110mm- (4.2-inch) tubes. Keeping to a five-to-six-yard interval along the march, struggling up the terrain, with many a helping hand, the Rangers tackled the treacherous route, facing death if they so much as tripped. The temperature, writes Captain and journalist Ralph Ingersoll, was ideal for climbing: It was neither too hot nor too cold, but simply fresh and clear. He could only see a few men ahead of him but heard the sighing shuffle of hundreds of feet and the little clickings of the rocks. Later on, the moon came out and it was very beautiful marching through the mountain. Roughly twelve arduous miles, with mountains ranging from 600 to 1,000 meters in height later; and, at dawn, the Rangers collapsed at their destination. Catching their collective breath and final checks done, they prepared for the exhilaration and fear of the impending attack into the rear of the unsuspecting Italians. Darby, with two officers and his walkie-talkie man, was beyond pleased as he realized the incredible achievement of his boys. "He spoke in a loud whisper, and there was a note of almost exultation in it. He spoke as if to old friends, abruptly and without introduction. 'Do you realize what we have done, men! Do you realize! We've got five whole columns through!'" Hannibal crossing the Alps it was not, but it was truly a remarkable accomplishment for the men of the 1st Ranger Battalion. At the top was a bowl-shaped plateau parallel to the ridgeline of a higher mountain, and several blocks long, hard and rocky with flowers, daisies, and little pink and purple and white flowers ankle-high, and birds giving it life. At the far end, Darby and elements of his HQ company used field glasses to watch the unfolding scenes.

It was around 0600 hours and, "with the first gray streaks of dawn," writes Altieri, "a bugle call split the air and skirmish lines of black-faced Rangers surged down on the sleepy Italians." It was Darby who blew the call to charge. Crazed screaming at the top of their lungs, blackened Rangers destroyed the enemy. In typical close-quarter battle, the Rangers shot, threw grenades, bayoneted, and knifed the defenders in a ruthless display of superiority and brutality. Blue haze from gunfire drifted above the battle. Shouts from Darby of "Give them some steel," or telling Charlie Company "We need a little bayonet work," added to the frenetic, nightmarish scenes. Ingersoll overheard nearby Rangers: "I bet they don't bring them bastards back alive. I bet they kill them bastards. They don't like not to kill them bastards. You wait and see, they won't bring no prisoners back." And, proving the point, Shunstrom and his platoon from C Company led an insane bayonet charge across the pass against a machine-gun nest hewn into the rocks. Grenades, Tommy guns, and the meat of the glistening bayonets running red, the position was not destroyed but obliterated. Throughout the battle, there were a handful of bayonet charges, usually calmly ordered by Darby. Corporal Robert Bevan, using the old but favorite '03 Springfield rifle with telescopic sight, silenced a MG at 1,350 yards, proving yet again Ranger excellence in marksmanship.

The German 88s opened, firing at Darby's CP, but one was immediately attacked by two assault sections, one platoon basically, and silenced with the use of grenades and bazookas. Father Basil, along for the ride, spoke Italian, and he managed to get a number of them to surrender instead of being slaughtered. By 0830 the left side of the pass was in Ranger hands with 200 prisoners. "Scores of dead of the *Centaura* Division littered the mountainside, most of them grotesquely sprawled in front of their unused weapons." An hour and a half later, they had captured the right side of the pass. Down in the valley, a single 88 fired on them, but the excellent use of the mortars saw an end to the raid. Whatever prisoners were captured came to Father Basil. It turned out the Germans had taken all the Italian vehicles and abandoned their allies, who were veterans of several campaigns in North Africa, some 48 hours earlier.

Battles followed, with the Germans launching a strong armored counterattack, but the armor soon was destroyed by artillery and naval gunfire. During the battle, there were times when Rangers, including Father Basil, were surrounded, isolated by Panzer Grenadiers, but saved in the nick of time by furious attacks by Chuck Shunstrom and his men from Charlie Company, especially around Djebel Berda, a massive mountain. In typical fashion, Shunstrom and his men used grenades and the bayonet to wipe out the enemy. When one American battalion was overrun by the Germans, Rangers came and retook the position on the right flank, eventually screening the withdrawal of parts of the 18th Infantry. It was a bloody affair. One action by Rangers from B Company led to 70 or 80 German dead. By 27 March, the Allied advance resumed and passed through the 1st Ranger Battalion holding the flank.

The Rangers returned to Gafsa. Father Basil was busy, the battalion having suffered four more killed, SGT John Ball, SGT Leonard Sporman, Corporal Marvin Madson, and PFC Nelson Trent, and 18 wounded while serving in a line infantry role. One of the injured was Combat Camera Sergeant Phil Stern, who was severely wounded in his neck and wrist before the battle on Djebel Barda. Years later, he thought he had come as close to death as possible. This proved the end of his official attachment to the Rangers. "We would miss him," writes Arnbal, "as he was always around with a cheery disposition and was very proud to be able to wear the Ranger shoulder patch." The other photographer, T/4 Harry Launer, also with HQ Company, was struck at the same time. Both men accompanied infantry and half-tracks with tanks when they were noticed by German aircraft. Messerschmitt fighters and Stuka dive-bombers made the Americans pay a heavy price.

As the campaign went on, Rangers fought small skirmishes. A German attack was being turned back when Captain Martin from Battalion HQ drove up in his peep, ordering the radio man also from HQ to jump in. The problem was that Martin exposed the observation point the Rangers had been using to communicate with headquarters. A German shell smashed into the area, wounding Corporal Launer, the radio man. A torrent of abuse hit Martin from Platoon Sergeant Musgades and Lieutenant Larkin for exposing their position. Captain Martin drove off in a huff, bouncing the wounded Launer around as he made his way down the slope.

With the end of the campaign in North Africa coming to a rapid conclusion because of Allied successes, Darby told his men on 30 March, in the olive grove near Gafsa, that their fighting was over in Tunisia. The Germans and Italians had suffered an African Stalingrad, losing hundreds of thousands of men and huge losses in equipment. While recuperating at Gafsa, a large Arab caravan of 3,000 camels and hundreds of Arabs, who had crossed the Sahara and the large salt flats, came for their annual trade. It was a spectacular sight. Darby was awarded the Distinguished Service Cross, and many Rangers received long-delayed awards. The offer to Darby for promotion by General Patton, with a new larger command as a full bird colonel, was rejected, much to the joy of most of the men. They would keep "El Darbo" longer to themselves. Father Basil, on the other hand, was ordered to return to the British Commandos on 12 April 1943.

On outpost duty for the early weeks at Gafsa, the Rangers eventually moved by trucks, then rail boxcars, to Nemours, Algeria, to refit and recover, leaving on 6 April and arriving on 22 April. It was a seven-day voyage never to be forgotten, and it wasn't just the cold air and dust flowing into the boxcars, or the bouncing along on the tracks. No, it was the shooting of chickens and goats around the Arab encampments around the railheads. If someone spotted a shot chicken ahead of their car, they jumped out and retrieved it, to the curses and fist-shaking of the Arab owners. Fun was had, but not by the locals. Some of the Midwesterners did not participate, as they understood the value of animals to farmers. Some of the anger stemmed from locals stripping and looting the dead, even, at times, knocking wounded men out. It had been done since the beginning of mankind. Looting of alcohol along the way by the Rangers and hoping for paid sex with women were also common.

During the trip, Charlie Company, which had a reputation for being the toughest outfit, and one of the platoon leaders, Shunstrom, who was a "former boxer and all-round tough hombre," fearless and ready to do Darby's bidding, got into some kind of altercation with the other platoon. Traveling at 30 miles per hour, the sounds of grenades exploded nearby. The C Company Rangers threw hand grenades at each other from boxcar to boxcar. The grenade exchange wounded several men in the second platoon. The train screeched to a halt. Luckily for the wounded, they had a medic in the car and were off-loaded at the next stop. It was probably en route that Shunstrom also threw grenades at local huts near the tracks. The following morning, a formation with complete inspection was conducted.

Finally at Nemours, Algeria, having crossed the Atlas Mountains, the most important thing to Rangers came with a limit. Only one whorehouse was permitted and heavily monitored by a Ranger lieutenant, keeping venereal disease to a minimum. It was here that Rangers who had been wounded or left behind or gone AWOL for a short time slowly returned to their old outfit. Being AWOL during this more relaxed time for a few short days was not considered an issue. For their combat actions at El Guettar, the 1st Ranger Battalion received its Presidential Unit Citation.

It was in Africa that Captain Stephen Meade, A/1 Commander, had to undergo a hernia operation that did not go well and forced him into an extended stay at the hospital. In fact, it went so badly that he was on limited duty, to the annoyance of Darby, and was "poached" by General Ernest "Mike" Dawley, Commander VI Corps, making him his aide. Captain Earl Carran also transferred alongside Meade out of the Rangers. Darby came twice to get him back to become a battalion commander, but the general and medics refused to let Meade leave, as he had not healed. Another account provides greater details:

> While in Africa, Steve suffered from appendicitis and had to be operated on. Never a good patient, Steve suffered several setbacks and spent approximately three months in the hospital recovering. After being released from the hospital, Steve was not fit for active duty and was assigned as chief of staff to General Mike Dawley. Colonel Darby wanted Steve back in his unit. He twice approached General Dawley and advised General Dawley that Steve would be given his own battalion. Steve wanted that position badly. In retrospect, Steve would have been a part of the invasion of Sicily and

may have been killed there. Many Rangers were killed in that invasion. General Dawley advised Colonel Darby that Steve was not fit for active duty. Steve absconded with a jeep. He traveled to Tunisia and had Army surgeons check him over. They advised him, he was not fit for duty. Steve accepted General Dawley's decision.

Great plans had been hatched for the Rangers. They knew all about looting, drinking, and whoring, but what set them apart was their fighting. They truly were the best and toughest combat soldiers of Africa. They would expand, adding two more battalions, the 3rd and 4th Ranger Battalions, in preparation for the next campaign: Sicily. Darby was permitted up to 1,000 new volunteers. From 4 to 20 May 1943, Ranger recruits were assembled or recruited by officers like Captain Shunstrom with his good looks and toughness—his slick salesman performances encouraged soldiers to volunteer for the glorified Rangers. On 7 May, 36 officers and 185 volunteers began training, followed by another 369 soldiers and more to follow. Murray remembered that the Rangers drew more numbers than needed because they expected losses from some of the men who'd enjoy the glory but didn't want to do the hard training required.

One of the new volunteers was Cherokee Thomas Bearpaw, standing tall at 6 foot 2, who was a BAR gunner. During his time fighting the Axis forces, he had been left to guard a group of four German officers sitting in their captured staff car. One of the Germans abruptly reached for something on the floor and Bearpaw emptied his magazine, killing all four. He then discovered that the German officer had been reaching for a cigarette lighter. Bearpaw joined A Company, 3rd Ranger Battalion. Bearpaw was born on 18 September 1923, in Tahlequah, Adair County, Oklahoma, to Stand Watie and Sally Soap Bearpaw. Thomas grew up in eastern Oklahoma, and was born in a log cabin, as was common. His mother died when he was three, and he was raised by his grandmother. His father was a drifter and did not help raise the boy. Tom Bearpaw ran away twice from residential schooling because they would try to beat the Indian out of him. Running away a third time at 16, he joined the CCC (Civilian Conservation Corps), where he spent a lot of time in Colorado and National Parks building stone steps and other construction jobs. Bearpaw enlisted at 17 or 18, wanting to get away from Oklahoma to travel. He'd receive his Ranger training in Tunisia under highly acclaimed Captain Dirks after he volunteered for it on 19 June 1943. Dirks threatened that he'd make them Rangers or kill them in the process. T/5 Bearpaw's friends in the Rangers called him Chief or "that damned crazy Indian." He was always ready for a fight. Thomas Bearpaw served in the military police in postwar Japan and would serve as a Cherokee Nation police officer until 1993.

The old guys, the Originals of the 1st Ranger Battalion, were split up. Even though the unit expanded, it did not include the usual addition of a regimental headquarters: This was rejected out of hand because of the provisional status of the Rangers on 29 April 1943. Another request sent later was also rejected with a note sent atop the rejection letter of 18 October: "Back to where you were, Bill, a red-haired stepchild. Signed Moore." And, as such, LT Col William Orlando Darby retained command of the 1st Battalion, with C and D Companies as his core and cadre. Major Dammer became commander of the 3rd Battalion with A and B Companies, and Major Roy Murray took charge of the 4th Ranger Battalion with Easy and Fox Companies. Veterans were spread throughout, with experienced and capable officers taking charge of the newly founded battalions. "I had two green men for every one old man," recalled Darby. Before the hard training began, the Rangers celebrated their one-year anniversary. The men sang, ate a huge cake the Navy had brought along, with plenty of beer flowing and fights erupting. John Stanton, a former Minnesota Golden Glove Champion, was in the mix with various bets placed on the bouts.

The training was tougher than the Originals had experienced in the U.K.: After all, they were now battle-hardened top soldiers who had performed incredible feats with an amphibious assault on Arzew, a couple of crucial and daring nighttime raids, and fought the highly vaunted Germans and their allies into oblivion. Speed marches, obstacle courses, nighttime operations, and amphibious landings became all-consuming. Rangers suffered casualties during training. Six weeks of brutal training under the African sun forged the men into Rangers.

A new face joined the Rangers: battalion surgeon Captain Emile Shuster, from the 168th Infantry Regiment, an older man but one who was fearless in combat, something he'd prove over and over again, especially in the mountains of Italy. As some of the men had come from other units, it came as no surprise that a few of the Rangers visited their nearby old buddies. Sergeant Carl Lehmann hitchhiked to his old outfit, the 168th, when he was picked up by a jeep with a driver and a corporal. As they drove by an ancient Arab riding an equally ancient mule, the corporal kicked out, knocking the old man off his ride. Lehmann immediately pulled his .45, pulled the offending corporal out of the peep, beat him hard for good measure, then dumped him back into the peep. Lehmann helped the old man up as the driver hit the gas pedal, showering them with gravel. He found another ride. "Carl was a real and true Ranger!" One day, knowing of another impending invasion, one BAR gunner from D Company, while cleaning his weapon, shot himself in the calf. There were no witnesses to the shooting—it was D/3's first casualty and apparently self-inflicted.

Sicily was waiting . . . the first European cities were waiting to be liberated from the Nazi and Fascist scourge. And Rangers planned on being the first to land . . . as always.

PLAY IT COOL
Rome, Italy
APRIL 1944

The train ride to Rome had gone well. He blended in perfectly, except for his muddy Army boots. And his height. William Newnan was one of the smaller Ranger officers; but in this part of the country, he was considered large, tall and thin. He had swapped his Ranger jacket with a friendly farmer and could now look the part of an Italian with minimal means. His pair of glasses was another issue, and he traveled without wearing them. In this country, few people wore glasses, and it was a dead giveaway for a man pretending to be a poor Italian. In short, he knew, a man wearing boots and glasses, and of unusual size, was just someone who stood out.

The train had left at four in the morning to avoid Allied strafing runs. It was a short journey of some 30 miles. In fact, his Communist supporters had told him, no Italian dared to travel the train in daylight to Rome. The couple had purchased the tickets, and they all sat in the compartment. It was also them who told him not to wear his glasses. Not wearing them was a detriment, making him feel unsure of himself: Seeing things was crucial, but he'd just have to depend on his other senses and his compatriots. Blending in was key, and fortunately the very early morning departure meant that most people would be sleeping or still be very tired and therefore not paying too close attention to fellow travelers: At least that is what Newnan hoped for. He had managed to avoid the Gestapo only recently. He was cautious. Once he grabbed a seat, he took a careful look around. He was nervous but had been on the run for a while, so at least this was more comfortable than roughing it.

Things had been going well. They had walked through the streets to the local train station without being challenged; the couple bought their tickets; and the train was on time: Good thing, for Newnan was certain that if the train was caught during daylight, it was going to have the crap shot out of it.

Newnan watched a train conductor approach. Dammit. He tried to play it cool as the man stopped and checked someone's identification papers. Satisfied, he moved on, walking slowly down the middle of the car. Newnan looked at his two companions. She carried his uniform, wrapped in newspaper, under her arm. He tried to squint a little without arousing the suspicion of the conductor, who was looking and walking slowly down the aisle. No, he didn't see anything that'd give away what she carried. Still, he had no idea of what he'd do, should something alert the train employee. The conductor walked by without checking anyone. Newnan almost let out a sigh of relief, but didn't. The Ranger officer carried his own ticket, knowing it was required to exit the station, and he had put it in his pocket for safekeeping. The train slowed down as it rolled into Rome's central station. Nobody checked his ticket or gave him a once-over once they came to a stop. Excellent.

The riders got out, the hustle and bustle subdued, but there—it had been a short, uneventful trip. Newnan got out like everyone else and made it to the exit gates. He tried to keep his cool while he fished around in his pocket looking for the ticket. Nothing. What the hell? He checked again, double-checked, and the line moved forward. Dammit. There was no way he'd make it through the gate without his ticket. They'd ask him questions he couldn't answer. He frantically went through his pockets. The jig would be up, and he'd be caught because of a stupid ticket, because he had been careless.

6

ITALY'S BOOT

OPERATION HUSKY

By July 1943, the German and Italian forces had suffered some 620,000 casualties, with a further 275,000 prisoners in the North African campaign. The hard-fought victory came at a cost to the Allies with 240,000 casualties including 18,500 Americans in Tunisia alone. Just before this, in February 1943 at Stalingrad, Russia, the combined human toll was in the lower millions. But the German and Axis forces were hardly defeated. Enemy strength was estimated at 200,000 troops on Sicily. The Italian Sixth Army, under Alfredo Guzzoni, General Officer Commanding, had six Italian coastal divisions that were woefully equipped and trained and composed of very young or very old soldiers; and four Italian infantry divisions, of which only one had a reasonable TO&E. One Italian division didn't even have a quarter of the strength of an Allied one. Guzzoni did what he could with what he had: He even lacked concrete and heavy equipment to build better defenses. The coastal units averaged one man per 40 meters, one machine gun every kilometer, and one anti-tank gun every three kilometers for the coastal defense of the island. That is not to say that was the actual disposition of the units, but it presents a clear view of the limited resources available for the defense of Sicily. Two German armored divisions, the 15th and the recently reconstituted one, the Hermann Göring Division, were also in the area of operations. But each German division possessed roughly half the strength of one Allied division. Actual enemy strength at Gela was unknown.

The planning for the invasion of Sicily, which in strategic terms was like the island resembling an aircraft carrier, allowing for deeper penetration, reduced the Americans to a supporting role, protecting the British flank, as they had previously done in North Africa. The British Eighth Army under General Bernard Montgomery was to seize the southeastern part of Sicily, roughly three miles west of Pozzalo, and inland to Ragusa and Vizzini, with the intent to strike north and capture the valuable, and closest, port to mainland Italy at Messina. It was a key strategic objective for victory. Messina for Montgomery. For the American Seventh Army under General George Patton, this meant serving as a screen for the British, covering their left flank, the west, along a 70-mile front roughly from the Irminio River closest to the British to just west of Licata with Palermo his primary mission. Palermo for Patton. The U.S. sector of the initial landing phases did not feature large port facilities, forcing them to land on the beaches and to use them, and small ports, for landing men and war matériel.

Sicily is a beautiful, mountainous island that has seen numerous campaigns and wars waged on its territory throughout history. Sicily is ideally suited to control access in the Mediterranean, and as such is a vital center of gravity in terms of commerce and conflict. Phoenician and Greek colonies spread around the outer rim of the island, and it was also contested by Arabs and Normans. There are numerous standing temples and walls still visible throughout. Although for the most part hilly or mountainous, ranging from 1,000 to 3,500 meters in height with the volcano Etna the highest point, it has been heavily cultivated since ancient Rome turned it into an agricultural basket, destroying its forests in the process. Its mafia may have been involved with the Allied invasion. No matter. Gela and Licata were the key targets for the Rangers under Lieutenant Colonel Darby. The Americans, including the Rangers, the "best damned combat soldiers in Africa" according to Patton, were under strict directives. They were not to disturb or enter houses of worship, and women were to be treated with the utmost respect. Soldiers guilty of assault on women, or looting, were to be shot. Clearly there had been issues in North Africa.

For a handful of Rangers, the invasion of Sicily would be their third amphibious assault. Their experiences at the ports of Dieppe and Arzew differed starkly from this one. The Sicily mission had been rehearsed thoroughly in North Africa. The time had come for the new and expanded Rangers to test their mettle. Training at night included the use of compass, pacing, and stars. Terrain features were not used for night movements. Rangers used column formation for easier controlled approach and assault on the objective. The Ranger Battalions were separated for the nighttime amphibious landings in Sicily: They would not land as one unit. The key city of Gela was to be taken by Force X under Darby, consisting of the 1st Ranger Battalion, using red lights for recognition purposes; Major Roy Murray's 4th Ranger Battalions, with amber-colored lights; three companies of the 83rd Chemical Mortar Battalion; the 1st Battalion, 39th Engineers using blue; and the 1st Battalion, 531st Engineer Shore Regiment. This group also included the 1st Infantry Division, minus one regiment held in reserve, and was collectively called Dime Force; it was part of General Omar Bradley's larger Shark Force that also included Wolf Force and Cent Force. The Chemical Mortars became a near-permanent attachment to the Rangers. Its commanding officer was Lieutenant Col. Kenneth A. Cunin, a 1934 West Point graduate and friend of Darby's since they had served together in the 82nd Field Artillery in the States. Darby had the use of 60mm, 81mm, and now the powerful 4.2-inch, 110mm, mortars, trading mobility for firepower—contrary to Commandant Vaughan's suggestions at Achnacarry the previous year.

The Rangers at Gela were to seize the town, its high ground, and eliminate enemy defenses, and then move some 1,500 yards northwest to capture key points of high ground, and eventually the mountain fortress at Butera. Standing by for a worst-case scenario were the guns of the U.S. cruiser *Savannah*. Concerns about landing on time and in the right place were foremost on the minds of the senior Rangers planning their detailed assaults. Darby and Naval Captain

John H. Leppert had developed a training method for guiding and using the landing craft for the amphibious assault and had rehearsed it for nearly one month. Bing Evans was "a little more apprehensive but still we were doing our job, but by that time we had also been watered down a little bit" in terms of quality. Training did not help the Rangers and sailors with seasickness, because of a powerful storm that hit the fleet just before the actual landing. But just as the first shot disrupts all carefully made plans, the landings at Gela would not go well. The long central jetty served as a marker for the responsibilities of the Ranger battalions. Gela was cut in half in planning. To the left of it, west, including a gun battery, at Beach Red, was the area of operation for the 1st Battalion under Darby; the right side, east of the town, was the domain of Murray's 4th Battalion. The engineers in the second wave were to clear the mines and then prepare to hold the center (fighting as infantry), allowing for the heavy mortars in the third wave to set up to support the entire force. Cunin was the executive officer to Darby for this operation. Three distinct phase lines were part of the planning, with the first being the beachfront buildings; the second phase line was the main street just off the beach; and the last line was the northern edge of Gela, just shy of the plain. This system of phase lines allowed Darby and the battalion commanders to communicate effectively and quickly.

The 3rd Ranger Battalion, under Major Herman Dammer, was attached to Joss Force under the father of the Rangers, General Truscott, and his 3rd Infantry Division, along with Combat Command A of the 2nd Armored Division. This group was to land at Licata, near the Salso River, well west of Gela. These were classic Ranger missions in support of follow-on forces.

GELA

Gela, founded by the ancient Greeks or perhaps the ancient Sicilians, the Sicani, was a small fishing town of some 32,000 people near the mouth of the same-named river, which was just to the east. The town was a stone's throw away from the long, sandy beach, with sandbars and changes in gradient. A 980-foot jetty, pier, divided the beach in half. The jetty was 50 feet wide, reducing to 20 the farther it went to the sea. The shore to beach had a slow gradient with occasional dunes or seawalls rising up to 15 feet. The town rose out of the slopes until it reached 150 feet above sea level. Gela ran 3 miles parallel to the sea and was about 4,000 yards deep. Leading from the steel jetty to the town of Gela was a winding road with a ravine rising along its way to the height of the town. There were a couple of smaller winding routes off the beach, but the main one led neatly into the middle of the town, crossing a main road before entering the labyrinthine, narrow streets of the town proper. In the middle, and off to the right of center, stood the main cathedral in a plaza that would see heavy fighting. The buildings in general were two- to three-story affairs of various shades of sand or ochre. Outside the town, to the north, lay the plains featuring few trees but with wheat and grain fields in abundance. Beyond the plain rose the mountains, which provided excellent views of the valleys and of Gela.

One of the challenges was the proximity of the beach to the town, making an unnoticed landing a near impossibility. The sandbank also could force the Rangers to wade ashore from a distance, exposing them to fire from guns and machine guns situated along the road and farther inland. Although both sides of Gela featured gun positions, the one to the west was considered to be critical, as it was fortified and elevated and had a direct line of sight to the beaches and the vessels offshore and was part of the 1st Ranger battalion's mission. Concrete pillboxes at the inland edge of Gela covered not only the beach and street intersections, but also the plain to the north.

Allied planners anticipated the beach and access points to be heavily mined, something the Rangers had not encountered at Dieppe or Arzew. Subsequent photographic intelligence allayed those concerns, although there were gun batteries including mortars and 25 machine gun nests along with concrete pillboxes, some camouflaged with vines and brush, some concealed in huts. The road network included a coast road, Highway 115, and one northeast to the inland, Highway 117.

Numerous smaller roads and tracks dotted the town and surrounding farming areas. The Axis headquarters was at Caltagirone, some 30 kilometers northeast of Gela. The Rangers studied a relief model of Gela onboard the USS *Dickman*. The highly detailed scale model included the height of buildings, width of the beach, distances to various parts of town, and obstacles and enemy positions. Taking into consideration the proximity to town, or with 3rd Ranger at Licata the high grounds, plans were set in motion. The plan at Gela called for Darby's men to land on Beach Red 68, which was shorter than Murray's Green Beach, roughly 50 or 60 yards deep and 500 yards wide, leading toward a fort situated on a 150-foot-high slope with guns. The approach featured barbed wire and pillboxes. In fact, numerous pillboxes dotted the surrounding area in the slopes and past Gela.

Both sides of the 4th Battalion's area, of 500 yards by 100 yards, had defensive positions: On the right was a machine-gun position in a small stone fisherman's hut common throughout the area, with pillboxes running along the edge of town facing the beach and the plain. Murray's men were to land on Green Beach 68, to the right of the jetty, and tackle its defenses. Both battalions had to climb slopes or use winding tracks. In typical amphibious-assault fashion, the Rangers would disembark their transports just five miles shy of the shore. There, they would load into landing craft and proceed to their objectives.

This time, the 1st Battalion was using American Landing Craft Vehicles, Personnel (LCVP), while Murray's men used the British Landing Craft Assault type. Once they hit the LOD (line of departure) at 3,200 yards out, the vessels would form into waves for their final approach. Just before deploying for the operation, the officers assembled at the bow of the USS *Dickman*, where they watched anti-aircraft fire dot the horizon, peppering American paratroopers initiating the attack. The officers returned to the troops, readying them and checking their equipment before final departure. Captain Lyle and other company commanders led prayers for the men. 1st Battalion, leaving the *Dickman* accompanied by the tunes of Glenn

Miller's "American Patrol," would arrive in four waves with C, D, E, and F Companies in the first; then Able and Baker, who'd have to pass through the other companies on their route to their objective, the 77mm gun battery in the western part of the town, with support from the 4.2-inch mortars. The second wave, 30 minutes later, saw the engineers tasked with mine-clearing and disabling any explosive on key installations at the beach, including the jetty; while the third wave, to arrive 60 minutes after the first wave, carried A, B, and C Companies of the 83rd Chemical Mortars under Major William Hutchinson; and lastly, 90 minutes on would see the arrival of the 531st Engineer Shore Battalion.

The 4th Battalion, transported by the HMS *Prince Charles* and HMS *Leopold*, would arrive in just two waves, being the smaller of the two groups. Leading the way were A, B, C, and HQ elements, followed by Dog, Easy, and Fox. Their task was the seizure of the eastern part of town, to link up with 1st Battalion and its attachments to their left and form a defensive perimeter around the town. The three mortar companies supported in the following manner: The engineers in the center had A Company, 83rd Mortars, who also supported the two additional companies on the western side of town; B Company supported Darby's battalion; and Charlie supported Murray's men in the eastern part of Gela. Instructions from Darby were not to pick up any survivors in the sea and to land with bayonets attached. Speed and aggression were the key to success.

Dime Force's two Ranger Battalions, the 1st and 4th, immediately ran into trouble trying to navigate to the beach, despite the plains beyond Gela having caught fire because of air strikes. By sheer luck, Darby bumped into Captain Leppert on one of the boats; Leppert was guiding the third wave of the mortar companies forward. He was ahead of the first two waves at this point. Milling about for a short while in the aftermath of a storm that was still whipping up the waves around the flotilla and getting reorganized, the assault craft, finally in calmer seas, moved forward, landing in order and on time. Enemy gunfire showered the bay and beaches. Darby's memories of the landing were reflective.

We ran into Captain Leppert and he put us on course and we went and we had Gela. I might say that one of the wildest scenes I ever saw was that landing at Gela. We got in all right. The place was alive with searchlights. They had machine gun fire up and down the beach. Another thing I learned there has always made me feel sure that the best place to be in the landing is the first wave. If you have any luck at all, the first wave gets across the beach all right. Then with the second wave, the enemy begins aiming at them. Then the aim calms down by the time the third wave gets in there getting good.

Allied destroyers and cruisers hit the shores with return fire. Suddenly, the beast of a jetty blew into the air with an earth-shattering explosion, illuminating the crazed scene with its brightness and destructive power; all the while the sea was raked by Italian mortars and machine guns. Shells exploded near or in the vessels, a more violent experience than some of the Originals had experienced at Achnacarry. Others, some 500 yards out, fired back at the Italians with machine guns and 2.36-inch rockets attached to the craft. Darby's recollection of the night was vivid:

Going toward shore, we could see blue tracers cutting across the beach. The LCS leading us carried 12 rockets in two banks, about the size of 105-mm shells. It looked as if nobody could possibly live through all the stuff the Italians were shooting out across the edge of the beach, but the rocket boat rode onto the beach behind a wave firing six rockets, three from each bank. I was aboard the rocket boat and thought that it was a tremendous feeling. When the rockets went off, it seemed as if the boat had blown up. The rockets hit an ammunition dump in the town, blowing everything sky high and knocking out the defenses on that side of the beach. An entire block and a half of buildings was leveled. It was a lucky hit.

A destroyer raced by the landing waves, nearly capsizing an LCA, and hammered the shoreline with the destructive power of its five-inch guns. The plains beyond Gela lit the nightmarish landscape with its burning fields and tendrils of gray and black smoke blending into the sky. Mario Turco remembered that evening and the destruction of the long jetty:

> On the evening of the 9th of July, my dad heard some noises, sounds of movement coming from the street. It was the evacuees pouring into the streets. My father got alarmed, so he went out onto the terrace to see and ask what was going on. Entire families were being evacuated from their homes all along the coast, and someone told my father that they were making them flee because they were about to blow up a jetty. Others said that the soldiers had to blow up the marine hospice, once used to be a hospice for children with tuberculosis, and that the Germans later turned it into an ammunition depot. Around midnight the Italian soldiers themselves blew up this depot. Perhaps this is what Darby mistook for a lucky hit. And this was the first rumble that was heard that night.

GELA—EASTERN SECTION—MURRAY'S 4TH RANGER BATTALION

Murray's 4th came ashore on Green 68, by 0255 hours, with A, B, C, and HQs detachment, and six minutes later Dog and Easy. All companies had made it except for Fox Company, who contrary to orders stopped to help men drowning in the waters. Unbeknownst to them, but found out later with a painful toll, the beach was mined. Earlier photographic reconnaissance believed that since the beach had fishing boats on it, it was not mined. In fact, as the Rangers learned, the boats had been abandoned, and mines, anti-personnel and anti-tank, were everywhere.

Dog Company, 4th Ranger Battalion, hit the beach and ran straight into a minefield. Company Commander Second Lieutenant

Walter Wojcik, who had celebrated his birthday two weeks earlier, led his men off the landing craft into knee-deep water and struggled toward the beach. The Rangers carried a lot of weight with spare ammo and supplies, around 50 or 60 pounds, to be left at the beach. Some nearly drowned, while others scrambled forward through the water and onto the soft and sandy beach. Barely halfway to the main road, they stepped right into a minefield. Wojcik, the man who had risen from enlisted to officer and done an excellent job reconnoitering the route to attack Italian positions at El Guettar just a few short months before in Tunisia, was no more. Dead at the age of 21, on the beach of the soft underbelly of Europe. Triggering an anti-personnel mine, a Bouncing Betty, it had flown into the air and exploded, killing him almost immediately. During the unfolding carnage along the beach, it was First Sergeant Randall Harris who looked at his officer turning toward him, and, seeing that the Minnesotan had suffered a terrible wound to his chest (his heart was hanging outside of his shirt), uttered the final words of "I had it, Harry." Within seconds, Harris got hit by shrapnel, feeling as though he'd gotten hit by a baseball bat. The Rangers kept assaulting past the body of Wojcik, stepping on more unseen mines, killing four men, blinding the 1st Platoon leader, and wounding Harris with a terrible, painful cut just below his Mae West life vest, deflating it in the process. Harris ordered the men to stop. Clearly, they were in a minefield; clearly, cooler heads needed to prevail despite all the gun and mortar fire blasting the area. Harris took a moment to find his wound. Intestines were visible through his seven-inch-long abdominal gash. Having the sensation that part of his intestines were slithering out of the wound, trying to make sure they wouldn't spill out, he tightened his ammo belt over the wound, then took charge of his Rangers. Friends of his were getting hit. One friend, Platoon Sergeant Howard Andre, found a clear path, probably more to the right, and they got the rest of the men off the beach, over the dunes, to a dike or road along the edge of the shore some 15 feet high and flat on the top.

Second Platoon made it to their position, but the new platoon leader was in no condition to take charge. Fear had taken command.

First Sergeant Harris sent the unfortunate man back and took command of D/4. Harris and Sergeant Andre discovered several pillboxes along the road overlooking the beaches. Andre said, "Let's get them, Harry," and so the two Rangers started to methodically "clean" them, one after the other, alternating between kicking open the door while the other threw in grenades or dynamite charges, knocking out 12 of them in a row. Having been together in combat for a long while, they completely understood not just the training they had had and the previous combat experiences, but the intuitive understanding men in combat develop. Door, grenade, door, grenade, leapfrogging down the road. At the last pillbox, Corporal Peter Deeb approached while Harris was sitting in front of the slit to the pillbox and asked if this one had been cleaned. The answer was "No, you'd better take a look." Next thing, Harris recalled, a grenade went off and Deeb was saying that there were a whole lot of Italians in it with their hands up. First Sergeant Harris handed over command of the company to Andre and took 20 prisoners to the POW collection point, then sought medical help for his wound. Quickly evacuated by the battalion surgeon, Captain Richard Hardenbrook, Harris was operated on at a hospital ship, under German air-raid attack, having requested not to be anesthetized. First Sergeant Randall Harris remembered lights flickering on and off during surgery. He'd receive the Distinguished Service Cross and a battlefield commission to second lieutenant.

The first wave continued on and established a perimeter by 0330 on the eastern part of town.

1ST PLATOON, F COMPANY, 4TH RANGER BATTALION, GREEN BEACH, GELA, SICILY, 10 JULY 1943, 0300 HOURS

Streaks of blue, green, and orange from Italian guns, highlighted intermittently by the harsh glare of searchlights, painted the night's dark canvas around the assault boats. Just past the city in the plains, burning wheatfields illuminated the far distance with barely visible smoke tendrils atop its red fires.

A huge explosion on the left lifted 1st Platoon's British assault craft like a toy in a tub, slamming it down into the water with an ear-rending noise, buckling its armor plates and tossing the Rangers around. The bracketing fire welcomed the assault waves, showering the men with seawater.

Another explosion saw the end of another assault craft going down into the black, turbulent sea. The stench of cordite and gunpowder draped over the 34 men like a suffocating cloak while they watched the unfolding spectacle.

Fox Company was led by Captain Walter Nye, the tall First Lieutenant William Branson its platoon leader. NCOs included Platoon Sergeant James Altieri, and Sergeants Leonard Greene and Robert Wincompleck of 1st and 2nd Sections, respectively—by now all veterans. Altieri and other Italian Americans returned to their homeland, but in war. Would they kill distant family members? Would they be killed by them? These were common thoughts for Rangers with European roots.

They hit the beaches late, having picked up survivors some 300 yards shy of their objective despite contrary orders from their commander. Darby's words before the assault, ordering his officers not to stop for survivors, had echoed inside Nye's head, but he just couldn't let men drown. This delay inadvertently saved their own lives—just moments earlier, their sister company, Dog Company on the right, had taken serious casualties. In rescuing these men, Harris and Andre removed the threat of a dozen Italian pillboxes dotted along the elevated areas running parallel to the beach.

First Platoon, F Company, 4th Ranger Battalion landed unopposed in two-foot-deep water, luckily free of the dreaded mines that were littered across other beaches and had exacted a toll on the first wave of Rangers. First Platoon covered the roughly 80 yards of the beach in two files comfortably, but wet. The cold water, the fear of the unknown, and the anticipation of impending combat replaced the seasickness that had impacted many of the men.

They climbed up a wide path toward the cliff, where they encountered two neutralized pillboxes from which the smoke of hand

grenades still drifted into the night. They had been lucky so far, landing unopposed. The Rangers scrambled up to take position along a
stone warehouse just past the edge of the cliff. With that, Phase One
was complete. Somewhere to their left, C Company had landed and
advanced. D/4 was off to their right, while E/4 was the follow-on force
arriving soon. Battles were raging all around them, but their sector of
Green Beach was eerily calm.

Here they now waited for 2nd Platoon, somewhere behind them, to
leapfrog through their lines to capture the central square around the
cathedral (Chiesa Madre—Mother Church), which was 300 meters
straight ahead. However, timing was crucial for the follow-on Rangers
of E Company, who were to execute Phase Three: establishing a perimeter at the edge of town before enemy forces could launch anticipated
counterattacks. Crucially, E Company could not crowd on the beaches
or they'd risk exposure to Italian fire while waiting on F Company to
accomplish its mission. There was little doubt that the Italians moved
units to counter the numerous American threats around Gela. But
first things first—the cathedral.

It took five minutes for Captain Nye to order 1st Platoon of Fox
Company forward. Every Ranger had studied the plans of attack
in detail and was cross-trained for just such an event. Platoon
Sergeant Altieri informed his section (squad) sergeants, Greene
and Wincompleck. Within one minute, at 0345 hours, the platoon
advanced deliberately along the two- and three-story sandstone buildings typical of Sicilian towns. Watchful eyes captured every detail.
Ears were attuned to all sounds. Knuckles whitened on fists, gripping
weapons tightly. With wet feet and adrenaline soaring, they took comfort in their training and their Ranger buddy, waiting for hell to be
unleashed, aware that other armed men were ready to kill them.

The hell—for some, the love—of war was everywhere. But only
silence greeted these Rangers as they inexorably advanced toward
the central square. Three long blocks later, the cathedral was but a
stone's throw away.

The 34 men of 1st Platoon, divided into two sections, crept cautiously through the streets. Nineteen-year-old Private First Class

Richard Bennet was followed by Ranger Raymond Noel Dye, weapons at the ready. They were close now: The cathedral was just ahead. Bennet turned the corner of the south side of the square. He was immediately gunned down by an Italian machine gun, shattering their otherwise tranquil night. A volley of rifle fire added to the cacophony. The Italians had initiated an ambush. Combat at last.

There are differing accounts on Bennet's death. Both agree he turned the corner and was killed. Ranger Altieri writes that, immediately, Sergeant Leonard Greene had spotted the flashes of the machine gun's muzzle and expertly lobbed a hand grenade, killing its crew—a difficult feat, given that it was dark out, making accuracy challenging. Another account, by Dye himself, has him and Bennet turn the corner, where they encounter two Italian officers, who shoot the Rangers with their Beretta pistols. Both men were hit, and Bennet fell on top of Dye's legs. Supposedly, Platoon Sergeant Altieri then rounded the corner, killing both Italian officers. Bennet took a few short breaths, still on top of Dye, then died. Ken Conners and another Ranger saw Dye move and pulled him to safety, away from the corner. His injuries were minor, because his musette bag, filled with cast-iron grenades, had absorbed the rounds. His superficial injury was caused by a ricochet. He was taken to the beach, where he was patched up to return to the platoon later.

At the moment of contact, Officers Nye and Branson charged into the square, firing their carbines from the hip. Sergeant Greene's 1st Squad flanked to the right under covering fire from 2nd Squad under Altieri and Sergeant Wincompleck, who aimed at the flashes of Italian orange and green tracers piercing the night. It seemed as though the Italians were firing from every building surrounding the church. Hell had broken loose.

The arrival of Sergeant Gallup's section, with mortars, between the two squads allowed Wincompleck's 2nd Squad to advance on the left. It was a pincer movement toward the square, while Gallup laid down supporting fire from the middle. The Ranger sections broke into smaller two-to-three-man teams by their own volition and cleared buildings with hand grenades, Tommy guns, and rifle fire. In the city center, fighting was now house-to-house.

Despite the confusion and the lack of visibility, the Rangers proved successful in the ongoing street fight, clearing or cleaning buildings with assured confidence, a confidence built from their initial British Commando training and combat, and then by their harder and better training conducted when the new Ranger battalions were formed for the invasion of Sicily.

There were many examples of courage and individual initiative on that night. Two Rangers from Wincompleck's section were on the left, the western side of the Via Giacomo Navarra Bresmes, the main road alongside the cathedral. They climbed a rainspout to the roof of a three-story building across from the square where two Italian snipers caused the advancing Rangers serious trouble. From the edge of the roof, the two Rangers gently lobbed hand grenades inside the building, eliminating the threat. They then swung themselves into the open window, where they blew a hole into the adjoining wall of the next building, knocking out two more Italians there.

PFC Hoffmeister became separated from his Ranger buddy while running into another building firing his BAR from the hip, wounding an Italian. From here, he provided excellent support for Captain Nye and other Rangers, clearing yet another building near the cathedral. While doing so, another man suddenly kneeled next to him, firing his weapon in the same direction. When Hoffmeister addressed him, he discovered the man to be an Italian who, only then realizing his mistake, threw down his gun while screaming in terror. The Ranger chose mercy, knocking him unconscious with the buttstock of his heavy automatic rifle, and returned to action.

Corporal James Hildebrant and Platoon Sergeant Altieri moved toward another building when they heard footsteps from an alleyway feeding into the cathedral's square. The two Rangers slowly lifted their weapons, ready to engage and kill the four enemy soldiers. But instead, Altieri had an inspiration. Holding Hildebrant by his arm to stop him from killing the enemy, Altieri yelled in Italian for them to join him quickly, which they did. The officer clicked his heels to attention before realizing his mistake. "But we're Italians too," he said. The four Italians had been sent to defend the cathedral at all costs. They were lucky.

By 0405 hours, the Italian command became aware of American penetration into the southern parts of the city. Reinforcements were ordered to Gela to shore up the defense. "In the meantime, *Carabinieri* had entrenched themselves in the public gardens, joined by *Guardie di Finanza* (customs and finance guards), Blackshirts, and some armed civilians. After about two hours of fighting, the *Carabinieri*, having run out of ammunition, were surrounded and then overwhelmed, while the young people from Gela who had come to their aid managed to take refuge in the bell tower of the Mother Church, from where they continued to resist by throwing hand grenades." Decades later, an Italian researcher located the teenagers who had indeed been in the tower where they had thrown a couple of hand grenades before immediately fleeing from the church, thereby saving their lives.

Elsewhere Italians continued to put up a stiff resistance to the merciless, professionally trained Rangers. Along the main western road, the Via Giacomo Navarra Bresmes, running alongside the cathedral, "Lieutenant Filippo Lembo, a 33-year-old reserve officer from Catania, was surrounded by the Rangers while he was trying to reach his command along with his men. The Rangers and Lembo's men engaged each other in hand-to-hand combat until most of the Italians were killed, some of them in front of the steps of the nearby cathedral. Lembo, who had retreated to a nearby depot with some survivors, had his throat slit while firing the last rounds of his Beretta."

After a tough hour of urban combat, the Ranger pincer movement succeeded, virtually ending resistance around the blocks of the square with the only holdouts left in the cathedral. Incoming fire from the various levels of the tower and from within the cathedral through the slightly ajar doors peppered around the Americans. "Bitter fighting was already going on in the main street, between the Rangers and the *Carabinieri* [later identified as soldiers of the *Livorno* Division by the Rangers] who had entrenched themselves near the *Chiesa Madre* and the former *Trinacria* Hotel. People of all sorts died in those confused moments caught in crossfire; among them the young mother Carmela Ferrara, 20 years old, with her two children Grazio and Lucia, one and three years old, respectively."

Only the dead had seen the end of war.

A purplish dawn, writes Altieri, arose over Gela, and the Rangers had to clear the cathedral, which was still being stubbornly defended. Sergeant Wincompleck, Corporal McKiernan, Allen Merril, and Lloyd "Big" Pruitt, led by Altieri, met with Captain Nye and Lieutenant Branson just short of the cathedral's doors on the other side of the tower. Here they were safe from the Italian rifle fire. Time had come to finish it.

It speaks volumes that Jim Altieri took the lead, exposing himself to danger, instead of sending someone lower-ranked and less experienced. Flat against the stone wall, he prepped his fragmentation grenade, kicked one door wide open, and tossed in the explosive device, immediately throwing himself back and away from the opening. Before the debris even had time to settle, he rushed into the church and fired off eight quick rounds into a corner. The other Rangers flooded in quickly and bounded over the altar's rails, firing at two Italians in the sacristy. They then battled their way up the winding tower stairs while Altieri remained below. At the end, they captured three die-hard Livorno Division soldiers, dressed in blue uniforms. The other two soldiers lay grotesquely dead by the altar. Wincompleck moved the prisoners out, and Altieri used the quiet moment to cross himself and to kneel at the altar in silent prayer. For a Catholic Italian American, this had been especially difficult, fighting in and around a place of worship, killing potential family members or being killed by one. But he had done his duty and would do so for his men and country until his dying breath if need be.

The sun arrived, banishing the battle-scarred night and purplish dawn away, when Altieri emerged from the *Chiesa Madre* out into the previously embattled square. Clusters of Italian dead littered the square alongside battle debris. Enemy wounded were tended to, and 40 captured prisoners were guarded in a nearby sweet shop. Tired

Rangers leaned or sat where they could, some reflecting on the battle, others perhaps thinking of sleep or loved ones, while some undoubtedly had enjoyed the fight, the adrenaline rush of cheating death and killing. Sergeant Greene and his Rangers arrived at the square, having cleared nearby rooftops, with 11 additional prisoners. Phase Two was complete, and time had come for the Rangers to execute the next phase: a defensive perimeter on the edge of town toward the fired plains of Gela.

"Parts of the city were burning, with clouds of billowing smoke poured into the sky." But Altieri didn't notice any of those signs of death and destruction. No, as the Rangers prepared to move to the outskirts of Gela, Altieri could only focus on the anguished, anxious civilians who hesitantly approached the square filled with American soldiers and Italian dead. He wrote, "Two old ladies, sobbing loudly, approached two bodies lying on the cathedral steps. They knelt, crossed themselves, and began crying out their saddened hearts to God." He barely understood the Sicilian dialect, and he wished he did not. "Please, God, bring an end to this terrible slaughter of your children. *Dio Mio . . . Beca . . . Beca?* [Why, why?]" Altieri reflected on the tragedy unfolding in front of the *Chiesa Madre*. "How can anyone understand or care which side is right or wrong, when one must witness the slaughter of human beings in and around a place of Christian worship, a citadel of faith and spirit and peace and good will to all men on Earth?"

He turned away from the tragic scene to encounter one even worse. "A handsome young Italian sergeant lay in a puddle of blood just to the right of the Cathedral entrance. Bending over him weeping was a swarthy, smooth-complexioned, young Sicilian woman, with straight long hair; she wore a plain black dress and long black stockings. Her head buried in his chest, and she was sobbing: *Giovanni . . . Sienti . . . Alsata . . . Veni . . . Giovanni, beca le non sienti?*" She was asking him to listen to her and get up, not to lie there like that. I couldn't take any more of this. It is bad enough for a soldier to be compelled to kill; but to witness the bereavement of the enemy's women is an anguish too torturous to endure."

Phase Two was completed by eight in the morning. The sun had washed away the frightening night, along with the horror of battle, but Fox Company's 19-year-old Private First Class Richard J. Bennet never saw the sun rise that day, nor would he ever again. The so-called soft underbelly of Europe proved anything but. The worst was yet to come.

GELA—WESTERN SECTOR—DARBY'S
1ST RANGER BATTALION

For the 1st Ranger Battalion to the west of the pier, things also did not go according to plan, although landings occurred around 0300 hours. One landing craft capsized after hitting the sand bar although there is an account that an artillery round severed the cable and lowered the ramps, filling the vessel with water, leaving 16 men and Lieutenant Joseph Zaloga, Easy Company, to die in a miserable way, by drowning. "Only the coxswain survived, being pulled into another craft." Men had jumped off, thinking they were close to the beach. Those were E/1's first casualties. Other LCAs got hit on their approach around 700 yards shy of the beach as the Italians opened up with just about everything but the kitchen sink, coastal artillery pieces, cannons, mortars, machine guns firing blue tracers, and small-arms fire as the dark night had been lit by their searchlights—some were shot out with return fire by naval elements. An LCA of the 39th Engineers also took a hit, but the men survived. Other boats stopped to help the men struggling in the waters. Because of this delay, A and B of 1st Battalion, who were originally part of the second wave, landed before the other companies, and had been assigned to pass through those companies on their way to silence the gun battery to the west of Gela. The other companies landed under heavy fire, requiring individual work to silence machine-gun nests and pillboxes just like the 4th Battalion had encountered. Sergeant John Van Skoy single-handedly eliminated a pillbox, capturing about a dozen Italians. Another Ranger sergeant, Steve Yambor, attacked a position on the left with a hand grenade, having crawled to within a foot of the pillbox, then prepped two grenades; one after the other, he dropped them through the firing slit.

These actions enabled F/1 to advance, hot on the heels of the Italians withdrawing through Gela, fighting house to house. "The Americans," recalled Angela Bruccoleri decades later, "when they landed, did not enter our house through the main door but through the roof of the building where we lived. In fact, they came down to our dining room but the whole family had already been woken up by the noise of the planes, and Dad told us all to gather around the table. At one point, we heard a dull sound of footsteps—from their boots—on the roof and then on the wooden staircase leading to our terrace. We little girls were so scared, we were terrified! Through this staircase they managed to enter our house; all of a sudden, they kicked through the door and entered the house. They were armed to the teeth! They came from the building next door, the one where uncle lived; they had first entered his house, and then through the rooftops they came to ours."

A AND B COMPANIES, 1ST RANGER BATTALION—GUN BATTERY, WESTERN PART OF GELA

A/1 and B/1, under Captain James Lyle, made notorious by a request from General Allen for a hairy-chested commander right after the landings at Arzew to tackle Vichy French opposition elsewhere, were tasked with eliminating the gun battery, no matter the casualties as Darby had said.

> You have observed the fireworks are short, and you can see we're not going to have an easy time tonight. You were selected for the gun-battery mission because you are one of the old-timers of the outfit and I have confidence you will find some method of destroying that gun position. As you will know, we have a great number of officers who have not had any combat experience. I expect you, and the enlisted men who we can class as old-timers, to guide the green officers and enlisted men alone. It has been reported that the gun battery will be a hard nut to crack. If you recall, I have made the same remark a number of times during the

planning of the invasion. During the landing and capture of the gun battery, you will probably lose a great number of personnel. You must expect this. The Rangers, as you know, have never lost very many officers or men during any one operation. Tonight you must expect to lose from one to 75% of both companies. But don't forget, that gun battery must be destroyed! If casualties are high, it will not be a reflection on your leadership abilities; and if you find need of assistance, contact me promptly, and I will try to fulfill your request. May God be with you, young feller!

If Sergeant Szima had been present, he would have recalled Lord Mountbatten's dispiriting yet prophetic words of anticipated casualties of 60 percent achieved at the raid on Dieppe, and he probably would not have been impressed with Darby echoing similar sentiments.

As it turned out, much like other companies, A and B under Captain Lyle had their own adventure. At 1,500 yards, two searchlights hit the approaching waves, and Lyle could not find anyone from the first wave ahead of his. Naval gunfire showered the beach area. At 700 yards, a naval support craft used its rockets to knock out searchlights for a while. Five hundred yards, machine guns from defensive positions opened up and were attacked with 2.36-inch rockets from the landing craft. The Rangers spotted a red guide light (submarine), and the coxswain adjusted to the left. Hitting sandbars, with half of them seasick, some 75 yards short of the beach, these Rangers un-assed their landing craft, as some sank knee-deep or up to their necks in the water, and struggled toward their objective, maintaining radio silence until they were on the beach, only communicating once they had hit their phase lines. Captain Lyle, in charge of A and B Companies, wrote that, firing from the get-go, they moved to the beach, while the Navy shot out a glaring searchlight on the left that had illuminated the men, like the sun had suddenly appeared, exposing them to deadly fire.

There was no first Ranger wave, later discovering that they had lost two landing craft. Unperturbed, they charged forward, up a drainage ditch in between several machine-gun emplacements, with such speed that they overran the two nearby machine-gun positions before the Italians could adjust their automatic and mortar fire. Perhaps it was on the far end of town when Italian defender Cesare Pellegrini gave up his life:

> Corporal Cesare Pellegrini, 34 years old, a Tuscan from Seravezza (Lucca), manned a machine gun in a pillbox near Porta Marina. He put up a stubborn resistance, hampering the landing on the beach for over four hours with the fire of his machine gun; the landing operations in the area that he kept under his fire had to be temporarily suspended. More American troops, however, had already entered other areas of Gela, and were already approaching Porta Marina; Pellegrini's companions felt surrounded and fled, and he remained alone. An American patrol, led by a non-commissioned officer, identified the source of the fire, worked around it, and then the NCO penetrated the pillbox and stabbed Pellegrini in the back. Cesare Pellegrini was left clinging to his weapon, stiffened in death. In a corner of the pillbox, there was his open briefcase, letters scattered all over the place, and his dogtag on the ground near the machine gun. He was posthumously decorated with the Bronze Medal of Valor.

Getting onto the main road, the second phase line, with single-file columns on either side to move west, they encountered numerous Italian soldiers running in and out of houses, being shot down by the take-no-prisoner, shoot and kill everything order of the fightin' and killin' Rangers—they had to get to the guns, no matter what. Bodies littered the street, and it was clear the enemy had been alerted. A pillbox roadblock at the road junction of Butera, the northern road, and Licata, the southern road closer to the beach, was in the process of getting its crew inside and about to lock its door when one veteran Ranger sergeant prevented its closure, kicking the door open,

spraying the interior with lead from his Tommy gun, followed immediately by a grenade, the reverse of what Harris and Andre had done
on the other side of town. The position's two heavy machine guns and
47mm anti-tank gun were destroyed as the Rangers continued moving
forward in columns alongside the main road.

Within a few short moments, although it probably felt like a long
time, the gun battery became visible to the south, closer to the beach.
A and B formed a line facing the rear of the battery, which faced
the beaches and was completely surrounded by barbed-wire entanglements. Unable to communicate to call for fire from the 4.2-inch
mortars assigned to them, because the radio was lost during landing, Captain Lyle, in good Ranger manner, used what he had—his
own four 60mm mortars set up near the recently captured road
junction, which peppered the battery. As the mortars were firing
and Bangalore torpedoes were placed around barbed-wire obstacles,
scouts returned having discovered a nearby ditch leading to the rear
of the well-defended battery. This was preferable to attacking over
the open ground that they otherwise would have had to cross. Proper
infantry tactics were used, with Lyle ordering the bulk of his force to
lay down heavy suppressing fire onto the battery as another section
with Bangalore torpedoes moved to the rear of the defensive position,
to the right of A and B Companies when viewed from their position
looking south to the beach. Once they had arrived, the Rangers would
fire a flare, signaling the main group to shift its fire away from them.
As this was going down, the USS *Savannah* opened fire in that area.
Captain Lyle and his men believed it to be short rounds from the gun
battery, but they soon discovered it to be friendly fire. Finally able
to communicate with Darby, Lyle informed him of the impending
catastrophe. The guns ceased firing shortly thereafter.

Lieutenant Donald Anderson, whose platoon had been interrupted by the friendly fire, led his men forward. The lead section
crawled out of the ditch and took one killed in action. The enemy
machine gun was silenced by two grenades, with the section advancing. An enemy mortar crew was discovered and also destroyed with
hand grenades just past the MG position, west of the battery. Moving

along the wire, the section discovered a gate, moved through it, and settled on top of sandbags. The Rangers fired the first flare, with each man throwing two grenades at the Italian positions, then charged over the sandbags, using small arms and bayonets to kill what was left of the crews. The second flare was launched, followed by the near-simultaneous explosion destroying the entanglements. The main force immediately assaulted the three 77mm-gun battery, capturing it by 0630 hours, moving through the fortified positions, cleaning house in Ranger fashion. The sights and elevating mechanisms had been removed by the Italians, or perhaps were missing. Lyle's A and B Companies then set up a defensive perimeter on the western part of town, establishing contact and tying in with the rest of the companies of the 1st Ranger Battalion to its right.

By 0830, 10 July, the Rangers had accomplished their missions and their heavy mortars of the 83rd were set up and used when needed, despite the casualties the mortar detachment had taken while landing. The hasty defense perimeter was established as intended, with A and B Companies on the far left, with three 77mm guns, the 4.2-inch mortars moved forward to them, followed by a gap to the right with the rest of the 1st Ranger Battalion. Hopefully the captured Italian guns and 83rd Mortars could contain any assaults through the gap. Both Ranger battalions covered the edges of the town, with the engineer attachments in a secondary position behind the main perimeter, locking down the center. During this time, battle correspondent Don Whitehead had made his way up to Darby's HQ:

> The civilians had swarmed out of their hiding places when the first wave of fighting ended. They cheered and wept and surged through the smashed streets in a frenzy of welcome. The American boys were bewildered. They did not understand at first these people were tired of fascism, tired of war, tired of giving their food and money and sons to the Italian army for a war for which they had little stomach. The Rangers knew how to slit a man's throat in the darkness, how to break a man's neck with a quick shove

of the knee, how to wipe out a machine-gun nest—but this joy-filled mob was too much for them. They did not know how to cope with the laughter and happiness of an enemy. . . . Then the Italians attacked. Eight light tanks broke into the town and ran through the streets spraying machine-gun bullets.

COUNTERATTACKS

The Rangers at Gela experienced three somewhat confusing counter-attacks. The first attack hit them within a few short hours of landing; the others happened the next day, with one traveling down the north–northwest road from Butera to Gela composed of the first battalions of the 33rd and 34th Livorno Division, the second attack with the 3rd Battalion, 34th, attacking along Highway 117 at the center of Gela, including a larger one from the area around the Ponte Olivo Airfield with a number of tanks including German Mark IVs.

The first and immediate threat to the Rangers came at 0900, 10 July, when Lyle reported the approach from the northeast of some 9 to 12, perhaps even as many as 16 light 11-ton hand-me-downs from the French the Germans had captured years earlier, tanks armed with 37mm cannons. The Italian tanks were accompanied by infantry moving south down Highway 117 from Niscemi and was the right arm of Mobile Group E. Five thousand yards out of the town, four tanks stopped in a small group of trees while the remainder trucked toward Gela. The tanks in the trees were out of range for Able Company, 83rd Chemical Mortars, but Lyle ordered the platoon commander to fire anyhow with the round landing short. Pushing the technical and mechanical abilities of the mortar to near the splitting point of the tube, the first round went over the target. With some tweaks, the rounds hit the area, setting one tank on smoke, forcing the other three to retreat. It was here, and a bit later, that Lyle's captured guns did their work. The enemy light-tank force of three reappeared at the same location. Fortunately, the Rangers under Lyle had diverse military backgrounds, so they were able to get three 77mm guns near the gun battery they had captured, although without optics but with plenty of ammo, and owing to the Rangers' diverse military background, they got them ready, alleviating the pressure on the 83rd who were running low on ammunition. Captain Lyle had established an OP on a two-story building overlooking the approaches into town. When the previous tank column returned, the 77mm guns were used when Lyle called for them. The first round hit his OP, angering the officer a bit, ordering his artillery crew to adjust to greater range. Five rounds later, they found their range. A large number of the artillery shells turned out to be useless, but enough rounds were sent downrange to force the tanks to retreat.

Meanwhile, the five other tanks had advanced into town, where they were pummeled by dedicated men bent on destroying them, on holding on to the turf they had bled and died for, including Darby and Shunstrom using a 37mm anti-tank gun and thermite hand grenade in close-quarter battle. The 4th Battalion bore the brunt of that attack. "The most frightening thing, and I'll never forget, is that wave of tanks coming across," said James Altieri 50 years later in an interview. Jack Belden was with Darby and recounted the action in great detail:

> "Well, it was sort of rough for a while," he admitted. "About 9 o'clock. I thought we had resistance stamped out so I sent the town crier through the streets to shout news and tell the people that we were Americans that had come to help them. That brought the people out," he paused and wiped his hand over his face, "and about then eight Eyetie tanks—there were real Fascists in those babies—came down from the hills and started zoomin' through the streets. They raised hell," he laughed as if remembering something. "We didn't have a damn thing ashore. I told everyone to get inside the buildings. But hell I didn't have to tell them. You should have seen them run. They climbed up on roofs and hung out the windows, throwing down hand grenades, and firing machine guns at the tanks. They might as well have thrown cream puffs at them

for all the effect it had. I saw one tank coming down the street and I chased around the block in my jeep, swung around the corner, ran up on a sidewalk and started shooting at him with my .30 caliber machine gun. I must've fired 300 rounds at him. It wasn't doing any good and the tank still kept coming on. I ran like hell then." He laughed again. "And I drove right down to the pier and found an antitank gun there and loaded it up on my jeep. I picked up Captain Charlie Shunstrom and we went after the tank. Every time we slammed a shell in that dismounted gun, she recoiled Shunstrom and knocked him ass over teakettle into the back seat. But we hit the tank and knocked it out. After that, we got another tank cornered right in the middle of the street. We must've put it out of commission because it wouldn't move. But nobody would come out of it either. Everyone was firing rifles, machine guns, and hand grenades at it, but that damn tank just sat there and no one came out. I said: Here let me fix 'em and I fired an assault grenade at the tank, but that didn't budge 'em either. They were tough guys all right! Seeing they wanted to play rough, I thought I'd play rough too. So I took an incendiary grenade and walked up and slapped it on top of the tank. It began dripping down inside and we saw a little smoke coming out of the tank; then the turret opened and they all poured out screaming like they were mad. After that we got another tank, and the rest ran away. It's been pretty quiet since then." A sergeant, who entered during Darby's speech, had waited in silence for his superior officer to finish speaking. But now he interrupted him in some impatience. "Tanks are reported coming up the highway north of us," he said in the tone of affected nonchalance. [The new attack occurred on 11 July, when this interview took place.]

The Italian perspective on this death ride into the gauntlet that was Gela details the death of one tank commander, Angelo Navari, who made it into the main square near the Ranger headquarters across from the cathedral on 10 July.

> During the American landing in Gela, the coastal defense tried to repel the invader. From Niscemi the Mobile Group E of Captain Giuseppe Granieri moved, comprising 12 "Renault" R/35 tanks led by Lieutenant Angelo Navari. The Italian tanks initially prevailed against the American defenses that were forced to ask for the intervention of the naval artillery, which unleashed a heavy bombardment with over 500 large-caliber rounds. For infantry, riflemen, and tank crews it was a massacre, but from that hell of fire Angelo Navari's tank managed to advance, overwhelming the first American outposts. At a certain point the tank stops, the driver, in an attempt to restart, is killed, but Lieutenant Navari continues to advance, enters the city, arrives alone in the main square of Gela despite the cross-fire. That tank seems invulnerable and continues to make room in front of him, shooting with the machine gun, now it is there, a stone's throw from the enemy headquarters, surrounded by the Americans. His tank is hit by several bazooka shots, it stops (it is not clear whether because of the shots or a mechanical failure), Angelo Navari comes out of the turret with the gun in his hand, but is immediately shot dead. An unreal silence falls in the square, among the Americans who surround him in silence a few words of admiration for that officer.

Time went by and there was a lull in fighting until, around 1400 hours, the Luftwaffe attacked the ships in Gela Bay, having already sunk the destroyer USS *Maddox*, killing over 200 sailors, and, despite anti-aircraft fire, managed to sink two transport ships, then proceeded to also attack the town. That night, apart from sporadic sniper fire by civilians as well as soldiers, the Rangers patrolled the town continuously.

On 11 July, a twin attack was launched with two battalions on the left side: the 3rd Battalion, 34th Livorno straight down Highway 117 and its western plain; and the other featured a large number of tanks, around 20, including the highly vaunted Mark VI tank that approached from the western side with a counterattack launched against the Americans on the right side of Gela and the town itself. But this German-led drive was delayed by fighting American paratroopers in the northeast and also by the terraced landscape dotted with olive trees that made movement difficult for the German tanks. Patton came into town, barely avoiding a handful of German tanks, and found Darby at his headquarters in the main square of Gela that had seen heavy fighting. The counterattack launched against the 1st Infantry Division included parts of the 15th Panzer and of the Hermann Göring Divisions. "They penetrated the positions of the 26th Infantry and the Rangers who were north of Gela and almost reached the beach. As a matter of fact, our defending troops were on the outskirts of Gela. General Patton was ashore at the time, and I am convinced that his presence had much to do with restoring the situation." At least that was the opinion of Major General J. P. Lucas, deputy to General Dwight Eisenhower, Supreme Allied Commander.

What had happened was that a twin attack started with Italians and Germans coordinating a simultaneous pincer movement. Twenty-five hundred yards north of Lyle's location, hundreds of Italians of the 3rd Battalion, 33rd Infantry Regiment, Livorno Division formed to launch a counterattack from a farmhouse to the left, west of the highway into Gela. They had left the Butera area around 0437 hours, reaching the northern slopes of Poggio Lungo by 0800 and taken under fire shortly thereafter. Yet again, Lyle turned their own artillery on them, and, after five rounds, effective fire rained down, dispersing the Italian force. About 200 soldiers rushed out of the farmhouse, scattering everywhere, into ditches and defiles, out of sight.

Also on that day, another column emerged between the two high points from the Butera area along the road toward Gela. This seemed also part of a coordinated attack with the Germans to the east. Captain Lyle estimated it to be regimental in size—a very large force, pitted against his 120 Rangers holding the western section of the town. It was the infantry of the Livorno Division. The attack came from the 1st Battalions of the 33rd and 34th Infantry Regiments of the Livorno Division, supported by tanks, and was directed at Lyle's western perimeter. Darby was unable to support, as the other companies of the Ranger battalions and attachments were neck-deep in fighting off attacks, including tanks from the 3rd Battalion, 34th Infantry Division, coming down on the right, the eastern part, of Gela. The 3rd Battalion, 34th Infantry Regiment was led by Lieutenant Colonel D. U. Leonardi, who was attached to the Livorno Infantry Division, which had deployed in Sicily in November 1942. The division was at nearly full strength; the artillery, engineers, and four out of six infantry battalions were fully motorized, unlike the other divisions throughout, many of whom had antiquated equipment and some did not even have shoes. The coastal units who had been driven back were composed of very young or very old men with terrible organization and support. This attack was made by the best Italian division in Sicily, as it had been picked out and trained for the intended but abandoned Malta invasion. At this time, the 3rd Battalion's strength was 34 officers, 1,100 NCOs, and enlisted men, with four 47/32 mm guns, six 81mm mortars, 12 machine guns, and a flamethrower squad. The Italian perspective on the battles was heartbreaking: They paid the ultimate price.

> I approached the 10th company, which had endured the hardest test. In all, there were just over thirty men. . . . We looked at each other for a long time, silent. No one dared speak. Our eyes, however, were teary with emotion at the memory of so many fallen comrades. Finally, I found the strength to speak. I don't remember what I said. I only remember that the soldiers did not let me finish: in a moment, they surrounded me in a spontaneous show of affection and understanding.

The corporal major, Spini Ermenegildo, a proud man of Milan, clasping me around my neck, said: "I was alone here; all the other members of my squad were dead or wounded. All the same, I continued fighting, dragging behind me a submachine gun and box of ammunition. I arrived here alone, always firing to avenge my companions. Here is the smoldering submachine gun and the empty ammunition box!"

"Bravo!" I replied. "You are a brave man and you will be rewarded for gallantry."

He said "It is not a medal I seek; if anything, I prefer promotion to sergeant because it would give me more chance to help my wife and my daughter."

I stared at him, almost lost. Those words reminded me that just a few months earlier, I myself had judged Corporal Spini "not suited to be sergeant in that he lacks military culture!" Now, I felt guilt and answered: "You will be promoted to sergeant for your war exploits," but I didn't hear anything more about major corporal Spini. The battle, unfortunately, was not yet over—and in the evening it would suddenly come to life and last the whole night. In the morning, the III Battaglione of the 34 Reggimento Fanteria Livorno of the 34th would no longer exist.

That force (III/34 of the Livorno) had approached in unusually tight formation, exposed to every weapons system of the Americans. To the GIs it had seemed as though they had a death wish. In the meantime, the 39th Engineers and Quartermaster units formed a small, interior perimeter behind the Rangers, just in case the attacking Italians were lucky or courageous enough to punch through the main line of resistance. Ultimately, the Livorno Division lost 2,000 men in a few short hours. This was shock and awe during the early days at Gela.

Lieutenant Colonel Darby took General Patton to Captain Lyle's OP, where Lyle was knee-deep in directing 77mm and 4.2-inch

mortars against the enemy counterattack, the 1st and 3rd of the
Livorno, now some 800 yards away, with a battalion deployed in a
skirmish line and the rest following in closed formation. The Italians
were unimpressed by the incoming mortar and artillery fire from the
captured 77mm guns, counter-firing at the Ranger position. Here,
another typical Patton-versus-Rangers moment occurred. Lyle had
loosened his chinstrap because of incoming rounds, when someone
behind him noted it. Without turning around, Lyle responded with
"Hell, yes, we always unbuckle the chinstrap when receiving incoming artillery or mortar fire." Hearing a loud clearing of the throat,
the captain turned around to see the glorious personage that was
Patton. He immediately briefed the general while buckling the straps.
Satisfied with the short brief, Patton left and said, "Kill every one of
the goddamn bastards." This was accomplished, around noon, with
the arrival of a naval fire control officer saying, "Having trouble, soldier?" who then got the naval guns working the area to Lyle's front,
as the mortars had run out of ammunition. The salvoes provided
enough shock and awe, enveloping the entire force in black smoke
and dust, throwing a number of body parts into the trees and littering
the grounds with torn bodies, for Captain Lyle to lead his Rangers of
Able and Baker in a countercharge, and, without firing a shot, 400
prisoners were taken.

The gap between them and the rest of the 1st Ranger Battalion was
filled by the 1st Battalion, 41st Armored Infantry Regiment. As the
unit prepared to move out under orders from Darby with Lyle present
at Force Headquarters, Patton made another memorable impression.
He told Darby, "Colonel, your outfit will make another attack in the
very near future. After the attack, I want to see Blood and Guts hanging from every man's bayonet. Do you understand?"

Italian and German counterattacks, one from the northwest, the
other from the northeast, were beaten off with a combination of small
arms, mortars, and naval gunfire evaporating the attacks starting at
0700 and again at 1500 hours. Through a combination of mortars firing smoke to add to the confusion, the destruction of the German-led
force ultimately came from supporting naval gunfire. With the

streaming in of American troops, reinforcing and taking new objectives, the battle for Gela ended fairly abruptly. Much like Darby had been the mayor of Arzew, here at Gela he, too, was tasked with administrating the town. When battle journalist Jack Belden made his way to Darby's HQ in the main square, he observed Darby listening to complaints of the Sicilians. Later that day, warning orders were issued to prepare for movement for another attack and to make the captured 77mm guns mobile. Mules and horses were requisitioned and late on 11 July, the 1st Ranger Battalion with its now-mobile heavy artillery moved out for another attack. Darby was happy with his newfound artillery.

MARCH UPCOUNTRY TO BUTERA

The town and plains were under American control, but the rising slopes and hills north of the plain were still under Axis control, with some fortified positions providing excellent vantage points of the Allies in the bay and movements across and around the landing area. Needing to seize the high grounds of San de Cola, Mount Della Lapa, and Del Zai, elements of the Ranger battalions advanced toward San Nicola fortress about several miles northwest along the Gela–Butera Road and left of the twin peaks. During the attack on San de Cola, Darby learned a lot, considering that he had been artillery officer and seen the Navy's gun batteries' impact in repelling tank attacks at Gela. But here on their way north to ultimately seize Butera, he became an even greater convert to firepower, especially of the Navy's.

> I had no artillery other than the artillery we had captured in these forts, and my boys I found weren't too good artillerymen when we got to shooting. We got to San de Cola. I made a night attack and got one battalion on its objective during dark. But my left flank battalion got caught in the plain and down we went. We almost got wiped out for keeps. We were in a very desperate situation with ½ of my force committed on the high ground and the other half

down in the plain. We just couldn't move. They had a tremendous amount of small-arms fire and they had very well dug and well-built positions—concrete emplacements, pillboxes and all. I had this little lieutenant of artillery with me, who had all the naval gunfire of the *Savannah* at his control, and decided to put him to use. I had one of my men in position on top of the hill up here and who could see the gun boundaries that were firing on us, some five 149 and 150 howitzer batteries that were blazing away. So with my forward observers, so to speak, giving me directions, we started working on the *Savannah*, who was cruising at that time back and forth south of Gela, of course. I never realized naval gunfire could be so accurate. We started firing with the *Savannah* before we finished, we had knocked out—or, rather, the *Savannah* knocked out, with my boy who was a simple infantryman company commander sitting on top of the hill, spotting these shots—and forced five batteries to stop shooting.

They needed to take the mountain fortress of Butera, which was 15 miles northwest of Gela, along the same road, and leading to the city of Enna, the hub of eastern Sicily's road network and location of the Italian command. To that end, Darby had to capture the high ground along the route. He sent three Ranger companies to the right side of the peaks. These companies were Dog, E/1, and F/1, with Captain Ralph Colby of D/1 in overall command. The fortress itself was to be seized by 1st Battalion of the 41st Armored Infantry attached to Darby's force. Along for the ride were engineers and parts of the 83rd Chemical mortars.

Around midnight, the Ranger commanders met at a rendezvous point with their companies and reviewed plans of action, finalizing their movement and attacks at 2330 hours with the attack launched at 0430 on 12 July. Keeping 100 yards in between the companies, they advanced at night for four miles, encountering the horrible carnage that had been wrought on the brave Italian soldiers who just a day or two ago had marched toward their doom in the failed attack on Gela and straight into the maelstrom of gunfire. The stench of decaying bodies was overwhelming; and intermixed with it was the ever-present smell of gunpowder, still fresh but not fresh enough to disguise the smells of decomposing flesh. Onward they staggered, and after a few short stops they reached their assembly point near the objective by 0430, 12 July. No rest for the wicked. F/1, thinking all was well on their way to their objective, encountered haystacks—some of which came alive with machine-gun fire; but F/1, putting their 60mm mortars into action, soon forced the Italians to surrender, while the other two companies reached their targets unmolested.

The regular armored infantry battalion, however, struggled with its assignment. Unaccustomed to night operations, it took them a bit longer, leaving them exposed in the daylight as machine guns, heavy mortars, and howitzers hit their area. Colby of D/1 observed the trouble from his excellent vantage point. He called Darby's HQ, which then relayed his request, and naval gunfire from the *Savannah* demolished the howitzer batteries in short time. Reinforced by the 1st Battalion, 39th Engineers, the 41st Infantry's 1st battalion attacked the hill fortification again and seized it by 1400 hours.

That same day, Lieutenant Colonel Darby was presented the Distinguished Service Cross and was yet again offered a new command, this time the 180th Infantry Regiment of the 45th Infantry Division, which was operating to the east of Gela. Again, the Ranger commander declined. Orders were issued to take Butera.

Butera, a Disney-like hill town, rests atop a mountain roughly 400 meters (or 1,300 feet) high and has strong walls and sheer rocky cliffs on three sides. A single winding access road led to the fortress and by itself also provided challenging terrain. The road was covered by intersecting machine guns and mines. The small town, perhaps 12 short blocks, was surrounded by stone walls approximately 12 feet high and several feet thick. The population was in the hundreds. The buildings were made of brick and stone and grew upward rather than outward because of the limited plateau available for building. Butera had a church with a garden. The height and strength of the fortress provided the Axis with excellent views of the plains toward the shores and as such provided superb observation for calling in artillery on advancing troops. To that end, the Rangers had to seize this important town—it was a challenging affair simply because of the terrain. The only intelligence available for planning was aerial photographs indicating the presence of roughly a rectangular town with three main streets running north to south labeled 1st, 2nd, and 3rd Streets while the lanes running east to west were called A, B, C, and D Avenues. The roads to this day are narrow, allowing usually single-car access only. Combat reporter Belden accompanied the Rangers for this operation and was with Darby when he conducted a leader's recon of the impending attack. "Lying on straw like a mountain Robin Hood, with a bottle of captured Italian wine in one hand and a map in the other, and surrounded by his informal crew of captains, lieutenants, sergeants, and privates, Darby told us the mission for the night. It was to attack the town of Butera, sitting like a sentinel on a rocky prominence overlooking the pass on the Gela-Enna highway. 'This is going to be a tough one, gang,' he said, and, with his finger and a flashlight dimmed with a red glass, he showed us the steep climb we had to make between two hills held by the enemy on either side of Butera. 'I don't know what is in Butera, and we may be sticking our necks in a trap,' he added, 'but that is the job we have to do.'" These words and thoughts would come to haunt Darby and his Rangers within a few short months in mainland Italy.

The main issue, apart from the terrain, was the single road littered with mines, laid by the Germans, and most likely not in the center of the road as it was harder to disguise them there. Mine clearing was conducted by Captain Frederick "Sammy" Saam, with a single-bar mustache highlighting his stature at 5 foot 3; and even though Darby did not want to risk his officer, Saam, a jack of all trades, who eventually became a dentist in California, took off and personally removed over a dozen mines, using his bayonet to uncover them. He was an expert in demolition and responsible for the massive explosion damaging surrounding homes during Ranger training in Scotland. Right after high school ROTC, Saam had been with the Michigan National

Guard, and after clearing those mines, "a short while later he was back twirling his mustache again. 'Funny thing,' he said, 'I reached down for those mines and the first thing I did was to shake hands with the arm of a Heinie. Then I found some more corpses in that minefield. Got some Lucky Strikes out of the pocket of one of the corpses. Here, have one,'" he said, producing the pack. There was no guarantee that all mines had been cleared, and therefore the Rangers still needed to advance down the center of the winding road.

This dangerous mission required a courageous, brave man to lead. A man who was not afraid to get his hands dirty, a man who'd do anything to please his commander. A man who was not afraid to stick a 16-inch bayonet into the gut of a man while potentially charging to his own death. Darby called upon Captain Shunstrom, though only 22 years old, and his hard-charging Charlie Rangers. How hard they were since the dilution of the Originals throughout the battalions was to be seen. Reinforced with a platoon from A/1, he was to proceed carefully up the winding road while the battalion would follow behind, ready to reinforce Shunstrom when called upon. The details about the kind of leader Chuck was, and the kind of environment they operated in, are well preserved by Jack Belden:

> Shunstrom was in great haste as he rushed through the explanation of the operation with his lieutenants and sergeants: "Only I will shoot red and green flares. Only I. Got that? Men will march with fixed bayonets." The men gathered on the road. Then stealthily, crouching like a cat, the first man went forward with his bayonet held in front and others followed. Behind them, Chuck Shunstrom's voice cried petulantly, "Get apart, get apart. If we are ambushed you'll want plenty of room." The men bent over double and shuffled forward in a slow creep. I fell into the column behind Shunstrom.

The hairy-chested tough commander Captain Lyle followed Chuck Shunstrom's company in immediate support. With Lyle were engineers tasked with mine removal and a platoon of 75mm half-track artillery in case they were needed to lay down fire and suppress the enemy. Darby had instructed Lyle to shoot at anything and every-thing while the battalion moved, as it was exposed on the single road. Somehow this filtered down to not taking any prisoners, something Darby had been known to order in previous campaigns. The order of movement was 1st Ranger Battalion, 1st Battalion 41st Armored, followed by the 4th Ranger Battalion, seizing the high grounds on either side if necessary.

The intra-battalion order of movement was 1st Platoon, followed by 2nd, a machine-gun section, followed by 3rd Platoon with three 6omm mortars, each keeping 75-yard intervals. Belden accompanied them on their march. "I want 15 yards interval between each man," ordered Shunstrom. "March at slow pace. We go in alone and with fixed bayonets." On the march, Belden saw debris and equipment strewn everywhere, and then the bodies of six men, in a narrow defile below Butera, where a shell had landed near two vehicles into the roadway. One was naked, his clothes either blown or burned off: "In a little while on our right we passed the remains of freshly wrecked vehicles. Sprawling on his stomach and face, with hand outstretched, was a figure in civilian clothing. Dimly near the center of the back I made out a dark stain. To see a civilian dead in a battle area is ten times as shocking as seeing a dead soldier and I had to swallow my desire to vomit." Another unsettling moment occurred en route. "The churned and chopped-up earth in the center of the road now loomed up directly beneath my feet. Sammy's minefield, I thought. I looked for the arm Sammy had shaken, and there it was like a ragged, bulky, elongated package and there also were shredded masses that were bodies. It was a grim scene in the moonlight, and dangerous too. In a moment we were through the minefield and breathed easier. We climbed steadily for two hours." They departed for the mission to the base at 0100 hours in the night. Shunstrom was in communica-tion with Darby in case they ran into trouble and needed artillery support—something Darby was fond of, being fanatical about power projection. Eventually Belden stayed with a small element well behind

Shunstrom and his scouts as they approached the base of the mountain. They then climbed one—less steep—cliff for four miles.

On Captain Shunstrom's climb, they bumped into an outpost, which they captured quickly. This may have been at 0235 hours when assault companies were fired upon by small-arms fire and overcome by 0300. Three Germans and one Italian were in their hands. Shunstrom, being hardly a dainty flower, forced his three men, all Originals, into killing them. He believed that no prisoners were to be taken. Ranger Edward Barbarino shot a German. Rangers Alvin Buie and August Passera shot two, with Chuck finishing off the last one. If this happened, it was when Belden was behind them with other sections. Reaching the top, Shunstrom deployed 1st Platoon to near the gate and 2nd Platoon to the left. The plan on the objective was simple. First Platoon would enter through the gate and clean the areas around 2nd and 3rd Streets, while 2nd Platoon would climb the walls, bringing along forward observers for the three mortars being set up. 3rd Platoon would reinforce the assault into the city by turning left from the gate. Chuck also wanted the mortars to fire 8 rounds each, in total 24, at the opening stage of the attack to sow confusion throughout the town.

At long last, at 0430 hours, 14 July, the attack on Butera crept forward. But as they approached the gate, Italian machine-gun fire erupted, hitting the platoon leader and the scout (radio operator), but the lead scout located the crew and its weapon and silenced it with his grenade. It was Ranger Sergeant Francis Padrucco, with the road-bound platoon, who encountered the enemy MG. "We got to a bend in the road, and a machine-gunner opened up on us at a range of twenty feet. He wounded my lieutenant and radio operator. But our scout with a Tommy gun let go with a whole drum of ammunition and he got seven." Belden, too, encountered adventures along the windy road. "At a sharp bend in the road, we abruptly ran into two anti-tank guns facing directly downhill toward us. With tightly gripped guns, our soldiers passed by them. Then appeared smashed trucks and, beside them, about ten bodies. Rounding a big curve, we stood at the entrance to Butera on the very face and edge of the cliff. Its buildings with blank walls faced us like a fortress. Through dark, narrow streets in which there was scarcely a sound, we made our way until a voice cried: 'Halt. Give the password,' and we shouted the countersign for the night. We had rejoined our first platoon."

The mortars fired their rounds and 1st Platoon, with one machine gun, charged in, with the latter establishing a line of fire down the south–north 1st Street, killing any and everybody entering the street. The Rangers cleaned houses between 1st and 2nd Streets while 3rd Platoon with a machine gun followed suit, turned left, emplacing its automatic weapon down 2nd Street. The last platoon climbed the walls near the church and garden and covered 3rd Street with their automatic rifles. The bell tower of the church had someone in it, perhaps a sniper, and Ranger Hummer was ordered to fire his bazooka into it. No one cleared the bell tower. All streets going north south were under fire. The mortars, having fired their first barrage, moved into town, keeping in touch with Able and Charlie Companies. Lyle wisely kept his company outside to avoid confusion and friendly fire. He was close enough if Chuck Shunstrom needed him to deploy into the town quickly. Shunstrom yet again led a furious, murderous charge into the heart of the enemy. "Shunstrom was poking a gun around street corners, then darting quickly across open spaces and constantly whirling and turning to face any possible ambush. He looked like an agile young killer."

Once Charlie Company cleared buildings and moved forward, Able came in to handle any unseen or hidden enemy forces in the areas that had been swept through. In hard-learned and -earned fashion, the Rangers house-cleaned as they knew how—hard and furious, sometimes resorting to grenades to gain access into houses. All the while, the machine guns and BARs kept an eye out for enemy troops in case they needed to suppress them, covering their comrades. Bazookas were used to blast out a machine-gun nest, while other Italian crews fired at Ranger BAR men on rooftops. Once the Rangers who had moved north reached the end of the town, they redirected to the left, east of the town, and engaged enemy forces there. This type of fighting required tactical awareness, target acquisition, and excellent communications, and all the platoons executed their plans well, going from one side of the town to the other. A couple of Rangers saw an argument between Italians and Germans, and one Italian-speaking Ranger yelled at them to surrender. Instead, they fled.

The 75mm half-tracks by now had deployed forward to the walls of Butera, while a 105mm howitzer battery of 2 guns was within 500 yards. The fight for the town lasted three hours and resulted in 100 Italian POWS, a third of the Garrison (the town's population probably did not exceed 500 or 600). The dead were unaccounted for, but there were a number of dead littering the streets with their now-decomposing bodies. It was a brilliant raid. Some 77 enemies killed and 14 captured, the town in their hands, the Rangers were exhausted, having fought for 4 days. Gino Mercuriali recalled some of the after-action events:

> At Butera, the seemingly inaccessible hill town, I experienced again the type of people that can be part of a great outfit, but I wasn't particularly in agreement with their action. After the action, which was mostly sniper type, I left the area and retraced a part of our approach. I came upon the body of a German officer and a short ways away that of an Italian. The German officer had a small *chez* [this was probably a Czech CZ-27, 7.65mm] pistol in holster on his belt. This I took. I also noted he had a large diamond ring on his finger, but I was squeamish about trying for that. As I walked away, another Ranger went directly to the German and cut the finger off for the ring. As for the Italian soldier, he appeared badly wounded but alive. I administered him with a morphine shot and a medical doctor was near. I told him about the Italian but he only made a "so what?" gesture. I've always had mixed feelings since then, as to whether I should have or shouldn't have taken the ring. There were few times that I would not consider relieving a dead German of anything for two reasons. One, unless he

was a fresh kill, he may be booby trapped and the other was that any additional burden was not desirable. In addition, I would think, why the hell go to the trouble, I may not even make it back, in spite of my promise to my mother that I would return.

After the battle of Butera, the 1st Ranger Battalion stayed in place as all the other attachments returned to their parent units. On 20 July, Darby was given command of a larger force called Task Force X. It consisted of the 1st and 4th Ranger Battalions, the 39th Regimental Combat Team, and the 1st Battalion of the 77th Field Artillery Regiment. Less than a week later, Task Force X included all three Ranger battalions. Larger units came to the forefront instead. Darby's Rangers moved to different locations. Darby CP with HQ Company were at Castelvetrano, A/1, B/1, and C/1 located at Gibellina, with F/1 at Caltanissetta. Their job was the less-than-glorious task of guarding prisoners, a job they never had relished. Murray's men of the 4th Ranger Battalion were also on guard duty—guarding supply depots and POWs with patrols from Ninfa to Ponte Biddusa.

Despite these successes, there were troubling issues to Darby and, without a doubt, issues that affected the Army in general. "We are severe in our punishments. Summary court used considerably. Infractions of discipline, military courtesy, and uniform violations are dealt with quickly and rather severely. Accidental discharge of firearms is reduction and $40 fine. The officers must bear down on these things. The Army has not stressed strict discipline enough and without it you are lost. I find my men slump after battle. I believe most of it is forgetfulness." Good thing for the Rangers that Dammer and Murray were there to smooth infractions over: Without these two men, more Rangers would probably have quit.

LICATA

The story of Major Herman Dammer's 3rd Battalion was equally stunning. Herm had been awarded the Silver Star for actions in Tunisia and with the command of the newly activated 3rd Battalion when the Rangers expanded. He was a tactical mastermind and an organizational *wunderkind*. It comes as no surprise that he was handed a key operation, the seizure of the port and town of Licata, near Mount Sole. To take the town, they decided to use the sandy beaches west of Licata at San Mollarella. The old Rangers looked at the impending assault with their previous combat experiences in mind while the new Rangers were more apprehensive.

The overall operation plan for the seizure of Licata and surrounding areas was divided into four main beaches. On the far right, and closer to U.S. forces operating around Gela, was Beach Blue, some five miles east of Licata. This was assigned to the 30th Infantry Regiment of the 3rd Division. To its left, moving closer to Licata, was Beach Yellow, tasked to the 15th Infantry, minus one battalion. This area was but two miles from Licata, and its taking involved sweeping inland and attacking Licata from the northeast. The actual town of Licata was not going to be directly attacked. The key beach was labeled Green, and that was the Ranger Battalion, followed by the 2nd Battalion, 15th Infantry Regiment. Beach Red was to the left of the Rangers, five miles distant from Licata. The inner two beaches of Green and Yellow were tasked with capturing the town.

Licata was smaller than Gela in terms of size and population, but it featured a small port, and a rail and road network. The headlands, cliffs, rose sharply from the sea and were up to 40 meters high, with rolling hills and high ground up to 1,600 feet about 5 to 6 miles in the distance. Small creekbeds and ravines dot the area. None of this should have caused the Rangers problems, as they had practiced and trained in the tall Atlas Mountains near Nemours, Algeria, and the coastal areas of Bizerte, Tunisia in the run-up to *Operation Husky*. An unfinished airstrip was two miles to the northwest. Dammer's 3rd Battalion's mission was to seize the nearby beaches, just to the west of Licata, and then secure the high ground, allowing for follow-on forces to capture Licata and its port. Aerial photography had been used in the planning and training phase, which readily identified enemy positions because of the usual barbed-wire entanglements.

The beach they were to land on also had a terrain feature for the Rangers to identify and help land in the correct spot. Instead of a long jetty, as was in Gela, at Licata it was a rock, a promontory, sticking out into the sea, Rocca Mollarella, connected to the mainland by a low sandy isthmus cutting the beaches in half. It is 250 meters wide by 45m deep, with steep cliffs seaside, rising into the sea by 82 feet. The rock is just over 5 kilometers away from Licata. It was fortified with defensive positions of pillboxes, machine guns, and strings of barbed wire. The beaches, labeled 71 and 72, were thought to have been mined with anti-personnel and anti-tank mines, and featured wide bands of double-apron barbed wire for waterline defenses 20 yards inland. On the reverse slope, protecting them from overhead fire, they had good lines of sight to both beaches. Defensive positions including trenches were emplaced in the rolling hills and surrounding high ground. The left-sided beach was bow-shaped and 500 yards long, while the right was a half-moon-shaped beach nearly 650 yards long. There were few homes in the San Mollarealla, and as such it was less challenging than seizing the beach at Gela. However, the beaches near Licata were nestled into surrounding high ground, hills and mountains. The high ground on their left, west, was Mount Poliscia, rising to 365 feet or more, and it was within 300 yards of the water's edge. It needed to be seized.

Third Battalion's Able, Baker, and Charlie were to land on the left side of the rock under Dammer, while new Executive Officer Captain Alvah Miller was with Dog, Easy, and Fox on the right. Each group had demolitions sections with them. These two sections were tasked with the destruction of wire entanglements and to put up lighted beach markers as soon as possible. The high ground that needed to be taken was through Mount Sole on the right, the east, nearly 600 meters tall.

In typical fashion, the battalion was offshore about three miles out, having suffered through a storm, and transported in the HMS *Princess Astrid* and *Princess Charlotte,* each holding seven LCAs and one Landing Craft Support (LCS) with twin .50 machine guns in a turret. There, they cross-loaded into the British landing craft and headed for the two parts of Green Beach divided by the rock mass. All six companies landed abreast in one wave, driven by the excellent crew as though they themselves were Rangers. According to Major Dammer, the Navy had done a beautiful job.

The attack had each company assigned to a specific task. Able was to take Mount Poliscia to the left of the beach and take positions along its northwestern slope, protecting the beach. Baker was to breach the wire, move around the eastern slope, the right side, of Poliscia, and clear the western portion of a hill farther inland about 1,200 yards to the northwest. Once cleared, the company was to occupy it, in effect protecting the left side of the landing sites and assault forces. Charlie Company, minus 2nd Platoon and the mortar section, had the hard job of cracking the nut that was the defense of the rock, while the 2nd Platoon and mortars breached the wire, moved inland some 400 yards, and awaited orders in case C/3 needed help reducing the rock.

The boys of Dog, on the other side of the beach, like everyone else, had to breach the wires, clear any resistance from the basin's center, then move to the high ground and take position on the right of Baker Company. Captain Alvah Miller's remaining two companies, E and F, were to breach the wires and move to the right flank (the eastern part of the basin), destroy the enemy, and hold two ridges on Mount Sole, overlooking Licata. These two companies had the longest distance to cover. Once the beach had been secured in 20 minutes, the 2nd Battalion of the 15th Infantry was to pass through Easy and Fox on the right to capture Licata.

The search lights in the hills skimmed the area, but no incoming artillery followed. There was a mist hanging off the shore. The LCSs swung into line and approached the beach slowly, due to its narrow maritime approach. At 0255 hours, the Rangers hit the beach, but long swells bumped some LCAs together. A single machine gun shot at the Rangers but stopped upon receiving return fire. A Company breached the wire. Two machine guns and a 47mm cannon opened fire from the slopes of Rocca Mollarella. Two craft received holes blasted into them by 47mm gunfire, and the crews received numerous casualties. At that moment, the LCS from the *Princess Charlotte* opened fire on the machine guns. One of the guns was silenced. This action enabled B Company to breach the wire and clear the beach. D, E, and F Companies landed and quickly cleared their area. Neither of the beaches was mined, unlike Gela.

Charlie Company (minus) landed while the LCA swung back into the surf and provided covering fire. The Rangers on the left suppressed the eastern (left) part of the rock, while only one enemy machine gun returned fire, but it was too high on the slope, sending its rounds into the center of the beach well over the heads of the attacking Rangers. One section provided suppressing fire, while the other used Bangalore torpedoes to blow through the wire entanglements. The Rangers succeeded in climbing the rock on the eastern and northern side while under fire and captured the 47mm gun emplacement that was in the process of being manned. The assault sections cleared the rock of enemy positions.

It took a little while for other companies to clear the beach, encountering light resistance; then Able moved east to Mount Poliscia, eliminating enemy positions, then climbed west to take up their defensive positions, per the assault plan. On the right side, but left of the rock, D Company tackled mortar positions on higher ground. The various small buildings that the Rangers encountered were cleaned from the top down, climbing up on the outside and going downstairs. Some Rangers heard the heavy gunfight at Gela, and barely visible in the west were American paratrooper planes getting shot down by friendly fire. Easy and Fox cut their way through barbed wire on their way to eliminating two machine guns, which was done by Easy as it was closest to those emplacements that were on the right side about 1,500 yards out and on higher ground. One Ranger, T/5 Fernand R. Sylvain of E/3, was seriously wounded and died of his wounds in the fighting to silence the MG nests. The 3rd Ranger Battalion cleaned out most of the resistance by the time follow-on forces landed on the beaches. Licata would fall into Ranger hands quickly. No doubt, recalls Ranger Arnbal, upon entering Licata and discovering a "house of Joy," that it would serve as Charlie Company's headquarters.

Hammer's force took nine casualties, of whom one died of his wounds. Pulled back into reserve and guarding Licata, the area came under Luftwaffe attacks. A U.S. vessel returned fire, and a round fell short on a house, wounding eight Rangers of D/3. In the heat of the aerial battle, U.S. anti-aircraft opened up on two American fighter planes who were hot in pursuit of the Germans. Unfortunately, friendly fire led to the lead American pilot getting shot down, crashing, and burning on impact. The second fighter, enraged at the death of his comrade, opened fire on the American AA unit responsible. Dammer's battalion was ordered to division reserve south of San Oliva, where it established a bivouac. The battalion commander was very well aware that at Arzew and at Licata they had only fought against less dedicated enemies, the French and the Italians. The battalion had yet to face tough opposition. Setting up bivouac three miles west of the beach they had invaded, several Rangers stole a calf and killed it. In the midst of this, Captain Alvah Miller, along with some 3rd Infantry Division officers, arrived, confiscated the carcass, and reminded the men that the Army did not live off the land. They were supposed to have been punished, but Miller did not. Darby, on the other hand, would have done something to enforce his disciplinary standards.

MONTAPERTO—MASS-A GRAMAGLIA— PORTO EMPEDOCLE

Not content to shield the western flank for the British, General Patton, under strict orders to do just that, decided to bend the rules and conduct a reconnaissance in force. Truscott was ordered to capture the mountain city of Agrigento while the 3rd Ranger Battalion was to seize Porto Empedocle and its port. Agrigento, high on a mountain, served as a key rail and road junction vital for the Americans to continue their drive west and north in an effort to outrace the British to the central key objective of Messina, the port closest to the mainland. Messina, under the duplicitous Mamertine mercenaries, started the First Punic War between Carthage and Rome for control over Sicily in 264 BC. Messina had always been of great strategic value. The capture of Porto Empedocle, some three miles south of Agrigento, was intended to cut the line of retreat farther west. The valley north of Agrigento held enemy 177mm artillery. Third Battalion therefore was to take part of the overall assault plans by seizing Porto Empedocle on its own, going through enemy-held countryside. Orders for movement to the objective arrived on 14 July, early in the morning. The U.S. command did not wish to have a major battle at Agrigento, but a reconnaissance in force was acceptable. The objective, after all, was to the north, not the south, to Palermo for Patton and not the western coastline. Attached to the 7th Infantry, 15 July, at 1730 hours, the mission was then to recon the Agrigento area, moving south along Highway 122 to the major hill city, but to bypass it and to capture the small hill town of Montaperto to the west, and from there to move south to capture the port town of Porto Empedocle.

The plan called for the Rangers to march north and then west and then south, bypassing Agrigento, and striking at Italian and German observation posts and defenses toward the port. They marched to Campobello, using Highway 123, where they took trucks to Naro, arriving at 2330 hours. The hasty plan did not include a route for the 3rd Ranger Battalion to move to Favara, other than that they were supposed to occupy the high ground of Hill 313, 1,000 yards east of Favara before their next movement. Dammer decided on the spot to march along the rail line of Naro-Favara to Hill 313, where they then were to use the Agrigento-Raffadali route north of Agrigento, on to Montaperto for their move south to Porto Empedocle. At midnight, the battalion moved in columns, with Able leading and Fox bringing up the rear. About a mile and a half out of Favara, the Rangers discovered a tunnel. Concerned that it might be mined, they moved overland, costing them an extra 30 minutes and, with the delay, raising concerns that if they had to fight to seize the hill, the assault would negate the Rangers' favorite time to attack, in darkness just before dawn. The hill was undefended; and from there, Dammer and staff saw the town still asleep at 0530.

Major Dammer and one company advanced into the eastern part of Favara, where they discovered a radio patrol from their battalion signal section that had just entered the town. They established contact with patrols sent to the south with the 7th Infantry just after noon. The rest of the battalion assembled on the eastern side of Favara at 1300. Here the Rangers were reminded that there was to be "no dropping out of the unit, stealing or harassment of the civilians." Clearly the leadership knew their men. The villagers looked and dressed like the poor they were, but this didn't stop some Rangers from stealing cheese—but, later on, finding the cheese to be too strong for sensitive Ranger stomachs and palettes. An extended rest was ordered, with many men stripping their boots, leggings, and socks, and attending to their troublesome blisters and whatnots. It was hard work for First Sergeant Merritt Bertholf to deal with some of his squad leaders, who ignored him about the state of their men.

The 3rd Ranger Battalion assembled on the western part of Favara at 1900 hours and moved out in column formation, the only formation favored by Darby for night movement and attack, with A, D, C, B, E, and F/3 bringing up the rear.

Rangers Joe Shuff, Larry Sausen, and Johnny Stanton all decided to find wine in Favara, and ducked away from the battalion as it departed. They missed the subsequent deployment. Interestingly, once the three men recovered from their drunken stupor they tried to find their battalion and, while marching along, rounding a curve, they encountered a jeep from the 82nd Reconnaissance with the driver and a first lieutenant dead. The damage on the vehicle indicated heavy rounds having been fired at them, not just infantry small arms. Soon the three Ranger *amigos* spotted the armored vehicles responsible for their deaths, just past the curve. Armed with 37mm guns, these seven vehicles seemed only guarded by a lone sentry. Since the vehicles were operational, it seemed the battalion had missed them or avoided them by marching around the Italian vehicles. Knowing they had gone AWOL, they felt that perhaps by destroying the vehicles, all would be forgiven. Experienced battle-hardened Ranger veterans that they were, Johnny Stanton killed the lone sentry—one presumes Commando style—whereupon the other two joined. They hastily dropped grenades into the open hatches and took off—like a Ranger speed march. Hustling down the road, they heard sounds of battle and bumped into a Ranger company and bumped into Lieutenant "Bing" Evans, an Original. They were the rear guard. Evans gave them a Ranger talking-to and pointed them to their company. Once their seemingly tall tale was verified, the Rangers were forgiven, with Sergeant William Lawrence Sausen receiving a Silver Star for the action, although later they found out that the 82nd Recon lieutenant received a DSC posthumously for having knocked out all those tanks. Sausen would be killed in Italy.

Three miles west of Favara, they came under sporadic incoming fire. Dammer made allowances for the scout to recon the forward areas, including terraced vineyards, and thus the column moved at a slower pace. Finding deep ravines four and a half miles out of Favara, they encountered a blown bridge. This meant that armor support was no longer available if needed. Reaching the intersection of Highways 122 and 118, which went north, they bypassed Agrigento just to their south. East of the highway junction, at 0030 hours, 16 July, they encountered a roadblock. It was defended by a small-caliber cannon and a machine gun only about 30 yards away on each side of the roadblock on higher ground. The entrenched enemy, on the right side, opened fire, leading to immediate counter-attack by A/3, screaming Indian and Rebel yells while charging along the road to destroy the roadblock, while D/3 tackled the enemy on high ground, holding their fire as they approached the telltale signs of gun flashes from the Italians, and then they unleashed a furious barrage, silencing the enemy. C/3 passed through D to take the hill facing the junction of the two highways. The Rangers captured 165 Italians, probably survivors of the 10th Bersaglieri Regiment, who were marched back to Favara under guard and handed over to the 7th Infantry.

The 3rd Ranger Battalion occupied the position to the north of the road junction until 0600 hours. In the early morning hours, Dammer's force moved down the western slope toward Montaperto. They then took a hill to the west that was 1,800 yards distant, moving down the slope when they received sporadic and ineffective long-range artillery fire.

Passing through a culvert under Highway 118, and some 200 yards west of the road, the Rangers spotted an enemy column coming around a bend 500 yards to the south. The column had 10 motorbikes with sidecars, and two trucks filled with troops that traveled without security elements. The majority of the battalion was on the slope, and quickly it was decided to let the enemy column come directly to their front, as the Rangers intuitively hid behind the rocks strewn about. The enemy was ambushed by all four companies from the hills, obliterating them, littering the highway with a great number of their dead. Forty POWs were taken and kept with the column as it marched on.

MONTAPERTO

Moving on, the Rangers finally hit the northern side of the hill town of Montaperto. Advancing into the small town, they went forward to the southern edge, overlooking the area toward Porto Empedocle. It was a grand view of the entire area. In the large valley below, they spotted four batteries, 12 guns, of enemy artillery—a clear threat to any invading force approaching from the south. The Rangers engaged them with small-arms fire and 60mm mortars, blowing up the clearly visible batteries, and hitting an ammunition dump, resulting in a big explosion followed with thick smoke. Few Italians escaped; a number had been killed while under fire, and the rest surrendered while struggling up the hill.

MASS-A-GRAMAGLIA

The next stop was the rock formation known as the Mass-a-Gramaglia. On this formation, the Italian command had set up a headquarters in several small buildings, supplemented by tents, which included a radio communications setup and what was believed to be a coastal-defense station. The view toward the sea was spectacular. The sheer cliffs of approximately 100 feet surrounded it and fell sharply off to the west into another valley running mostly to the south. Dammer tasked

Charlie Company to take the hill and, once taken, advance south to rejoin the battalion as the rest of the battalion moved alongside the west (right) side of the hill to their assembly point closer to Porto Empedocle.

The mass also featured large boulders, four to six feet in diameter, and spread from the base to about 100 yards out. A small tunnel located to the north was located near the junction of three small tracks. From there, a stairway led to the top of the hill. Just out of the tunnel, 15 yards or so, was a low stone wall. Charlie Company, 3rd Rangers, under new Company Commander Captain Ed Kitchens Junior, moved up to the base of the hill with two platoons abreast, keeping to 10-yard intervals. Mortars were on standby at the foot of the cliffs. On approach, an Italian on top of the rock mass yelled at them when the Rangers were 300 yards away to retreat or be fired on. The Charlie Rangers took cover around the boulders. Near the three-path junction, Company Commander Kitchens Jr. led one section into the tunnel, fearing for the worst. He should have—Kitchens wrote a few years later—sent in scouts or, better yet, personally conducted a leader's recon before committing his men. If he had, they would have discovered an easier access point to the mass: The eastern-side edge had no sheer cliffs. They moved slowly into the staircase hewn into the rock, finding it empty. The low wall was to their front and provided some cover. Kitchens's section fixed bayonets while in the tunnel. The captain sent a runner to grab the other sections of the company to join him. The Rangers flew out of the tunnel, screaming their lungs out. That was all it took: Before the first section had even cleared the tunnel, the Italians surrendered, with only one sniper offering resistance, leading to his death. The Italians turned out to be the command group from Agrigento. Thirty-six were captured, including the commanding colonel and 19 officers. However, not all ended well.

Three Italian soldiers had escaped and headed down the hill, coming into contact with elements of the 3rd Battalion. Kitchens radioed Dammer, but by then the Italians had opened fire with their machine guns, hitting Lieutenant "Bing" Evans in the helmet, temporarily stunning him. New Ranger Lieutenant Raymond Campbell volunteered to take them out but was promptly killed at 400 yards from the MG nest, leading his platoon from F/3 in the assault. The three Italians surrendered but seemingly did not survive the day.

PORTO EMPEDOCLE

The assault on Porto Empedocle moved from north to south. After all, that is why the Rangers had taken Monaperto and Mass-a-Gramaglia, thus avoiding Italian defensive positions looking to the south and the shore. Charlie Company moved out of the mass and by 1400 hours had rejoined the battalion that had stopped at vineyards first, then at an almond grove, 2,000 yards north of the sea town.

By 1420, the attack had commenced. Empedocle was nestled among and below rocky hills with a deep ravine, running perpendicular to the beach, dividing the town into near-equal parts. In traditional Ranger fashion, the battalion advanced in two columns astride the ravine, deploying for attack. The town had a German battery facing the sea (this was the first time 3rd Battalion had encountered Germans) and other defensive fortifications including pillboxes and machine-gun emplacements. The information about a German battery was gleaned from a local Italian. The battery was roughly a mile west of Porto Empedocle and was to be Captain Alvah Miller's target. The plan called for Major Dammer to lead A, B, and C Companies east of the dividing ravine, while Captain Miller, with the rest of the battalion, D, E, and F, attacked the western part. Supporting mortars, with a range of 1,800 meters but running low on shells, were set up 600 yards north of the town, where Rangers also guarded the accompanying 800 prisoners. Here the battalion divided and approached Porto Empedocle.

A sharp skirmish ensued. A/3 encountered machine-gun fire that was immediately silenced. Another was taken by surprise as it set up to fire on Charlie, who had just defeated the Italians on the Mass-a-Gramaglia. Reaching the main street overlooking the beach, Dammer's Charlie Rangers found unoccupied anti-aircraft positions and pillboxes set up to cover the beach and captured three Italians after blowing off the door of a pillbox.

Miller's men, D, E, and F Companies, faced stiffer resistance as they approached a walled cemetery at the northwest edge of town. Here the Axis forces fired small-arms and anti-aircraft weapons at the attacking Rangers. Easy Company assaulted the position with suppressing fire, isolating and trapping the enemy. There were additional prisoners taken while the rest of the group and the other force spent 40 minutes clearing houses throughout the town in typical Me and My Pal fashion. The new Rangers acquitted themselves very well despite earlier concerns that they had not really been tested in combat at the beach landings of Licata.

At 1600 hours, the Rangers held Porto Empedocle. A defensive perimeter included captured machine guns and saw B, C, D, and E Companies on the edge of town preparing for any potential counter-attacks while Able Company built or supervised the building of a POW camp for its 91 Germans and 675 Italians they had captured in their assault on the town. But not all things ended gloriously, as communication problems with the 3rd Infantry Division did not alert higher authorities to the fact that the Rangers had been successful.

After an aerial drop of leaflets urging the defenders to surrender, naval gunfire from the cruiser USS *Philadelphia* hit near Charlie with Carl Lehmann seeing a house he was observing disappearing into a gigantic cloud of smoke and debris, despite Dammer's frantic or frenetic attempts to alert the Allied force offshore. After the initial barrage, the American cruiser allowed for the surrender of the defenders, during which time desperate attempts were made to spell out "Yank" and "U.S. Troops" with oil drums. Around 1800, two small seaplanes flying white flags landed inside the jetty, to the anger of Rangers who had captured the town four hours before.

During that night, four, some reports say fifteen, Renault tanks with the standard white death's-heads came into contact with a Ranger patrol of three, one officer and two enlisted, looking to link up with the 3rd Recon Troop of the 3rd Infantry Division and their three vehicles, near a blown-up bridge over the San Leone (Drago)

River. This was two miles south of Agrigento, and the attack began on the Porto-Agrigento Road. Here they were overtaken by the light tanks. Halliday would receive the Silver Star for his actions. During the combat, it reads, T/4 Halliday "showed extreme presence of mind and without regard for his own safety, ran along the side of the leading tank and thrust a grenade into an open port. He thereby killed or disabled the crew resulting in the tank crashing into the gorge. He continuously exposed himself to cannon and machine gun fire while he assisted in removing wounded men to safety." The Americans received serious casualties, but between the 3rd Recon Troop and Ranger Communications T/4 Robert H. Halliday, who dropped a grenade through the lead tank's port, perhaps simultaneously the tank was hit by machine-gun fire from a lieutenant of the 3rd Infantry Division, which led to the lead tank plunging into the embankment. Lieutenant David G. Waybur of the 3rd Infantry Division received the Medal of Honor, an award not handed out to any Ranger during the war. A conclusion on the new Ranger Battalion's actions was drawn by Kitchens, who did not spare criticism of his own actions as a company commander:

> During this operation, the absence of determined resistance on the part of the enemy gave the majority of the battalion an erroneous concept of combat. This concept could have been largely eliminated during the short pause following this operation through proper orientation on the part of the leaders and the experienced cadre. This attitude had no effect on this operation unless it was instrumental in causing the company commander of C Company to act without a proper estimate. However, when determined resistance was encountered, there was a reaction of surprise that such could happen. Though not having a marked effect on the battalion there was an unnecessary period of readjustment. The individual soldier must be trained to expect the enemy to fight with all the means

available, and that ingenuity must be combined with an aggressive spirit to defeat him.

In typical Ranger fashion, some of the men had taken over the local bar and looted a clothing store. Dressing like respectable men, they supposedly fooled a visiting general into believing they were the leaders of the town when the general came through Porto Empedocle. He was none the wiser by the time he left.

SICILIAN MANEUVERS

The Rangers moved westward and secured the Belice River, captured Castelvetrano and its airfield, then continued their advance to Mazra-Ponte Biddusa-Salemi. This was done to allow for Patton's forces to launch their attack north to Palermo and from there to Messina. Dammer's force captured Marsala. Murray's 4th Battalion patrolled the coastal regions from Ninfa to Ponte Biddusa in the Trapani province, capturing more prisoners; feeding and guarding them became their routine. They also seized Salemi without resistance, taking large quantities of war material and machines as well as capturing 250 German and Italian prisoners on 21 July 1943. Prior to this, and after the landing at Gela, Murray had been patrolling— and reinforcing U.S. troops—the Niscemi to the north, and the easterly Comiso area and its airport earlier during the campaign. Roy Murray's son, a colonel (retired) with Special Forces, also named Roy Murray, remembered:

> The 4th was in the Comiso area. In fact, there is an interesting story on how my dad almost became a Ranger Ace. He and his driver made a wrong turn and came upon an Axis airport near Comiso. He and his driver captured about 100 Italian Air Force members [his father recalled 150 Germans], who were extremely happy to be captured. Included were 3 Italian planes. They also captured a German bomber crew with working bomber. They were

not at all happy to be captured. My father being a quick thinker drove the jeep at the head of the POW column and his poor driver walked at the end keeping a close watch on the Germans. One of the few times I know about where the officer got over on the enlisted man. In the small world arena, I later on was negotiating with a housing developer to build housing at Comiso to house the personnel running the Ground Launched Cruise Missile system that was being emplaced there [treaty signed that un-emplaced all the GLCM systems in Europe later]. Houses were built but the local population got the benefit.

The 3rd Ranger Battalion moved north through Montarporte to Raffadali and reached their assembly area at Mount Sera northwest of Cattolica Eraclea. It secured a road junction at Calamonali and ended up guarding POWs at Sciacca, having captured near 4,000. It had been a hard march leaving the Rangers, tired and aged, with salt- and dust-encrusted uniforms and boots: Sicily in the summer. The Italian prisoners suffered as well, with dehydration and food insecurity and, importantly, unsanitary conditions by not digging trenches and burying their feces. Flies were everywhere. The local brothel in town was frequented by the Rangers. The guard detail was hated, and Rangers had to loot American convoys at gunpoint for water and food for the thousands of prisoners and themselves. Arnbal records one Ranger captain from C/1—perhaps this was Shunstrom—who, along with other Rangers, delivered rations and was swarmed by the prisoners, whereupon he emptied two clips of eight rounds each into the mass of Italians. Lieutenants Larkin and Cannon of the two companies, previously assigned as guard detail, ordered their men to have nothing to do with the changeover to the other Rangers. Joining the rest of the 3rd Battalion in bivouac, the strength of one company of 3rd Battalion was under 50 men.

General Patton captured Palermo and then drove east to outrace British general Bernard Montgomery to Messina. The 1st and 4th Battalions found themselves at Corleone and did not participate in the drive to Palermo or Messina. It was here that a training program was initiated for needed replacements, as well as for the notoriously lax Rangers who needed a reminder of discipline. During live-fire training, two Rangers were wounded by .30 cal machine-gun fire; Shunstrom visited them at the hospital and apologized for the accident. The 3rd Ranger Battalion was ordered to move from Menfi to the northeast at Coronia as attachment to the 3rd Infantry Division. En route, Captain Kitchens and his driver were sitting in their vehicle not wearing their helmets when none other than Patton, sirens blaring and traveling at high speed, led to Kitchens running alongside his truck column, banging on them for the men to put their helmets on. Running back to his vehicle, he threw on his helmet, chinstrap and all, but the ever-watchful and wrathful Patton stopped by his vehicle, casting his hawk-like eyes on the scene. While Kitchens saluted, the general barked a question as to what outfit this was. Hearing it was the 3rd Ranger Battalion, he replied with "It figures," and drove on.

Third Rangers encountered civilians who looked gaunt, thin, poorly dressed, and unwashed. Children would beg, and some mean Rangers gave the kids halazone tablets, intended for water purification, that would cause stomach pains. Others would sometimes hand out hard candies. The fact was the natives were poor and owned nothing of value, meaning the Rangers had nothing to loot.

Many Rangers were lost due to muscle cramps and fallen arches . . . fatigue was evident. First Sergeant Bertholf used a stone to drive a tent peg into the ground and injured himself so badly that everyone heard him scream, and he was whisked away in a jeep with a medic, never to be seen again. "We would all miss him, as he was always trotting up and down the ranks on our long marches, sweating and red-faced, cajoling the troops, urging them onward. Those of us from the original Company B, 1st Ranger Battalion, missed him the most; the short-statured ex-artillery sergeant was always able to keep up on our long speed marches and was the butt of many jokes about his sexual prowess. He was also one of the six enlisted men from the company who had been on the August 17 [19], 1942, Dieppe Raid."

The 3rd Ranger Battalion reinforced with F/1 and Darby were attached to guard the inland flank of the 3rd Infantry Division as it advanced east to Palermo. This meant 140 miles of gut-wrenching mountains the Rangers had to cover. According to Altieri, this force became known as "Truscott Trotters." To that end, 50 mules were attached to Dammer, Darby remembers 200, with an additional 30 for F/1 to act as mule resupply column. The beasts of burden carried the heavy equipment and supplies the Rangers now required. Most of the mules would die horrible deaths in the mountains, with one shot by a German MG leading to a Ranger shooting the animal in the head between the eyes, and others falling thousands of feet to their presumed deaths. War is hell. Darby once was an artillery man with experience in using mules. Occasionally he would ride one. Battalion surgeon Sheldon C. Sommers wrote: "So the Col[onel] being from the artillery always wanted to use pack artillery; he got some of these disassembled, packed on mules and sent a company of temporary Ranger mule-skinners along the north Sicilian coast up in the hills alongside the 3rd Div on the coast. Since I was very bored, he let me go along as 'doctor for the Mules.' It was fun, we only picked up German stragglers, and the mountain artillery was never fired."

The Rangers encountered some enemy actions around Popo di Marco, four miles southwest of Capo d'Orlando, a commune of Messina. Struggling onward, the Rangers encountered German resistance on and off, capturing Germans along the route with Dammer, speaking German, interrogating the prisoners. For about a week, 3rd Rangers "fought and marched over almost one hundred miles of steep mountains and jagged ridges." Dammer's Rangers "were called upon to march cross-country through the high mountains parallelling the coast and to seize several important road centers and strategic enemy positions." They were up against German veterans of the Eastern Front who "made stubborn suicide stands on almost every hill and mountain that could be defended." German soldiers hid out in the many caves in the mountains of Sicily. Twenty-year-old Iowan Corporal Jack Hall, D/3, was involved in clearing out those pockets of enemy forces. That took about a month. One night Jack was asleep in a foxhole and a German soldier tried to sneak up on him. A sergeant in the foxhole with Jack shot the German; but as he fell, he gave Jack a bayonet wound in his leg. He was from the Hermann Göring Division. Jack did not go to a hospital: A medic "taped it up." Another time, a wounded soldier from the 15th Infantry Regiment was found with Ranger Dr. Emile Schuster trying to save him. After a short attack by small arms and mortar barrage, the man was killed.

They helped relieve a battalion that had been trapped after an amphibious assault at Cresta di Naso, moved through San Angelo di Brolo, the northern part of the island, with their mules all the way to Patti. One Ranger company was down to 47 enlisted and three officers. The 3rd Battalion was at 350–360 from an original strength at Licata of about 465 Rangers. The mountains included Monteforte and Mount Balavaggio to arrive at Falcone. They moved southeast of the mountains to Sanbruca (Darby), Sambuca, that lay north-northwest of Highway 113. They were four miles west of Messina. Here two companies were tasked to guard the road junction while the rest of the exhausted Rangers finally came to rest at a cemetery in town.

On 18 August, Dammer was ordered back to Coronia, then to Corleone on the 21st to join the other two battalions. The 1st and 4th Ranger Battalions were at about 40 percent understrength, while Dammer's battalion, which marched all over Sicily including the tough mountain ranges, was 50 percent understrength in killed, wounded, and non-battle injuries. At Corleone, Bill Darby was again in command of his Rangers. Refitting and finding replacements to train, the Rangers had little time to prepare for the next invasion: mainland Italy and its even-harder underbelly made up of mountain ranges galore. Mosquitoes buzzed the Rangers, eventually causing malaria for many of the men. Court-martials, promotions, and transfers were ongoing.

Photographer Phil Stern, although no longer attached to the Rangers, took some of the finest photographs of this campaign, now on permanent display in Catania, Sicily, in a large wing of the World War II museum. He was offered a place within a family of farmers. No doubt other Rangers were tempted, too, as desertion was not uncommon. In North Africa, for example, when two men had tried to flee to

Spanish Morocco but were captured by military police and brought to Lieutenant Colonel Darby, one of them, an amateur boxer, threatened Darby. Darby removed his rank insignia and "knocked the hell out of the man"—Darby took no shit. Corporal punishment existed. Marcel Swank was so afraid to discredit the Rangers and Darby that it did not occur to him that he might get killed at Dieppe. Sometimes punishment was less brutal. "He got angry very seldom; once when Gorski, a medic driver, creased the throat of a Col's driver while playing with a Beretta pistol, the Col had Gorski take off his shirt and sit in the broiling Sicilian sun for some three hours, getting a dandy sunburn." Ranger Edward Barbarino remembered Darby's small scar over his eye and "when he got mad, the scar turned white." Drunken Rangers were not tolerated while on duty and many a drunk Ranger would find himself in full pack marching in front of a jeep until he sobered up.

The next invasion saw the creation of a larger, heavier Ranger force, now dubbed Ranger Force: It included the three Ranger battalions; the 83rd Chemical Mortars, who had been exceptional in their support; a small tank unit; a detachment of the 82nd "All American Paratroopers"; and engineers. Darby, ever the heavy-artillery man, added a Ranger Cannon Company under Charles Shunstrom. It consisted of four self-propelled 75s, manned by volunteers knowing that wherever the action was hottest, Shunstrom's Rangers would be there. The interesting thing about Chuck Shunstrom was that despite his tremendous bravery, near recklessness, "none of the battalion commanders really wanted Shunstrom [as company commander or in general] because they considered him a loose cannon." Roy Murray's son Roy Murray wrote, "He was an exceptionally brave and reckless officer who they thought would get Rangers killed needlessly. I guess Darby had a good idea to put him in charge of the Rangers' cannon element." That was probably why Darby had him previously assigned to the hairy-chested Captain James Lyle, who was able to handle Shunstrom's eccentricities. Forget personalities, replacements, training, and other parts of life—another invasion was on the horizon. Mainland Italy: the Amalfi Coast.

The worst was yet to come.

TOWARD THE MOUNTAINS
A Hamlet near Sansepolcro, Italy
9 APRIL 1944

Technical Sergeant Robert Halliday and Staff Sergeant Dale Greenland couldn't believe their bad luck. Easter Sunday had seen them sitting on a sidewalk bench as churchgoers walked by, having left service. Their traveling companion, who spoke Italian, was New Zealander Norman Hellings, and had been captured in North Africa two years ago. They had traveled for a month by now, en route to the Adriatic. A local police officer, a *carabinieri*, on patrol approached them. Three unknown young men drew his attention. And that was that.

Now the two Ranger sergeants sat in jail, rotting away until they'd be handed over to the Germans, no doubt. The Kiwi was being held somewhere else. That also sucked. The Americans were in the village's small jail. So far and yet not far enough, they rued their misfortune. Both Third Battalion men had survived the killing fields of Cisterna and had made their way this far. They heard a commotion, soon followed by an upset and irate and perhaps even flustered chief of police. He was indignant from what the Americans could make out. They were interrogated, with the chief being absolutely worried about the presence of Americans in his area of operations: his territory. Satisfied with what he had learned, the chief of police left.

And Halliday and Greenland got everything they could have dreamt for: food and smokes. Throughout the day, they ate like kings with all sorts of food, the excellent wine, and cigarettes. It was a miracle. But they knew they had to build up their strength and rest, because tomorrow they felt they'd be in a far worse situation: in the hands of the Nazis. And their treatment of escaped prisoners was, at times, horrific.

Night encroached and cloaked the town. They heard a guard approach. He unlocked the cell and motioned for them to follow. Halliday and Greenland exchanged looks: What the hell was going on? Were they to be handed over to the Germans now? Whatever it was, it wasn't going to be good. They were surprised, and little surprised veteran combat soldiers. Right before them stood the Kiwi. Wry smiles were exchanged between the three. Together again, they were certain that something bad was about to happen. Why would they have been moved at night instead of the following day? The Carabinieri marched them along and out of the village.

The police officer came to a stop just outside of the last building. He looked at them. His hand rested on his holster. He pointed toward the mountains, telling them which way to go, and to get out of the district before they were caught again. The last thing the chief of police wanted was trouble from the nearby Germans: not in his district, not partisans. He did not want his villagers shot by the Germans for any anti-German activity. The direction they were told to use got them well out of any guerrilla activity in the nearby areas. Off they went, not believing their luck. The Germans who were nearby guarded one of the headquarters used by Field Marshal Albert Kesselring. No wonder the local police chief was concerned.

━━✦━━

7

OPERATION AVALANCHE —

SALERNO, ITALY

THE MAJORITY OF GERMAN AND ITALIAN FORCES EVACUATED FROM Sicily to the mainland while the Allies watched. The desire by the American war planners to invade the European continent through France in 1944 was counterweighed by the British immediate desire to remove Italy from the war. Plans to invade Italy proper were made and code-named *Operation Avalanche*. Although it was a two-pronged assault, the preparations for the invasion of the European continent outweighed the material needs for the invasion of Italy. Therefore, the two assaults occurred distinctly and separately with the British Eighth Army under General Bernard Montgomery landing in the toe of Italy in Calabria. The U.S. Fifth Army under Lieutenant General Mark W. Clark would strike around Salerno, south of Naples, almost a week later, on 9 September 1943. The hopeful idea was that German forces would be weakened, having to fight against two landings, and being trapped by the two main Allied forces.

However, German Army High Command under Generalfeld-marschall Albert Kesselring decided on a wiser course of action. Prepared, and aware of impending Allied landings, and also being very well aware that the Italians might surrender, the decision was made to make the Allies bleed for every hill and river they had to cross on their way to the Italian capital city, Rome. A string of defensive lines, along mountain ranges and rivers, was prepared and constantly improved upon with plans calling for fast reinforcements rotating in during the subsequent campaign. These seven lines came one after the other, traveling north, and would ultimately make this one of the bloodiest campaigns of World War II. So much for the soft underbelly of Europe. The reconstituted Hermann Göring Division that had battled Rangers and other American troops around Gela in Sicily, and had escaped, was quartered around Naples, some 60 kilometers north of Salerno. The Rangers, accustomed to routing the Vichy French and Italians with a sprinkling of German forces, were now facing the professional, veteran German Army.

For the Rangers under Lieutenant Colonel Darby, who was busy recruiting and training desperately needed replacements, this operation called for him and the various units under his command to seize the small seaside town of Maiori on the Amalfi coast, north of Salerno. Maiori, and its funnel-like draw leading northward to the peak of the Chiunzi, the pass alongside it, was unpaved and tortuous, dropping steeply down to Pagani and into the plain of Naples. The pass dissected Mount Chiunzi to the left and Mount San Angelo di Cava on the right. The Rangers were tasked with capturing the town and one of the three routes cutting across the mountain range immediately beyond it. Additionally, they were to sweep and control the small coastal highway to the east and west. To the left of Maiori were the small villages of Minori and Amalfi, both vital in controlling access along the narrow coastal road. It had been cut into the base of the mountains, zigzagging along its sheer cliffs along promontories and inlets. Rangers had to contend with access routes up the mountain chain overlooking the Amalfi coast, including Maiori and the Chiunzi Pass, which was the key objective for Darby's Ranger Force. The stony mountains were up to 1,000 meters tall with their peaks stretching to the west into the Sorrento Peninsula. Driving along the Amalfi coastal road would lead to Sorrento on the far edge of the peninsula, sticking out like a thumb, and then north to the German-held city of Castellammare, sitting on a vital road junction. The coastal road was a two-lane road at best, lacking guardrails; one had to drive

carefully, especially when trying to pass armored vehicles. Fourth
Ranger Battalion Commander Major Roy Murray recalled the road
being very poor, no wider than 30 feet. Most of the small villages dotting the shoreline featured small beaches, with the villages themselves
nearly hewn into the mountainous rock rising behind them.

To the Rangers' right, Royal Marine Commandos of No. 2 and
No. 41 were tasked with the seizure of the fishing village Vierti and its
road sitting on a defile between the mountain ranges running north
to Cava and Nocera Superiore. The Rangers and Commandos were
responsible for the western flank of the Fifth Army invasion force
centered below Salerno. They needed to hold the high ground, interdicting any German movements or operations aimed at the Allied
beachheads of Salerno. The geography of the region stood against
invading forces.

For Darby and his planners, who previously had flown to Algiers
for finalizing the operation, it meant they needed to take a number of issues into account. Maiori was a small fishing town with its
black shale beach, perhaps founded by the ancient Etrurians, at the
mouth of the Reginna Maior river, flooding and destroying most of
the city in 1954. A seawall and promenade ran parallel to the shore,
and the main road from the beach to the mountains cut the town
in half. The main road followed the river from the mountain to the
sea, ending at the beach, also cutting it in half. Closest to the sea
and the coastal road, this river had been paved over, but it could still
flow underneath the road into the sea. Following the road alongside
the river, and toward the mountains, it wound its way up the Chiunzi
Pass, passing the towns of Vaccaro, Sala, and S. Egidio, which leads to
the massive plain beyond the mountain and the towns of Pagani and
Nocera. Along the way, and to this day, the surrounding areas have
hundreds of terraced landscapes that add vibrant colors to the scen-
ery with their citrus, olive, chestnut, almond, and walnut trees, the
vineyards, and the vegetables that are grown at the foot of the trees
or poles. Key towns of Pagani and Nocera sat on vital road junctions
just at the other side of the mountain. Once across and to the west lay
the remains of the ancient Roman city of Pompeii. Visible, and just

to the north of Pompeii, was the massive volcanic Mount Vesuvius, which had rained rock, ash, and lava onto the ancient Pompeii, neatly preserving it beneath the layers of debris. If Mairoi was defended, it would be a nightmare to land and push German forces out of the town and the high ground. Capturing the high ground and using it for observation to interdict the Germans was vital. Darby, ever so in love with firepower, made sure he had one of his radio men with his own equipment on the battleship supporting him for fire missions. Good ship-to-shore communications were vital, a hard-learned lesson by Darby and his HQ elements. The three main routes across or through the mountain range were the Cava-Nocera Pass for the Commandos to seize and hold, the Chiunzi Pass in the middle, and lastly, on the far left, the Pimonte Pass, which led to Castellammare. Once on top of the mountain, it was "an artillery man's dream." The power of this kind of support is clearly seen in a message sent from Roy Murray to Snow White (Darby). It reads, "The mission of the 4.2's at coordinates given flushed out 350 Germans who were seen moving toward Pagani carrying their wounded."

Surrounding the coastal road with its many smaller towns or villages, the Germans had observation posts and defensive positions that could look onto the various bays, beaches, and landing zones with absolute clarity. This meant, of course, the vulnerability of the Allies to German artillery barrages. The amphibious landing and seizure of the high mountain was ideally suited to the Rangers, for they had trained and fought in the mountains in North Africa and Sicily. The major difference now was they'd be head-on fighting the experienced and motivated German soldiery. And there was a manpower shortage in the U.S. Army.

On 8 September 1943, days after Italy's surrender, a fleet of 450 vessels was en route through the Tyrrhenian Sea toward the Gulf of Salerno. Things did not go well for the main invasion forces, with the Luftwaffe sinking 13 ships and damaging more, and the German mobile defenses, reinforced daily with new troops, nearly pushing the Allies back into the sea. It would be a blood-letting south of Salerno and its beaches.

For the Rangers, on the other hand, things started off very well. The forces under Bill Darby's command were the 1st, 3rd, and 4th Ranger Battalions, with a fighting strength of about 1,100 men, the No. 2 and No. 41 Marine Commandos, and two companies, Charlie and Dog, of the 83rd Chemical Mortars. Although detected during the afternoon en route from Palermo and despite repeated attacks into the night, the Rangers did not suffer any losses in personnel or material. In the usual fashion, they climbed into their LCAs, British this time, while they were attached to the side of the ship. Once fully loaded, the LCA was dropped into the sea eight feet below with a resounding splash of water. Once all the landing craft were in the sea, they came alongside their main ship and drove forward in two columns. In the lead boat was Darby, always keenly aware of the importance of landing on the correct spot to the point where Darby "got awfully obnoxious." At a naval conference in 1944, "your compass," Darby said, "no matter how many times you swing them, in a small craft are practically worthless after 35 soldiers with helmets and rifles and everything else that contains metal get into the boat." To that end, the accompanying destroyer set the course and got them oriented until they were about one mile offshore; then the LCAs were on their own, basically going straight forward. The Allied landing in the northern sector was supported with a prearranged 15-minute barrage.

The operations order called for Roy Murray's 4th Ranger Battalion to lead the assault onto the beach and securing the flanks for the 1st and 3rd Battalions and attachments to move inland. The landing hit Maiori at 0310 hours on the 9th of September, two months after the invasion of Sicily, which had concluded by the end of August. Not much time, in fact only four weeks, had been available to train the new Ranger replacements. Murray's 4th had to secure the beachhead, eliminate any coastal defenses, establish a roadblock on the narrow coastal road to the west, the left side of Maiori, and protect this flank from any counterattacks. The 1st Rangers were to land 15 minutes later, make it up the pass for about 10 miles, and occupy the right side of it on Monte San Angelo di Cava, overlooking Route 18 between Cava and Nocera. Lastly, Dammer's 3rd Battalion was to follow 30 minutes after Murray had hit the beach, move inland, and occupy the left side of the pass on Monte di Chiunzi and be prepared to attack the town of Pagani.

Occupying these two peaks would protect the flank of the Commandos and the anticipated attack inland. Company B of the 83rd Mortars was attached to Dammer. From that location it could reach Pagani and Nocera with its 4.2-inch tubes. The newest addition was the Cannon Company (provisional) comprised of four 75mm half-tracks under the command of the bravest of the brave, Captain Charles Shunstrom from the 1st, and Lieutenant Otis Davey of the 3rd Battalion. This mobile artillery unit was to land 60 minutes after the initial landing, and drive up the narrow and tortuous dirt road to a point where it snaked its way to the slopes of Monte di Chiunzi and the Plain of Naples below. This mission called for Shunstrom to protect the Rangers deployed around the pass and to protect the beachhead from approaching German armor, traveling south. Having experienced vulnerability during the armored counterattacks at Gela, firepower was a welcomed addition. Whether or not Darby was the creator of the unit is unknown, but it certainly must have appealed to him. Dammer recalled Darby saying he wanted cannons after those tricky first days. Additionally, being on the far flank of the invasion meant that the Ranger battalions were isolated and reinforcing them would be problematic, other than with naval gunfire, which did prep the immediate area 15 minutes prior to the assault. Hence the additional four 75mm half-tracks.

The planning and use of the Rangers for this operation was not what the Rangers had been intended to do: quick, daring, night-time raids by a light-armed, highly mobile strategic strike force.

> Murray believed Darby never stressed the Rangers' uniqueness to its fullest extent. Murray thought that Darby chose not to emphasize the Rangers' special character out of fear that they might draw hostility from more conventional commanders and their units. If true, Darby was a more timid man than his other behavior indicates. More

probably, Darby was growing to see the Rangers as less unique than many Rangers would like to believe. Dammer, who spoke of Darby as having a "fetish for firepower," was underscoring an essential element of Darby's military background—he was an artillery man by training and previous assignment. As such, he may not have had a doctrinaire commitment to the idea that the Rangers were by definition a light Commando-like strike force. They were being used too often for conventional missions, and Darby wanted them armed heavily enough to succeed in those missions. He acted pragmatically; lightness was traded in favor of greater firepower, and the Rangers grew to resemble a conventional regiment in organization, as well as in function.

In the early hours of 9 September, by around 0320, the 4th Ranger Battalion had landed without any problems, although there were the sounds of fierce fighting at Vietri and at the main landing beaches south of Salerno. All Rangers carried extra ammunition and mortar rounds for sustained combat operations. These supplies were left once they passed the highest watermark. Murray's battalion encountered no resistance. The beaches were not mined. They cleared and secured Maiori by 0345 hours with B, C, D, and E Companies occupying the higher ground at the back of the village. During the initial landing, 22-year-old Iowan F/4 Sergeant Don Earwood, who had been attached to No. 3 Commando at Dieppe, encountered an Italian near a lighthouse to the east along the coastal road, shouting that Germans were in the building. The Germans became alerted and opened fire, but the MG nest at the base was immediately silenced by Earwood with a grenade. Running up the circular stairs to the top, he threw in another grenade. And that was that.

Subsequently, B/4 swept through the town again during daylight, just making sure no enemies were left behind. A/4 used the coastal road toward the next small village west, Minori. Minori featured a smaller beach, and A/4 quickly moved into the mountain range. Here they set up on the high ground overlooking the town and the coastal road, where they also established a roadblock, supported by their own demolition teams. Sergeant Wilbur Gallup and his mortar section, using two carts, found a group of 11 Germans asleep who had mined the cliffs near Minori. A German vehicle approached, and the driver was killed. Clearly, the Germans had no idea Rangers had landed along that part of the Amalfi coast. The landing went so well that the Rangers captured two German officers asleep in a hotel in Amalfi, which was just past Minori. Murray's standing orders to his patrol were, he recalled in 1997, "that whenever they caught any German headquarters to look and see if they had any cigars, the cigars were to be brought to me and the information given to the G2. And the fellows have never forgotten that. They send me cigars to this day as individuals. Really, I get maybe 10 to 15 cigars a month from different fellows. It's, I guess, a standing joke."

In the meanwhile, Murray had sent F/4 in the other direction toward Salerno, to neutralize two enemy observation posts and one machine-gun position. They were then to contact the Commandos at Vietri. En route, they ambushed a German motorcycle with side-car and its three enlisted men traveling toward them. The Germans intended to go to Napoli and then on to the island of Capri just outside of the Sorrento Peninsula for rest and recuperation. A few miles on, the Rangers spotted a fortified observation post manned by 11 Italian soldiers, probably unaware that Italy had surrendered. The Rangers killed one, while the rest fled. Shortly thereafter, the front elements of F/4 near Lanterna were hit by small-arms fire from the second observation post held by Italian naval person-nel. The company organized and launched an assault, killing four Italians, with the sole prisoner confirming that they were unaware of Italy's surrender. The Rangers of Fox Company tied in with the Commandos who had landed at Marina Cove near the fishing village of Vietri at 0330 hours, successfully seizing and blocking the road from the fishing village to Cava north of it and blocking Route 18 going south to north. The Rangers set up a roadblock to the east of the Commandos on the windy and narrow coastal road leading to

Salerno by 0600 hours, less than three hours after loading onto the assault landing craft.

With the 4th Battalion executing its first mission, the 1st Ranger Battalion, under Darby, landed later than scheduled. By 0355 hours, the 4th Battalion had guided in the wave of 1st Battalion using color-coded flashlights. The 1st Rangers reorganized and moved inland quickly as planned, seizing the road from Maiori north to Vaccaro where they then established positions on Mount San Angelo. From here, they could interdict any enemy forces using Road 18 from Cava to Nocera—in effect picking up, and tying in, the northwestern section of the road beyond the southern section that was under Commando control. Once the Allied main landings were successful, the mission for the Rangers was to assault downhill and seize Pagani, a suburb of Nocera, to help the Commandos keep the vital road from Vietri north open for the Allied advance.

The Rangers set up in Maiori: Darby in the ramshackle San Francesco Hotel, with others settling in the Palazzo Mezzacapo, today's town hall. They set up camps in the "vegetable gardens" along the seafront and set up their hospitals in the public gardens and in the church of San Domenico. Some trucks parked in what is today Piazza Mercato (Market Place) and served as warehouses. A room on the first floor of the Palazzo d'Amato became an officers' club. "The events of the landing and the advance to the Chiunzi pass still remain imprinted in the minds of the older generation but also of children and grandchildren who have often heard them told. There are those who remember that the Germans had mined the Sant' Antonio bridge, in the Ferriere di Tramonti area [along the Chiunzi Pass]."

The next morning, Baker/4 cleared Minori, capturing one colonel and three enlisted men. Joined by Able/4, they moved closer to Amalfi, establishing a roadblock where they were joined by Charlie and Dog Companies in Amalfi.

The 3rd Battalion under Dammer landed at 0400 hours with the mission of capturing the high ground overlooking Pagani. They encountered no resistance and by 0900 had made their way up the tortuous path north with one company south of the pass, three companies on the ridge north of the pass, and two companies in reserve. One hour later, Dammer had to commit his two reserve companies to cover a wide draw giving access to his position from the Naples Plain below them. These two companies were also tasked with recon patrols to ascertain routes to Pagani and Nocera Inferiore. By 1700 hours, 9 September, Darby had sent A and B Companies of the 1st Battalion as a reserve. They ambushed a three-man patrol and noted the movement of another. The next day, the Rangers drove off a large German patrol of 30 men.

Fox Company of the 1st Battalion was the lead element for the battalion's mission up the winding Chiunzi Pass northward. Following behind were E, D, B, and A Rangers along with C/1 in reserve. Following behind the column was Charlie Company, 83rd Mortars who were vital in this kind of mountainous terrain, being able to lob shells over impediments and ranges.

Captain Chuck Shunstrom's four half-tracks, named after the four card suits, Ace of Diamonds, Ace of Spades, Clover, Club, initially moved west to prevent any enemy armor traveling along the coastal road from the Sorrento Peninsula to Maiori. Soon they were divided into two groups, with one moving up the windy dirt track of the Chiunzi Pass in support of the battalions occupying the mountain ranges.

F/1 bumped into light resistance struggling their way up. They, along with Major Bill Martin, the XO of the 1st Rangers, came onto a German command car, killing one, capturing six others. The vehicle was used by the mortar crew who were lugging up their equipment. Two armored cars blocked the road farther ahead. Using a bazooka, one vehicle was blown up, with the other retreating. The wounded and moaning Germans in the damaged car were killed with a grenade— dropped on top of them by Sergeant Van Skoy. Eventually the battalion moved east and seized the high ground of Mount San Angelo, soaring to 3,000 feet, as planned. The 1st Battalion occupied the high ground opposite the Chiunzi Pass. The 1st and 3rd Rangers held the mountain range. This was accomplished by 0900 hours. They sat on top of the vital real estate crucial for *Operation Avalanche*. The Plain of Naples lay to their front with roads and towns clearly visible. From here on in, patrols and counter-patrols would bump into each other. An unidentified German battalion defended the exits of the mountain passes in front of the Rangers.

Along the Chiunzi Pass, on the western side of it, sat a two-story stone house with thick stone walls, still present today, with steep cliffs on the side of the house and road. It provided a vital observation post for the Ranger headquarters. This property became the aid station for 35-year-old 3rd Ranger Battalion Surgeon Dr. Emile G. Schuster, who'd earn the Distinguished Service Cross, and was aided by Staff Sergeant Robert Reed. Schuster was fearless and greatly admired by the men. He would die of a heart attack on 23 December 1949, at the young age of 41 in Oakland, California. Darby and his call-for-fire element, including British teams to control gun fire, used the upstairs and its clear vantage points. Battle reporters spent considerable time here accompanying Darby and the Rangers, dubbing the house Fort Schuster, as it withstood heavy bombardment by German artillery. Some of the nearby Rangers dug holes or used existing caves dug into the rock alongside the pass. The 83rd Mortars set up well here, protected from direct German artillery fire, and was talked onto targets from the various observation posts dotting the ridge lines. Throughout the day, German counterattacks battered the Rangers. Nighttime patrols tried to infiltrate the Ranger lines and ascertain their locations. Signal flares illuminated the night, not penetrating the mountains as well, but well enough to cast eerie light and shadows across the mountains. To no avail: The experienced and well-entrenched Rangers fought them off. At the dawn's early light and the day, the Germans paid a price with the 83rd Mortars hitting roads and rails in nearby Pagani and Nocera. From the mountaintop, Darby and his HQ saw the ships out at sea. He sat comfortably on the ridges with massive firepower. The 83rd, the Cannon Company, and naval gun fire were available, the latter directed with the help of British fire-control parties. There were problems utilizing this power at night, but it was clearly a force multiplier for Darby. And, of course, he had the bravest of the brave.

Shunstrom's half-tracks wreaked havoc with the Germans. There was never a break, as every single action was part of his tactic of firing his guns, retreating as the German counterbattery opened up, exposing their positions to Allied gunfire. Using his jeep, the Joker, he'd drive back and forth looking for targets. Then he'd order his half-tracks out of their protected positions, hammering the Germans, then retreating. This tactic was employed day and night, and a few Rangers hated the young captain because of it. The Germans would batter the locations the 75mm tracks had occupied before withdrawing, but the Rangers in the mountains had no places to retreat to and suffered throughout the continuous German bombardments instigated by the Cannon Company commander. Needless to say, though, it was Darby who did not put a stop to it. The incoming German rounds sounded like a "boxcar going sideways." Neither a man nor a vehicle of Cannon Company was hit by returning German fire.

Even though the Rangers did their best to occupy the reverse slopes of the ridges, it wasn't always possible, and casualties were inflicted. The greatest threat to the Rangers were the German 88's anti-aircraft or anti-tank guns that fired flat trajectories, unlike mortars or howitzers. Throughout this mountain gun duel, each side tried to shoot through the open channels of the Chiunzi Pass, sometimes with disastrous impact on the Rangers who could not always escape or detect the incoming rounds. Many artillery pieces could not elevate enough to shoot over the ridge, unlike mortars or howitzers, and therefore straight-fired artillery shot along the Chiunzi Pass, which was like an alley, whenever possible. It was here that young Thomas Sullivan, who had saved Bing's life, was killed by an 88 shell when returning from a combat patrol in the Chiunzi Pass—his brilliant life snuffed out and blown apart on 16 September 1943, a week into *Operation Avalanche*. The duels with the Cannon Company resulted in the identification of German locations, and those were passed along the chain of command until the fire-control parties called in fire missions. One such position was an 88 hidden inside a haystack near a typical farmhouse; another example was an ammunition dump in Nocera hit by naval gunfire. Resupply up the mountains was as brutal or more so than it had been for 3rd Battalion in Sicily. Here, too, mules were forced to carry supplies, leading to their many deaths.

One of the first replacements for the degraded Rangers was George Sabine, born 17 May 1922, from New Haven, Connecticut. He joined Fox Company, 3rd Ranger Battalion, where he was treated very well and given instructions by his company commander, 1st LT Warren "Bing" Evans. Training was minimal and consisted of scouting and patrolling taught to him by his company commander and the first sergeant when they went out and consisted of a lot of talking and looking. Sabine called it Boy Scout work. "They needed warm bodies," he wrote years later. Interestingly, for him and some of his replacements, there was no formal integration. He recalled an order issued for the Salerno mission—"shoot anyone opening a window on our line of march." Having returned from a night patrol, he fell asleep or took a nap on his back in a wooded area to the right of the pass—where his battalion occupied the mountain. Some kind of noise woke him up to see a big German soldier with a submachine pistol, looking at the sleeping Rangers. The man wore a bleached Afrika Korps cap and was so close to Sabine that the Ranger made out the blond hair and blue eyes of the soldier. Sabine had screwed up, because his rifle was four feet away. Jumping up, he raced to it, startled the German into action, who fired and killed the second in command behind Sabine, before Sabine shot the German veteran dead. This was his first time in close combat. Sabine's rifle never left his side again. Dragging the corpse away, George Sabine's hands became covered in the dead man's blood. There was no water available, and the blood dried on his hands, unwashed, leaving a permanent nightmare with him. Sabine recalled a fight on 10 September, where they were able to drive off a German patrol, and this might have been when they had fallen asleep after their own patrol. "I never have been without a tool to protect myself from that day on." In combat, he wrote, "you had no choice, you did your best to stay alive, you tried to uphold the standards of your unit, your fellow soldiers meant a lot to you." He rated the German soldiers excellent. He had problems adjusting to life back home. "I could have done better, I could have shot when I didn't." George G. Sabine Jr.

was wounded on 8 December 1943 on Hill 960 around San Pietro. "We were making a night attack and I got hit with a hand grenade, set off a mine first and that knocked me out and then I—it didn't knock me out but it disoriented me. And then my platoon squad sergeant and I got hit with a hand grenade." He ended up fighting with the American-Canadian 1st Special Service Force in the Second Company of the First Regiment, and in A Company of the 474th Infantry Regiment, in France and Germany, before shipping home.

There were individual acts of bravery or perhaps stupidity; but whatever they were, they were Ranger in nature. One such affair saw an unhappily drafted Technician Fifth Grade William J. Fox of Easy 3, formerly with the artillery, desire to go out on patrol, which was denied. In somewhat typical Ranger fashion, he decided to ignore the order and moved down the mountaintop to the heavily bombarded town of Nocera—one of the key interdiction points—where he entered an abandoned home. Changing into civilian clothing that he had found, Fox decided to establish an OP and recorded German movement. Not being the type to sit still, he moved through the town and bumped into an Italian garrison. It bears to point out that some Italians were not inclined to surrender. Some were hardcore Fascists. In this case, the entrepreneurial T/5 Fox managed to find the one unit that was willing to surrender without being killed or shot at. Insisting on an officer to provide a map with all the details of German troop deployments, he promised in return a cessation of bombardment. He and the Italian lieutenant moved back up the mountain, where Fox was promptly arrested for disobeying orders by Lieutenant Larkin. At Darby's HQ, the intel from the Italians was fed to the fire-control teams, who subsequently demolished the German positions. Fox was released and put forward for the Distinguished Service Cross. Interestingly, Fox later thought it had been a mistake to have joined the Rangers, but he wanted to fight the enemy to end the war. Like most, he enjoyed booze and women and noted that there were no Black Rangers, and Blacks were considered inferior to whites, although he felt there was no internal discrimination. T/5 Fox thought the Rangers' combat performances were excellent. He, like others, experienced friendly-fire incidents and eventually would suffer from battle shock and difficulties adjusting to civilian life. He would be wounded on 8 December 1943 and captured on 30 January 1944. He'd make his escape to the Soviet army in April 1945. His experiences at POW camps, including Stalag IIB Hammerstein, West Prussia, Germany, were horrific, as he recalled: "I was in a Jew concentration camp. If I told you, you wouldn't believe the terrible things that happened in these camps." William J. Fox retired to Naples, Italy. Reflecting on the war, he wrote: "Overall, if I had to do it all over again, I would not have joined the Rangers. I would have not joined a combat unit. I would have avoided the draft and service. I would have stayed in the U.S. as a civilian, lived a good life and endured what hardship shortage of goods there were at the time. I said all this, but remember I am the most combat-decorated enlisted man Ranger [of] WWII [in] Italy." Fox was awarded the Distinguished Service Cross, the Bronze Star, the Purple Heart, the Combat Badge, and the Italian War Cross of Military Valor.

On 10 September, Darby requested motorized infantry to patrol various points along the coastal road more effectively. Much to his surprise, Fifth Army accommodated, and attached the 1st Battalion of the 143rd Infantry of the 36th Infantry Division, a tank company of the 751st Medium Tank Battalion, a company of the 601st Tank Destroyer Battalion, Battery A of the 133rd Field Artillery Battalion, and Company H of the 36th Combat Engineers, the latter two in support of C Company, 83rd Mortars. "On the Eleventh, the 1st Battalion, 143rd Infantry, was shifted by LCI's to Maiori and arrived just in time to help beat off an enemy attack south of Pagani." Before their insertion, the advance group of the 143rd found Darby at the Hotel San Francesco, which at the time only had eight rooms with two baths. (Today it is a four-star hotel.) Here, "Colonel Darby greeted us warmly. We all sat down at some tables and discussions were started as to where and how TF 1/143 could reinforce the Rangers. We were now working on a co-equal basis with Darby's Rangers, reporting directly to Headquarters Fifth Army [like the Rangers]." In fact, the 143rd operated independently without any interference or attempts to exercise command over them. Darby and his staff made suggestions, and they learned to listen to Darby's advice. During the meeting, a notable incident occurred, and was preserved by 1st Battalion, 143rd Infantry's intelligence officer Richard Burrage in his memoir, *See Naples and Die!*:

> Colonel Darby spent much of his time driving up to Chiunzi Pass in his Jeep, which was outfitted with a calibre .50 machine gun on a pedestal mount. He was usually upfront with his troops, encouraging them and seeing they were cared for with whatever was available. I well remember that on one occasion when Darby was in his headquarters in the San Francesco hotel conferring with our staff when his driver rushed into the room and told Darby that one of their men had been badly wounded, and the other Rangers had moved him to the ditch alongside the road down in front of the Chiunzi Pass. The driver and Colonel Darby raced to the vehicle and left in a hurry up the road toward Chiunzi Pass. Going down the road Colonel Darby started spraying .50 caliber cartridges on both sides of the road toward suspected enemy positions. They arrived at the area where the wounded Ranger was lying. While Colonel Darby continued his firing, the driver put the Ranger in the back of the jeep. The driver then started in reverse back up the hill with Colonel Darby still blazing away with his machine gun. He passed the blockhouse in Chiunzi Pass in a cloud of dust and continued on downhill, still in reverse, to the local monastery in Maiori where the 10th Medical Unit (Br) was located. This was typical of Colonel Darby's support of his troops. They believed in him and knew that if they got in trouble up there in the hills he could and would come to their assistance.

The cooperation between the Rangers and the Dogfaces went well. Staff of the 143rd accompanied Darby on tactical walks covering the terrain. Their medical doctor worked out an evacuation plan with 3rd

Ranger Battalion's medical officer, Captain Emile Schuster. Medical facilities were set up in Maiori's monastery. The reason the 143rd was sent to the Rangers was that at that time the floating reserve for the landings at Salerno had been committed elsewhere. On 11 September, Ranger outposts reported the movement of 200 Germans through Sala but timely arrival at 1100 hours, by the 1st Battalion, 143rd Infantry added to the defensive perimeter of 3rd Ranger Battalion. This in turn allowed one Ranger company to move south to reinforce the southern part of the pass. By midafternoon, at 1430 hours, a small enemy patrol exploited a gap between the two Ranger battalions but was driven off by mortar and Cannon Company fire, leaving behind a German captain and one enlisted man from an unidentified unit of the Hermann Göring Division. Despite the reinforcements, the bulk of infantry fighting in the mountains remained with the Ranger battalions, who were constantly exposed to incoming rounds. During that time, the 4th Ranger Battalion acted as a Fireman's Brigade. Two companies pushed toward Sorrento, where they found it unoccupied and ate a dinner at the Tromantano Hotel, after which they took control of a trolley car and set up a roadblock at Vico Equence just in time to destroy an armored car with bazookas. With the help of engineers, elements of the 4th Battalion destroyed a bridge where the Amalfi drive cuts across the Sorrentine Peninsula from the north.

Captain Alex Worth writes in the Infantry Journal in 1945 that "from September 9 to about September 18 we plastered that valley with naval guns chiefly, because during that time most of the targets required long-range artillery. Convoy after convoy, and armored column after armored column, were fired upon." The brutal exchanges of artillery barrages saw the Rangers suffer heavily too. The terrain, the weather, the rounds fired directly through the Chiunzi Pass, coupled with other incoming artillery and German combat patrols, reduced the Rangers' strength. The mosquitoes in Sicily had added their firepower in reducing Ranger numbers with malaria and diarrhea. Poorly supplied, the Rangers endured worse than they had in training in the highlands of Scotland. During this time, noted Ranger historian Bob Black writes of a memorable encounter for Ranger

Lehmann—the Ranger who had been kind to an elderly Arab in North Africa. Lehmann remembered an old Italian farmer fondly. The old man crawled around the Ranger foxhole positions, dragging a basket along with him, handing out cheese balls. He did not speak English but exchanged handshakes with the men. Other men suffered through the arduous combat against Germans with small firefights erupting throughout their positions.

One Ranger, Ron Yentzer, killed a German but was badly wounded when his weapon malfunctioned, sending his helmet downslope. He had to put his fingers into his wound, watching the Rangers battle Germans from a foxhole. He watched as one Ranger picked up a bazooka and jammed it into the ground, ignoring that it required an unobstructed backblast area, and fired it—causing it to explode and tear off the man's head. The Rangers moved, having to leave Yentzer behind after patching him up briefly and probably giving him morphine. He remembered a German soldier looting him of his watch and wallet. Finally, the Rangers returned and Yentzer was placed on a make-do shelter half cum litter, but the litter bearers dropped him when hit by shrapnel from nearby explosions. Coming to, he saw Germans carrying him who also dropped him when incoming fire hit the area. He was sure he had been captured but was informed otherwise. Making it to a boat, he was hoisted up and promptly dropped by sailors when the Luftwaffe attacked the boat. He survived.

As the campaign raged on, Darby received more attachments to his command to protect the flank and hold on to gained grounds in the Sorrento Peninsula. The 325th Glider Infantry Regiment, minus one company, of the 504th Parachute Infantry Regiment, along with more artillery and signal troops, arrived. At this point, Lieutenant Colonel Bill Darby commanded over 8,500 men, and this after the Army had refused to grant him a regimental headquarters for his three Ranger battalions. From 13 September over the next 15 days, the Germans launched attacks, probing for gaps, to drive the Rangers out. Darby's naval guns supported for the better part of 19 days, hitting the most beautiful targets, and here at Salerno all the previous ship-to-shore errors were made up for.

The fighting was vicious and was a signal of things to come. The Report of Action of the 1st Ranger Battalion dated 29 March 1943 details the minutiae of the fights from 8 November to 13 December. Firefights between combat patrols, artillery exchanges, air attacks, and even the use of a loudspeaker to speak to the Germans—the Germans reached back out with heavy fire. It was a sign of things to come while fighting in the mountain ranges of Italy. An observation point on the northern ridge of Mount Chiunzi was overrun, forcing the Ranger from the post.

Meanwhile, the left, where Murray's 4th Rangers were, had to deal with Germans swinging around the Sorrento Peninsula, trying to exploit gaps between the 4th and 3rd Ranger Battalions. Murray moved fast, sending A, C, and D Companies inland through the Agerola road in the Lattari Mountains, going north through the Pimonte Pass. Here they established a roadblock on 12 September, at a crucial tunnel forcing the Germans to use the coastal road, where they encountered stiff Ranger resistance along with two 75mm half-tracks of Shunstrom's Cannon Company. All of this was happening within a few short days of the landing. A/4 occupied Mount Pendola, E and F/4 seized high ground off the coastal road overlooking Castellammare on the Gulf of Naples. A patrol was sent to reconnoiter the town but found it occupied by the Germans. In the ensuing firefight, 12 Germans were killed with one Ranger killed in action, forcing the Ranger patrol to withdraw. Stealthy Ranger scouts stayed behind and gathered intelligence, noting them with sketches of anti-aircraft positions. The last patrol into the town made a quiet entrance, riding a streetcar before getting off and buying ice cream at a local stand. The Italians did not seem to notice they were Americans—and if they noticed, they certainly remained composed. Oddly, Germans were not to be found in the immediate area.

The Ranger OPs on the high grounds caused the Germans a lot of trouble, leading to vicious counterattacks, 12 according to Darby. And at one time, his units were cut off and almost ran out of ammunition. One handwritten message on Italian stationery, labeled "Amalfi"— *Panorama e Terra dell'Albergo Riviera*—says "could use more troops I'm spread out like a fart PS send tobacco." The Salerno Landings detail the first few hectic days for the Rangers:

Sep 11—0208 hours

Darby's Ranger position intact on high ground south of Pagni-Nocera. Reinforced it this afternoon with 82nd Airborne Division detachment of 450 men. Will also reinforce Rangers tomorrow over Maiori beach with composite U.S. force taken from VI Corps of one infantry battalion reinforced with tanks, tank destroyer and artillery. Aerial reconnaissance today indicates many motor movements from south of Salerno sector to the north and from Eboli area to the east and north through Potenza. Other motor movements observed are from north to the south in the direction of Salerno. It may be deduced from this that new German strength from south may avoid the Salerno area and pass around into the Naples area.

    1946 hours

Rangers are very short of ammunition

2300 hours

German resistance throughout has been determined.

Sept 12—1200 hours

LCTs transferred weapons and troops from X Corps beaches to Rangers at Maiori.

For the Rangers at the base of Chiunzi at the town of Sala, three Germans destroyed a vital bridge, but members of 3rd Battalion killed one of them, a member of the parachute division of the HG Division. This was on the 12th of September, when 3rd Battalion was in fisti-cuffs with units of the Hermann Göring Division. One small German patrol was ambushed and its leader killed, revealing him to be a parachutist of that division. This 0600-hours engagement was followed by a much larger attack of 200 troops who were routed by the concentrated fire of six 60mm mortars. Captain Kitchens, the foolish young officer from Mass-a-Gramiglia, had learned his lessons well and ordered a massive resupply of grenades, fighting off 200 soldiers of the Hermann Göring Division, showering them with grenades rolling down the slopes—instant artillery, followed by the pre-designated 60mm mortar fire. At least nine Germans lay dead at the bottom of the slope with bandages littering the area indicating heavy losses.

By this time, all forces, including any and all rear-echelon troops, were mustered to the front as riflemen throughout the Salerno landings as the Germans pushed to expel them. The Germans looked close to succeeding at pushing the Allies into the sea, forcing General Mark Clark into a hard decision—to abandon or stay and fight. It was the latter, with reserve units pushed into the bloody fray.

On 14 September, the 4th Ranger Battalion was relieved from duty on Mount Pendola by the 504th PIR and rejoined the other two Ranger battalions and took up positions northwest of Polvica. A/4 and D/4, along with H Company of the paratroopers, attacked German positions at Gregano, but were pushed back to Mount Pendola. From 15 September to 27 September, Murray's battalion fought numerous engagements against German paratroopers.

Darby ordered elements of the 83rd up the tortuous pass with Italian civilians laboring the heavy equipment up the steep and winding road. This was done to be able to engage German targets farther inland. Three days later, some of the 4th Ranger relieved the 3rd Ranger Battalion to bivouac west of Polvica. On 18 September, nine days after the landings, the 325th Glider relieved the 1st Ranger Battalion that had seen and fought off seven counterattacks.

The same day, Dog/4, with one engineer officer, one signal officer, and five enlisted, attached and moved down the Chiunzi Pass toward Sala to reconnoiter the road to discover any obstacles from bridge demolitions to minefields and other emplacements. In a quick and nasty firefight, the Rangers were driven back by heavy resistance, suffering six wounded in action and three Rangers missing.

Eventually the Rangers would have to return to push the Allied offensive inland. The 1st and 3rd launched an attack and overcame what little resistance there was, all the while exposed to heavy artillery and mortar fire. But this attack was launched at night, the preferred Ranger time to operate. Despite this and to the credit of the German soldier, a number of Rangers were killed and wounded in this action. By now, the Ranger battalions had been steadily losing men to combat, but also to disease and exhaustion.

There was little activity on the 19th of September 1943, and several battle correspondents arrived in Maiori visiting Darby. Among them were Richard Tregaskis and Robert Capa of *Life* magazine, as well as Will Lang. They moved up to Fort Schuster, also known as Schuster's Mansion, or Land's Lodge, named after the Battalion XO of the 143rd who had said "see Naples and Die," after staying at the old stone house and overlooking the valleys below. Major James L. Land, of Chester, South Carolina, would die at Guigliano, a suburb of Naples, along with 11 others. The journalists met legendary Ranger officers Schneider, Murray, and Shunstrom during their visit to the embattled area. The pass the Americans occupied was so vital, Tregaskis notes, that the "Nazis are struggling feverishly to recover." The drive to Mairoi was breathtaking in the "steepness of the cliff, and the jewel-like brilliance of the blue Gulf of Salerno." At a ramshackle Victorian house, presumably the Hotel San Francisco, they met the hero of Gela, Colonel Darby, who moved quickly and spoke with decision, briefing them on the campaign so far, pushing off the Heinies from the surrounding mountains including a German engineer battalion and the counterattacks the Rangers had fought off successfully so far. They departed with Darby telling his staff, "I want to give this a hell of a pasting. I want to start out with the mortars again tonight. I want to blast the crap out of this hill, and the living daylights out of that hill. The chemical mortars will cover that one with WP (white phosphorus)." They received a tour of the local hospital set in a church where "human limbs in heavy casts protruded in grotesque positions."

By nighttime, the journalists had made their way to Fort Schuster again and its three-foot-thick walls. Frank Capa writes about the difficult conditions the aid station operated under. "There was a large table in the middle of the room that was used for emergency operations. When I entered, the medics were preparing some wounded for the trip down to the church of Maiori. I had been taking pictures of war and blood since Spain [civil war], but even after seven years the sight of torn flesh and fresh blood brought my stomach up close to my eyes. Near the door, the dead, in the center, the wounded, and in the far corner, the barrels [of wine] and the photographer."

Some more details were preserved during their visit. They met the staff of the 143rd and were briefed about their mission to reinforce the sector. Major Max Schneider joined them to give the newly arrived unit the "dope" on the situation. The location was ideal for them to observe the nearby 4.2-inch mortars hammering the hill, exploding with "showers of white clouds rising like luminous fountains from a spur on the slope which led to the plain of Naples. The big WP shells lit up the area like a photographer's bulbs flashing in the dark." It was also during their stay here that battle reporter Richard Tregaskis watched Cannon Company in action:

> This evening I had a chance to watch one of Captain Shunstrom's half-tracks in action. I heard the rattling and roaring of the vehicle as it moved into position in the pass, shortly after dark, and began firing. From the front door of Fort Schuster, I could see the flashes of orange flame just beyond the cleft of the pass. Each blast of the big gun illuminated not only the vehicle itself, but the open mountainside around. Anyone on the far-stretching Naples plain below could have seen the blast. The crew knew they were inviting counter-fire. But only by pushing their half-track smack into the open could they train their gun on the nose of rock below, where there was supposed to be a concentration of German troops. For a long time, the crew worked feverishly by the light of the blinding cannon flashes, firing as rapidly as they could; they were working against time. Sure enough—the German batteries began to boom, and shells whistled our way. The half-track rattled and clattered through the pass in reverse, like a boxer side-stepping a counter-blow.

There were some Rangers, Les Kness and Randall Harris of Gela fame, both serving with the 4th Battalion in Italy, who thought Charles Shunstrom to be a psychopath or impulsive, endangering the lives of Rangers and occasionally causing near-fatal friendly-fire incidents, although others, including Alex Szima, thought otherwise. "Every recallable incident of the Maiori landing and the highlight all Rangers will agree, was Capt. 'Chuck' Shunstrum's Cannon Company. Chuck always fought the war to the tune of 'Audacity' and a 75mm cannon just meant a bigger weapon." But it was also Kness, who was at the Chiunzi Pass and under heavy 88 shelling, who had threatened to shoot a medic if he failed to join his wounded comrades to patch them up. Things were complicated in combat.

Richard Tregaskis made his way back to Ranger Battalion Headquarters at the hotel. He encountered Majors Max Schneider and Roy Murray deep in discussion about the intelligence they had received in the form of two ragged Italians looking over a map spread out in front of them. One of the Italians spoke with a Brooklyn accent, while Schneider handed the journalist a note the men had carried from Angri, a town of 20,000, to the southwest of Pagani. The letter asked for the Americans to shift their gunfire, sparing the town and its residents where many had been wounded and killed and buildings destroyed. Murray wrote a note to be taken back. It read: "We will try to respect your wishes, as we certainly do not intend to harm the Italian population." Visiting the hospital one more time, on 21 September, he encountered a young lieutenant from the 143rd he had met at the shell-battered stone house of Fort Schuster. "I noticed almost immediately that he was a case of battle fatigue. He looked lost. His eyes were sunken; his chin and neck jerked nervously in spasms, like a turtle's head poking out of its shell. But he recognized me, and confided 'It's the God-damnedest feeling. I can't sleep, and I can't rest. I can't stop the jitters.'"

Four days later, there had been no changes to the Ranger battle lines. Captain Worth of F/1 wrote, "The one time a force was strong enough to jeopardize our positions, actually penetrate through our line, a final telling blow was awaiting them. The force of about three hundred German with LMGs [light machine guns] and mortars in support was allowed to pass through a gap upon which the fire of twelve 60mm mortars, four 81mm mortars, and two machine guns was amassed. The result was devastating. From observation of the shelled area we believed that only a very few, if any, Germans returned to their lines."

On 26 September, the eastern half of the troops on the Sorrento Peninsula were under Darby's command. An overall Allied attack was launched the following day, since the Germans had started their withdrawal three days earlier, with Fifth Army finally muscling its way forward. Slowly but surely, the Allies broke out of their respective areas of operations while Darby remained in the Sala-Polvica-Pigno area to protect the flank of the offensive. During this time, the Rangers lost the town of Sala on 27 September at 2006 hours and recaptured it the next day by 1728 hours—all within the space of half a day. Three days later, the Rangers came down the mountains into Pagani, and then headed west to Castellammare, where they established bivouac. Murray's battalion joined them there.

On 1 October, Allied forces entered Naples and moved on to the next German defensive line—the Volturno River. By 2 October, Darby's Rangers moved into Naples, past the ruins of Pompeii. The port lay in utter destruction. But the Rangers had done their job and settled in the botanical gardens about 10 acres in size. The Germans, during their retreat, had booby-trapped a few houses, and, fortunately for the Rangers, Darby cut them no slack and made them live in tents. Once cleared, the Ranger officers established their Officer Mess in a restaurant where they did what Rangers do: drink to excess, with Herm Dammer leading others, including experienced singer Alvah Miller, in belting out German songs, with the musically inclined Darby chiming in at the appropriate times with *"Ach du Lieber."* Thinking those were Germans left behind, some paratroopers barged in, and its commander, a fellow West Pointer who was not close to Darby, got into a heated argument that eventually simmered down. Back to drinking. Many of the enlisted Rangers visited local whorehouses.

For some of the Rangers, this had been their fourth amphibious assault: *Jubilee* at Dieppe, *Torch* at Arzew, *Husky* at Sicily, and *Avalanche* at Salerno. For most, it was their second. The battalions had lost at least, if not more, 28 killed, 66 wounded, and 9 missing, not including non-battle-related injuries. The battalions had been ground down in the tortuous mountains of the Amalfi coast and used as line infantry fighting veteran German troops. Roy Murray wrote "that a report cannot begin to describe the rough terrain that the troops operated in. The men of the battalion, I feel, should be highly commended for their splendid spirit they showed working under extremely difficult conditions." There were far more casualties because of malaria, jaundice, fallen arches, non-combat injuries, and whatnot. They needed to recuperate from their fight to capture and hold the Sorrento Peninsula, which secured the western flank of the hard-fought, and nearly lost, Allied invasion. For this combat action, the 1st and 3rd Battalions received the Presidential Unit Citation, the second award for the 1st Ranger Battalion, and Darby was awarded his second DSC and a promotion to full-bird colonel. Murray's men were allowed to wear mustaches. They had done so since their founding at Nemours, Algeria, with Murray taking command on 29 May 1943. "All men in the 4th Rangers wore mustaches. Only unit in WWII to do so. Not approved officially but tactically allowed."

During recuperation, for the 4th this was in beautiful Sorrento, 27 NCOs of the Ranger Force were awarded battlefield commissions. While here, Major Max Schneider, the executive officer for Roy Murray and a highly rated officer by Vaughan, Darby, and the men, was transferred to Supreme Headquarters in London to assist in planning the Normandy invasion slated for mid-1944. Schneider would prove to be an excellent commander during that landing, leading the 5th Ranger Battalion on its glorious amphibious assault at Omaha Beach:

> The President of the United States of America, authorized by Act of Congress, July 9, 1918, takes pleasure in presenting the Distinguished Service Cross to Lieutenant Colonel

(Infantry) Max Ferguson Schneider (ASN: 0-384849), United States Army, for extraordinary heroism in connection with military operations against an armed enemy while serving as Commanding Officer of the 5th Ranger Infantry Battalion, in action against enemy forces on 6 June 1944, at Normandy, France. In the initial landings in the invasion of France, Lieutenant Colonel Schneider led the 5th Ranger Infantry Battalion ashore at "H" hour on D-Day in the face of extremely heavy enemy rifle, machine gun, mortar, artillery and rocket fire. Upon reaching the beach Lieutenant Colonel Schneider reorganized his unit. During this reorganization, he repeatedly exposed himself to enemy fire. He then led his battalion in the assault on the enemy beach positions, and having accomplished this mission led them up a steep incline to assault the enemy gun emplacements on the top of the hill. The destruction of these enemy positions opened one of the vital beach exits, thereby permitting the troops and equipment which had been pinned down to move inland from the beach, with the result that reinforcements could be landed from the sea. Lieutenant Colonel Schneider's leadership, personal bravery and zealous devotion to duty set an inspiring example to his command and exemplify the highest traditions of the military forces of the United States and reflect great credit upon himself and the United States Army.

Max, a Darby Original, the recipient of the Silver Star and Distinguished Service Cross, would die by suicide with a self-inflicted gunshot wound while on peacetime active duty in South Korea in 1959. Perhaps it had been battle fatigue, perhaps it had been the surgically implanted silver plate in his skull—no matter the reason for his suicide, he was an exceptional Darby Ranger.

Worse was yet to come.

A BROKEN WINDOWPANE
Stolpmünde, Germany
MAY 1944

The 60 miles north had been covered. The plan had gone well. North was their escape route. North to the Baltic Sea, north to neutral Sweden. They were close. Throughout their trip, Carl Lehmann had cut quite a swath in his wake, from burning down barns to cutting phone lines and emplacing stakes on rail tracks. He was a Ranger's Ranger.

By now, Lehmann and his non-Ranger partner had survived a night up in the trees after his partner had killed a piglet and its mother was rightly angry. They only traveled at night and only for short distances. Taking a short break to orient himself, Lehmann climbed a tree, and, lo and behold, before him was the Baltic coast. They had made it this far. Soon they'd get to the shore and find a way north. Now in the deep woods, and coming just around a sharp bend, Lehmann froze. A beautiful, no, magnificent buck stared back at him. Both creatures on the run from death, wanting to live without interference. For ever so brief a moment, there was a connection with the animal; then it took a great leap and disappeared. Moving on, at dawn, he and his partner found small summer beach houses common in the area. Here, they slept for the first time on mattresses. A luxury for Lehmann, who had spent considerable time on the ground and in tents.

The men woke to a forceful wind accompanied by pelting rain that made it hard to see or hear; but soon enough they found a boat house with a small boat with mast and sail, ready to be pushed into the sea to freedom. But his partner did not want to leave under these conditions. Lehmann argued. Here was an opportunity instead of walking in enemy-held territory to Sweden. They returned to the small beach house and argued intensely. The storm, like their anger, rose.

They decided to follow the original plan and to conduct a reconnaissance of Stolpmünde, which was very close. Lehmann led the way to the river's mouth, where they found boats: But the weather conditions were admittedly lousy. They spent a few days observing, ready to hide in a departing boat soon. But the Ranger admitted temporary defeat, and they retreated back to the row of beach houses near the town with the ongoing storm savagely whipping the area.

It was a black night as they got close to one of the small beach houses. Lehmann froze. Something wasn't right. He sensed it. He smelled it. He slowly crept forward, the darkness cloaking his well-practiced movements. Closer and closer . . . a broken windowpane. Okay, he thought, as he moved forward. He could take a quick look inside the house and see what had alerted his Ranger senses. Lehmann leaned cautiously forward . . . Germans!

The Mother Church of Gela. This square saw heavy fighting with the Italian defenders and, subsequently, with the heroically desperate tanks during their attempts to dislodge the Rangers. (US ARMY SIGNAL CORPS)

One of the German-captured French tanks, the R35, given to the Italian army early in the war. It was woefully inadequate as the war progressed but still posed a threat to the Rangers in Gela. The Italian tankers paid dearly for their valiant efforts to drive the Rangers out of Gela. (US ARMY SIGNAL CORPS)

The first of two beaches at Rocca Mollarella. Behind the camera is the town of Licata. On the other side of the rock is the second beach. In the background is part of the higher ground surrounding the area which the Third Ranger Battalion needed to secure to capture Licata. (AUTHOR)

The Disney-like mountain fortress of Butera just inland from Gela. It was a key objective. Reporter Jack Belden accompanied the Rangers on their night operation who noted the death and destruction the battle around Gela had inflicted on the Italians, and Shunstrom added to his lore during this action. (AUTHOR)

Oklahoma Cherokee and Ranger Thomas "Chief" Bearpaw as a military policeman in post-war Japan. A veteran of the North African campaign, he joined the Rangers in time for the invasion of Sicily, Mairori, Chiunzi Pass, Anzio, and the final battle at Cisterna where he was captured. He fled in the last days of the war and was rescued by approaching American tanks. He was inducted into the Oklahoma Military Hall of Fame in October 2024. (GEORGE BEARPAW)

Battlefield commissioned Lieutenant Gino Mercuriali, who was an original Darby Ranger. He was present in all campiagns except for the final one at Anzio. He had suffered trench foot in the mountains of Venfaro a few months earlier. (US ARMY SIGNAL CORPS)

Mairoi with its rocky beaches and the incredible challenging terrain of the Chiunzi Pass and mountains the Rangers had to secure and hold during the invasion of nearby Salerno. (AUTHOR)

The saddle, almost half-way to the top, and in between the two rock formations, was Darby's command post during the heavy fighting of the Winter Line near Venafro. It was located on the southern slope of Mount Corno. (AUTHOR)

The Roman trail in 2024. (LUCIANO BUCCI / WAR MUSEUM WINTERLINE VENAFRO)

A Ranger litter party at the Roman trail. To approach the area there were only mule trails. Here is the most important one, the Portella pass, which linked Venafro and Conca Casale. The Portella pass is a natural creek on the trail used by the Rangers as a First Aid station. (LUCIANO BUCCI / WAR MUSEUM WINTERLINE VENAFRO)

Luciano Bucci, President of the Association of Winterline Venafro, and author walking the Ranger area of operations. (AUTHOR)

Battlefield commissioned James J. Altieri. An "Original" and veteran of North Africa, Sicily, and Italy, he served in Roy Murray's Fourth Battalion from Sicily on to the bitter end at Cisterna. (ALTIERI/BAHMANYAR COLLECTION)

January 22, 1944, American engineers at work to install the tethered balloons at the Paradis on the Sea, the White Casino, headquarters of the Rangers Command. The White Casino was the center of the Rangers' amphibious landing at Anzio where Darby landed. (PATRIZIO COLANTUONO, ANZIO MUSEUM)

Airforce veteran and good friend Angelo T. Munsel on the left, with President of the Anzio Museum, Patrizio Colantuono, and author on the right. Angelo had previously accompanied the author in 1999 to Anzio and Cisterna. (AUTHOR)

Angelo Musel, who served for many years as superintendent of the American Battle Monuments Commission, Alberto Augstini, property owner, and the author on the Cisterna battlefield. This field is just south-west of the Calcabrini House, which served as HQ for the beleaguered Rangers.(AUTHOR)

The Mecca of the Rangers, the Black Rock, at the former site of the Sunnylands Camp, Carrickfergus, Northern Ireland, 1992. A 50th Anniversary reuinion saw a dozen of Darby's Rangers visit Carrickfergus. To show their appreciation, Carrickfergus Borough Council erected a permanent granite memorial stone. Two years later the US Rangers Museum was opened on the grounds of the Andrew Jackson Cottage, in Boneybefore. (THE CARRICKFERGUS MUSEUM & CIVIC CENTER)

8

THE WINTER LINE AT VENAFRO

THE BREAKOUT FROM SALERNO, COUPLED WITH THE GERMAN WITH-drawal, saw the Rangers in bivouac. The attritional campaign, one of the bloodiest of the war, was to continue against the Germans' clever use of terrain to slow the inevitable Allied advance. Since the main campaign was to be in France, it came as little surprise that the Italian campaign was always a secondary front. The buildup of the invasion force in the United Kingdom kept draining matériel and men from the Italian front. If the fighting in the Sorrento Peninsula was hellish, then the next fight was hell frozen over. The valuable lesson German commanders learned from their defeat at Salerno was the overwhelming power of Allied naval guns. To that end, for the Germans, the fight had to be taken away from the coastal areas and moved inland. Defending successive lines of fortifications intended to make the Allies pay for every advance to the north—to Rome. Yet, the Germans knew their own weaknesses of needing to hold key terrain. They also knew the Allies held the initiative and that the German divisions were nowhere capable of withstanding any heavy attacks. Morale was not the best and any successes would probably not increase it.

The Rangers had entered Naples on 2 October 1943. On the 11th of October, Darby was tasked with getting his three Ranger battalions ready for the next phase of combat. For Darby, this meant he and others, notably the good-looking Captain Charles Shunstrom, started looking for replacements to fill the depleted ranks. Throughout the war, like all wars, the bloody infantry suffered the greatest casualties.

For the Rangers, this was a harder loss to overcome. New blood was needed and had to be trained. This would often not be possible. But a Ranger-thing was the return of wounded or sick men who came back to their Ranger units, even so far as by going Absent Without Leave. It helped fill the ranks. Two Ranger battalions were ordered to be ready for combat deployment by 20 October, while another was to be ready by 27 October. The 1st and 3rd Battalions were stationed in San Lazzaro near Amalfi, with the 4th at Sorrento. There was not much time to refit and prepare the Ranger Force for upcoming combat operations.

Slowly but surely during the middle of September, German troops had withdrawn north of the Volturno River. The river stood 130 meters above sea level, and the valley running through it was flat, sometimes rising to 40 meters. The river had a width of 150 to 200 feet with a depth of 3 to 5 feet. Its embankments rose 5 to 15 feet, and during autumn's rainy season it could swell and move swiftly. Rivers thus were an excellent means of slowing down advances. The purpose for the German command in defending the Volturno Line was simple: It had to buy enough time to build out subsequent defensive lines to the north. The series of defensive lines relied on the mountainous terrain and rivers, running east to west, starting, for the Americans, at the Volturno River, and all the way to just north of Rome. The two main routes traveling north were Highways 6 and 7. The effort to dislodge the defenders became attritional. To get to Rome, the key objective, the Allies had to cut through the defenses of the Volturno/ Biterno Rivers first, then move north against the Barbara Line until they hit the Gustav Line, which was the main defense that cut Italy in half using the Sangro River as its marker. To its front was a bulge of a defensive line, centered around Cassino—the Bernhardt Line. There would be two or three more lines to cross after that to reach Rome.

The first obstacle for the Americans coming out of Salerno and Naples was the Volturno River. Beyond it were the mountain ranges of Monte Cassino, Monte Sammucro, and Monte Corno. It was at Monte Corno where Darby established his command post at the *Passo Del Urso*—the Bear Pass—during the heavy fighting. The mountain range was continuous, with few gaps in between. Nonetheless, gaps existed. In the American sector, this was the Mignano Gap and Highway Six to the left of Monte Sammucro. On its slope was the village of San Pietro, which saw heavy fighting and was made legendary by war correspondent Ernie Pyle and filmmaker John Huston. Perhaps the greatest and most honest—and depressing—American WWII film, based on Pyle's accounts, was *The Story of GI Joe*. It is based on actions in North Africa and around Cassino. Two of its technical advisors were Roy Murray and Charles Shunstrom.

The Mignano Gap, named after the town on the highway and rail tracks, ran northwesterly from the generally north–south Volturno Valley. The surrounding mountains rose up to 1,000 meters. To its right stood a chain of mountains above Presenzano and Monte Cesima, Cannavinelle Hill, Monte Rotondo, Monte Lungo, and Monte Sammucro. To the left, southwest of this gap, were Monte Camino, Monte la Difensa, and Monte Maggiore. As was the case at the Chiunzi Pass, he who controlled the mountains would control the universe, in this case the lush valleys, Highway 6 traveling north, and the actual Mignano Gap. To the right of Monte Sammucro were the mountains of Corno, followed to the right by Monte San Croce. Off the base of Monte Corno lay the village of Venafro and its railroad. These geographical locations were just across the Volturno River. This, then, was the terrain that would be part of the Winter Line, a place that would be synonymous with a meat grinder of men and beast.

The Fifth Army pushed north of Naples to cross the natural defensive barrier of the Volturno River, to the gap to interdict Highway 6. The British Eighth Army was tasked with breaching the German lines on the eastern side of Italy, then to drive into the Germans' rear while they were busy battling the Americans, whose aim was Rome. The geography of the river dictated combat operations. The 3rd Infantry Division was outside of the loop of the river when it veered south, thus not needing to cross this obstacle. The units inside the loop were the 45th and 34th Infantry Divisions, who'd have to cross the swollen river. All the divisions were overstrength, but not the Rangers. Replacements and their training remained a continuous problem.

In any event, the 4th Ranger Battalion was the most prepared for combat, since it supposedly had not been as active in the fighting in the Sorrento Peninsula, although its casualties exceeded that of 3rd Battalion. Murray's mission, which he chose to accept, was the seizure of high ground near Vallecupa south of Venafro, by crossing the back of the Monte Sesto Campano. Once there, the Rangers could interdict any travel on Highway 6. The old military saying of "We ain't training if it ain't raining" came to the fore. This time it was heavy rains, flooding all-sized waterways, streams or rivers, and cold weather started to flow into the misty mountain ranges, aiding the Germans. Tracks, some still built up by Roman stone steps, were washed out, mud was everywhere and on everything and on everybody, the biting cold numbed the body and the mind. The mountain ranges became casualty central. Getting supplies of any kind seemed Sisyphean. Typical of the narrow tracks and roads that peppered the mountain ranges, so, too, did the defenders pepper the attackers with minefields, pre-designated mortar and small-arms fire, and, cruelly, the ever-present and frightening 88 adding to the misery and death of American soldiers. Battle fatigue would sweep through the companies. For the Rangers, these battles would become a series of confused, messy fights in the freezing mountains near Venafro against a determined, well-prepared enemy. The Ranger battalions were just a small cog in the giant green machine that chewed them up and spat them out without remorse. But these things were yet to come.

Leaving beautiful Sorrento on 1 November 1943, Murray and his mustachioed boys had enjoyed a wonderful time after the tenacious battles they had fought in the area. Trucking 70 miles to their new bivouac area near Ciazzo, the 4th along with the 180th Infantry of the 45th Division hashed out plans for the crossing of the river. Company F, 180th crossed on 2 to 3 November. The Rangers crossed, with little trouble, at 1800 hours on 3 November and were on their way over the mountains west of Sesto Campano toward Highway 6.

Combat was nearly instantaneous. The Rangers marched in single file up the 12 miles of tortuous paths, carrying double loads of ammo and rations. They moved silently, and by dawn they were behind enemy lines on the eastern slope of Monte Cavallo. At 0600 they hit three separate German combat patrols advancing toward them; as Jim Altieri writes, they "were quickly cut down with BAR and rifle fire." Ranger scouts advanced to scope out the area on the summit of Monte Cavallo—and what they saw was a German company in extended formation climbing the eastern slope. Immediately, Captain Walt Nye, Murray's XO, led three companies toward the enemy. The prepared Germans zeroed in with mortars and 88 direct fire while at the same time hammering the strung-out and advancing Rangers with machine guns "from mountain tops on both sides of the wedgelike Monte Cavello." The Rangers immediately took two killed as Nye's D, E, and F went straight at the Germans on the left slopes while Murray with the other three companies assaulted the right side. The attack on the left, western, slope was beaten off by the Germans, with Easy Company getting pinned down during the withdrawal. Simultaneously, another company of 80 Germans arrived on the scene and to the rear of the Rangers, forcing them to retreat in small groups. Here, seven Rangers were captured, while three, including Altieri, stayed low and hid until nightfall. On their way back to their own lines at Monte Sesto Compano, they captured a three-man patrol. During the fighting, the Germans were like fleas on a dog, crawling over the mountains. The Rangers did not make any contact with American units on either flank. The dreaded 88 fired "point blank at individual Rangers, so bitter was the battle." Captured Germans were surprised at the audacity of the Rangers who infiltrated behind their lines unnoticed, and so high was their confidence that they believed "the [Ranger] Battalion was doomed." But the Germans were impressed by the swiftness of the American attacks and their desire for close combat.

The Rangers dug into the mountainside and set up outposts and patrols. Murray made plans with his company commanders during the approaching night—the plan called for an audacious assault onto Monte Rotondo at the juncture of Highway 6 and the San Pietro–Venafro road. The area they wanted to seize was pounded by a sustained 60mm mortar barrage while three companies provided covering fire for the other three companies advancing. Typical infantry tactics, not necessarily Commando-style raids. Spread out in skirmish lines, the Rangers initially surprised the Germans, who recovered very quickly and began to hit back. The incoming fire was too intense for the Rangers to continue their assault. Mortar and machine-gun fire sprayed all around them, killing C/4 Commander Lieutenant James O'Neil. Highly mobile German reinforcements streamed down from surrounding slopes, ready to entrap the 4th Ranger Battalion. A desperate fight was on with BAR men and expert riflemen earning their Ranger Scroll. Outgunned and definitely undersupplied, the Rangers made a tactical withdrawal instead of risking decimation. There were no naval guns to save the day this time around. Murray's men retreated under fire, carrying their wounded back from Monte Rotondo to Monte Cavallo, and, finally, back to Sesto Campano. The wounded were dropped off at a church converted to an aid station under Battalion Surgeon Captain Richard Hardenbrook, who had helped Randall Harris with his gut wound at Gela. There was no rest for the wicked as the German artillery hit the town, wounding more men and destroying the church. The bitterness inflicted on the Rangers in the mountains was hard to handle. "From the good life of Sorrento to the hell of Monte Rotondo was a jarring experience for most of the Rangers involved and only a foretaste of what was to come during the bitter Italian campaign," reflected Altieri years later in an unpublished Ranger history.

Within two days, by 0400 hours on 6 November, Murray's battalion incurred 7 killed, 9 missing, and 21 wounded in action. Considering how small Ranger battalions were, these losses were not insignificant. During those 80 hours of combat, the Rangers had not been resupplied whatsoever. This was the Ranger curse, as it was a redheaded child to the large divisions upon which they had to rely for everything. Murray asked for his battalion to be relieved—which it was, by units of the 30th Infantry Regiment.

On the afternoon of 8 November, Lieutenant Colonel Bill Darby's 1st Ranger Battalion plus elements was attached to the 45th "Thunderbird" Division from Oklahoma—a veteran unit having fought in Sicily and Salerno. Their original patch was the Native

American Swastika: For obvious reasons, this was changed to the Native American Thunderbird. Originally a National Guard outfit, it, too, became federalized. During the Sicilian campaigns, some of its soldiers executed 74 Italian and two German soldiers at Acate, near Ragusa. Nonetheless, the division fought in the bitter Winter Line campaign all the way to the end of the war, liberating the Dachau concentration camp. It was decided that the depleted 4th Ranger Battalion would go back into combat despite Darby, and his XO Major Martin, reminding higher-ups that it was "short of weapons and not in good shape."

The task at hand for the 1st and 4th was to hold a two-mile-long ridge on a north–south axis to the west of Ceppagna, with 1st Rangers relieving in place the 1st Battalion of the 180th while Murray was to hold the unoccupied southern half. The 4th Battalion, with one company of the 83rd Chemical Mortars, and a minesweeping element of the 120th Engineers, took the ridge without encountering any Germans. From there, Murray sent out patrols to the north and west toward Monte Summacro. On the 9th at 0925 hours, they established a roadblock at Ceppagna–San Pietro Infine road at the southern ridge the 4th Rangers held. Things went deceptively smoothly.

For Darby and his 1st Ranger Battalion, things went flawlessly. The battalion moved to Sesto Campana at night on 8 November, and on the next day, when it was safer to do so avoiding friendly fire, relieved the 1st Battalion of the 180th Infantry. The two Ranger battalions were now roughly abreast but holding too much terrain for their small size. That night, the 83rd dropped some mortar shells, but there was no significant action whatsoever. A recon patrol discovered a forti-fied German OP on a ridge of Monte Sammucro overlooking Venafro to the east and San Pietro Infine to the west. The Rangers attacked and drove the Germans off the ridge toward San Pietro Infine, but two days of intense fighting followed. Since they were stretched out, Darby had the men consolidate as much as possible. Realizing the need for more men, Corps HQ attached the 509th Parachute Infantry Battalion to the 45th Division, who in turn sent them to Darby to fill his lines. The next few days saw strong German counterattacks, and since Murray's battalion had already seen hard combat, Darby had his men conduct patrols in front of the 4th's sector to identify any German movement and to give Murray's men some respite. A German counterattack on 13 November drove them out of Ceppagna, but the Rangers reinforced their lines and, coupled with the 83rd flinging death, held on. Early on 14 November, the 4th Ranger Battalion was relieved by the 3rd Battalion, 180th Infantry, which was attached to Darby's command.

The Fifth Army also encountered similar problems as the Rangers. Whatever momentum the Allies thought they had came to a screeching halt within two days. Men were exhausted and needed rest. Replacements and supplies were needed. On 16 November, units were held in position, command was changed, and sectors were reorganized and reassigned to the American divisions. A new offensive was to start at the end of November, permitting time for new personnel and war matériel to be integrated. Aggressive combat patrols were to be maintained throughout this time, to not only probe and locate enemy lines but to also keep the enemy from resting while the Allies regrouped.

During this phase, Lieutenant Colonel Darby sought to have the worn-out 4th Ranger Battalion replaced by Dammer's 3rd. Although approved by the 45th Division and VI Corps, decision-makers at the Fifth Army rejected the request. As Darby biographer Michael J. King notes, "This demonstrates how little control Darby had over the three Ranger battalions." Murray would stick by Darby's side, with the 1st Rangers handling a few more tasks. During the reorganization of the Allied offensive, Darby and Murray had little action in their area of operations. This changed within a few short days when, on 20 November, the Rangers noted an increase in German patrols and infiltration attempts. Clearly, the Germans sought to take advantage of the difficulties being experienced by the Americans. Bitterly fought firefights resumed. The 1st Rangers and the Germans battled it out over defensive positions that were too close to the Rangers. These fights did not find clear winners. Some Rangers who had suffered friends killed in combat didn't want to take German prisoners—the officers talked the men down from their frenzied talk of killing them. Two days later, the 4th joined the action with Able/4 and Charlie/4 securing the 1st Battalion's left flank, while Darby's men continued their attempt to dislodge the Germans entrenched on Monte Corno. Able/4 used mortar fire and expert rifle fire to clear the Germans off the American side of the mountain. Baker and Charlie of the 4th Battalion established an outpost line on the southern slope of Monte Corno. Lieutenant Walt Nye, Murray's XO, noted that although the battalion's morale was good, its "combat efficiency [was] poor due to recent losses," which it had incurred during the early battles.

The brutality of the fighting in the mountains also hit the 1st Rangers hard. Between 21 and 22 November, it lost 9 Rangers killed with 19 wounded. And there was no sign that the Germans would discontinue their attacks. Continuous assaults hit the Ranger positions, finally ending on 27 November. During this week of continuous fights, the Rangers lost at least 70 killed and wounded. Interestingly but not surprisingly, most were fragment wounds, not penetrating skull wounds. Doctor Sommers noted several scalp creases from deflected bullets and shell fragments. The helmet provided very effective head protection. The following day, the 4th Ranger Battalion was relieved by the 3rd Battalion, 180th Infantry, and retired to Caiazzo, 27 miles to the south, to refit and recover. The 1st Ranger Battalion's Report of Action details the variety of combat situations:

> 21 November 1943. At 1800 we shelled enemy positions with 60mm fire and was unable to dislodge them although we had a number of direct hits. At 1200 hours a patrol of Company B made an attempt to drop Molotov cocktails into a cave which was occupied by the enemy, but were driven back by shellfire and fire from auto weapons. At 1400 hours E Company started to sweep to our right to come from behind to the enemies' left. Contact with E Company was broken and we ordered artillery fire to give them cover. At 1750 E Company reached the ridge and said it was clear of enemy, but were not strong enough to occupy

ridge to prevent the return of enemy. During the day very severe heavy caliber shell fire came in our sector and continued intermittently throughout the night.

1 December 1943. At 1655 we sent a patrol from Company A to toss Bangalore at enemy in cave. Company D drove off a counterattack by 1710 by rifle fire. Shelling continued during night.

2 December 1943. At 1040 we sent eight snipers from different companies to go into valley. They met a group of the enemy on patrol and killed six of them. The others ran off.

3 December 1943. At 1515 enemy artillery shell our area. At 1530 center patrol from F Company to attack enemy who are waiting to ambush mule train, but patrol was seen by enemy and they ran off. Enemy continue to shell the battalion area.

10 December 1943. At 1200 gunner on defensive position fired or rocket gun, but she failed to detonate because of soft ground at 1145 patrol from Company D into the southern end of Concasasalle but could not contact the enemy.

11 December 1943. At 1200 the battalion was dive bombed and strafed, but the morale of the men was improved due to the slackening of enemy shelling.

The 1st Ranger Battalion *Log of Action at Venafro, Italy*, beginning 8 November, presents even greater detail, logging in any incident the battalion encountered. It has 10 entries, for example, for 10 November, from the Cannon Company ordered to protect the flanks from Ceppagna to Pozzilli, to the last day's entry of three killed and two wounded. Some entries included lengthy reports observing enemy activity. One highly detailed one, nearly a page long, observed Germans with mules coming in and out of the town of Conca Casale. During that time, it seemed animals were butchered in a house. Another one has recently promoted Lieutenant Van Skoy's patrol waiting to ambush a mule train, only to hear two sharp whistles with enemy MGs opening fire, followed by an attack of unknown number. The enemy suffered two dead, with no casualties for the Rangers. Van Skoy's men were unable to retrieve any papers from the dead and also discovered barbed wire, about one and a half feet off the ground with a nasty surprise: Attached to it were TNT charges buried in the ground. The same day, on 3 December, Captain Shunstrom talked to a Lieutenant of Infantry regarding the use of grenades and firing when orders were not to fire unless the enemy was too close and impeded their withdrawal. Twenty-three minutes later, Shunstrom threw grenades and drew machine-gun fire from behind a rock.

The 4th Ranger Battalion's Operations Journal records similar events. One, early in the campaign, on 12 November, details standard actions. "At 0430 A and D Cos moved to F Company position. Following artillery and mortar preparation A Company with D Company in reserve attacked along ridge line to Hill 630. Slight resistance but no casualties for us. Three enemy killed and 5 officers and 40 men captured. About 30 enemy retired toward S. Pietro Infine." Another entry shows the desperate state and fight the Rangers were in with strong German attacks against their positions. On the 13th of November, a heavy barrage hit all of 4th Ranger Battalion's positions. The right and left flanks rolled back while the center held firm. The enemy attacked in waves of company lines. "Position critical and reinforcements requested of 180th Infantry. Four companies, approximately 148 men, covered front of over 1500 yards." Mortars of the 83rd hit the Germans hard, and, along with accurate fire from small arms, they stopped the assault and entrenched. The journal notes the Germans attempted to withdraw under "protection of two white flags." No such luck, as the Rangers inflicted heavy casualties on them. On this day alone, the 4th suffered five killed, 36 wounded and evacuated, and 3 missing. A couple of weeks later, on 26 November, the Rangers captured a deserter who was an Austrian national serving with the 7th Company, 2nd Battalion, 71st Panzer Grenadiers of the 29th Division.

Major Roy Murray wrote a letter, dated 28 November 1943, outlining issues the Rangers had. The most immediate one was that they were supposed to be a Commando-type unit but lacked a clear directive to do just that. Replacements required a month's worth of training, which was impossible as long as the battalion remained in combat. Therefore, he suggested, some of the new Rangers trained in the U.S. should be plugged into the replacement line for Darby's three battalions. Combat-experienced junior officers from Darby's Rangers should be given command of new Ranger battalions, while older Ranger officers should be sent to Camp Forrest, Tennessee, to train new Rangers. Additionally, the lack of a regimental headquarters needed to be addressed. The administrative aspects also needed be addressed: planning, intelligence gathering, and, importantly, decide if a mission was appropriate for the Rangers. There seemed have been no response to his letter.

The 3rd Ranger Battalion, under Major Dammer, had its own operations. From 29 November to 13 December, they conducted two reconnaissance-in-force patrols against San Pietro Infine and launched an attack and defense near Monte Sammucro at Hills 950 and 1205. "That night the Rangers moved up from Venafro through Ceppagna, and at 2230, led by guides from the 180th Infantry, they began the steep descent toward San Pietro through rain and mist that reduced visibility to a few feet." As they approached the Rangers, though supported by B Company, 83rd and the 133rd Field Artillery, they were pinned down by heavy artillery and mortar fire about a mile east of San Pietro. The purpose of this reconnaissance in force was to make the Germans believe the Allies intended to attack through that area. The next night, the Rangers withdrew with 10 killed and 14 wounded. On 7 December, Dammer's battalion left their assembly area southwest of Venafro, traveled on the road to Ceppegna, where they then turned north at the village, which was nestled along the lower slopes of a ridge leading to Hill 950. Two Rangers, PFC Swain and "Original" Platoon Sergeant Anders Arnbal, both D/3, carried 10 pounds of quarter-pound TNT blocks, taped into one-pound blocks, and a roll of fuse. The detonators were carried by two assault sergeants. When they left, D/3 was the largest company of the battalion, while one company had only 22 enlisted men left. The combat

operations on 8 December, at Monte Sammucro, were initially successful when at 0400 hours the Rangers charged 1,000 yards at the
two machine guns that had opened fire. It took some time, but by
0750 hours and despite the stubborn German defenders, the Rangers
seized the ground. A German counterattack from the northwest
arrived an hour later and drove the Rangers to the northeastern
slopes. They reorganized but failed in their night assault to dislodge
the enemy, where they dug in and waited for the mortars of the 83rd
to arrive. To their great credit, the 83rd dragged their heavy equipment up the tough trails where they then set up to support the Ranger
attack on Hill 950. The next attack occurred in daylight on the 10th
of December when 3rd Battalion launched another assault onto the
crest of the hill. This time they were supported by two battalions of
artillery, firing over 1,600 rounds. They retook the hill and fought
off severe counterattacks over a four-day period. Ranger losses were
severe.

That "damn crazy Indian" T/5 Tommy "Chief" Bearpaw of Able/3
under Lieutenant Palumbo was part of this assault. As a BAR gunner,
he was crucial in ground assaults. Bearpaw carried 14 loaded magazines, 12 in his harness with 2 in his hip pockets. He also carried a .45
pistol with 4 clips of ammo. Additionally, he had 6 frags (fragmentation grenades) on him, along with his Fairbairn-Sykes blade. They
made their way forward, infiltrating German lines until they spotted
a German bivouac with soldiers from the Hermann Göring Division.
Fortunately for the Rangers, the Germans were asleep in their tents
with their rifles stacked in between. The Rangers threw grenades and
fired their guns as the Germans rolled out of their bags, screaming
and shouting. Return fire sprang up and the Rangers started to take
casualties. Pulling the trigger back, Bearpaw and other auto gunners, including Tommy gunners, emptied their magazines rapidly.
Overwhelming firepower was needed and dished out. Still, word was
passed to move to high ground and dig in. But German artillery soon
found them, inflicting casualties on them. The Germans prepared
for a counterattack, but the Rangers of A/3 withdrew under massive
covering fire from what was left of their small-arms ammunition. T/5

Bearpaw fired all but two of his magazines during this fight. The two mags were needed in case he became isolated and had to make his way back to friendly lines. Half of his squad did not return from this action. American artillery batteries hammered the German positions. Tommy Bearpaw made it back to his lines, near the kitchen, and found a tree to slump against. He fell asleep immediately. (Sleeping in a combat zone, although sometimes necessary, could prove fatal, as it nearly had for Ranger Sabine in the Chiunzi mountains.)

During this deployment in early December, heavy shelling impacted the Rangers. Eight men were sent to Ceppagna with battle shock by Medic Sergeant Tom Prudhomme: This included Company Captain Charles Cannon, Staff Sergeant Keberdle, Sergeant Oslund, Corporal Pestotnik, T/5 McMahan, PFC Ford, and Privates Sipes and Roberts. Men had been killed and wounded. Battle fatigue or shell-shock were part and parcel of combat, as were non-battle-sustained injuries. D/3 was left with 24 enlisted and one officer. It was during this time that an Italian attack against the Germans at Monte Lungo met with disaster. Things were bleak. For D/3, however, one night was memorable. At 0400 hours on 11 December, a German patrol approached, consisting of at least a dozen men. Much to the Rangers' delight, the men were close to each other, unusual for the disciplined Germans. Platoon Sergeant Arnbal writes "their helmets [were] glistening in the light mist and their hobnailed boots noisily striking the solid rock trail. Our BAR teams opened up on them simultaneously; others threw fragmentation grenades, the British plastic concussion grenades. Private First Class Swain and I lit our one-pound TNT packets and threw them among the Germans thrashing about below us. It was all over in less than a minute, a mad minute."

During the night of 13 December, they moved to bivouac at Venafro. Roman steps had been hewn into the trails zigzagging up the mountains. Even mules struggled and, at times, refused to stagger up the mountain. During one mission, a sergeant from the 45th Division led the Rangers to San Pietro but got lost and they never completed their mission.

The men loved Darby, not just for being at the front all the time, or for rejecting command of other units: They loved him for being a Ranger. Medic Sergeant Thomas Prudhomme, of Natchez, Louisiana, of Dog Company, 3rd Ranger Battalion, saw Lieutenant Colonel Darby dress down some officers who were drinking coffee. During a particularly nasty winter day, the mess tent supposedly only had black coffee. His hawk eyes noted that the color of the coffee the officers were drinking was not black but suspiciously lighter, so he asked them what was wrong with their drinks. They were dumbfounded, not understanding the question. "'I don't see how in the hell you can drink that coffee without it being black. Everyone else has black coffee.' Shamefacedly, the offending officers spilled their cream coffee out and replaced it with black." And that's the way Colonel Darby was. "How can you keep from loving a man like that?"

First scout of C/3, Melvin Dodge from Fairport Harbor, Ohio, just a few months past his 20th birthday, observed Darby after the ugliness of Venafro. A new captain had joined the Rangers, and he believed his rank entitled him to cut to the front of the chow line. Darby had none of that. In the Rangers, no man was better than any other. The new captain was sent to the end of the line.

Medical surgeon Sommers spent time with Darby not just in Sicily during the great mule trek of the 3rd Ranger Battalion, but also in the bitter fighting in the bitter cold mountains. "Col., Master Sergeant Ehalt, a couple of others, and I were up on top in a dugout shelter. Nothing special about that; Col. was always at the front or in front. I remember Col. taking a crap on the rocks and looking back south at all the hills we had climbed. In a rear area, perhaps at Caiazzo, the Col and officers were together one night. The Col got a mandolin and accompanied himself singing old Army and West Point songs I had never heard before. He had a good singing voice and was an accomplished musician."

During this time, until 14 December, the 1st Ranger Battalion was on the defensive with little action to their front. From the start of the campaign through 13 December, the Rangers suffered enormous casualties as they were ground down in line-infantry combat, though punching well above their size. Twenty-seven men had been killed, with 121 wounded and over 200 non-battle-related injuries. Artillery barrages took their toll, killing two Rangers and wounding three. In turn, the Rangers had killed six Germans who patrolled too closely to their positions. Journal entries included Darby having diarrhea on 30 November, sending his medical officer to inspect the mess's sanitation. 4 December saw him order two men to make a Ranger Christmas card. "The next day he sent an officer to 'eat the ass out of the cooks' and teach them the right way to cook ham. A class on cooking ham began the next morning." 11 December 1943 had him receive the promotion he deserved to full bird colonel. Two days later, the 3rd Battalion, 180th relieved the 1st Ranger Battalion and was removed from VI Corps back to direct control of Fifth Army. All three battalions assembled at Lucrino; this was the first time, since Salerno, that they were all under Darby's command.

Staff Sergeant Wayne Ruona had a lot to say about his experiences with the Rangers. Like Szima, he was a man not afraid to speak or to write down his thoughts. He wasn't too fond of the new replacements he had seen. The ugliness of deadly combat impacted morale. This hit the young men especially hard, with some crying, and scared, pulling back from their frontline positions. He understood the dynamics involved, for he had volunteered for the Rangers lacking the training he had received. To him, and probably other older veterans, the 18- or 19-year-olds were too young to take the place of the older, more mature individuals and therefore were not reliable. "I threatened to shoot one before I got him to stay in his allotted position. They were a detriment to the veteran. In comparison to those of us that had Ranger training, they were not to be trusted in combat because their training was so inadequate and their fear so real that it was difficult to lead them. They replaced where a fill-in was needed. And they were given as much responsibility as training permitted." Despite their flaws, the veterans accepted them, hoping that with experience they'd mature. Yet some would break down and cry. They were emotionally immature, he thought. This lack of qualified replacements impacted the unit cohesion and morale that the old-timers had—and it was missed by them. One company had 26 replacements without any combat experience, out of 42 men.

Having experienced the brutal nights on the mountains of North Africa, Ruona said those nights were colder than hell but worse in Italy during winter. There were, he laments, "no clothes to provide comfort at these times." He thought highly of the sergeants who did a commendable job; but commissioned officers, he wondered how they got there. He never received a battlefield promotion but knew that the Ranger noncoms made the best officers. "I found that men that had been trained the most and were combat-experienced were relied on to lead those with less experience, and in the Rangers the noncoms naturally did the leading." Kitchens, who was the CO of C/3 through Sicily, told him after the war that the Rangers siphoned off too many top-notch soldiers and placed them in lower positions than their abilities could command.

Religion, despite Father Basil and other chaplains being available to the men, was not for Ruona. He was not religious, and neither were his buddies. In fact, he said that with one of his friends, during the few times they did discuss religion, it was about "the false premises preached in church and not about religious convictions." And, of course, the Rangers cussed a lot.

Ruona had been an old-timer, older than most by four or five years. He had started as a BAR gunner in Bravo/1 and ended as a staff sergeant with C/3. He was an admirer of Dammer, especially during combat. He would be captured by the Germans after a horrific battle, but that was to come. Still, he reflected, "front-line and POW living conditions are inhuman and should not be tolerated." He'd catch a serious disease before imprisonment. Things would be hard, but he was a hard man. He never experienced shell shock or battle fatigue, but he did observe that fear; and after months of combat duty, some Rangers had a mental breakdown and went berserk. "But I think it is downright inhuman to force anyone to deliberately have to force himself to advance toward rifle, artillery, or any other type of killing device. We in a supposed civilized society still have to resort to such inhuman methods of exterminating ourselves?"

Battalion Surgeon Sommers commented on battle shock.

> Yes, there were some cases but never that I remember in an amphibious attack or a night raid, or a patrol action—what the Rangers were trained for. The battle fatigue or burnout cases were when the Rangers were used as line infantry in a holding position for long periods, particularly the 90 days at Venafro. Some very good noncoms would come to me and say something like Doc I can't take it anymore. What we did was to keep these good soldiers at the medical tent, talking to the medics and sick and casualties, and their duty was to make coffee. After a week or so in what they regarded as a rear area, say 200–500 yds from the front, they felt better and went back to their company. A worse instance was Master Sergeant Ehalt, as brave and tough a soldier as I ever knew. After a shelling on top of the hill at Venafro, he got to shaking so bad that I sent him down the hill with a medic escort.

Bob Ehalt would return like so many Rangers. He would make history by being the last man to talk to Darby on a fateful day near Anzio.

For Sergeant George G. Sabine Jr. with Fox, 3rd Battalion, Venafro held a special memory and reminder. And it was not about falling asleep and nearly getting killed for it. On 8 December 1943, he and his section sergeant were lead scouts in an attempt to take Hill 950. Moments earlier, Darby had left when a buzz saw of German fire stung the area, driving the Rangers off. He and the sergeant, side by side, made haste to get away, scooting on their stomachs, triggering a mine or hitting some kind of wire coming down the slope. The explosion blasted both men into the air, slamming them flat on their backs. Sabine scooted down behind a protective boulder. He sat there for a while, dazed and clueless as to where he was. Midnight approached. During the night he heard some kind of tin bouncing down the hill, hitting his arm. It was a grenade. It went off and injured his arm. A sniper from their right fired, and one bullet creased his pants. He spotted four, five guys near him, just below from another company. He told them they had to get out of there, and they should try to escape once the fog descended onto the mountain. Once it did, they took off with one getting shot, with four puffs of smoke hitting his back, but he managed to go on. His sergeant was in bad shape, back on a ridge with his company where he refused to let the company medic cut off his clothes because of the cold and he needed them. He sat there throughout the night, and then the next day they carried the wounded down the hill to the aid station. He was transferred to Santa Maria, outside of Naples, an evacuation hospital, overflowing with casualties. He stayed there until after Christmas, but in typical Ranger fashion a blue-dyed bottle of medicinal alcohol was found, cut in half and cut in half again with lime juice. It was a pleasant Christmas Eve for the 20 wounded men in that hospital. His fighting days were far from over. He joined the Devil's Brigade, the American-Canadian 1st Special Service Force, and the 474th Infantry Regiment fighting through France and Germany.

Gino Mercuriali, who had recalled the flaming onions flying at him during the raid on Dieppe, was promoted to second lieutenant on 19 October 1943, just in time for the grueling winter campaign. When he later passed away, he left behind a number of floppy disks filled with information about the Rangers and his time in service. He recalled vividly their operations around Venafro when 1st Battalion took trucks, on 8 November, for a 30-mile run to Venafro. "Back to the hills," he wrote, to relive various infantry companies of the 45th. He was happy to still have the highly respected 83rd Mortars attached to his battalion. The 83rd seemed to have become a permanent feature to the Rangers. "This was the beginning of 35 days of intensive activity with the action confined to the battle area around Mt. Corno. German rifle and machine-gun fire wounded one and killed three of our Battalion on the 10th of Nov. I was assigned to retrieve the 3 killed from a wooded area. This was accomplished with the help of mule skinners to carry the bodies out. I took over, as I wasn't babying those mules. At our risk. We were harassed by ME 109s diving bomb attacks and overhead artillery explosions about tree height." He recalled the proximity of the lines to each other at Monte Corno, with Germans barely 200 feet away from D/1. Gino suffered from malaria and diarrhea, but he kept up with his men and never fell out. But the mountains were kicking ass. "The life in the mountains," he observed, "in the severe cold rain, meager food supply at times and the need to ration your water supply or replenish it. From dangerously close German troops you could hear their conversation and possibly they could hear your canteens knocking against each other." Eventually the diarrhea and frozen feet took their toll. During patrols, he no longer felt his feet and thought he was walking on stubs. The diarrhea and environmental conditions sucked out his strength, and he lost a lot of weight. The battalion doctor hospitalized him, and Gino Mercuriali, one of the old-timers, was shipped to North Africa to recuperate. He would rejoin the battalion later, after it had been further decimated. In a letter sent to historian Bob Black, Gino provides an assessment of his time during the war:

> The Germans were good fighters, and I'm sure made up of every type just as we were. Much of our opposition was Italian and the Baltic slavs, which sure didn't have much heart for the war. I have not dwelled on the many aspects of combat itself. . . . Suffice it to say that even if not for the shellings, airburst, strafing and personal contact that the living conditions alone in rain sleet and freezing weather, the chow, sanitary conditions, etc., were bad enough when endured weeks months at a time over a couple of years. On the other hand, we had a hell of an experience and having met with Free French, Poles, Indian-Indians, British, of course, New Zealanders and Australians. Even the American Japanese. Then the various countries, Northern Ireland, Scotland including far north and billing in civilian homes in Dundee, England, including London, and Brighton, the trip through the Mediterranean Sea, Algeria

and Tunisia, North Africa, Sicily, including Palermo and Italy, including Naples and Mount Etna. Now, I think it's great. Sadly, I'll never have grandchildren to pass any of this down to them.

Colonel Darby had all his battalions at Lucrino near Naples for a well-deserved rest. One can imagine what the Rangers did during the brief lull in fighting, but such activities were not limited to the enlisted, as Battalion Surgeon Sommers remembers well: "Then there is the party that the Rangers gave for the nurses at a castle south of Naples just after Venafro. The 225th Station Hosp. had just arrived from the States; it was an unequal contest, battle scarred Rangers versus impressible nurses; I draw a curtain over the details but it was quite a party."

The Rangers had bled on the mountains and thrown themselves against German defenses. Now it was time to refit and recuperate, but recruiting officers needed to find replacements. Everyone understood that training saved lives. Plans were afoot for the next operation to break out of the deadlock of the German defensive lines. The Allied planners thought of an end run, bypassing the defensive lines, and attacking the Germans from the rear.

Worse was yet to come. . . .

THEY TORE THE ANIMAL TO PIECES

The Walter von Alton Farm, Rachdammietz
Pomerania, Germany
LATE JULY 1944

Private First Class Clarence Goad, of the 3rd Ranger Battalion, missed Major Alvah Miller, the man who had recruited him into the Rangers for the invasion of mainland Italy. Oddly, he was one of the few who had 10 days of training at Achnacarry that did not involve Darby's Rangers, and that was what had caught Miller's attention. He was near Miller when he got killed at Cisterna. And now here he was. Stalag IIB at Hammerstein with Russian prisoners in cages—the men were starved to death. The POWs looked and smelled like death. Goad saw them lure a guard dog to them: And once it was close enough, they tore the animal to pieces, eating it raw. Typhus raged, and he helped bury 120 Russians a day, lugging 10 men at a time on an unsteady wheel cart, with the corpses held in place with a rope all the way to a pit. It was pure evil.

He woke up from his nightmare. He had been transferred to a work farm, a Kommando, as food shortages ravaged the lands. He trusted no one, there were stool pigeons at the Stalag, he was hungry as hell, and his previous two escapes had been crap. The last one included a savage beating with fists and clubs and a promise that he'd be shot the next time. Well, the next time was today.

Goad had regained strength, weighing in at 110 to 120 pounds for his next attempt. He lacked food, and the conditions he lived in didn't allow the body to heal. But he was determined. Since he was forced labor, he thought he could pass as a local potato-digger. He moved around the area and found a boat that he was going to use, but he was hungry. And he desperately needed to eat. Not just now but later once at sea. Anything would do. It was just before daylight when Goad found a field with potatoes laid out. He started to dig. Suddenly, and out of nowhere, an old German rode in on a thin-legged horse. The man wore a long green coat and a spiked helmet and carried an old rifle. He gave Goad a careful once-over. The old man's sharp eyes and instincts detected that something was off. *Shit*, thought Goad. The German asked him what he was doing. It was forbidden to take things from the field, he said.

Twenty-three years of age, Goad was savvy and tough. Still, he couldn't believe his bad luck—but maybe he could bullshit his way out. He did speak Platt-Deutsch, a northern Old German that farmers used in the region and he had picked up. Goad said he was hungry and that he was from southern France, but the old German simply told him to march. And march they did, for four long kilometers while the German rode on his horse, of course.

They arrived at the local police station. Goad trusted his instincts. The officers interrogating him kept pointing fingers at him, yelling in German; all the while, the old man told them that his prisoner spoke German. But Goad didn't answer in German. They thought he was a spy—one who had landed behind enemy lines using a parachute. The Ranger knew spies and escapees were often shot, and he didn't want to die. The police officers got frustrated with him. Goad stuck to his guns. He didn't see the blow that hit him in the back of his head, but he sure as hell felt the heavy blows pummeling his face, shattering his teeth, before passing out. . . .

9

ANZIO

OPERATION SHINGLE

The gargantuan slaughterfest that had become the mountainous war-fare near the Gustav Line needed something to break the German defensive lines north of the Volturno River. Division after division bled itself dry, lacking the numbers required for an assault against a well-entrenched enemy, using every piece of terrain to exact an enor-mous human toll. The British on the right, the eastern side of Italy, struggled as much as the Americans did. To offset this imbalance and to break down the German troops into fragments, the idea was con-ceived to do an end run around the Gustav Line and land somewhere north of it. The "it," it was decided, was to be an amphibious assault at Anzio and its beautiful beaches ideal for such an operation. The limitation of war matériel to deliver a large force was only part of the problem. The intent was to trap German forces retreating from their lines, as a simultaneous push from the southern Allied divisions was to be made to dislodge them with the landings at Anzio, threat-ening the German rear. The major issue, however, proved to be the plan to seize Rome, to be a morale boost to the Allies and a blow to the Germans, instead of driving south from Anzio into the rear of the Gustav Line. As most things badly conceived, Prime Minister and blowhard Winston Churchill, who had been the architect of the poor decision to strike into the soft underbelly of Europe, was also involved in the push to land at Anzio—despite resources being thrown into the northern theater, preparing for the invasion of France. "It is hard to understand how Churchill and many higher Allied commanders so late in the war so badly and repeatedly underestimated the German will to resist stubbornly any large-scale threat to the Gustav Line. But perhaps the single biggest mistake was on the part of the Allied high command, in assigning inadequate forces to the Anzio-Nettuno landing and not ensuring that it could join with the Fifth Army within forty-eight hours." A stronger force might have been more successful and cost fewer lives. But that was to be revealed over the next few days, then weeks, and finally months with Rome liberated on 4 June 1944.

The man to lead the invasion was General Mark W. Clark of the Fifth Army, who was placed in charge of planning and executing the attack on Anzio code-named *Operation Shingle.* It involved three beaches and two towns, with a road network leading to the Alban Hills, some 20 miles inland, between Highways 6 and 7, and a key strategic point for Clark's plan.

The Rangers had done remarkably well so far in the war, considering that their conceived purpose was to be raiders from the sea or land, and not regular line infantry. The Ranger Battalion was smaller than the average American infantry battalion. The average Ranger received more training than the average Dogface; but as the war continued, the Ranger replacements did not always get that specialized training. Often it was on-the-job learning. That is not to say replacements did not enjoy the benefit of the training and experience the Originals, and subsequent Ranger veterans, had, but there were certainly issues getting personnel the time for training. Darby and his staff did their best to get the men what they needed—in training as well as other support. After the attrition of the Ranger battalions on the Winter Line, they all were relieved by 20 December. *Operation Shingle* was scheduled to take place on 22 January 1944. About a month to find new soldiers, train them, and refit the battalions that had suffered near 40 percent casualties. Three to four weeks of training was available but certainly not nearly as much time as they had had for the invasion of Sicily, which had been three months.

The operations at Anzio were under the Fifth Army's VI Corps under Major General John P. Lucas, and were coordinated with a simultaneous attack on the German winter lines by V Corps. The landings themselves were divided into sectors. To the left-center of Anzio was the British 1st Division on Peter Beach, a mile and a half long, and five miles northwest of Anzio, with the American 3rd Division, under Major General Lucian K. Truscott Jr., to take the right center at X-Ray Beach, two miles long, three miles east of Anzio and two miles east of Nettuno. Linking these two divisions were the Rangers, specifically tasked with seizing Anzio, then Nettuno to the right of Anzio.

Darby's command was now called the 6615 Ranger Force (Provisional), composed of all three Ranger battalions, rested and refitted. The biggest change was the authorization for a regimental headquarters, the 6615th Headquarters and Headquarters Company, Ranger Force (Provisional), with an authorized strength of 10 officers and 100 enlisted men under Colonel Darby and Executive Officer Lieutenant Colonel Herm Dammer. Prior to the creation of the Regimental HQ, Ranger battalions had had a problem administering the units, as well as in planning operations. Attached to the Rangers were Captain Charles Merton Shunstrom's Cannon Company of four 75mm-mounted half-tracks; the 509th Parachute Infantry Battalion, under the father of the modern Green Berets, William P. Yarborough; the glorious blood-brothers of the Rangers, the 83rd Chemical Mortar Battalion; and, last but not least, H Company of the 36th Combat Engineer Battalion. Included in the group were 27 men of the 57th Signal Battalion and a three-man team of the 163rd Signal Photography Company, scheduled to land at 0200 hours at Anzio. As always, communications were a key part of the planning, and orders for *Shingle* were precise: "to install, operate and maintain signal communication between the units in Ranger Force and Ranger Force Headquarters." It was a strong force led by battle-savvy and hardened leaders, officers, and non-commissioned officers, across the board.

Anzio was to be a classic Ranger operation, the kind that they had been created for and had executed at Dieppe, Arzew, Sicily, and Salerno. This was, for some of the Originals, their fifth D-Day.

The mission at hand was to capture Anzio and the town to its right, Nettuno. The landing, departing from the warm and sunny city of Pozzuoli, on the Gulf of Naples, was aimed directly at Anzio's beach, centered to its large white casino. The 6615 was tasked to seize port facilities with the engineers to clear mines and explosives throughout the beach, docks, and surrounding areas. As usual, they were to destroy any and all gun batteries. The beachhead needed to be secured for follow-on forces and matériel with roadblocks along the coastal road. Then the Rangers needed to link up with the British 1st Division with two Commando units, to their left, and Truscott's Trotters of the 3rd Division to the right. Famous war photographer Robert Capa tagged along for the ride.

As was done at Gela, the Ranger battle plan called for the 1st Ranger Battalion, now under West Pointer Major John Dobson, to land on the left side of the beach code-named Yellow Beach at about half a mile long, with the 4th Battalion still under Major Roy Murray to take the right side while Ranger Headquarters was in the middle. The HQ Ranger Force's Landing Diagram to Accompany Outline Plan *Operation Shingle* shows the 4th Battalion on the left side of Yellow Beach with the 1st Rangers on the right—HQ with Darby was smack in the middle. And the second wave on the left, the 509th, and to the right the 3rd Rangers. The lack of landing craft meant the 3rd Ranger Battalion, now under Major Alvah Miller, had to land with the second wave, which also included A/1, C/4, the paratroopers, the heavy mortars, and engineers. For the Rangers, this was a staggered landing. Phase lines as a measure of advance were also used.

The Ranger Group's landing was handled by Capt. E. C. I. Turner, Royal Navy, and used 2 LSI(M), the *Royal Ulsterman* and the *Beatrix*; 1 LS(L), the *Winchester Castle*; and featured, overall, 1 Landing Ship Tank, 32 LCI (Large), 22 LCT, 1 Landing Craft Gun, 1 Landing Craft Flak, 1 Landing Craft Tank Rocket, 4 Patrol Craft, and 6 Submarine Chasers.

The first of two Ranger waves hit Anzio at 0200 hours and dumped the extra 60mm ammo at the beaches. Their landing did not feature any naval gunfire because the ship was off course. The relationship Darby had developed with the Navy proved its value when guide boats were at their correct locations, waving in Darby, who landed within feet of his target, the big, white casino just on the other side of the coastal road. Sergeant Gustave Schunemann wrote about his experiences with the Rangers:

On January 20, 1944, we boarded the British commando ship *Princess Anne* and set sail for Anzio, a resort town on the coast about 30 miles south of Rome. With the coming of dusk, speed was stepped up and the final rendezvous near the enemy-held shores was breached. At midnight, moonless and starless, we were silently lowered into assault boats for the ride to the beach. Combat engineers, God love them, had gone in before us and cleared the beach of mines. They left small lights, one red and one green, at each end of the cleared area for us to guide on. We were about half-way in when the Allied rocket ships opened fire with a barrage that sounded like deep claps of thunder. Concussion from the exploding rockets shook the area for miles around. The enemy returned fire briefly with anti-aircraft guns, shooting across the water, causing air bursts. That really got our attention! I don't think their blind firing hit anything, however. By the time we hit the beach, they were long gone and hard to find. The landing came as a complete surprise to the enemy, so there were not many troops on hand to provide the reception we were accustomed to. It was so dark, I couldn't see my hand in front of my face. Once on the beach, we moved forward through streets and alleyways, holding on to the pack of the man in front. I tripped over something and fell on the cobble-stoned pavement, crushing my right fingers under my rifle. I could tell my hand was bleeding but had no idea how bad it was. At dawn, our medic cleansed and bandaged my badly cut fingers and

I was okay. He wanted to make out an EMT tag, which would get me the Purple Heart, but I refused. I felt that the award was intended for people with wounds much more serious than mine.

By 0202 hours, an amphibious vehicle had run into mechanical troubles and had to be abandoned—it carried some of the 4.2-inch tubes, and 57mm anti-tank guns. The 4th hit the port facilities. There were no mines on the beaches and little resistance. Renzo Mastracci, a 36-year-old, deaf electrician caught at the landing was killed, mistaken as German. He, and Remo Mattioli, both employed by the Roma Electric Company, had been summoned by the German commander to fix an issue that evening. The Germans were partying with several women and ordered them to evacuate after they had addressed the electrical problem because of the anticipated attack and the German decision to blow up key installations. Remo left but returned to Anzio around dawn to retrieve his coat from home. He was captured by Americans but released once they confirmed he was an electrician. Remo was released in front of the white casino where dirigibles were in the air. Here he found the body of his dead friend Renzo who had returned earlier to Anzio. There were only 40 Germans at Anzio. Two Germans were killed by the 1st Battalion on the road to the east. Perhaps one of them was Renzo wearing overalls, misidentified as a German soldier and unable to hear commands or perhaps he was simply killed during the initial attack. Elements of the 29th Panzer Grenadier Division offered weak resistance.

An hour later, at 0300, the "Bastard Battalion," the 83rd Chemical Mortar, minus C and D Companies, landed, carrying extra ammunition; and fortunately, 30 minutes later, the disabled vehicle carrying the tube and anti-tank gun was towed to the beach. At the same time, 1st Rangers fired on a German wheeled armored car directly behind the casino. The occupants were killed. Roy Murray radioed that his men had hit their first phase line around 0240, leading to the second wave carrying five companies of 3rd Battalion, headquarters, and A/1 using the same landing craft the first wave had used. Fourth Battalion expanded the perimeter around the town, with 3rd cleaning houses and the town itself of anyone missed in the early sweep through it. Miller's Rangers then were tasked with protecting the vital port facility. As more troops came ashore, the three Ranger battalions prepared to move north. Skirmishes occurred. The 4th encountered Germans at a footbridge north of the railroad tracks, which grew into a larger fire fight with the Rangers forcing the Germans back. Ranger logs annotate the early action details: One German communication crew was killed and its radio-equipped vehicle captured; small, uncoordinated, and scattered attacks by the Germans. Clearly the Germans had been caught out.

Darby set up his headquarters in the casino. 0445 saw the arrival of two companies of the 509th, F/4, and more men of H Company, 36th Engineers. There was minimal resistance throughout, as more troops and equipment came ashore using the port that was cleared of demolition charges by engineers. By seven in the morning, Darby's men had cleared their areas, including 3rd Rangers capturing a four-gun 100mm battery on the left side, west of Anzio, where they killed 5 and captured 12. First Sergeant Arnbal of 3rd Rangers recounts the moment his men took out a German bunker at the edge of town. Splitting the platoon into squads, they approached from the left and right sides of the fortified position. On the inland side, he and the squad found the entrance. It was too dark to see if the door was open or shut down in the stairwell: He ordered one man, Feigenbaum, to fire his Tommy gun, hitting the closed metal door. Next, Arnbal ordered PFC Swain to throw his dynamite block. The blast ruptured the door. Corporal Eden and his assistant came up with a flamethrower toward the broken door, leading to shouting from inside. Once the flames died down, a solitary man with a flashlight approached, revealing a dimly lit room. The German soldier, looking very pale, said, "*Was ist los? Heraus Kommen, du Amerikaner?*" To which Arnbal answered, "*Ja, Feldwebel.*" Nineteen surrendered, of which half were Poles. No one had crewed the anti-aircraft position. By 0800, Darby ordered the 509th to sweep to the right to seize Nettuno, which they accomplished within a few short minutes. The Germans shelled the beachhead throughout the night.

Despite this tremendous achievement for the Rangers, the worst was yet to come. The Germans cobbled together units and built, as quickly as possible, lines with interlocking defenses centered around surrounding villages and farmhouses able to withstand a lot of fire. Behind those lines of resistance, they organized troops for eventual counterattacks. The buildup made the German reaction look relatively static for at least a week. Perhaps it deceived Allied planners for upcoming operations. The Germans marshaled over 20,000 troops by the end of the day, with more reinforcements to pour in from France, the Balkans, Rome, the Adriatic, and from northern Italy. There were hundreds of the dreaded 88mm anti-aircraft guns in the area. These were the guns that could also shoot at a flat trajectory and had caused problems for the Rangers in the Salerno area.

The assault was the smoothest for the Rangers yet. The nine-mile stretch around Anzio was guarded by one German company. Forty Germans were killed, 9 vehicles and 24 prisoners were captured, and 5 Russian POWS were sent to work the docks. Later that day, the bag had increased to 32 German and 18 Russian prisoners. There had been little resistance. The Ranger battalions patrolled the edges of the beachhead between the Anzio and Nettuno roads. The beachhead expanded to a half-moon shape, seven miles deep, but enemy activity also grew, with constant bombardments and traffic throughout. There had been more serious resistance at the other beaches. The Allies built up their forces, landing more troops and equipment, and advanced slowly as the Germans organized and regrouped their newly arriving units. "All VI Corps objectives were taken by noon as the Allied air forces completed 1,200 sorties against targets in and around the beachhead. On the beach itself, the U.S. 36th Engineer Combat Regiment bulldozed exits, laid corduroy roads, cleared mines by 0320 hours, and readied the port of Anzio to receive its first landing ship, tank (LST), an amphibious assault and supply ship, by the afternoon of D-Day. By midnight, over 36,000 men and 3,200 vehicles, 90 percent of the invasion force, were ashore, with casualties of 13 killed, 97 wounded, and 44 missing. During D-Day, Allied troops captured 227 German defenders." The German situation during this time: "At 1900 on 22 January, the troops of the 14th Army began to leave their areas in northern Italy. On 23 and 24 January, the transportation of troops from France, Germany, and the Balkans began. These forces arrived in Italy by 31 January, despite constant enemy air attacks on roads and railroads. By this time, the advanced detachments of these units were already employed at the beachhead."

The next day, the Rangers moved north to relieve 2nd Battalion, 7th Infantry Regiment, and established contact with the Scots Guards on their left.

There were two key terrain pieces in the Anzio area; both had substantial road and rail networks. To the north was Aprilia, known as "the Factory" because of its cluster of brick buildings, significant for any action for the Alban Hills—it would be won, and lost, then won again—and to the northeast the town of Cisterna. Highways 6 and 7 were crucial to interdict, and vital to control for future operations against the Germans. Past Anzio, the land was as flat as the 88 could shoot. It was farmland stretching to the Alban Hills in the distance. A flat piece of terrain without cover or concealment, unlike the crevices of mountains that might cast a protective cloak from prying eyes and shells—or allow one to oversee the enemy in the valleys below. Small farmhouses dotted the lush green fields, littered with ditches and canals and footbridges. The large Mussolini Canal, built to drain the Pontine Marshes, started at the seacoast 10 miles north of Anzio and made its way south to the sea 11 miles on. It featured numerous footbridges as well. It was not a deep canal and therefore did not impede operations in general. The Mussolini Canal, like others, had a number of drainage ditches with one neatly leading to Cisterna.

Over the next few days, as the beachhead expanded and Germans organized their reinforcements, the Rangers patrolled their areas and Darby plugged gaps in the lines with the 509 Paratroopers. A bitter blow struck the 83rd and the Rangers when 303 men of C/83 and D/83 were killed when the LST 422 (landing ship tank) hit a mine, as did the LCI 32 (landing craft infantry) when it came to assist. One of the survivors, Sergeant Clark Riddle of Dog Company, 83rd, located a lifebelt and bedroll that he placed under each arm to keep afloat until rescued. For a week the Ranger sector was on the plain between two roads—one to Cartoceto 10 miles away, the other from Nettuno to Spaccasassi, a town that was 8 miles beyond the Alban Hills.

The Rangers were tasked with supporting and covering the right flank, the left of the Ranger position, of the British advance aimed at Cartoceto on 25 January. Murray, along with the 509th and a platoon of 601st Tank Destroyers, was dispatched. By eight o'clock, they had bumped into slight resistance at Padiglione, to the right of the British advance. The 3rd Division under Truscott had started their attack the previous day. As the Allied advance progressed, with the British re-seizing their objective, Truscott's Trotters advanced faster than their British counterparts, forcing Darby to fill the gap with three companies of the 1st Ranger Battalion to establish a line to the right with the 3rd Battalion, 7th Infantry Regiment. During these days, advance elements of the 1st Armored Division and 45th Thunderbirds began to land while receiving incoming artillery. The Bastard Battalion of the 83rd supported Murray's task force. Soon the 1st and 3rd went into reserve as the 3rd Infantry Division was fighting hard and doing well enough.

The next day, the 26th, with worsening weather conditions reminiscent of the Venafro Mountains, the 4th Rangers dug in anticipating a counterattack, which came and hit the British and 4th Rangers, but was fought off. As usual for all infantry, and especially the Rangers, non-battle injuries reared their ugly heads: Trench foot, diarrhea, malaria attacks, and new mosquito attacks from the Pontine Marshes started to impact them. The muddy terrain was a curse to the crews of the heavy mortars. The dawn of 27 January had the 3rd and 4th Rangers and paratroopers in a skirmish line moving from Cartoceto eastward, fighting Germans in foxholes and farmhouses while the British shelled the factory area of Cartoceto. The next day witnessed increased German activity with constant artillery and mortar fire.

Troubling for the Allies was the German defense. Within three days of *Operation Shingle*, by 25 January, they "had almost twenty-six thousand combat troops on the line. Instead of weakening the Gustav Line, the Germans had brought in some thirty-four thousand troops to the area. Elements of eight German divisions were facing Anzio, and five more, with many supporting units, were on the way. This number was much larger than Allied intelligence had believed possible. The Allies had estimated that German commitments in northern Italy and elsewhere would limit reinforcements to only two divisions from north of Rome, and those not for sixteen days." For the Allies, and especially for Darby's Rangers, it would spell disaster.

During the landings, the Germans did not sit idly by. Kesselring moved the newly activated 4th Parachute Division and replacement units of the Hermann Göring Division into blocking positions on approaches from Anzio to the Alban Hills and Rome. But the Germans knew that units of the 4th Parachute Division and the Panzer Division Hermann Göring were not completely up to strength, nor trained. Micromanager Adolf Hitler authorized units for the defense to Kesselring, including the 3rd Panzer Grenadiers, the 71st Infantry Division, and the bulk of the Hermann Göring Division from northern and southern Italy. The German main line of resistance (MLR) went through Cisterna and Campoleone. Additionally, they flooded some fields, making the road network crucial—which favored the Germans.

The next attack of the Rangers was to the north again, starting at Carpoceto for about 1.5 miles on the road leading to Cisterna. They were close to within seven miles of the town, about two miles north of the Mussolini Canal. At the crack of dawn—when the French and Indians used to attack during the French and Indian Wars in North America—of 27 January, Murray's battalion and the 509th Paratroopers advanced into combat. Our hero of Gela, Randall Harris, who had suffered a terrible stomach wound, was now a lieutenant and led the charge against a well-fortified road junction using a chain of stone farmhouses. In between them were well-camouflaged "grass cutter" machine-gun nests. Harris, and his XO Lieutenant Andre Howard of Pennsylvania, along with their platoon leaders, led the way and paid the price. During the engagement, three Rangers were killed: 23-year-old Howard Andre, who had participated at Dieppe; Sergeant James Hildebrandt, 20, from New York; and PFC

Bosika. Six Rangers were wounded. The Germans were driven off the road junction, but this was a high price to pay. The Rangers and Paratroopers fought their way to the objective as the enemy grew in strength. In four days of fighting, three lieutenants of the 4th Battalion were killed, including 23-year-old Texan Lieutenant Louis Harper. The open terrain and the scattered farmhouses provided bunker-like defenses for the Germans to exploit. It was evident that only heavy artillery and tank destroyers could handle the defensive positions comprised of farmhouse and other entrenchments south of the German Main Line of Resistance.

In the meanwhile, the beachhead expanded to 11 miles deep, and incoming artillery and mortar barrages became routine. Fourth Battalion captured prisoners, and the Germans complained about the foreigners—in fact, three out of nine were former French soldiers, and one was Polish. The After-Action Report of the 4th noted that a German officer was combative. This was not going to be an easy fight, not that any of them had been. But clearly the Germans were not defeated; they were motivated. The British on the flank dealt with a main German counterattack; and two Ranger battalions had moved or strayed temporarily into the British territory during the confusing situation of combat, to where 3rd Battalion was shot at by British artillery. No doubt Darby did some ass-chewing and, once settled, the Rangers tied in with the Scots Guards to their left. They were to defend their sector.

"Probes by the 3rd Division toward Cisterna and by the 504th Parachute Infantry Regiment toward Littoria on 24–25 January made some progress but were also halted short of their goals by stubborn resistance. Renewed attacks on the next day brought the Americans within three miles of Cisterna and two miles beyond the west branch of the Mussolini Canal. But the 3rd Division commander, Maj. Gen. Lucian K. Truscott, Jr., on orders of the corps commander, called a halt to the offensive, a pause that later lengthened into a general consolidation and reorganization of beachhead forces between 26 and 29 January."

As Darby was now officially a regimental commander, and Herm having returned to being Darby's right-hand man with the creation of a regimental headquarters, West Pointer Major John W. Dobson was handed command of Darby's 1st Ranger Battalion on 12 January 1944, with Dammer's 3rd going to Major Alvah Miller. Captain Shunstrom became attached to the 1st Battalion, and the Cannon Company was handed to First Lieutenant Otis Davey. There was some grumbling among the Rangers that Dobson, an outsider, had been given command instead of someone being promoted from within. One observation made by Dobson was that almost "all the Italians in his area were Fascists." Dug in, the Rangers—like everyone else—got battered by continuous enemy artillery fire. This was not to Darby's liking: He wanted to dish out heavy-caliber shells, not be on the receiving end of them. After a few ass-chewing sessions with 3rd Infantry Division and his own liaison fire control officer and Lieutenant Colonel William S. Hutchinson Jr., of the 83rd, things were going to change a little.

The 28th of January saw more German combat patrols probing the Ranger positions and all along the Anzio beachhead. Artillery fire took more Ranger lives. Raiders from the sea, night-fighters with blackened faces, were ground up and slowly but surely decimated. Never mind malaria, trench feet, colds and fever, and more. That night, Darby was ordered to move his battalions to an assembly area eight miles southwest of Cisterna, after being relieved on line by a British reconnaissance unit. Trucks were provided for the move, although D/3 had to march four hours to get to the area because of a lack of vehicles. At the assembly area, the men shaved, cleaned, got haircuts, rested, wrote letters, and bullshitted while some sang favorite songs like "Pistol-Packin' Mama." Most of the time was used to prepare for the attack. Weapons were checked and rechecked, while staff was planning the mission, looking over the maps.

Dog Company, 3rd Rangers, lost their commander, Captain Cannon, to malaria with former-Platoon-Sergeant-turned-Lieutenant Bill Musgades taking over. But not for long: During a briefing with First Shirt (Sergeant) Anders Arnbal, Musgades was wounded by falling shrapnel from anti-aircraft shells during the aerial battles taking place over the harbor. Things were not looking great. . . .

The Germans, on the other hand, brought forward more units. The old favorite Hermann Göring Division was in the area, along with the 26th and 29th Panzer Grenadier Divisions and the 1st and 4th Parachute Regiments. German artillery, radio-controlled glider bombs, and Luftwaffe attacks contained the Allied advance, while E-boats and U-boats made the waters unsafe for the Allies. Bob Black neatly sums up the situation: "Pinned against the sea, General Lucas could not break out unless he had stronger forces, but the beachhead was already crowded and had become a German-controlled shooting gallery." Things needed to change.

Major Alvah Miller of Michigan sat with pen and paper in hand, finally committing to a final version of his work that he had been pondering for a while. He looked at the pages and felt satisfaction. He was a man of great depth, capable of expressing his deeply held emotions, if not in speech, at least on paper. Alvah missed his wife, Loretta, and his young boy, James Patton, both at home far away, far from danger. He thought of his parents. All of them safe in Saginaw, Michigan. . . . Soon the war would have to end. He had been with the men he now loved seemingly since forever. Since Northern Ireland, those early days at Carrickfergus interviewing volunteers after he had been hand-picked by the brave then-Captain Darby. He remembered the questions asked of the young men. Could they kill? Could they kill with a knife? Could they . . . and they did. Despite the horrors of Dieppe, the Originals had performed beyond expectations in Algeria and Tunisia; the new Rangers had done remarkably well in Sicily with the Originals spread throughout the battalions. The brutality of the mountains and the Germans at Maiori and Venafro had bled them, but they had remained a good outfit. It had been his job to integrate the new men, to lead them in combat as he had done under Dammer, whom he greatly admired. And now at Anzio he had been given command of the 3rd Ranger Battalion, and he was proud of the men. He cared for them greatly. He understood the demons of the war inhabiting the souls of his men. They had seen much, done much. . . . The men of his command.

The Men of My Command

'Tis midnight and I stand
Amid the sleeping forms of men—
The men of my command.
And, as their troubled murmurs stir
The quiet of the night,
I wonder at the subject of their dreams.
What matter if tomorrow I command again;
This one—the father lying at my feet
Laughs and plays (in dream) with the son he's never seen. (God
    grant his safe return)
And over there, a dozen paces to my right,
A boy—a man now, he's just passed twenty-one—
Sobs a name, his brother's.
Today's long looked-for mail notified him of his
Brother's death.
And on the other side—
But what was that? A child's frightened cry?
No! I see from whence it came,
That youngster there who's writhing in his sleep.
(He's dreaming of that shelling we received the other day And who
    can blame him, 'twas his first.)
"Marilyn!" Whose voice cried out? Oh, yes!
I know the man. and the name he speaks—his wife's.
Spoke in remorse for that last letter, penned in anger's heat. I cen-
    sored it, you see, and know its content.
He'll be glad tomorrow when I give it back.
I withheld it from the mail, for I knew his anger'd cool,
And he'd regret the sending of it.
But now my reverie is broken;
Other thoughts and sounds impinge upon my mind, (The distant
    sentinel's sharp challenge;
The jackal's cry, the scudding clouds that chase the Moonlight from
    the sky, to let it reappear again To form a new kaleidoscope
    of sight.)

And all my present sons lie quiet in their sleep.
I'm thinking now about an absent son—My own—who sleeps so
* far away*
Beneath the same deep, scintillating canopy To which I turn my
* eyes*
To ask God's blessing on all my sons. Both here and there—
Those whose dreams I'll share
(God willing)
And pray that I might be a faithful father, now— And then.

Tomorrow was another day, he thought to himself, as he put the paper away.

Near the end of January, the advance from Anzio had been stopped. Things also did not go well against the German defenses in the Winter Line. At Anzio, the German strength increased daily, pinning in the Allies. Soon the very real possibility of being destroyed or pushed back into the sea could happen. A decision was made to punch through the German lines surrounding Anzio and the mountains to the south that were bleeding the Allied armies. "Lucas still believed that a quick linkup with the main Fifth Army in the south was possible. Yet German resistance all along the perimeter was growing stronger, not weaker. Further, and unknown to Lucas, his attack would be aimed directly at thirty-six German battalions massing for their counterattack."

A plan was hatched to push forward on 29 January with a two-pronged attack toward the Alban Hills, vital to their success. On the left, a combined group of the British 1st Infantry Division, reinforced by the newly landed Combat Command Group A of the American 1st Armored Division, was to push directly inland toward the Alban Hills. The British, closest to Anzio, were to push forward, while the Americans were to conduct a flanking maneuver to the far left, the western flank. Truscott's 3rd Division was to attack to the east and seize the vital road-and-rail transportation hub of Cisterna. He was reinforced with the Rangers and the 504th Parachute Infantry

Regiment. Darby took a visit to Truscott for the planning details. He wasn't happy. He needed more time for the men to recover and, importantly, more time to conduct a recon of their objective.

CISTERNA PLAN

The Allies' breakout plan took place from 29 to 31 January 1944. Darby's Rangers, supported by the 7th and 15th Infantry Regiments of the 3rd Division, along with some elements of armor, were tasked to seize and hold Cisterna. The basic concept of the mission was a proper Ranger one: an in-depth infiltration at night through enemy lines that were also deep, not just one line, to seize a strategic objective. In the lead, advancing in column, was the 1st Ranger Battalion, scheduled to move out at 0100 hours on 30 January 1944. Fifteen minutes later, the 3rd Battalion was to follow. While the two battalions advanced, Lieutenant Colonel Murray's 4th was to move along the Conca-to-Cisterna Road at 0200 hours, following the general advance of the Allied attack that was taking place across the front. On the left side of the Rangers, the 7th Infantry Regiment, 3rd Infantry Division, was to support the attack and seize the northwestern sector of Highway 7, while the 15th Infantry Regiment of the 3rd Infantry Division was to do the same but on the southeastern sector. Both flanks then would secure the roads leading in and out of Cisterna, which was going to be held by the Rangers. The mission of the 504th PIR was the seizure of Highway 7 and to relieve the Rangers in Cisterna.

SITUATION

All three Ranger battalions assembled near Nettuno on 28 January 1944 to prepare for the attack. The mission had one flaw, and that was intelligence. Prior to all previous Ranger attacks, there had been detailed recon missions and leader's reconnaissance to help plan and brief the men. This time, the Rangers depended on 3rd Division's intelligence for the infiltration route and defensive emplacements they might encounter. There seemed to have been a gap between German defenses to the eastern, right, side of the Conca-Isola Bella-Cisterna Road. "The German situation map for 26 January 1944 clearly shows a 3,500-meter gap between strongpoints, directly on the route used by the infiltrating Ranger Force." The battlefield was a fluid, organic creature. Once a bullet was fired, things changed drastically, and war was not something that could be controlled. Nonetheless, proper reconnaissance by the Rangers had always been done well. Darby's intel provided by some of the patrol indicated something 3rd Infantry Division did not provide: It showed considerable enemy presence in the area they were to move through and in front of Cisterna. But higher authority argued that in fact there was no undue hazard for the mission. In fact, 3rd Infantry Division's detailed intelligence argued that the Germans were on the defensive, not aggressive but weak, with desertions happening, as well as the continuing struggles the German army, the Wehrmacht, had in integrating Poles into their combat groups. It argued that a major enemy counterattack did not seem probable.

Furthermore, the German MLR was five miles north of Cisterna, and not on flat terrain but on the hills beyond the town. This meant that the Ranger attack would not meet heavy opposition. Intelligence was aware of units from the Hermann Göring Division to the front and to the right of the American sector; but the German tanks and artillery losses were at higher rates than those of the Americans, implying that the Allies had more firepower and armor. The Germans did enjoy superiority in terms of observation from their high points. And finally, German counterattacks were not probable, and the Germans would resort to delaying actions, possibly leading to a retreat. Things looked good for the Allied advance across the board.

"As usual," writes Altieri in an unpublished manuscript, "Darby exuded confidence. If he had any compunctions about the suddenness of the mission, about the hazards, about the lack of time to do a thorough personal reconnaissance, as he and his Rangers had always done before an operation, he did not reveal them to his commanders." Although, there are several accounts that indicate he was less than pleased, in fact mad, according to his driver, Carlo Contrera. But there they were. The Rangers did manage to conduct a small recon for themselves, but not in detail. The 29th was spent in reconnaissance and preparation for the attack on the following day. It revealed very little, but did lead to the 83rd not being attached to the 3rd Ranger Battalion. They also spotted a burned-out tank and vehicles blocking the main road. Shells landed nearby, indicating that German artillery was zeroed in on the roadblock. Whatever the case, Darby and Dammer planned and detailed the upcoming mission and were to use "previously reconnoitered routes" to Cisterna.

But unbeknownst or not interpreted properly, despite reports of digging along the railroad tracks west of Cisterna, was the German planned counterattack with 30 infantry battalions, armor, artillery, and with six more infantry battalions in reserve. These units were positioned on the MLR in front of Cisterna and Campoleone, directly in the path of the impending Allied advance. Originally, the German counterattack was to be launched from north to south along the Albano-Anzio Road, with the main concentration on either side of Aprilia. "The date of the attack was to be 28 January, but in a meeting between Army and Army Group Commanders on 26 January D-Day was postponed to 1 February so that reinforcements would be available. These reinforcements were: 1027th and 1028th Infantry Regiments, the Special Artillery Demonstration Regiment, the Special Rocket Projector Demonstration Battalion, and the 1st Battalion of the 4th Panzer Regiment. These units left by train from Germany and are expected to pass through the Brenner Pass on 26 and 27 January. The plan of attack as proposed by the 1st Parachute Corps follows."

The Ranger strength was tabulated by Ranger researcher Julie Belanger. The strength of on-duty men the day before Cisterna on 29 January 1944 was 1st Ranger Battalion: 510; 3rd Ranger Battalion: 501; 4th Ranger Battalion: 568; Ranger Force HQ: 57; for a total of 1,636 on duty. Five hundred eighteen Rangers were absent and not on duty. Combining these numbers, the Rangers had 2,154 men on their rosters. Absent from duty were the 1st Ranger Battalion: 181; 3rd Ranger Battalion: 107; 4th Ranger Battalion: 115, making it 518.

TERRAIN AND WEATHER

The terrain just beyond Anzio and Nettuno was flat farmland dotted with streams and ditches, with a number of stone-and-brick-walled farmhouses typical of the region. Colonel Darby called it a "billiard table" with hills and mountains just beyond Cisterna. The terrain was wet, muddy, had seen—and still had—some snow, creating cold conditions, and was accentuated with a light fog. The wet and soft dirt provided difficulties for heavy mortars and armor. The sky was moonless and cloudy. Sunrise for the attack was 0715 hours, with sunset occurring 12 hours later at 1712. In essence, the infiltration started at night in typical Ranger fashion; and when twilight hit, the Rangers would just about have started the fight, using the approaching dawn to further exploit their combat gains.

RANGER FORCE UNITS

Tasked yet again with the seizure of a vital asset, Colonel Darby had all his battalions available directly under him. The 1st Ranger Battalion was under Major Dobson; the 3rd was commanded by Major Alvah Miller; the mustachioed 4th Rangers were under Major Roy Murray; and, lastly, the Ranger Regimental Headquarters was commanded by Colonel Bill Darby, who was wired in with Truscott's 3rd Infantry Division and had radio communications with his battalions, as well as gunfire support. For this mission, the Rangers carried two extra bandoleers, fragmentation grenades, Sticky grenades, and bazookas for anti-tank capability, without any machine guns because of weight and noise discipline while carrying them. But available were the 60mm mortars they had often used to suppress the enemy during their assaults. The Cannon Company, under First Lieutenant Otis Davey with its four half-tracks, completed the Ranger force. Attached again were elements of the 83rd Chemical Mortar, minus Cos C and D, and minus one PLT from Company A, lost during landing, ready in trucks to support when called upon. Two armor units were made available, 601st Tank Destroyer Battalion represented by one platoon of M-10s and one platoon of Sherman tanks of the 751st Tank Battalion, but the armor was only available along the road from Conca to Isola Bella, the latter well shy of Cisterna. The 7th and 15th Infantry Regiments were also supported with similar attachments.

RANGER INFILTRATION

Darby's plan called for the 1st Battalion to advance from the Line of Departure (LOD) at 0100 hours. This line was four miles south of the town of Cisterna. Since the flat terrain offered no protection whatsoever, it dictated the use of the canals and ditches that had been reconned by the 3rd Infantry Division earlier. Dobson's men were to avoid any contact with the enemy, as they were the lead element tasked with driving out the Germans and capturing the town, not to get drawn into battle while moving to their objective. Once in Cisterna, the 1st Rangers were to hold the northwestern part and repel counterattacks. During daylight hours, the Rangers were then to link up with the 7th Infantry Regiment who had been tasked with the seizure of the northwestern part of the highway.

Major Alvah Miller's 3rd Ranger Battalion was to follow in the footsteps of the lead battalion and would therefore depart 15 minutes after the 1st Battalion had left the LOD. The primary mission was to allow 1st Battalion to seize Cisterna unhindered, and this meant that Miller's men were to fight off and engage any enemy forces encountered. In effect, the 3rd Rangers were the muscle in the mission. After any entanglements had been defeated, they were to join Dobson in Cisterna and establish link-up with the northeast with the 15th Infantry Regiment occupying their sector of Highway 7.

Any support needed for the two battalions was provided by the 4th Ranger Battalion under Murray. His battalion was to move from the LOD at 0200 hours, fully one hour after the 1st Battalion had started its movement and at the same time as the general Allied advance began. Attached to them was a minesweeping team and the 83rd Chemical Mortar, as the ground was too soft to accompany 3rd Battalion. Murray's battalion was to march along the Conca-Cisterna

Road and eventually become the reserve force at Cisterna, which at that time was to be held by the two other Ranger battalions. Available, along the Conca-Cisterna Road, to the 4th was the Cannon Company with 601st Tank Destroyers for anti-tank protection.

The Ranger Force RGT HQ under Darby advanced earlier, at 2315, and established a command post on the right side of the Conca-Cisterna Road by 0125 hours. In typical fashion, the Ranger command had a final briefing for the impending attack. At midnight, all three BNs were at the road junction near LOD for a final last-minute brief, and, importantly, a communications check. The Rangers, especially Darby, knew of the importance of having good communications. Radio silence was to be observed by the two lead battalions until the 1st and 3rd were northeast of Isola Bella, a small grouping of farmhouses along the Conca-Cisterna Road, which the Rangers dubbed Jerryland, and two miles south of the target, Cisterna. The sign and countersign for the operation was the prophetic Bitter, Sweet. Colored flashlights were employed with the letter R used for identification purposes. All the lessons taught and learned were used again. As a contingency, once Cisterna had been taken and communications were unavailable, the Rangers were to fire a series of red Very flares, a system the Rangers had used since the early days of their amphibious assault on Arzew in November of 1942.

Both the 1st and 3rd Battalions moved out on time, but German interdicting artillery fire disrupted their movement from time to time. The battalions moved in single file, like a slithering snake, on the western part of the Mussolini Canal, finally making it into the Pantano Ditch to the right, the east, of the Conca-Cisterna Road. A few times, Rangers hugged the sides of the ditch, keeping quiet, as German sentries walked by on its bank. Luminous tape on the packs and helmets aided the men, but it was a dark night. Attention had to be paid not to lose the man directly in front of you. It was a winding ditch, with water and mud. The Rangers embraced the cold and terrain and moved silently forward. Eventually, they'd have to abandon the shallowing Pantano Ditch and move west, the left, across the road, into deeper ditches running toward Cisterna. The Rangers moved through the ditch. The ground was soft, and the canal trail was slick from light showers. Perfect Ranger weather. A light mist helped conceal them. Lieutenant Clarence Meltesen of 2nd Platoon, C/3, writes, "We were silent. No sloshing of water. We slithered in mud at times. If anyone lost their balance, there was no cursing. There was no rattle, squeak, or creak of weapons or gear." Interestingly, Sergeant Clarence W. Eineichner with 3/HQ, who decided for no particular reason to tag along with Major Alvah Miller, thought, "Stealth, so necessary on our previous successful operations, was not evident as we moved toward Cisterna. Although, with all the chaos, it appeared as if the enemy was not aware of our movements, or was he playing cat and mouse games?"

Nearly two hours into their movement, at 0248 hours, four radio operators who were intended to be with the 3rd Battalion unexpectedly reported to Darby at his Command Post. They had become lost and returned. How this happened was never made clear. In any event, the First Rangers passed by a German *Nebelwerfer* (rocket launcher) battery on their right just before daylight, around 0545 hours. The silent Rangers remained undetected, but they came so close to the Germans that they heard them speak. However, this caused a delay in movement and minor breaks between the companies as they stopped, took a knee, or remained still, until the order was passed down the line to advance again. Dobson considered turning around and sweeping through their position; but, unable to call Darby, he stuck to the original mission.

Halfway through this movement, while still in the Pantano Ditch, the lead elements of the 3rd Battalion lost sight of 1st Battalion. Loss of intervals was rare for them, but this night there were some serious problems. Unbeknownst to them, the 1st Ranger Battalion was half a mile ahead of them and had broken into two units. Each had three companies. What had happened was that German traffic along the Conca-Cisterna Road, which needed to be crossed by the Rangers to then continue their advance, caused problems. Not only were vehicles moving up and down the road, but the Germans also captured a recon troop of the 3rd Infantry Division—43 men with only one escaping. "They heard rather than saw the capture of a large motor patrol of the 3rd Prov Cav Squadron led by Major Edward C. Haggard. Dobson considers this recon patrol on our axis of advance was a major blunder that definitely tipped off the Germans to the coming action in the neighborhood." Things were messy. F, E, and D/1 had made it across the road, just north of Isola Bella, with C/1 stuck at the ditch and the road, followed by B and A Companies. A/1 was just south of Isola Bella. Captain Shunstrom, who had been transferred to the 1st Ranger Battalion, perhaps to give his experience to the new battalion commander, was ordered by Major Dobson to find the trailing three companies somewhere to the rear. Shunstrom moved back, reestablished contact, then sent a runner to get back down the line and establish contact with the trailing 3rd Battalion. 3rd Battalion tried to cross the road and ambushed a vehicle with three staff officers and pushed it off the road. "It was dark, and they stopped. Acting as to need to check and verify something. The driver dismounted, pretending to check his tires, while he checked the ditches. 'So!' Somebody whispered [that] the Germans 'had made the column,' and a fusillade took out the driver and the officers with the motor still running. Then the platoon moved across the road into the left ditch and the canebrake."

Major Miller, with a small command and radio team, crept along the ditch until they approached the road junction. Miller pulled over to the side of the road and began the procedure to transmit. Now with the increasing light, the group moved toward cover in the high ditch, and at the same time they now saw a German tank parked on the side of the road. Sergeant Eineichner was communications sergeant. Miller tried to establish communications with Darby's CP. Focused on it, he didn't hear the warning. A tank nearby the ditch rolled forward and fired a round at the command group. Miller never knew what hit him—his head was torn off by the German shell, which wounded a number of others.

The details of Miller's death are preserved by T/S Dominick F. Poliseno. He was a runner for 1st LT Alfred J. Reid, commanding C Company, and was covering Major Miller at that time. He saw the tank and shouted, "Hit the dirt." Miller was totally involved with trying to reach Force Headquarters by radio and missed the alert. The tank fired a single round, killing the major. Sergeant Eineichner was wounded at the time Major Miller was killed. Lieutenant Jensen was killed by the same round and died in Sergeant Burke's arms, after which the tank was taken out by the 1st platoon, C/3, now in the low (left) ditch in that vicinity. Staff Sergeant Wayne Ruona ordered his grenadier to fire; the man failed to pull the pin but did bounce the grenade off the tank. Ruona then climbed onto the tank deck to drop a phosphorus grenade into the turret.

St. Eineichner recalled, "After checking Major Miller, and realizing we couldn't do anything for him, his body guard removed his map case and some personal items. We moved him to the side of the road to prevent additional future mutilation to his body."

Daylight approached while the 3rd was still two miles out of Cisterna. Things got worse. "The 1st Platoon of C/3 while advancing into the canebrake was shattered by a direct hit of a single German 150 artillery round. This happened while the company was close to catching up to A/3 in the canebrake of the left ditch, and was just after Major Miller was killed." The 3rd had suffered a tremendous loss including casualties inflicted on the company and platoon leadership organization. Ruona reorganized the group and was stopped in crossing the road again when a staff car drove by. B/3, however, managed to clear a group of farm buildings of snipers and machine gunners. Gunfire was all across the front. The constant traffic was a clear warning to everyone. Lieutenant Meltesen recounts the details of his platoon, crossing the heavily trafficked Conca Road:

> I led the second platoon of C/3 and was now guided under the Conca Road and turned right to go up the ditch on the left side of the road. Everybody hit the dirt now as a large German troop carrier headed for Isola Bella came into view and halted. This was the "grosse truppenwagen" of the Nazi street parades in the German newsreels. Three full-sized bank seats. A driver and assistant were up front. There were three riflemen in the middle seat. Two staff

officers were fiddling with maps in the back seat. They had stopped on the Conca Road jog just south of the bridge/overpass and had a fair view, looking back, of some 30 of us in the lower ditch. I did a very slow roll to sight my carbine on the starboard rifleman and checked to see if any of my men were masking my field of fire. T/S Poliseno was in the upper ditch and watched. As the officers moved their maps, the driver dismounted and looked around on his side, and the soldiers began to climb down. Our men on the other side of the road (A/3, B/3) passed the word quietly that we were made and then delivered a fusillade.

The runner Shunstrom had sent found them just after the incident.

The last three companies of the 1st Rangers and the 3rd Battalion closed up again, and advanced toward Cisterna, using ditches dotting the farmland to the north and east. A developing firefight to their front about 300 yards away told the 3rd Ranger Battalion that things were not getting better. The approach of two German tanks prevented them from moving forward. The tanks approached from the right and were just 50 yards away. The Rangers destroyed them quickly using bazookas.

The lead companies under Dobson advanced to the farm fields on the southern edge of Cisterna. Dobson decided to move quickly before the full light of day exposed them. The town was the apex of a triangle—the left was the Ponte Cotta Road, and the right was the Conca-Cisterna Road. Each was roughly 1,000 yards per side. It was the Triangle of Death. The lead companies used a series of trails on the west side of the Conca Road, moving past a small number of farmsteads and homes, skirting by the western side of the Calcabrini House. Here, to the surprise of Fox/1 in the lead, a German self-propelled gun was bivouacked. Scouts who had been stalking in advance of the Ranger column had crept upon several German sentry groups and knifed them before they could spread the alarm. "A sleeping unit was surprised." Gus Schunemann said that the point found a sentry sitting under an olive tree. First Sergeant Mattivi tried to silence him, but the sentry broke the grip and let out a scream. T/S Gilbert indicates that the bivouac was that of a self-propelled gun detachment with four guards posted. All the German guards were taken out by F/1, the point company. "It was just a little before dawn," recalls T/5 James P. O'Reilly of B/3, "when we crossed a small tree-lined road and took to a narrow irrigation canal. We heard a lot of screaming up ahead—the boys were using plenty of knife work. Continuing our march, we passed several artillery and mortar positions, but we had orders to bypass everything, unless absolutely necessary to do other-wise, until we reached Cisterna. Most of us thought we should have knocked the [bastards] off anyway." Fox Company's Lieutenant Fowler and his point men were tasked with the silent removal of sentries. They bumped into two groups. He killed two sentries by slashing their throats, but another German in the second group shouted while being stabbed in his leg by a Ranger, ending the concealment and alerting the encampment, with many asleep in their foxholes. The details of this mishap are well preserved by Schunemann:

> My unit, F company, was the point or lead unit, so I was one of the first Rangers into the area. It was near dawn, about 0500, when we came upon a lone sentry sitting under an olive tree. As our First Sergeant, Frank Mattivi, tried to silence him, the sentry managed to break free of the grip over his mouth and let out a scream that transformed a peaceful rural setting into a living hell. Machine-gun fire opened up from all directions. Unknowingly, we had walked into a well-camouflaged airborne division. They had dug trenches six feet wide by three feet deep, covered them with planks and dirt, and planted cabbage in rows. Except for small openings at each end of the trenches, they were invisible. We caught them asleep, but they woke in a hurry. We were completely surrounded. The air was alive with bul-lets whizzing over our heads like a swarm of mad hornets.

The Rangers smashed through the startled enemy, firing from the hip, emptying magazines and throwing grenades in a mad rush through the encampment. Ranger Carl Lehmann, the man who had helped the old, abused Arab in North Africa, describes the initial stages of combat while firing one and a half of his two bandoleers:

> I sprang running to the left right through an enemy bivouac (no tents, just men lying under blankets), astonished at Germans rising all around, running away with hands in the air, crying "Kamarad!," as I ran through them, shooting from the hip. By the time I had expended the clip from my M1, I had run completely through the camp area, coming to a shallow hedgerow running generally parallel to the ditch, although now I was more than a couple of hundred yards from it. I continued my run up the hedgerow until my attention was caught by the clatter of a flack-wagon which pulled into view on a low ridge perhaps 100 yards to the left. Dawn was just breaking, and the flack-wagon was silhouetted against the lightening sky. I dropped, reloaded, and commenced firing at the soldiers trying to unlimber a brace of automatic guns in the open body of the truck. They were in plain sight and easy targets, and beat a hasty retreat to the far side of the ridge. It was then that I became aware that a line of Rangers had followed me up the ditch, many doing the same as I. (I had no squad at the time and was attached to Company HQ, carrying a load of demolitions). We had quite a successful shoot for several minutes, at Germans whose heads we could see, but who could see only our muzzle-flashes in the dark of the swale. All the metal of the M1 was hot and the wood was smoking.

By 0330 to 0400, the lead companies of the 1st Ranger Battalion were south of town, which turned out was full of Germans; and now a footrace to Cisterna, 600 to 800 yards away, was on.

The Ranger companies moved quickly forward, realizing the game was up and only speed and violence of action would give them the reward they sought: Cisterna. Most Rangers in the lead companies got to within 200 yards when hell broke loose and the Germans hammered them with small-arms fire. "Evidently the enemy had also detected the Rangers' approach through their lines and had had time to prepare an ambush." Fox Company led the charge forward as others hit the ditches or road to return fire. As F/1 pushed through the open toward a white house just north of the road junction and before the rail lines, two lieutenants were killed with two others wounded. One of them was First Lieutenant James C. Fowler, who led his men toward the white house when incoming fire stopped them, with the men hitting the dirt. At this point he tried to reach for his radio, and never got up again. The other killed was Second Lieutenant Harry A. VanSchriver. A handful, perhaps eight Rangers, made it into town. They were either killed, wounded, captured, or driven back. Things turned into a confusing mess. Quickly the Rangers got organized, with company mortars setting up and plastering the Ponte Rotta Road to the front and left of their advance. But ammo ran out quickly at their rate of fire.

That's how desperate the situation had become. Dawn approached and lit the stage for the impending battle. Fox, Easy, and Dog of the 1st Battalion were in an open brawl with the defending Germans—the ones who were supposed to be well north of Cisterna, ready to retreat.

RANGER SUPPORT

Just before the battle developed north of Isola Bella, east of the Conca-Cisterna Road and south of Cisterna, the 4th Battalion left its Line of Departure on time at 0200 hours with the order of movement with C/4 leading, followed by D, HQ, A, B, E, and last Fox Company. After 500 yards, it divided into two groups; C, D, HQ, A, and B moved 300 yards east of the road, then north, paralleling the Conca Road; while E, F, and HQ, followed by Force HQ, continued north on the road. Three hundred yards of slow, careful movement forward, they got hit with stiff resistance at 0315 hours that was as close as 200 yards. They were hit at the German Main Line of Resistance, here manned by a Parachute Machine Gun Battalion with about 100 yards space in between them, and with riflemen every 10 yards. Their positions were in depth and well camouflaged. And the machine guns fired about one foot above the ground. Simultaneously, the advancing flanks of the 7th and 15th IRs didn't even get that far. The 4th, still not at Isola Bella, bumped into "an iron ring around the town." Nearly three hours later, at 0600, attempts to flank to the left, the Germans' right, failed with heavy casualties just before the 1st Battalion passed the *Nebelwerfer* battery.

Seeing the 4th in trouble, Darby ordered two half-tracks and two tank destroyers forward on the Conca-Cisterna Road. The Germans had not been asleep and had mined the road. The toll was one vehicle each lost to the buried mines. Otis was in the Ace of Diamonds when it blew up. Jumping into the nearby ditch, roughly one foot deep, some of the survivors crawled back under fire. One Ranger from the destroyed half-track grabbed the .30 cal off it and prepared to fire—it jammed. For some, it took three hours to make it back to friendly lines; others were captured. During their escape, a German sniper appeared who stood up in front of the fleeing men and "one of the Rangers calmly took aim and shot him with a .45 automatic." And in an odd incident during the retreat, Tank Destroyer Sergeant Larson heard a Ranger yelling to an unseen Kraut, "Are you an American?"

At dawn, the 4th ground to a stop. Unable to push forward, they dug in about one-and-three-quarter miles south of the few farmhouses called Isola Bella, east of the road junction. The distance from the 4th's position was four and a half miles south of Cisterna. The road was blocked by three abandoned vehicles, two peeps and one Italian truck, covered by German fire. There wasn't a way to push through this without major artillery support and armor. The entire American sector was bogged down in its drive to Cisterna. Since Darby was not able to communicate with the Ranger battalions somewhere to his front, he wasn't able to call for fire.

By 0622, Darby had reported to 3rd Infantry Division that he was out of comms with the lead BNs. Within a few moments, Darby was able to get six or eight tanks from the 751st to clear the road-block at 0635 hours. They assumed a holding position on the road behind the 4th Battalion. Finally, Colonel Darby had a short situation report with Dobson at 0700. The 1st Rangers were 800 yards south and battling enemy forces. The 3rd Battalion was to his right and his battalion still attempted to move toward the town. Suddenly, communications dropped and were lost again. In daylight hours, 0720, repeated attempts by Cannon Company to break through the German lines clogging up the route to Cisterna failed due to heavy incoming fire. A tearful First Lieutenant Davey, of Orange, New Jersey, and a couple of months shy of his 25th birthday, joined Darby in his HQ inside a farmhouse. Finishing his report of his four failed attempts to punch through, and wiping away his tears, he moved out to report to 3rd Infantry Division. He was killed by a sniper as he exited the Command Post just before noon. At around noon, an artillery barrage killed Major Bill Martin. Another one killed Darby's field clerk, Corporal Presley Stroud. Both Rangers were Originals; all the while, all three battalions bled. At the same time, Ranger Force HQ notes, "The force had been badly shot up and was surrounded. Enemy tanks and Self-Propelled guns were causing great damage." At 1259 hours, Ranger Private Kembler reported to the Force CP. He was concerned about stretcher-bearers for 3rd Battalion and said casualties were very heavy, and he took it upon himself to get aid for the wounded. When questioned, Kembler said that he had only seen three casualties. He seemed nervous and unsure. Dammer ordered him to remain at the Command Post. Dammer understood the young private.

Onward they fought: The 1st and 3rd Battalions were by now all on the left side of the Conca-Cisterna Road, north of Isola Bella, but short of Cisterna. Captain Shunstrom looked and found Dobson. The situation was that the three lead Rangers companies had two companies facing to the front in a battle with Germans, while the third company swung to the left, trying to work its way to the flank and drive into the German side. The battalion commander believed that the enemy fire came from no more than 100 yards across the Ponte Rotta Road, from a heavily wooded area. It seemed the Rangers were receiving fire from two 20mm machine guns and three smaller-caliber machine guns. To the left front, Dobson noted two more MGs with infantry trying to infiltrate through Rangers. As the briefing was happening, an alert was called out that three tanks were approaching from the Ranger position's rear right on the road, traveling with 100-yard intervals—obviously making it harder to hit them. Both officers took off to set up company defenses. During those confusing moments, Corporal Mosier saw a building when it got light and spotted a tank he thought was friendly, but then it fired on his group. The Rangers attacked and destroyed it, but more tanks approached with infantry and auto weapons.

Dobson was almost immediately wounded, either by shrapnel from incoming artillery, as per Shunstrom's After-Action Report, or by shrapnel from personally destroying a tank. With the 1st Battalion's leadership decimated and Shunstrom unable to find the executive officer next in line of command, one Captain Saam with his macabre sense of humor, Shunstrom himself took command of the battalion. During this melee, 3rd Rangers destroyed one of the tanks while the 1st Battalion boys took care of the other two, using bazookas and white phosphorus grenades—Gela-style—hand-to-hand and up close and personal. After all, those tanks had tried to kill them. It was after this, around 0700 hours, that Dobson, who was now wounded, was able to contact Colonel Darby and apprised him of the situation. Things were dire.

The detailed look at the battle saw the 1st and 3rd within the Triangle of Death. By daylight, the trailing three companies of the 1st Battalion had arrived and slotted into the line to the southwest, with F/1 across from the white house representing the far-right flank of the two Ranger battalions. The white house was just south of Cisterna's rail station and north of the Conca road junction where it split into two. The left went to the Ponte Rotta Road, and the right to Cisterna. During this time, "Colonel Darby was on the radio, frantically calling for us to direct artillery fire to enemy positions. The battalion commander told him we couldn't use artillery support, as we were in a hand-to-hand situation. We were pinned down in a cabbage field, and the Germans were making sauerkraut out of it with machine guns. We were also firing in all directions; however, they were so well hidden, they were difficult to spot. We managed to inflict heavy casualties on the enemy, however, even though we were greatly outnumbered." As the Rangers were so close to the German lines, any artillery support would have been "danger close," meaning the Rangers would be exposed to its deadly fire. The same applied to the Germans. The only difference, and it was a major one, had German tanks and self-propelled guns available to drive up and down the roads shooting at the Rangers holding road embankments, ditches, and a few of the farmhouses. When the shit hit the fan, Dobson had established his headquarters at the small house owned by the Calcabrini family to this day—it would be known as the Calcabrini House, one the Rangers had overrun. It sat 1,200 yards southwest of Cisterna. Right behind the far-right flank manned by Fox, 1st Rangers, was an aid station, which would fill quickly with the wounded battling hard and in close quarters with the continuously reinforcing German troops and armor. Small-arms fire, grenades, and bazookas were the only weapons available to the Rangers, as their mortars ran out of rounds, so heavy was the fighting. Dobson saw at least 15 German vehicles within sight of his CP.

The movement and actions of the 3rd Battalion started even before they hit the triangle: Their leadership had been devastated early on. Nonetheless, Rangers led the way, and Able/3 crossed the Conca-Cisterna Road and moved forward and to the right of the 1st Battalion. At this point, the 1st Rangers were spread from right to left, with F/1 on the far right; moving left, E, D, C, B, and A/1 on line to the west. A/3 dug in to the left of A/1. Baker/3 had a firefight on the right flank of the Matto Creek, which was the boundary to the west and south of the Rangers. B/3 used mortars to destroy a flak wagon that had been interdicting movement to the Calcabrini House and the Anima Jante Creek, which ran from the road in a northwestern direction with the Calcabrini House sitting on the right side of the creek. Charlie Company, 3rd Battalion, stopped at the Conca/Ditch

Road where Battalion CO Miller had been killed, with Captain Joe Larkin taking command. Here they also destroyed a German staff car, one tank, and one self-propelled gun. Charlie crossed into the Matto Creek, where it got almost immediately hammered by German mortars, but it linked up with B/1 and then became flank security for both battalions now inside the triangle. Actions within the triangle were as confusing as any battle ever had been or would be, and this was no exception to Carl Lehmann:

> There was a tall barn nearby, and I climbed to its second floor, which had a door looking south the way we had come, but another window higher up and facing west, which I attempted to gain for a better look with a handy ladder. I had no sooner started up the ladder when I heard the ungodly clatter of an armored vehicle outside. I abandoned the ladder and stole a peek through the door, which revealed a self-propelled gun with a driver and a 4-man crew in the back, working about the gun, directly under me. I dropped a grenade in it and hit the ground running on the other side of the barn before it exploded. I did not inspect the results. I was running here and there like a scared rabbit, but I had a good excuse: I was looking for my Company. I finally found Bills, a wounded Lieutenant Rip Reed, Scotty Munro, Larry Hurst, Hodel (the only ones I now remember for sure) and the remains of Bills' platoon, on the extreme right of the battlefield, and dug in with them there. We were about a hundred yards southeast of the farmhouse [Calcabrini House] where, I learned later, Ehalt and his radio were. We could see distant scurrying German vehicles on the road to our right—out of rifle range, and all of the action was now going on to the north and west of us.

During all of this confused fighting, a flak wagon constantly fired at the Calcabrini House. Dog/3 provided rear and flank security. E/3 set up to the left of A/3 at the Ponte Rotta Road while F/3 settled in just behind E/3 along the Matto Creek, securing the far-left flank of the battalions. The Rangers were battered by heavy barrages and armor sorties. Ten minutes after comms with Darby had been lost, the Rangers had created a crescent-shaped defense along the Ponte Rotta Road, anchored on the right by the Conca-Cisterna Road and the left by the junction/bridge of the Matto Creek intersecting the Ponte Rotta Road. Rear and flank security was provided by three companies, B, C, and D, of the 3rd Ranger Battalion. "Their shit was weak" as tanks, flak wagons, and SPs roamed the area, discharged all their ammunition, only to depart, refuel, rearm, and return to hammer the trapped Rangers over and over again. The only hope was for 4th Ranger Battalions and other Allied forces to punch through the German lines and relieve them of the continuous German attacks. The overall situation was dire, with German veteran reinforcements of the Parachute Lehr Battalion and the Hermann Göring Division moving into line. The Calcabrini House became a strongpoint for the Ranger defense, able to withstand some punishment.

Meanwhile, the 4th Rangers, and the Dogfaces of the 7th and 15th Infantry Regiments of Truscott's 3rd Infantry Division, all were stuck barely beyond their original lines of departure. At 0800, communications with the 1st Ranger Battalion were reestablished— they were "fighting to gain a foothold in the outskirts of town in the vicinity of the railroad station. Artillery concentrations were requested and fired on the northern and western parts of town. Fire was discontinued since observation was reported impossible." By 0805 hours, one Sherman tank retreated alongside the 4th Rangers. The desperate situation was recorded in the 3rd Division journal. "MG fire both flanks, shells everywhere perhaps 170s. 4th boy that is in the jam."

Eventually the report would read "4th Battalion well shaken up." Five minutes later, Darby ordered the Bastard Battalion of the 83rd Mortars forward to set up behind Murray's unit. Darby's words to Hutchinson were, "Hutch, get a couple of co's up here right away. Drive them as far as the [Mussolini] canal and put them on carts with plenty of ammo. I'll deploy them after they get here." Here they did what they could, pounding various targets and areas with 250 heavy shells. This, despite the terrible quagmire of terrain. They dug deep trenches because of the heavy incoming artillery and were ready to act as riflemen, but it was too late. There was rapid dialogue between Dammer; Murray; Walt Nye, Murray's XO; and Hutchinson during those tense moments: "1122 Hello Hutch; this is Roy. Will you put that smoke down now? Hutchinson, this is Nye. As soon as you give them W.P. I want you to pour on W.P. until I tell you to stop; then give me ten rounds of H.E. Hutch responded with, Okay Nye. In about three minutes. Dammer communicated at 1145—this is Col. Dammer. Tell Murray to stay in the C.P. until the tank officer gets there. Hutchinson, please. Murray, the tanker reports that W.P. is landing on friendly troops across the mined area."

Darby did not quit his beloved Rangers. By 1045, he again had comms with 1st Battalion, where he received updates of their dire situation near Cisterna, and he also received updates from the 4th Ranger Battalion. Darby was determined to get the armor he felt was needed to punch through the German lines to free his entrapped boys. Thirty minutes later, he tells his trapped battalions to hang on as tanks were on their way. He repeated this at 1144 but that the tanks were now 2,500 meters out from them. If only they could hold on like they had at Gela. But the farmlands were not Gela. Still, there was hope, as some beleaguered Rangers saw tanks moving along the Conca Road, much to their relief and joy—joy that turned into tears: German tanks rolled up. Three were destroyed by the fightin' and killin' Rangers. "Lacking antitank guns or heavy weapons, the Rangers fought back with bazookas and Sticky grenades. One enemy tank was quickly set aflame. As a second tank rumbled down on a squad commanded by Sergeant Thomas B. Fergen, he hit it with a Sticky grenade. One of his men blasted it with a bazooka, and another finished the tank off by climbing up on it and dropping a grenade down the turret."

It was hard to fill in the gaps of leadership, although plenty of Rangers stood up to lead the men in the bitter fighting. Leadership losses included, but were not limited to, 1st Battalion CDR Dobson, who was wounded; the horrible death of 3rd Battalion CDR Alvah Miller; E/1 CO CDR CPT Bev Miller, KIA; killed also was F/1 CO CDR 1st LT Fowler, who early in the op had killed a couple of German sentries with his knife; C/1 CO CDR 1st LT Kendrick, WIA; and also wounded D/1 CO CDR 1st LT Magee. Significant losses.

The Triangle of Death now saw the companies dug in, but the perimeter dwindled down to 300 yards in diameter. The After-Action Report written by Captain Shunstrom provides the on-scene dramatic conditions and actions.

> There was a great deal of enemy automatic firing coming into our positions. When the enemy had pinned us down with automatic fire, we would hear single shots as they sniped at men in our position. So far, both battalions occupied an area of about three hundred yards in diameter. At this time, Capt. Saam, executive officer of the 1st Ranger Battalion, came back from a patrol. He immediately took command of both battalions. Captain Larkin, the executive officer of the 3rd Ranger Battalion, had assumed command immediately after the death of his battalion commander, Major Miller. Capt. Saam immediately took two companies of the 3rd Ranger Battalion and sent them to a position about three hundred yards in our rear, with a mission of closing the gap in the circle that we had formed and to dig in and hold at all costs. He informed Captain Shunstrom that C and D Companies had been unsuccessful in their enveloping movement to the flank, and that he had ordered them to dig in and hold the ground that they had. This left four companies of the 3rd Ranger Battalion in the immediate vicinity of the command post in reserve. He then gave orders that the radio operator call back for reinforcements on the radio. A battalion aid station was set up in a building

where the radio was kept about 25 yards from the command post's position.

Neither Ranger officer sat in the Command Post at the Calcabrini House. "In the D/1 area, Corporal Kenneth W. Markham had been firing along with Captain Charles W. Shunstrom and Capt. Frederick J. Saam from a ditch position. During the day, the Captains had argued dates of rank while sniping and being sniped at."

There were lulls in incoming barrages but always, always, these lulls were followed by heavy ones (barrages). The Rangers were low on ammo, despite the extra load they had carried into the mission. The three reserve companies handed over half their ammunition to the front-rankers. Desperate times. But worse times were ahead, as German reinforcements from the east came down Highway 7 and attacked the rear of the Rangers. This was the highway that had to have been cut by the other units from the 3rd Infantry Division and paratroopers. Sometime during a lull in the fight, a patrol from the 15th Infantry Regiment made it into the perimeter but departed quickly with German prisoners as the Germans finally started to shut the trap completely. The worst had come.

By noon or 1330 hours, as per AAR, the Germans had captured Ranger prisoners growing from 12 to 80 in but a few moments. The German paratroopers drove their prisoners in front of their armored personnel carriers toward the center of the Ranger lines, from the rear, demanding their surrender.

Sporadic small-arms fire was heard all during this operation. Two of the German guards were seen to fall. Immediately two more German soldiers bayoneted two American soldiers—who were then prisoners with their hands in the air—in the back, killing them. The Germans formed the 10 men into ranks and marched them toward another position that Lieutenant Evans, Company Commander of the 3rd Ranger Battalion, occupied. Lieutenant Evans's company refused to surrender. Instead, his company ambushed the guards, killing two more. The Germans retaliated once again by bayoneting two more of men in the back. Lieutenant Evans's company was very low on ammunition and eventually ran out and surrendered.

The Germans by now had about 80 American prisoners and formed them into columns of four and immediately started to march them toward the center of the Ranger position, where the command post was. Captain Saam immediately dispersed the four remaining companies that were in reserve and planned an ambush for the oncoming German soldiers who were guarding the American prisoners. Lieutenant Evans was made to lead this column up the road. The Germans kept shouting "Surrender or we shall shoot the prisoners. All this time, small-arms fire was coming into our positions from the enemy to our front and flanks, keeping us well pinned down."

For Carl Lehmann, the actions so far had sucked up all his adrenaline:

> I was dozing from exhaustion in the early afternoon, when, after the events at dawn and shortly thereafter, I settled with the remains of Bills' platoon, taking an occasional shot, mostly long-range, at vehicles on the road. I woke to Bills' excited scream, "Them bastards is givin' up!" By "them bastards," he meant our guys who were being marched toward our positions, bare-headed with their hands clasped over their heads. We jumped to our feet as one and started running in the opposite direction— toward the beachhead. No one of us tried to shoot through the prisoners.

Dozing away wasn't just Lehmann but also Ranger Dominick Poliseno, who awoke when he heard Germans marching prisoners near the abandoned house he had fallen asleep in. A German paratrooper was backing into the door when Poliseno heard a captured Ranger sergeant on the road yelling at him not to shoot the men because they would be killed. He hid his weapon and carried out a wounded comrade. Poliseno would eventually escape through the advancing Russians to American troops in the west. Half-tracks and armor rolled about, with one tank with loudspeaker calling for surrender. At least twice, the Rangers killed Germans approaching them with their prisoners. Both times, the Germans bayonetted the same number of Rangers in return. There was no messing about. There was a final attempt by Shunstrom and Saam to stop the surrender, but the fire discipline of the Rangers broke down with some men shooting early, and also killing their own held prisoners by the Germans. Yet again, the veteran German troops killed Americans in return. Tit for tat—bullet and death for bullet and death, or bayonet and death. Ever brave and ever angry at anything failing the Ranger standard, Shunstrom, and probably Saam as well, shot at their own men—but to no avail. The mass surrender had begun. What Shunstrom did to his personalized .45 remains a mystery. He may very well have buried it. The men that had set up in ambush immediately ceased firing, and a few of them who were evidently new in combat immediately got hysterical and started to leave their positions and surrender. All attempts to stop this disobedience of orders failed. Eventually, all men surrendered and were taken prisoner by the Germans.

During those fatal last moments, hard as nails, and at one time battle-fatigued, Sergeant Major Ehalt called Darby, after a captain from the 1st Ranger Battalion was too overwrought and weeping, and the sergeant major apologized for their surrender. "Some of the fellows are giving up. Colonel, we are awfully sorry. They can't help it, because we are running low on ammunition. But I ain't surrendering. They are coming into the building now." Ehalt had only five men left. "So long, Colonel, maybe when it's all over I'll see you again." Years later, Ehalt wrote a short account of that moment. Once he had informed Darby that it was all over, Darby replied, "Ehalt, I leave everything in your hands. Tell the men I am with them to the end." The radio went *wham, wham* and went dead. He had destroyed the radio and weapons. Ehalt—Silver Star, Bronze Star, and Purple Heart recipient—would spend 16 months in prison camps until liberated. When he finally arrived home, nobody offered him a seat on the subway, and a cab driver refused to take him. In later years, Ehalt reflected on his time, and came to the conclusion that "the real thing [war] is never told. They glamorize the game of war. They never tell of the heartache." Unlike Ranger Bill Fox, Ehalt would do it all over again. He was deeply patriotic and identified as 100 percent American. He was not in favor of Americans being sent to fight somebody else's war; but, if attacked, every man, woman, and child should fight to the death. He favored a draft. He wanted all immigrant children to speak English.

During the close-quarters fight, Ranger Richard Glasscock of Able 3 had been an assistant rocket-launcher gunner; but when his gunner was killed, Ranger Tom Bearpaw took over as loader. They carefully waited until the tanks rode by, exposing their rear, then the bazookas were fired. All crew that climbed out of the tanks or vehicles were cut down. "Lieutenant Charles Palumbo and Lieutenant Paul Johnston of Able 3, with the assistance of a Ranger, knocked out a German vehicle and took five prisoners. As they were being marched away, the Germans made a break for freedom and were shot." Despite having carried extra ammunition for the mission, everyone was running short, from riflemen to mortar gunners to rocket-launcher teams. Tom Bearpaw, like many others, tried to make a break for it. His buddy, PFC August Cordaway of A/3, might have been with him. Bearpaw had no ammo, no weapons other than his .45, and that was down to a few rounds in his magazine, and that probably wouldn't stop a tank. He crawled into a ditch, where he bumped into two other Rangers, one of whom was wounded. And so was Bearpaw. His left thigh and leg had been hit with shrapnel. Bearpaw and his companions were taken captive. One did not survive, despite Bearpaw's best efforts. Cordaway was captured and ended up at Stalag VIIA.

Tom Bearpaw of Oklahoma became a prisoner of war and was imprisoned at Stalag IIB at Hammerstein. The Germans had an affection and fascination for Native Americans, and Bearpaw was treated well by the guards. He learned pidgin German from them. When he was interrogated after his capture, the Germans wanted to know why Natives fought for the Americans, considering that the "Indians" were slaughtered, treated like animals, and kept on reservations. Tom Bearpaw, deeply patriotic, simply said, "I'm an American." Those types of questions were always asked and answered the same way, perplexing the Germans. The guard Tom Bearpaw remembered vividly was Otto, who respected Indians and knew a bit of history. Eventually, Bearpaw and two others made good their escape, ironically just two weeks before the camp was liberated. Ranger T/5 Thomas Bearpaw remarkably survived 14½ months as a prisoner of war in Stalag IIB, near Poland, and survived the 1,000-mile Black Death March from Poland to Germany. On 15 April 1945, Thomas and two other Americans escaped during a bombing raid and hid out for about three weeks. One day while hiding in a cellar, they heard tanks rumbling through the town. Thomas ran out and flagged down one of the tanks. The tank commander of the 5th Armored Division stopped and asked who he was. Thomas said, "I'm a Cherokee Indian from Oklahoma." The tank commander tossed him a bottle of confiscated champagne and yelled, "Here, have one on me!" and raced on to battle. Minutes later, the three escaped prisoners were safe with American troops.

After his liberation, Tom Bearpaw volunteered for duty in the Pacific but ended up as an MP in Japan after the war. Thomas Bearpaw's name sits on a brick that makes up a memorial created by the Cherokee Nation in Oklahoma, and he was inducted into the state's Military Hall of Fame in October 2024.

The Panzer Division Hermann Göring report not only notes the final moments of the battle at Cisterna, but also lists some of the hard-core units the Rangers fought:

> The first attack force had made several penetrations, which were repulsed by local counterattacks. Enemy units which advanced to Cisterna were destroyed. During the morning, the enemy began a new counterattack, with a strong infantry force, northeast of di M Garbaldi - Isola Bella. Our forces counterattacked and fought heavily until darkness. A defensive front from Isola Bella to benchmark 45 (3 km southeast) along the Canale Mussolini to north benchmark 31 (6 km southeast of Isola Bella) was restored. An enemy breakthrough from the beachhead had to be prevented,

and a closed main line of resistance in the sector of the 3rd
Panzer Grenadier Division had to be restored. In the sector
of the Panzer Division Hermann Göring, the 26th Panzer
was to counterattack the 3rd American Infantry Division,
which had penetrated south of Cisterna. The 26th Panzer
Division was concentrated in the area north of Cisterna and
units of the 114th Jager Division, which had arrived in the
region south of Velletri, were attached as Regimental Group
Berger to the Panzer Division Hermann Göring.

One German account claimed the Allied advance was supported
by massive artillery and tank support. We know this not to be true for
the Rangers.

The battle certainly left an impression on the Germans.
Oberleutnant Opel, one of the Lehr regiment's company commanders, said:

> We had no heavy weapons, only FG 42 submachine guns.
> We were deployed to protect the counterattacks of our
> tanks. I only remember one episode of these actions. To
> check a force of Rangers who had thrust into the posi-
> tions held by a neighboring company, I launched a coun-
> terattack at one of their flanks, thus cutting off a large
> number of Americans from their unit. About four or five
> hundred Americans fell into our hands. However, others
> had escaped and entrenched themselves in surrounding
> farms. They surrendered after a heroic stand. During this
> action, I was shot twice, but kept on fighting until relieved
> by reinforcements.

Another German account mentions that Lehr paratrooper
Lieutenant Herbert Joswig hit the Rangers in the flank and captured
400–600 prisoners.

For Carl Lehmann and many others, the key was to survive the initial moments once captured. It was not uncommon to shoot enemy prisoners after a heated battle.

> We got at least a quarter-mile back toward the beachhead before we were pinned in a plowed field by machine-gun and rifle fire from concealed positions. I was straddled with a burst and a bullet hit Larry Hurst. It was hopeless; and while somebody waved a white piece of paper (all our handkerchiefs were OD) we lifted our hands. Before doing so, I managed to bury a Luger which I had carried through Sicily and Italy, but forgot something else which damned near got me executed. The first German I saw was an officer in a leather coat running, pistol pointed at us, screaming, "Are there any more Americans out there?" Hodel answered inanely "No capisce!" Shortly thereafter, we were marched into a farmyard and searched, during which I for a time believed I was about to reap my final reward. This little Kraut who searched me looked about fifteen, and he dearly wanted permission to shoot me because of "scalps" he found in my shirt pocket. The "scalps" were the Nazi wings worn on breasts of the tunics and coats of the Germans. During the time before we went on this last expedition, I had been the first in a hastily evacuated German position—a barn obviously used for sleeping, where numerous tunics and overcoats were scattered about. I stripped them all before anyone else came into the position. After separating me from the others, the little Kraut took this handful to the Feldwebel, begging him for permission to shoot me. The Feldwebel shook his head with a "Nein!" But the little bastard kept it up, drawing more headshakes and quiet "Neins." Before this played out, I was blessing the Feldwebel's obviously sainted mother for having birthed him. Before we were marched out of the farmyard to the rear areas, the Feldwebel came close and smiled at me. "You haff a Churman name, Karl!" That and what went

before was worth the snappy salute I delivered and which he
returned.

Experienced or savvy Rangers destroyed radio equipment and
weapons, while others booby-trapped gear. It was a miserable end to
the greatest fighting outfit of the Mediterranean Theater.

Back at the Command Post, Darby kicked his staff out as he wept
bitter tears for the loss of his beloved boys. A few hard moments later,
he alerted 3rd Infantry Division to the destruction of the 1st and 3rd
Ranger Battalions, and his lack of communications with Murray's 4th.
What was left of his command reorganized. B/Company 83rd closed
the gap between the 4th Rangers and the 15th Infantry Regiment on
the right to prevent German penetration. Eventually, and with little
if any satisfaction, the 4th Rangers and the 15th seized Isola Bella,
capturing 250 Germans, of whom 150 were from the 1st Parachute
Regiment and the rest from the Hermann Göring Division. The
Americans remained in position until 4 February 1944.

The Ranger Force casualties at Cisterna are subject to debate,
although perhaps 737 Rangers were unaccounted for or MIA: 1st
Battalion, 21 officers and 370 enlisted, 391 total; 3rd Battalion, 18
officers and 328 enlisted, 346 total. There were then 737 in the 1st
and 3rd Ranger Battalions. Another source, Julie Belanger, a Ranger
researcher, lists 765 missing in action. Killed in action: 1st Battalion,
4 officers and 12 enlisted, 16 total; 3rd Battalion, 1 officer and 9
enlisted, 10 total; 4th Battalion, 3 officers and 10 enlisted, 13 total;
RF HQ, 2 officers and 1 to 4 enlisted, 3 to 7 total. In total, then,
there were 42 to 46 killed. Belanger puts this number at 56 killed in
action. The myth of only 6 Rangers returning also needs a closer look.
Rangers either in service or returning from the battlefields were: 1st
Ranger, 185; 3rd Ranger, 155; 4th Ranger, 505; Ranger Force HQ, 54.
For the 1st and 3rd, this meant 658 prisoners, 56 killed, 51 wounded,
escaped, or returned. The 4th Battalion started with a hefty 568 and
suffered 20 killed in action or dying of wounds, with 53 wounded.
Some 548 Rangers were still around. Hundreds were wounded but
exact numbers, even the ones above, are not absolute. A number of

Rangers made their way back to friendly lines, while others escaped, creating more legendary tales of Darby's Rangers—these men were dubbed the Houdini Club.

Although not the end of the Rangers, as a fighting force it was finished. The 4th battled on, as was noted in their Journal of Operations, with combat patrols and under enemy shelling. On 10 February, the 4th Ranger Battalion was attached to the 504th PIR, and the Bastard Battalion of the hard-fighting 83rd went to the 45th "Thunderbird" Infantry Division. A week later, on 17 February 1944, Colonel Darby became the commander of the hard-suffering 179th Infantry Regiment of 45th Infantry Division. He would reform the unit under his leadership. By 27 March 1944, 19 officers and 134 or 137 enlisted men of the 4th Ranger Battalion, always commanded by the great Roy Murray, left Anzio for Naples, where they then were transported to the United States. Eighty-seven (perhaps more) original Rangers from 1st Ranger Battalion made it home. Others with less time in service joined the FSSF, which itself was short of men and on the chopping block by higher-ups until the arrival of the Ranger replacements. The fabled Ranger battalions were officially deactivated at Camp Butner. The 1st Rangers and 3rd on 15 August 1944, and Murray's 4th Battalion on 24 October 1944. Nine hundred sixty-two former Rangers went on in combat with other units.

WHAT HAD GONE WRONG FOR THE RANGERS?

Primary blame can be assigned to faulty interpretation or analysis of otherwise sound intelligence reports by the 3rd Intel staff. In particular, a story circulated about a Polish prisoner, Stempkofski, who, upon capture, had informed them of the German reinforcements to the front lines and planned counterattack. Lieutenant Colonel Herman Dammer said that he had heard of a captured German officer who was supposed to have stated that the attack was anticipated, and therefore Germans reinforced the sector and ordered the men not to engage the Americans, even if they pushed well into the rear. Dammer was not able to verify the report.

But the very poor timing of the Allied attack hurt. An earlier one might have been successful, or it might not have been. "The Germans had planned to attack from north to south along the Albano-Anzio road, with the main concentration on either side of 'the Factory' at Aprilia. The original date for the attack was 28 January, but on the 26th Kesselring [Field Marshal] and Mackensen [Major General commanding the 14th Army] postponed it to 1 February to await the arrival of the reinforcements. The German plan called for three main phases: Phase I (3–10 February), preparatory attacks to cut off the British salient at the Albano road and to capture the Factory; Phase II (16–20 February), penetration of the enemy perimeter along the Albano road; and Phase III (28 February–2 March), an attack on Cisterna and penetration of the beachhead defenses along the Mussolini Canal."

The Germans supposedly detected the infiltration one mile south of Cisterna and set a trap. The Rangers, however, were able to sneak into a German encampment just outside of Cisterna, slaughtering 100 soldiers in their sleep. So, the infiltration seemed to have gone well enough. More probable cause for their defeat was the amassing of German troops and the lack of enough armor and artillery support. Considerations need to be given to the lack of radio communications with forward observers. Although during the battle several shells were fired by the Navy, they could not assure its accuracy and therefore shelling was abandoned. There was no air cover provided to the infiltration force. One key reason for the loss was the German reinforcements arriving on the scene without much interference. It was far easier for the Germans to move their units around and entrap the Rangers, who had slinked through their lines. Perhaps the Rangers suffered from a lack of good replacements, and no doubt some of that had merit; nonetheless, the Rangers managed to infiltrate silently through unanticipated German defensive lines. Additionally, the battalions may have been understrength; but if they had managed to get into Cisterna, they would have fought tooth-and-nail and held it for follow-on forces. Yet the overall Allied advance stalled completely. Even though the two Ranger battalions lost many leaders in the early phases of the fight, there can be little doubt that those holes were plugged by veterans capable of leading men in dangerous situations. Darby may very well have thought this to be a poor mission because of the lack of time to properly recon the area and to give his men the time to refit and regroup prior to the attack; but he and his staff did what soldiers do: They obey. "The Rangers were not ambushed, but their infiltration tactics were not suited for use against the prepared defensive positions of the Germans." One thing is for certain: The Germans bled themselves out against the Rangers. The fight forced a postponement of the previously planned counterattack when the Rangers went straight into Combat Group (KampfGruppe) Konrad in Cisterna. Konrad had parts of the HG Panzer Division and 114th Infantry Division, totaling four battalions with tanks and self-propelled guns in their TO&E. Combat Group Konrad also had more support from 32 15cm guns, 42 10.5 cm guns, 3 10cm guns, 11 8.8 cm AA, 9 3.7cm, and 31 2cm AA. During the battle, the Hermann Göring Division was reinforced by elements of the 114 Jager Division, and the 26th Panzer Division, which was part of Konrad Group but had been stationed north of it. The mission itself was a perfect Ranger operation that almost succeeded against an overwhelming force of veteran German troops and armor.

But the fight for some Rangers was far from over. Duty, honor, the kind of special volunteer attracted to dangerous men and dangerous missions, were to add to the woes of Nazi Germany by tying down thousands of soldiers hunting down those courageous men who escaped their prisoner-of-war camps. The Rangers of the Houdini Club.

10

THE HOUDINI CLUB

CAPTAIN CHARLES MERTON SHUNSTROM

Headquarters, First Ranger Battalion

Shunstrom escaped on 7 February 1944 from the Laterina camp in Italy. He was the first to do so. He stuffed all the valuables he had managed to hold on to around his toes in his shoes—insignia, watch, and rings. He then joined the enlisted ranks doing manual labor, until he made his way to a barn and found a plank. He used the board to lift the first wire of the fence, bluffed the guard into believing he was an Italian laborer repairing the wire, and then he used the same technique to get out of the camp. He walked to a nearby barn, knocked on the door, and asked for help. He was given food and a rough direction of travel by the woman at the barn. She pointed to a road into the mountains and told him to follow it until he came to a particular house. At the house, which was part of the Italian resistance and British Special Operations Executive, he was given civilian clothing, money, and directions to the coast. He moved at such speed that any other Ranger escapees were well behind him.

He traveled for 12 days, walking from 0700 hours until 2000 hours daily, toward the Adriatic coast over the snowcapped mountains; at times the snow was five feet deep on the trails. And he did get lost at times but managed to always get back on the trail. He covered some 350 kilometers, and, at times, was on mountains that were 700 to

1,000 meters in altitude. Shunstrom was a hard, hard man and possessed great strength. He pretended to be an Italian, whistling Italian songs he had picked up while walking, and learning a few words here and there during his movement. He had scrounged over 200 cigarettes by the time he ended up around the Ravenna area and the Communist partisan Garibaldi Brigade. There he was carefully interrogated, since he could easily have been a Fascist spy instead of an American.

When Shunstrom realized that there were no boats available at the time to take him to Allied forces, he took another course of action. He had heard that the infamous Axis Sally had mentioned his name, and he fully knew that his reputation would be exploited by the partisans for more money from the various Allied intelligence services operating in the area. He negotiated with the partisans and insisted on a more robust presence before he signed off on a supply request, which they forwarded on to the intel operatives. He participated in sabotage activities for the next six weeks, blowing up trains, raiding towns, and kidnapping mayors who were then given a fake trial and executed—no mercy—all-around wreaking havoc using all his skills. He helped a Russian nurse move through the lines to eventually get to her husband. She stayed with the medical station at the guerrillas' base in the meanwhile. The German response was clear. They found the local band and attacked its patrol base. Shunstrom told the woman to leave, but she did not want to abandon her patients. He found an oxcart and moved her and the patients away from the base as the Germans attacked. The fighters sent the Germans reeling back temporarily, sniping at them and attacking the tanks.

Time had come for Shunstrom to continue his original mission: to escape. He asked for a boat ride or help in crossing the line to the beachhead. He was offered a ride to a boat and covered some 150 miles in the German rear area until they were stopped at a checkpoint. The truck slowed, and the German guard made the mistake of lifting the tarp—a burst of fire killed him. Shunstrom did not mess about. Six Germans were killed, and the rest of the band scattered. He was on his own now.

The young captain moved south through the Arezzo-Rimini area, pretending to be an Italian worker on his way home. His looks certainly did not arouse suspicion, and by now he spoke enough Italian to get by and even spoke to Germans when getting water from one. He was staying in a town when a local boy who had been hired to bring him figs told him about three British soldiers next door. A German patrol found the three soldiers. He watched them shoot one, with one escaping. The third man was captured. A German walked up to Shunstrom's house and knocked on the door. Inside, Shunstrom knocked the man out and fled. He moved on and suffered through a bout of malaria. He hired himself out to build defensive fortifications closer to the front. He hid in a cemetery between two defensive positions; and the next day, with the sun shining brightly, he walked to the front and in between German posts as if nothing was out of place. He kept walking until a shot rang out and then he sprinted. Sprinted straight into a position held by Rangers who greeted him: "How come you're still alive, buddy?" It had been two months and eight days since his capture.

The bravest of the brave was an exceptional Ranger forged and destroyed on the anvil of war. The Clinical Findings of him conducted right after the war in the United States noted:

> He would often volunteer and would go out alone in the night with a knife in his hand, trembling, shaking like a leaf nervous, but he would never tell anyone about his nervousness and would go on. He became known as the solo killer. He never took prisoners, always killed them; the more he killed the more excitement he found in it and began to actually crave to kill. He was getting one commendation after another and would often risk his life for the purpose of showing off. Yet when one of his men was killed, he would blame himself and could not take it. He felt fidgety and worried a great deal. He became more and more nervous, could not sleep, and finally complained to his chief. And during the attack on Naples, he could not

remain away from his men and would often go to the front where he would direct them personally.

Shunstrom tried to explain his emotional state during the sessions:

> I feel very guilty. I never was fair about it in killing the prisoners of war, not the way I did it. All I thought was kill, kill, kill. I'm trying to forget that. I don't want to talk about it. The more combat I had, the more I wanted to kill them, I got crazy. I used to mow them down. I had them lined up and ordered my men to kill them. It wasn't fair. I will never be the same. I have no feelings any longer. I was nervous and I often felt like crying, but I had rather commit suicide than make a fool of myself. I kept awake nights. I couldn't see the fellows being killed around me, but the more nervous I became, the more I fought it. I did go to the Colonel: "I'll try to get it off my chest," but he had no time to listen to me. I can't get together with my wife because I have no feelings for her—I realize she is the only girl, but I can't be with her because I only hurt her continuously [spousal abuse].

After the war, having been denied entry into the electrical union in Hollywood, and unable to start an acting career, Chuck went on a crime spree robbing numerous gas stations at gunpoint. His criminal trial was the first time post-traumatic stress disorder was used in his defense and led to changes in the California criminal code. He did not serve time in jail and was found innocent of all charges due to temporary insanity brought on by his combat experiences. Roy Murray, Walt Nye, and other Rangers attended the trial and gave evidence in support of Shunstrom.

Charles "Chuck" Merton Shunstrom was born on 26 November 1920 in Boston, Massachusetts, and died on 4 December 1972 in Buffalo, New York, in a liquor store, dying of a heart attack.

His decorations and citations include: the European-African-Middle Eastern Theater Ribbon and five Bronze Service Stars

(Campaigns); a Distinguished (Presidential) Unit Citation and Oak Leaf Cluster; the Silver Star and Cluster; the French Croix De Guerre with Silver Star (Divisional Dispatches); the *Croix du Combattant* (Combat Service to France); Purple Heart with Oak Leaf Cluster; Combat Infantryman Badge; Bronze Star Medal; American Theater Service Ribbon; Allied Nations Campaign Ribbon; Expert Infantryman Badge; American Defense Service Medal; American Campaign Medal; Honorable Service Lapel Button.

Chuck was denied entry into the Ranger Hall of Fame. A shameful betrayal to the bravest of the brave. Like a Houdini he had escaped combat and imprisonment but not the curse of battle-fatigue and life itself . . .

A TRIBUTE TO CHUCK SHUNSTROM: 1920–1972

By: A Ranger Buddy (probably Peter Deeb)

A few days ago they cremated him. There was no pomp or pageantry. It was a simple service with only his aged father and youngest sister present. Three old Rangers were there at the wake the evening before to pay their last respect to a fallen comrade. They spoke of him quietly and with reverence as should befit a true hero, If, in the annals of the history of World War II, there could be a hundred men who were heroes in every sense of the word, Chuck Shunstrom would certainly have to be one of them. At one time he was the youngest combat Captain in the European Theater of Operations. At nineteen he went to war and as was his nature, gave everything he had to give to the cause of the America he loved and cherished, He earned medals for bravery above and beyond the call of duty. He led men, many years his senior, into some of the fiercest fighting of World War II, and came through unscathed. He landed in North Africa, chased the Nazis from the Tunisian desert, knifed through Sicily and stormed the beaches at Salerno. He single-handedly stopped German counter-attacks at Chiunzi Pass and slogged through the mud at Cassino and Venafro killing Germans wherever he met them. He was captured on the Anzio beachhead when he no longer had ammunition to fight back, and escaped from a prisoner of war camp. He was a man's man and a soldier's soldier. He always believed the only heroes in war were those who died fighting for their country. This man who did all his country could ask of him, and much more, came home from the wars and the killing and the bloodshed with scars, that although unseen, were there in his young-old face, never to heal. In talking to him on quiet evenings years later I found no bitterness in his recollections of the past, no hatred for the war he'd been so cruelly involved in, no malice for the lost and lonely years. But there was no peace either, no content-ment that the peace should bring after the fighting is through. He was placid now I found, heavy of heart, sad-lonely, full of war memories that would not let him rest easy,

Finally, he found comfort in the confines of a bottle. He drank to erase the chaotic past but it only came back more vividly and violently to the surface. It was the only way he knew how to fight it. Ultimately he could no longer control his hopes and fears and lost himself com-pletely to that elixir of life that so many of us these days find solace in. For him the war was never really over. He re-fought it from day to day, through long, lonely sleepless nights, from bar to bar and he left a lot of terrible memories in empty bottles across the country. In the five decades he was here perhaps a handful of people knew him well. He left us in his prime but the legacy he gave to those few can never be forgotten. May God grant that he find the peace and comfort and quiet contentment now that he was unable to find while he walked among us.

Sunday – December 10, 1972
Buffalo, New York

PRIVATES FIRST CLASS EDWARD PAUL FEIGENBAUM AND FRANK A. DUFFY

D Company, 3rd Ranger Battalion

"I still have physical and mental scars from the fight at Cisterna and being a prisoner of war," writes Feigenbaum in his three-page mem-oir. Both men were part of a fire team and veterans of the Sicilian,

Salerno, and Anzio amphibious assaults. Both were captured at Cisterna. Feigenbaum was concerned about his last name sounding Jewish or German—either way, he had thoughts on it. He decided to lose his government-issued dog tags and told his captors his last name was Finnegan. His early recollections of those traumatic days were probably shared by many other prisoners. He and several other Rangers were placed on the top floor of a building they were being held in, the Germans aware that the buildings were strafed by Allied planes regularly. In the building, he fought other prisoners, perhaps even Rangers, for honey that oozed from some of the boards. He, like others, was slapped around during interrogation.

The Rangers and other POWs were trucked to Rome, where Feigenbaum and Duffy were thrown off the truck against a wall of the ancient Coliseum. Here, against the old wall, they thought they were to be shot, but instead would feature in the German triumph through the street of Rome like victories Roman generals had celebrated since forever. The large column of prisoners, five-wide, marched through the streets, and Feigenbaum felt the hatred of the Italians who, he writes, spat in their faces.

"Hunger is a terrible thing," as it reduced one to an animal state. Spiritual belief and mental strength were crucial to survive the terrible conditions prisoners experienced at the hands of the Germans and Italians. To both Rangers, survival was key, and all the suffering they had to endure made their resolve even stronger to get revenge and to get back at the hated enemy. The constant screaming and denial of basic human needs burned deep within him and Duffy.

Many Rangers ended up at a POW camp near Laterina in Italy where they were searched yet again, with the guards taking whatever they wanted. Sustenance was nearly nonexistent. The Rangers were given some "ersatz" (replacement) coffee made of burned barley and chicory first thing in the morning, then in the afternoon they got a small loaf of bread that had to be shared between five men. A small cup of soup made of dehydrated cabbage and dried peas was dished out into their issued tin can. The can and half a blanket were all they were handed by their captors. If a POW did not have his tin can with him during the roll call, he'd receive no food. Sleeping arrangements were less than Spartan—straw on top of pallets. As it was brutally cold, the Rangers burned the wood for heat. "We smoke anything that would smolder. Pine needles were smoked." There were roll calls without notice, which occurred roughly three times daily.

Standing in formation during that time was a brutal experience since they lacked winter clothing or proper blankets. During these times, a strong mind was required. Feigenbaum notes that thoughts of suicide were not uncommon amongst some of the prisoners. No doubt he and Duffy, who had been buddies and were captured together, were extremely important for each other. The Me and My Pal system of Darby's Rangers was one key to their survival. Another thing that stood in their favor was having been raised during the Great Depression, lacking the comforts of life since both their families were poor. Being streetwise kids from New York, and trained to kill to survive, made both dangerous and strong-willed.

On 28 February 1944, many Ranger POWs were taken to the nearby rail station where they were crammed with 40 to 50 men into small boxcars known as Forty and Eight, "40-8," because they carried 40 men or 8 horses during the Great War. Inside, and in the middle of the car, was a small wooden barrel to be used as a latrine for the men, men suffering from diarrhea, malaria, chills, colds, fever, malnutrition, and other physical ailments. "There was lots of weeping and wailing from the men in the car. Most of them had given up hope. It was pitiful. The sounds were like children lost in the void. The morale was very low. Abandon Ye all hope who enter here. Most of the men laid down in despair." Lieutenant Clarence Meltesen, also a prisoner after Cisterna, notes in his exceptionally well-researched book on Ranger POWs, *After the Battle*, that this was not an unusual reaction of young men to an unknown future filled with horror and without leadership to help them navigate their fears.

But Duffy and "Finnegan" Feigenbaum were not those kinds of men. They stood against one wall of the car and searched for anything that offered hope of an escape. They found a metal piece where three boards joined. They dug their fingers underneath it and pulled and pushed, moving it inch by inch until they were able to snap it off and away from the wall. Using it as a lever, they and others managed to break off two boards, exposing everyone to the icy cold, with men complaining about it. This took time, and the train slowed and stopped occasionally with guards patrolling the perimeter of the train. When the train slowed, probably in Florence, Feigenbaum and Duffy replaced the boards and leaned against them to hold them in place until the guards hurried back into their warm car at the end of the train. Then the Rangers went back to work, enlarging the hole so they could manage to squeeze through.

The next stop, they decided, was it. And it took a while to happen. The train finally stopped; the guards did their thing and hurried back to their car. Almost timed perfectly to the disappearing guards, Feigenbaum and Duffy removed the boards, leading to more complaints from freezing men. Feigenbaum looked out and saw nothing in the darkness of the night. He climbed on top of Duffy's lowered back, through the hole, and turned around to face the boxcar, grabbing onto it for dear life. He released his grip and dropped heavily onto the cinders on the track. He stayed on his back, watching the train chug down the line. He heard something down a ways—Duffy—as planned. Reunited, they knew they had to leave the area as quickly and quietly as possible.

They needed food and clothing to blend in better and to survive. They found a small house on the outskirts of the nearby village where they barged in, ransacking the place of everything they could lay their hands on to survive their escape. Driving the older Italian man from the house ahead of them, they made it up a hill, where Feigenbaum killed him, probably using a knife. The shotgun they took from the man would have alerted neighbors.

The next night they were reconnoitering the outskirts of a town when Duffy got stopped by a German soldier. No doubt, Duffy, young and dressed like an Italian, ought to have been in the military or working on defensive fortifications for the Germans—young men did not escape notice by the Fascists or Nazis. Feigenbaum crept around the sentry and killed him quickly and quietly, like Rangers had been taught. They took the dead German's money, wallet, watch, knife, and pistol. Burying him under a pile of hay, the men took off for the hills. "We knew there would be no mercy now if we were captured. Freedom is precious, and we were totally selfish to preserve ours," Feigenbaum wrote in his memoir.

Hiding in trees and woods on the high sides of hills, and staying off roads and trails used by German forces, they made their way south, bumping into partisans and other Underground factions such as the *Carbonaios* (Charcoal Workers) and the Garibaldi Brigade, which was the Communist Party. The Americans learned about the various groups and their political agendas during their escape in the province of Romagna. They joined one group to conduct a raid but soon discovered that when the Germans arrived, the partisans fled, hanging Feigenbaum and Duff out to dry—to fend for themselves. When the mission called for the destruction of a rail track near Faenza using explosives, their partners fled midway through. This untimely event happened while Feigenbaum was packing explosives, getting ready to cut a fuse and crimp the detonator. He took just one moment to look away from his work. Good thing he did, for what he saw next was a pair of black jackboots with the German ready to capture the saboteur. Duffy killed him. The charges were set off, and the two Rangers fled the scene. Time to leave. The two Rangers went back to their original mission—returning to Allied lines on the West Coast of Italy.

Throughout their travails, they encountered numerous other escapees from America, the British, even Gurkhas and some others, including Italians who by then knew the war was over. The information exchange was helpful. The Ranger buddies were told of a local Underground band they joined near the town of Rocca Strad. Here they heard fighting to the south. They broke up with the band and each other. Duffy opted to wait for the advancing Allies, while Feigenbaum moved south to find them.

One day, Feigenbaum was hiding in a ravine, having built himself a hide-site with brush, when he heard American voices nearby. He carefully made it out of his hiding place and managed to turn himself in to his fellow countrymen of the 36th Infantry Division of the Fifth

Army without getting shot. It was a great feeling. It was 20 June 1944 when Feigenbaum returned to military control. Eventually, he made it to Fort Dix, New Jersey, where he met Frank Duffy who also had made it back alive the following day, on 21 June 1944. "Without each other, we never would have made it."

PRIVATE FIRST CLASS GUSTAVE E. SCHUNEMANN

F Company, First Ranger Battalion

The good looks and great speech Captain Charles Shunstrom had given to the potential recruits was enough for the 19-year-old Gustave Schunemann, of Manchester, New Hampshire, to join the Rangers in Naples in October of 1943. A veteran of the Winter Line Campaign, he took part in the landing at Anzio and was captured at Cisterna at the very front of the battle and close to the town itself. When the Rangers surrendered, they marched a mile, carrying their wounded, to an open field with a deep ravine running through it. Here they were forced into it while machine guns were being set up on top of it. The Germans were very angry at the number of casualties they had taken. Schunemann thought it was all over now—getting butchered and covered by dirt from bulldozers wasn't how he had envisioned things. Soon, German organization took over, with the wounded being moved out; and by night the Rangers marched again, but this time into a large barn and other buildings in an abandoned farm complex. A strafing run by an American P-51 plane the next day had Rangers running around the courtyard, frantically waving their arms. The attack stopped.

The second night, yet again in tightly filled trucks like sardines in a can, the prisoners arrived in the outskirts of Rome after a long drive. Here, he and many Rangers were paraded through the streets, flashing V(ictory) signs and the middle finger, along with shouting profanities, at the cameras that filmed the German triumph. Schunemann recognized the Germans' need for good news, since they had pretty much lost nonstop since the arrival of the green Americans in North Africa: It had been defeat after defeat on all fronts for the Nazis. Once the glorious triumph had been filmed and the Rangers had marched across the city, they were jam-packed into trucks again, standing room only. They un-assed at a compound where they were issued half a blanket to fight off the still-bitter cold of the region. Their buildings had no windows or doors, which exposed them constantly to the weather. Such was the life of a prisoner. After a few days of this at the "Holiday Inn," as Shunemann called it in his memoir, they moved, this time north, to another transit camp that this time had windows and doors. This camp administratively prepared the prisoners for their departure to Germany, requiring all the Allied prisoners to fill out identification papers and an official postcard announcing their status as a prisoner of war. Schunemann didn't experience any poor treatment at the hands of the guards, but the lack of food was disturbing. It was minimal at best. It didn't take long for the prisoners to mow the greens of the compound with their teeth—nothing green or edible was left in the transit camp. Hay, which was provided to sleep on, was full of large lice, adding more misery to the already miserable men.

On 28 February 1944, they boarded a train for their final ride to German POW camps. Escape would be much, much harder there. In typical fashion, as the prisoners made their way through a small gatehouse, they were searched. Quick-thinking Ranger Ray Sadowski, a buddy from Schunemann's squad, carried a small knife that he managed to throw surreptitiously over the fence to an already-searched prisoner. This effort required three men: the receiver outside the wire, the thrower, and one man to distract the guards. This small Army pocketknife would be a lifesaver for some of the Rangers. Fifty prisoners were crammed into each 40-8 boxcar. Inside, they took turns using the tiny blade. First, they battled the boards: impossible. Next, they took on a small window ventilation unit with barbed wire on the outside of it with the knife and a piece of metal they had pried from the floorboards. Success. While they were working, they had to put things back in place every 15 to 20 minutes when German guards patrolled the exterior of the train when it stopped.

The time had come. It was late, around 2200 hours, when the Rangers tore strips from the blankets and fashioned an ad hoc rope out of them. Tying one end around the biggest man inside the car, they tossed the other end out the window. Quickly, Rangers struggled through the opening and jumped off the boxcar. Schunemann was the fifth to get out. He held on to the rope on the outside as the train slowed its speed arriving at a station. Dammit. The young Ranger cursed his bad luck. On the platform were armed soldiers and civilians. Most didn't see him clinging onto the rope on the outside of the boxcar; a few civilians just stood there, mouths agape, frozen in place. The train accelerated again, went past the marshalling yard, then PFC Gustave Schunemann pushed off and went head over heels onto the railroad bed. He had been lucky: no injuries other than a sprained thumb, and he hadn't jumped off a bridge or jumped when in an underpass. He thanked God for his good fortune.

Time had come to move out. It was dark. Other Rangers were undoubtedly jumping off along the rail. He headed straight away from the tracks, roughly knowing which way the rail ran: He aimed to make it to the Adriatic coast to the east. Through vineyards, backyards, over roads and trails, he made it into the foothills away from everything that was behind him. The occasional dog barking had him move faster. Finally, a road sign informed him that he was at Pontevecchio, south of Florence. He crossed the Arno River at a place called Lastra a Signa where he spent the night in a haystack well removed from the highway. "My lice were delighted to meet some of their relatives, most of whom joined their friends on my body."

The next day, he walked through woods. He heard wood chopping and took a closer look. A 60-plus-year-old man was cutting away. He was Ugo Paci, and Schunemann managed to convey, with what little Italian he knew, that he was an escaped American prisoner. They walked to a farmhouse, where Ugo explained things to the woman. They asked him to sit and have bread and soup. The best he ever had. Of course, he could only eat so much because of his shrunken stomach. They handed him clean civilian clothes to get rid of his old uniform filled with lice. He spent one week with others, the Gradi family. Schunemann knew the danger the family was exposed to, should German or Italian patrols find him. He decided to move on. Two to three hundred miles south were the Allied lines.

But Ugo had other ideas. Other prisoners had been caught, he told the young Ranger, and shot. He asked the young man to stay and lie low for a while. Deciding that the old man was wise, Schunemann made a teepee-style home out of cornstalks, six feet in diameter, in the field. It fit in well with the general area. He spent those nights on the Rossi Farm, near the village of Bruccianese. Here he was able to join others in listening to BBC radio broadcasts in English. He discovered that Allied forces had landed in France, both in Normandy and in the south.

Later during his stay, he was asked by a local 100-man-strong partisan group, under the leader code-named Toscana and operating in the Prato area just northeast of Florence, to help sabotage the Germans. The men had no training whatsoever and exposed themselves to the enemy with blazing bonfires roasting chickens and rabbits. They also drank too much to remain tactically aware. Not a good thing to someone who had been on the run for four months. On their way down the mountain, they bumped into a small German patrol of six, leading the partisans to run in all directions like rabbits with the Germans taking potshots. And that was that for Ranger Schunemann. He stayed in his teepee hiding place and learned Italian and worked for the old man. The local Italians treated him like one of their own and came to visit regularly. One thing he learned was that the locals had an excellent grapevine system of whistles. They knew immediately who was coming and from where.

By mid-July 1944, nearly five months since his capture, enemy patrols had increased and Schunemann didn't wander around— movement meant capture. Twice he had escaped recapture when the Germans swept through the area. They weren't just looking for partisans or escaped prisoners; they were looking for young men in general who were capable of working on the defensive lines in the mountains. Schunemann decided to find a better hiding place. He found the ideal location. Inside the forest was a deep gully with a brook with thick brambles and large raspberry bushes providing excellent camouflage and concealment. He and his local friend, Ugo's son Geraldo, dug a cave six feet deep until a granite wall stopped them from digging even deeper. Inside the cave, a local boy chiseled "a beautiful scene of clouds, angels, and roses on the stonewall."

Unfortunately for Schunemann, his toe, on the right foot, had become infected from the wet conditions, and it got worse. On the other hand, there was good news, too, because by 1 August, Allied lines were within 30 miles of his location. The artillery barrages in the distance grew louder. He took some chances by doing what Rangers did, reconnaissance. He watched the unfolding scenes in the area, with German activity increasing, moving artillery, ammo supplies, mining bridges, and whatnot throughout as they tried to counter the Allied advance. The Ranger took notes.

A miracle happened on 10 August when Schunemann crawled out of his cave and saw a British jeep on the hilltop. They had advanced nearly 20 miles during the night. He hobbled up the hill and went straight to a member of a Canadian tank battalion. He was driven to the command post, where he was debriefed. Here, the Ranger pinpointed enemy locations and booby traps on their well-defined maps. He had done a great job locating potential problems. But it wasn't just locations he shared. No. Schunemann knew of a number of people who had worked with the Germans and Italian Fascists. He shared those names as well.

After the debrief, he was taken to the field hospital 30 miles to the rear, where he showered, was issued a brand-new British uniform and boots, and had his toe looked after. They put him on a truck heading south back to Rome, where, six months earlier, he and his buddies had been paraded through the streets and the Coliseum. Back in American hands, he was moved to sunny Naples. Debriefed by the Americans this time, he ended up at an Army hospital because of his pus-filled toes—the infection had spread, and he had been in tremendous pain for weeks. It took 10 days to reduce the infection. Gustave Schunemann was shipped to America and was sent to Fort

Devens for processing. He was issued a brand-new full set of clothing, took a medical examination, and received nine months of pay. Private First Class Gustave Schunemann made his way home. He visited his Italian friends in 1950 and retired as a sergeant major.

CORPORAL KENNETH M. MARKHAM AND PRIVATE FIRST CLASS ARTHUR L. LYONS JR.

F Company, 1st Ranger Battalion

Tennessean Ken Markham was the first one out of the boxcar, using all his strength to push away from the car and the wheels of the train. Having used a small pocketknife that belonged to PFC Sadoski of Connecticut, they, as a team, pried loose a piece of metal and, between it and the knife, made an opening through the ventilation window. Next off the moving train was Arthur "Red" Lyons of Massachusetts. Ranger Gustave Shunemann was number five. Lucky for Markham, he dropped just after the train had passed a bridge: The guard on top was unaware. Waiting in the dark, he heard Lyons creep toward him within an hour. They looked for a road and ran five miles to clear from the other escapees while shots rang out in the cold night air. They were in the Prato area.

The Rangers first bumped into an old woman who was too afraid to help. She said the Germans would kill them all if they found the POWs in her house. They moved on. But the next encounter, a mile on, at 0300 or 0400 hours, with a man on a bike going into a house, yielded results. As it should have, since almost no one was out and about at those hours. Clearly, they thought, he had connections to the Underground. From Tuesday through Sunday, they stayed at a barn that was attached to the house, where they cleaned their clothes and ate, regaining strength as Red had fallen ill. Both men were unable to eat too much. The man hitched up his horse to his buggy and was to go to Florence to contact the Underground. Markham mulled killing him. He decided on trust. The wife told him, in broken English, their son was a prisoner captured in North Africa and had written that he was being taken care of well. She offered to wash their clothing and let them take baths.

A member of the Underground arrived on 5 March, not only with tandem bicycles to ride but with civilian clothing for both. They did not have boots big enough for Markham's feet though. Riding parallel to the tracks, they, including their guide, made their way south and rode into the northern outskirts of the town near the main plaza. As they turned into it, they saw 100 German soldiers having a party. Fucking hell, the Rangers thought. They kept their composure and rode on. Three blocks later, they were in Florence and in a hotel. Red and Markham stayed until the end of March, sharing accommodations with three British soldiers and perhaps a Welshman. Markham wanted to get to the mountains, the Alps, and make it to the coast to Venice, but the snow made it impossible and traveling on the road was challenging at best with the constant patrols of German and Italian Fascists. At the hotel, they all received stipends to survive.

The British—some of whom spoke Italian—went out during their stay, while blond-haired Markham and redhead Lyons wisely stayed in. One night at a pub, the Brits were discovered by Gestapo agents who followed them to their billet. At 11 o'clock the following morning, the Germans surrounded their residence with machine guns covering the intersections around their block. The hosts, on the rooftop, tried to give themselves up but were murdered by automatic fire instead. Then they captured the British. Making his way up to the roof, a black-coat-wearing Gestapo officer with Luger in hand got the two Rangers some 45 minutes later.

Starved of sunlight in a dungeon-like civilian cell for 30 days, with a small bucket serving as a latrine, one of the British soldiers became seriously ill. They also underwent brutal interrogations. The more they beat them, the less they spoke. Corporal Markham communicated with one civilian guard about the man's serious condition—to contact the Swiss Red Cross. Only the intervention of the local Swiss Legation brought medical attention to him. The others were placed back into the regular prisoner-of-war system. The Rangers were moved to Germany, to Stalag VIIA, Moosburg, southern Bavaria. There the Ranger buddies were split up, with Markham, an NCO and considered a security risk, going to Stalag IIIB in Fürstenberg, 60 miles southeast of Berlin, while Lyons, the enlisted man, was shipped out to Stalag IIB, in Hammerstein.

The prisoners did have a radio and received sporadic news updates. With the advance of the Soviet army during the Winter Offensive of 12 January 1945, the Germans moved their prisoners west. For Markham, this meant a long march from Stalag IIIB to Stalag IIIA in Luckenwalde, 32 miles south of Berlin, reaching the latter on 7 February 1945. During the march, the guards shot anyone who fell out. No mercy whatsoever. The Soviets pushed harder and captured Luckenwalde on 22 April 1945. Liberation, however, was not to be had; instead, the prisoners were held hostage by their Russian allies until Berlin had been captured, and the war had ended, with the POWs used in future negotiations.

That was too much for the Ranger. Markham jumped the fence of the POW camp and walked away to the west to the Elbe River. He bumped into Russians and told them he was an American, but nothing happened to him. He wasn't recaptured and he wasn't given any help. He caught a ride west to Torgau, near the Elbe. Tens of thousands of German refugees fled before the advance of the Russian army. Desperate people tried to cross the river to British and American hands. They knew they would receive what they had dished out for years to the Russians. The advance elements of the Russian army did not allow him to cross either; so, in typical Ranger fashion, and not liking to be told no, he made his way up the river for a little while. Knowing he was too ill and weak to simply swim across the river, he found a log to help him float and used the current to cross the Elbe River—to freedom. The first American he encountered across the shore helped him up. The guy was a colonel who provided him with everything he needed, including his own quarters. Markham had lost 100 pounds. His Ranger buddy Arthur "Red" Lyons was also repatriated.

FIRST LIEUTENANT WILLIAM L. NEWNAN

B Company Commander, Third Ranger Battalion

He decided he would also escape from the Laterina Campo PG 61, northwest of Arezzo and 100 kilometers southeast of Florence. He and his group arrived on the night of 8/9 February having traveled nearly 250 kilometers in trucks and on a train. The shock of having been captured was almost worse than the thought of being wounded or killed. Rangers did not fully realize they could actually be captured. No matter, Newnan was ready. He had reconned the camp: two double-wire fences about 10 feet high and 10 feet apart between the fences; at the corners were guard posts roughly 12 feet tall with searchlights. The guards faced the back of the other guard posts. Along the fence line and 25 yards apart stood poles with lights on them. They had machine-gun posts and were equipped with small arms. The camp, however, was not in good shape, falling apart, and now had to hold 1,200 prisoners. The guard posts were falling apart and lacked searchlights. The fences were not nearly tight enough to prevent escape. And the Germans knew it, hurriedly repairing it, bringing in new rolls of wire, new searchlights, lumber, laborers, and, importantly for Lieutenant Newnan, he noticed the Germans were in the process of adding another ring of wire around the officers' barracks. The longer he waited, the less likely it was that he could escape.

At the morning *Appell*, roll call, in mid-February, he sneaked in with the enlisted men in formation, who never did as the guards asked, delaying the counting efforts and aiding officers and enlisted to escape. Obviously, some of the rankers knew who he was and did their best to support his movements. On his way out, a fellow Ranger asked if he could join him. Newnan rejected him, saying that it was a one-man mission and admonished the soldier to let him be and not to alert the Germans. He managed to make it into the motor pool where he hid inside a truck, with teeth chattering because of the cold, until lunch around 1130 hours when the Italian mechanics left the area. Fifteen minutes later, with the mechanics having cleared the area, he sat on the outside of the building, monitoring the guards and looking for a way out. He spotted a hole in the outside fence, then climbed a pole, dropped over it, and walked along it to some buildings. Rounding one of the buildings, he bumped into the Italian mechanics, who spoke quickly and loudly to each other as he took off and ran 200 yards to the hole in the second fence. Newnan then made his way to the double strand of barbed wire surrounding the camp. The shouts of the Italian mechanics finally alerted the guards. Moving at speed to the left, he struggled through a swift-moving ford of the Arno River, as lack of food started to take effect. Struggling in the water, a nearby farmer held out a pitchfork and helped him up. Newnan quickly ran another 500 yards and hid in a hide site on high ground as a six-man German patrol hot on his heels appeared and interrogated the Italian, who stonewalled them. The farmer told them he had seen nobody; satisfied, they left.

Newnan kept moving to stay warm, to not die of hypothermia. Knowing he needed dry clothing and aware of his uniform, he dared approach three workers. Together they walked to a farm half a mile away. Some men did chores while Newnan was plastered with wine and cheese with one of the laborers. For a brief moment, Newnan thought about killing the man, but decided to engage him instead. He traded with the worker, who had his eye on the Ranger's tanker jacket, in exchange for socks, pants, a mackinaw coat, a scarf, and a hat. Two days later, he wanted to move on. A neighbor's kid brought him a school atlas with a six-inch map of Italy.

He moved on and walked briskly, going the wrong way, north, not south. Newnan took another chance, and they took him in and provided a guide to take him to a local English captain operating in the area. His guide was a French soldier captured in Algeria who planned to stay in Italy and become a citizen. The captain turned out to be an enlisted man and was hiding out with six young Italians. They were going to stay and wait for the Allies to advance. Here, Newnan learned pidgin Italian. The Ranger wanted to leave.

He remembered how to use a watch as a compass. "Pointing the hour hand at the sun and bisecting the angle formed with 12 o'clock gave him a south line." It worked. He moved on and stayed clear of villages, staying on the ridgelines. He walked roughly seven hours daily, often taking a chance by approaching locals for food and shelter and engaging with them about all things America. He encountered gun emplacements and work parties the farther south he went in the Allerone/Chiusi area. He followed the rail line south. One of his farm friends put him in touch with a handler called Franco and other escapees hiding in a grotto. The men had tried to make it to Rome but decided to wait it out here. Franco held chits—IOUs that he would receive money in exchange for helping airmen. None of the money ever made it to the escapees, and Newnan was certain the man went to Rome and received daily compensation. The Ranger offered to help sabotage the Germans by blowing up bridges or attacking Germans, but no one was willing to take him up on the offer. He left five days later.

He joined forces with a submariner named Bennet, and they moved on south to Rignano. At a farmhouse Bennet spoke Italian when two women rushed out of the house and whisked them into the barn. There were three Germans in the house. Once the Germans left, they were fed and spent the night in a goat pen. A local Communist leader offered to take them to Rome. They accepted. Five days later, he returned with 100 lira and a new suit for each of them. In Rignano and part of the Underground, the Italian couple accompanied them to Rome with an early-morning departure to avoid Allied strafing runs. He nearly misplaced the much-needed ticket but found it at the last second and made his way through the gate at the station.

In Rome, he and Bennet separated. In the safe house, the couple managing it were nervous and asked him to stay in his room at all times. Here he met with officers working the Underground network. He was moved and given a stipend. Newnan also understood he needed a more expensive suit to move within certain social circles in Rome—and he was lousy, as in full of lice. A new suit and louse powder took care of those issues. He was now on the Via Flaminia, a main road through Rome with a ton of German traffic, with an equally nervous landlady. He left 10 days later.

At his new accommodation, a spacious apartment, he remained for two weeks. During that time, he walked the neighborhood, and occasionally he'd do his part of socializing with the officers in charge of clandestine services. He had a stipend to help make ends meet.

> One evening, I took a lady out to dinner at the Casino della Rosa. She called my attention to four men sitting at the next table, not over eight feet away. She said "Those are the head of the Gestapo in Rome and his three assistants." I got the impression that the chief Jerry was looking at me rather often, and I began to think of taking off. I was especially interested when he got up and left the table to telephone. I called the waiter over and asked him to check on him. The waiter came back in a few minutes and said "Routine call." A rather amusing picture—the waiter leaning over the shoulder of the chief of the Gestapo, listening to his telephone call, and the waiter and I conferring about the matter in English, with the three assistants only eight feet away. Even more amusing is the fact that all four of them hung their Lugers in the check room with their hats; same theory as the old Western practice of checking the revolvers with the barkeeper. There was no one in the check room, and I had an overpowering desire to take the Luger of the chief of the Gestapo as a souvenir, but finally conquered this desire when I realized that the Jerries would simply wreck the Casino della Rosa if this happened.

Naturally, his lady friend became rather nervous at the turn of events.

He moved to the French seminary near the Pantheon from the end of April until early June 1944. Here he stayed below the radar but had two close calls because of British escapees and their antics. Unfortunately, the billeting part of the Escape Line had been compromised. One of the key men was captured and turned. He then informed the Gestapo of the billets known to him; but fortunately for the Escape Line, they had an asset in the Italian operations center and were able to clear out many before the Germans raided the homes. One of the officers involved in the Underground was captured.

A bombing attack on German units led to reprisals and an absolute tightening of the various security cordons. Over 300 men were arrested, taken to caves, and machine-gunned. A number of the captured died of asphyxiation. However death came, it was permanent and brutal, conducted by the National Socialists and the Italian Fascists—the scourge of mankind. As the Germans tightened their security, so did the Underground, and it was discovered that an Edmund, 18, had stolen money from the room of Father Superior. Ranger First Lieutenant Bill Newnan was part of the investigative team. If Edmund would steal, what would stop him from selling 50 Jews, 1 American, and 6 Frenchmen? They found a letter indicating just that. Newnan considered murder. The decision was made to keep Edmund in the seminary under tight surveillance with windows screwed shut and a guard at his door. They organized guards and established a new hiding place. Newnan mentions in his memoir, *Escape from Italy*, the Italian Jews having their own guards who finally cooperated fully with them. Flashes of gunfire illuminated the nights. Soon the Allies would break through the German defenses.

Newnan could not move at the time because of the fierce battles raging south of Rome at Anzio. He witnessed Fascists corralling men on the streets who lacked proper papers who were then shipped to Germany. By 4 June 1944, more and more Germans retreated, taking any mode of transportation they could find. On 5 June at 0300 hours, local Italians told him to go to a plaza where a lone American stood. The soldier had gotten separated from his unit. Newnan told him to stand by and wait. The Ranger returned an hour later, but the American had disappeared. Lieutenant Newnan met with elements of the Fifth Army's First Special Service Force.

> I finally ran into some of the Special Service boys. This
> was a task force, half Canadians and half Americans. They
> were quite some chaps, particularly the top officers that I

later saw. They told me that the Rangers had all been sent home except for the men that had been in only a year and under, and that those men had just been automatically put in the Special Service force; they told me where their head-quarters were.

He found the FSSF's commander, General Robert T. Frederick, at his headquarters.

I got there, and there was Brigadier General Frederick and a few of his staff. He knew all about the Rangers and took good care of me. He was just nicked all over, though, and full of scratches, and he even had a bullet hole through the cuff of his glove. How he could get it through there I don't know, except that the glove must have been blowing out so it went right on through and never touched him.

Later that day, General Frederick took him through Cisterna. "I saw these towns flattened and finally we got to a place that was just a pile of rubble and the General said 'Do you recognize this?' I said 'No.' He said 'This is Cisterna.' Just flattened—absolutely nothing left."

They drove by Velletri en route to Fifth Army's headquarters. Once the HQ moved to Rome, Newnan took chocolate bars to the families and others that had helped him. From Rome he went to Naples, to Oran, Casablanca, Belfast, and, finally, arrived in New York on 18 June 1944. First Lieutenant William Newnan joined the Office of Strategic Services and taught Chinese troops in small-unit tactics in Burma and China.

TECHNICAL SERGEANT ROBERT HALLIDAY AND STAFF SERGEANT DALE GREENLAND

Headquarters Company, Third Ranger Battalion

The two non-commissioned officers led the way out of the 40-8 box-cars traveling from Laterina through Florence. They were not the kind of men who'd take shit lying down. They agreed with the others, who were also going to escape, to travel in different directions. This car had been used to transport horses, as it still had an iron ring bolted into a wooden panel. A small problem to overcome was the lack of belts and shoelaces that had been confiscated by the guards once Rangers started to disappear. But this wasn't a real problem. They had their mufflers and half-blankets for tools. They used them to loop through the ring, then to pull, jerk, and twist until there was enough separation for them to get fingernails, then fingertips, and, finally, fingers underneath the wood panel holding the metal ring. Once they pried the wood panel off the wall, exposing the hole and bringing in the cold air, they had to deal with the barbed wire that was nailed down on the exterior. They needed something to get through it. Lacking a knife—or anything, really—they volunteered Ranger Kenneth Tongate of C/4 as a battering ram. Lifting him up and battering the wire feet-first, the entanglement came loose almost immediately. The snowstorm, "like a bucket of ice," battered them as they held on to the outside of the car before they pushed off, using arms and legs to propel themselves away from the train, into the crap weather, where they then rolled down an embankment into a bramble patch. Weather that was perfect to hide them, but terrible to be in without clothing or food. Having survived their jump and rolling onto the hard turf, they moved laterally, 300 to 500 meters above Santa Margherita. Fortunately for them, the area they were in was above areas where local police patrolled, but not too high, where partisans were hiding out. They moved, as planned, to the southeast.

Stumbling on a shepherd's hut, the two Rangers soon discovered that they had been beaten to the spot by rats. Unable to sleep, Halliday and Greenland abandoned the hut and spent the night sleeping in the rough in a gully below the harsh winds. They moved on the next day and roughed it again at night, using the training they had received. The following day, they staggered on, finding a farmhouse in a small valley. The Rangers approached the owners and were treated well immediately. Unbeknownst to them, they were now in the embrace of the Underground network of the Resistance.

Here the men were given food, baths, and civilian clothing to camouflage their uniforms. A small map with directions to the next stops
to the boundary of the Resistance was handed to them. From here
they moved on, not affiliating with any local bands and thereby not
imposing on them with the needs of supplies and fake papers. The
map showed locations of friendly farms and even a priest to help
them navigate their escape. During their travels they were sometimes delayed, needing to acquire food. At one friendly location,
they spent 10 days at a farm, being taken care of by the family. At
another stop, a priest handed them a compass and map to help
them navigate. Unlike other escapees who had caused problems
or were rude, Halliday and Greenland were good in their interac-
tions with the locals. This was a crucial component to their evasion.
Another time, they stopped at a place where the hosts spoke English,
much to their relief. And they were surprised by a gift of cigarettes.
Throughout their evasion, the Rangers traveled cautiously near tree
lines and below the snow lines. This gave them the advantage to
disappear quickly should they encounter enemy patrols of any kind,
German or Italian. Food, and repair of boots and clothing, ate up
their time. They were occasionally dependent on guides to navigate
the ever-more-dangerous areas that saw German activity that they
had to cross.

In the early days of their travel, Norman Hellings, a New Zealander
captured in North Africa, dressed and fluent like an Italian, was
their companion for three to four weeks. Sitting on the roadside at
Sansepolcro watching churchgoers walk by after services were over,
they caught the attention of a local *carabinieri*, who promptly arrested
them. Although imprisoned, they were treated well and interrogated,
including by the regional chief of police. Later that night, they were
reunited with Hellings and released into the mountains, away from
the village, away from causing the local Italian police any trouble with
the nearby German units safeguarding one of Field Marshal Albert
Kesselring's headquarters. Luckily for them, the war was ending,
and people did not want to have any problems with the Germans or

fanatical Fascists still roaming the areas—thus avoiding anything partisan was the order of the day for many.

They made their way east to the town of Casteldeici. Desiring more assistance, the New Zealander knocked on the door of a house that, unfortunately for him, had a German patrol in it. They immediately grabbed him and chased after the Rangers, but to no avail. Halliday and Greenland moved on without their translator. They had each other, experience, and training. The one thing they could not stop was the onset of malaria, which took Halliday down in the middle of May. Fortunately, a friendly farmer bought quinine from the local black market. It took a week, but Halliday was back on his feet.

Onward they went, zigzagging across the peninsula toward Urbino, to contact a local resistance fighter operating in the Senigallia area. From 16 to 17 July 1944, they hid in a ditch along the coastal road in the northern outskirts of Ancona. The city itself had been taken by the Polish Corps on 16 July, but not the northern outskirts. Now Greenland got hit by the dreaded illness and was starting to suck wind badly. Things started to turn sour for them. Halliday considered surrendering to the Germans for fear of his buddy's deteriorating health. While hiding in the ditch, they heard German voices floating in the air. Fortunately, those voices came and went, drifting away from them. Next, they heard other strange sounds. Good enough, they thought—it wasn't German, and it wasn't Italian. The Carpathian Lancers were on the road on 17 July, moving north of Ancona, followed by the 3rd Carpathian Infantry Division. Carefully, Halliday rose and made himself known to the Poles. These were dangerous times, where one false move or the exigencies of war could easily lead to death. It was clear enough that they were not the enemy, but they had to wait for an officer who spoke English to come along.

The two Ranger sergeants were taken to the headquarters section, where they received medical treatment and the new clothing they so desperately needed. The two members of the Houdini Club then traveled to Oran, Algeria, and then on to the United States of America.

SERGEANT CARL HARRISON LEHMANN

C Company, Third Ranger Battalion

"It was one of the worst days of my life," wrote Carl Lehmann years after the war. The "it" was the parade of captured Rangers in Rome. He ended up at Stalag IIB at Hammerstein, Germany. Getting out of the boxcars, they were told to take off their clothes and put them on hangers for delousing while they were ordered to take showers. Years later, he understood that Jews had been told the same but with a far different, and horrific, outcome. Like others, Lehmann was sent to a work farm. This one was a massive feudal estate with a mansion, farm buildings, hundreds of cows, even a schnapps factory, and small buildings for the peasant workers. He and the other 21 Americans were housed in a two-story building surrounded by barbed wire. On the ground floor was the kitchen and two sleeping rooms for them. Above them were two German army guards.

One was fat and middle-aged, incapable of fighting at the front lines; the other was a blond, handsome Aryan-looking type with severe combat wounds who took a particular dislike to the Ranger. Lehmann's job was to milk cows and to clean the stalls. On his way to the dump to dispose of the manure, he located the loading dock of the schnapps factory. Frustrated at his inability to figure out how to get some and not be caught, for that was considered sabotage with harsh punishment to follow, perhaps even death, he drove a pitchfork into the barrel with great success. Alcohol was a precious commodity. Eventually the leaky barrel was discovered. The Germans thought it had been an accident, much to his relief.

Lehmann formulated an escape plan. He shared this with his chess partner, Jock, a Frenchman, and fellow American Bill "Sal" Space, because Space claimed boat-handling skills from fishing the Pacific Northwest between Seattle and Alaska. The plan was to move north to Stolpmünde, where a fishing fleet left twice a week. The details were that they'd observe the fishermen, eventually sneak on board, and, once out at sea, kill the occupants and take off for Sweden 80 miles away from Stolpmünde. The Frenchman had been captured early in the war and had privileges, including going to the local town to meet with other "froggies." He supplied a compass and a map but would not try to escape.

In early May, the time had come. They, Lehmann and Space, cut their way through the wire and took off to the north, traveling only at night. Nearly three weeks later, they completed the 60-mile trek despite having had to double back when a motorcycle rider spotted and shot at them, and another time when they were caught stealing water by a watchman and his dog. Rousing the village, the Germans, some with pitchforks, shotguns, and torches, walked down the dark road looking for the intruders, slowly walking past the escapees, who were hiding in a ditch filling their canteens. Another time, they spent the night in trees when Space had killed a piglet and its mother was furious, hoping to kill the murderers.

There was constant fighting between the Americans about leadership.

They finally were only five miles out of Stolpmünde, where they found beach houses. One contained a boat ready for sailing, but Space declined departing right then and there. A storm hit the area—it was an excuse but also a legitimate concern. Space admitted he had been full of shit and didn't know how to handle a boat. It was decided to stick to the original plan, and the two men observed the goings-on at the port for the next three to four days, hoping for the storm to abate. The next night was going to be it—they were going to sneak into one fishing vessel. The time had come to get back to one of the beach houses they had used, and rest during the night. Approaching the small house, Lehmann noticed the smell of ersatz cigarettes. The Ranger sergeant moved back into the woods while Space went inside to have a look. An hour later, Lehmann sneaked back and heard two voices coming from the window, one of which belonged to his American travel companion. To take a better look, he sneaked up the stairs and looked through the crack of the door, only to see Space and a bunch of German Luftwaffe personnel having a fine conversation and a good time. Turning away, he accidentally made a noise and was immediately captured and went on to proceed to participate in the conversation, to the delight of the Germans.

Things weren't that delightful the next day, when the entire local police force arrived, composed of two men, with one being the local chief of police, looking very much like the Kaiser, in an immaculate, bemedaled uniform, pickelhaube, and monocle. The old man screamed at the Americans all the way back to town, their hands shackled by a chain and a Luger pistol pointed at Lehmann's head. At the station, the chief made a phone call with much shouting that found Lehmann surprised that the guy didn't salute when hanging up. The experienced Ranger saw the chief of police clean up his desk and straighten things out, alerting him to the arrival of some superior officer. Sure enough, a small motorcade slammed to a stop outside, as heels clacked throughout the neighborhood. A German major spoke perfect English and asked the Americans how they had expected to escape. Lehmann only gave his name, serial number, and rank while at attention as though on parade. A few questions later, nothing had changed—at least not Lehmann's answers. Asking whether or not they had been treated well, he complained about having been shackled in violation of the Geneva Conventions. The major had them removed, after berating the old chief of police. The major then left, and the Americans were jailed, with Space warning Lehmann that he would get them killed with his attitude.

The next day was 7 June 1944. The invasion of France in Normandy had just happened the day before. Two guards from Stalag IIB arrived and threw them into the Kooler back at "home." At home, the Kooler was full and they, he and Space, were separated. Lehmann hung out with various nationalities and ethnicities. Finally, in the Kooler, he shared the accommodation with French Foreign Legionnaires, one of whom he dubbed Freddo. "He taught me to sing 'Belle Ami' in French, excised some awful, ragged warts that covered near my whole chin (by tying each with pieces of cotton thread, tightening each a little a day, until they dropped off), and cheerfully accepted defeat as I became chess champion of the barracks and he became the runner-up." Unfortunately, for Lehmann, Space was tossed into his cell, where things devolved into fights, leaving the Ranger bruised and battered, needing medical care. Malaria and dysentery struck as well; and by the time Lehmann was returned to his Kooler, Space had been released into the general population. Three weeks to go until he got out of the Kooler, since he spent most of his sentence in the medical facility. Lehmann worked out as best as he could in his cell and out in the yard, hoping for a rematch. This was helped along with rations being served by Ranger Joe Phillips, who also brought cheese, meat, and other edible stuff collected from the prisoners. Finally released, Lehmann found Space and clocked him into the netherworld. There would be no more fights after this.

The Escape Committee run within the confines of the prison didn't impress the Ranger sergeant, to the point where he threatened to report them after the war's conclusion. They fitted him out with identification papers as a paroled French POW permitted to travel the local areas, and handed him money, a map, and a compass. During his time, he worked details, digging ditches for repair work. Two clear memories stayed with him:

> Prominent in the fill which we excavated were myriad broken black marble stones, such as are used for storefronts. One side of the slabs had Jewish characters scribed into the polished surface. Clearly, the "Final Solution," here as elsewhere, included eradication of Jewish characters on storefronts. This then added substance to reports of the horrors of Jewish persecution of which we'd read and heard in newspapers and broadcasts back home. One of the fears we all had was for the Jews among us prisoners. Oddly, I know not of a single instance of mistreatment of Jewish POWs; actually, many were in superior positions because of their abilities to speak the language. Another memory that endures is of the sometimes multiple "funeral" processions down the street where we worked. The procession invariably consisted of a horse-drawn hearse, a carriage for the elderly among the mourners, with most trailing,

black-clad, behind. These were part of the ceremonies for
Krauts killed on the Russian and Western Fronts; of course,
there were no remains in the caskets, but all had a Kraut
helmet riding atop them. The same caskets were used over
and over. As the hearse went by, we all stood at attention,
with bared heads and solemn faces, singing softly, muting
the words: "The little black hearse goes riding by, And you
may be-ee the next to die." The mourners, as they passed,
smiled and nodded, "Danke . . . Danke . . . Danke" in appreciation of our "respect" for a fallen foe.

The second attempt came after this. At 130 pounds, well below his
fighting weight, Lehmann squeezed through a barred window and
wire, wearing his new Red Cross–provided Class-A uniform that had
been dyed into a nice reddish brown. A change in buttons and sport-
ing a spiffy beret made him the best-dressed "Froggie" in German
prison. Trying to bluff his way into a ticket to Berlin, the old employee
knew bullshit when he saw it and reached for the phone. "A large
stack of shit was about to hit the fan." He sprinted out of the station
all the way into the outlying woods. Back to the Baltic. Back to the
original plan. A few days of lurking about en route to his freedom,
he got hit with another bad case of malaria and fever. He woke up in
Stalag IIB's hospital. Soldiers had found him passed out along the
road. The Commandant gave him two weeks in the Kooler, which surprised Lehmann: He had expected more. The Commandant simply
said, "It is a soldier's duty to escape—but don't do it again, verstehen
[understand]?"

In his time as a single occupant, he read histories and whatever else he had access to. In the exercise yard, he met Jack Fisher,
a tail gunner who had survived being shot out of the air during
a raid. Thinking it was easier to escape from Stalag IIB's work
camps than from the Air Force POW camp he had been in, he
switched identity and was transferred as an infantry grunt to his
new home. He tirelessly asked Lehmann about his escape attempts.
Much to Lehmann's surprise, after the war he bumped into Jack Fisher

in Baltimore on a bus. Lehmann had become a lawyer, recently having passed his bar exam. Jack became his first client to help change his name.

But the Ranger sergeant was still stuck in prison. Here he bumped into old compatriot Ranger Wayne "Pop" Ruona, who was older by four or five years. Ruona was a staff sergeant with C/3. There was also Ranger PFC Joseph P. Kiernan of C/3, a replacement at Pozzuoli, and now full-time hustler. Prison government, like all governments, was far from decent, and as such Ruona, who had been ill and exempt from work details, and Lehmann ran in the next election. But before that happened, both were called in front of Sergeant Major Bob Ehalt, the last man to have spoken with Darby at Cisterna. They were told in no uncertain terms that they could not run, because the current leaders were in touch with the Secret Service: that, in fact, the Secret Service had ordered them to stand down before ruining everything. "As a part of their demonstration of the truth of the matter, we were allowed to listen to a clandestine radio, smuggled in part by part, inside bars of G.I. soap from Red Cross supplies." They were now part of the governing circle and Ehalt had a medic inject Lehmann with something that made his temperature rise so high that he was exempt from the dreaded work assignments.

At the end of 1944, the Soviets were marching across Eastern Europe. Because of that, Stalag IIB, along with others, decided to move their prisoners to the west. From January to March 1945, the prisoners, four abreast, were on the march through winter, poorly fed, and spending the nights in abandoned houses and farms. Fisher escaped during this time. Shortly thereafter, five prisoners did the same, although Lehmann wasn't too sure about escaping yet again— it was emotionally and physically draining and the potential for severe punishment was great. But Rangering on, he did. Three of the five escapees were Rangers—Ruona, Kiernan, and Lehmann. When the column surprisingly made a U-turn to go back the way they had come, the Rangers decided to use the moment the curl of their section happened, to jump into the knee-high vegetation off the road. Serbian soldiers, under Colonel Vladimir Sykovitch, behind them played their part. When the five rushed off, the Serbians marched in place looking straight ahead, giving nothing away to the guards whose views were obstructed. The Serbians marching and covering them was a picture burned into Lehmann's mind for the rest of his life.

The escapees staggered toward the sound of the guns, ever aware that they were in hostile lands. Finding whatever food they could in fields or abandoned barns, they struggled on—fighting off starvation and capture and death. One German farmer turned his back, deliberately avoiding eye contact with them. He wanted nothing to do with anything—perhaps he disliked Hitler and the war, or perhaps he was afraid of any action he took—whatever it was. They tried to stay clear of areas where they heard dogs barking while slowly moving south. They crossed a river and at one point were in swamps up to their necks when they decided to turn back. Another time they found two British escapees but parted ways to keep the numbers small. They observed a large bomber-and-fighter contingent, in the hundreds, in aerial combat with German planes.

The shell casings showered the men in their hide site. Another time, they were discovered by a Russian slave laborer who got them food, which they cooked in an abandoned house. In April, while they were deep in a forest and sound asleep, gunfire awakened them. Hearing men crash through the woods, Lehmann spotted three men wearing camouflage and Green Berets—a familiar sight. A lieutenant, a sergeant, and a private from No. 1 Commando. What a glorious sight it was. Lehmann chased them down. After a quick consultation among the eight men, it was decided to hunker down and await the Allied troops pushing east. The Commandos had played dead during an attempted river crossing where they had been ambushed and suffered casualties. Over two days, hundreds of fleeing German soldiers rushed through the woods, too afraid to look for anyone, just desiring to escape the clutches of death. During the lull of battle, the Americans were too hungry and too tired to wait any longer. The Commando officer recommended the men to carry branches resembling rifles and to march out like an armed party.

They marched. American soldiers, not broken by the Germans. After two hours they saw someone wearing a British helmet, and Ruona told the lieutenant to wave his yellow scarf that served as a recognition sign. They had made it. They didn't get shot crossing the lines. Instead, they were given a warm welcome. Declining rations, the Americans asked for any nearby functioning farm. They were pointed in a direction. A gorge-fest was about to begin at the farm:

> I walked into one nearby and told the man of the house that we wanted some meat and eggs. This old clown had a light patch on his upper lip directly under and limited by the width of his nose, from which he had just shaved a Hitler mustache. He pleaded that they were poor people, hated Nazis—particularly Hitler—and that they had no spare food. I flicked the safety off the Kraut burp-gun [small submachine gun] which I had recently acquired, and he immediately produced an egg apiece. "Nicht Genü[g]end,"—"Not enough," I said, and motioned him toward the cellar steps, following him down into the basement. It was loaded! Sausages, pork chops, vegetables—lots of glass jars full of goodies lined shelf after shelf! I had him load a large basket of these things, together with eggs, eggs, and more eggs! I ate three large breakfasts and vomited each, one after the other.

Onward they staggered, but this time they made it to the next village and took the mayor's car, acquired a new battery and gasoline from the British, and rode in style all the way to Brussels. In typical Ranger fashion of easy-come, easy-go, they sold the car and promptly lost all their money at a dog track. Reporting to the local British authority, they were given new everything, and after some well-earned rest they were flown to Paris. On the flight, the pilot allowed Sergeant Lehmann the co-pilot's seat and pointed out the old Great War trench lines below their flight. From Paris they made their way to Le Havre's Camp Lucky Strike to be shipped home. "The chow line was tended by Kraut POWs and, when I reached into the pot for another baked potato, a Kraut rapped my knuckles with a heavy spoon. I lost it; I wrested the spoon from him and beat him about the head until he was near unconscious. Until I was able to reflect upon this, I had been unaware of the hate that had built up in me. Much lasts."

PRIVATE FIRST CLASS CLARENCE GOAD

B Company, Third Ranger Battalion

Goad had been captured south of the Calcabrini House at Cisterna. He was a hard man who had joined the Rangers when Major Alvah Miller, the Third Ranger Battalion Commander, recruited him after seeing that Goad had been to a 10-day training program at Achnacarry. Goad, born 15 December 1922, from Bainbridge, New York, was a veteran combat soldier in North Africa and Sicily, and fought with the Rangers at Salerno and Anzio. It was during the phase of the Cisterna battle, where desperate, and dangerous Rangers threw everything at German armor, from small arms, to Bazookas, to grenades including the nasty burning white phosphorous ones, and killing any surviving crew that struggled out of the vehicles, that he got knocked out by artillery. Lucky for him, and unlike Alvah Miller, Goad did not have his head shorn off. Waking up, he saw guns pointed at him and he surrendered. They were warned, if one man escaped a bunch of them would be shot. The Germans weren't fucking around— they had taken casualties. Marching along the Coliseum, he ended up working in terrible trolley yard pits with 50–60 men laboring away. From there he went north by train, strafed at least once by Allied aircraft. Some POWs escaped, leading to the prisoners losing their shoes or shoelaces and belts to irate German guards. Nothing like frozen feet, as if the other issues weren't bad enough. Goad arrived at Stalag VIIA, Germany, after a few days, without food, and was then moved to Stalag IIB.

The situation at Stalag IIB, as was the case with most if not all German camps, was appalling. Russians in cages were starved to death. They managed to catch a dog that was torn apart and eaten raw—that was how dire things were and certainly opened Goad's eyes to his future were he not to escape. How many Russians were killed after the dog episode? He did not know. Unfortunately for Ranger Goad, he was part of the death detail, moving up to 120 corpses daily for burial. Some still alive as dirt was thrown on them. He did this for a number of days. In this Stalag, thousands of Allied soldiers came and went; some traded information for better treatment and food. Goad was having none of that. He trusted no one. He was hardcore. He was in a horror show of human depravity.

Goad was lucky enough to be sent to a German work farm for prisoners. The Walter von Alton Farm, Rachdammietz, in Pomerania (now Poland) grew potatoes and beets. Here were Americans, Lithuanians, Russians, and French, men and women. Goad was attached to a forest group, felling trees, using horses to move the wood for lumber processing. He also took care of the horses. Escaping was easy as there were only four battle-damaged German guards. But surviving in enemy territory and without food, as it was hard to come by, was another challenge altogether. His first escapee lasted about four days. Starving, he approached a farmed area and was spotted. In typical obedient and fanatical German manner, he was spotted by a civilian and captured. If he escaped again, he was told, it would be bad for him.

The second attempt occurred after Ranger Goad had given a careful thought about his location, trying to piece together locations and terrain from geography books he had seen. He took off again, this time lasting two days. Reconning a home, he spotted an old German woman with a pot, which she placed on her back porch. Open terrain and country, much like in the fields of Cisterna, were once again his nemesis. The old hag spotted him and called the local police. Rearrested, he was beaten severely by them. Crying out in pain only got more physical punishment. He learned to keep his mouth shut. After rotting away in the local, filthy cell, he was released back to the farm with a threat that he would be shot the next time.

The next time was after he had healed and regained some strength. Difficult to do under the conditions but he did and fled again. Hungry, and after having found a boat that he wanted to use for his escape, Goad dug in a nearby field for potatoes. He needed to eat not just now but also once he hit the water of the Baltic Sea. No such luck, as an old German cartoon of the Kaiser rode up on a thin-legged horse. The man wore a green uniform coat with a pickelhaube, the spiked helmet used by Prussians and Germans of the Great War. To enforce his will, the German carried an old rifle. Back to jail it was for Goad. He did speak to the old man in an attempt to bamboozle him into believing he was from France. Goad spoke an old northern version of German called Platt-Deutsch. This had been a mistake. At the station, the old man told the police that his captive spoke German. Thinking he was a spy that had dropped in with a parachute, the interrogations got louder and harsher, but Goad, typical hard Ranger that he was, kept his mouth shut. The favorite German way of hitting people happened to Goad again—from behind, into his head, knocking him onto the floor where more blows and kicks shattered his teeth and knocked him out. He hurt bad, Goade recalled years later. But he wasn't shot. So far.

During the next round of questioning, Goad tried to bullshit his way out, claiming he was a simple farmer, barely in the military, and he was not an escapee but simply got lost. The Germans didn't buy it. They thought him an idiot. An army officer arrived. To prove that he was a spy who had parachuted in, they took off his shirt, looking for the telltale signs of bruises on his shoulder that he might have gotten from the opening shock of the silk and its risers. Seeing the lack of bruises, the officer agreed that Goad was not a spy but a prisoner. Unhappily for his German brutalizers, Goad was sent back to Stalag IIB and put into a cooler using a ladder—it was an underground potato cellar made out of stone and concrete, eight to nine feet wide and ten feet tall. "This is where you are going to die," said a German soldier. Twenty-one long days, he was pulled out by two Polish POWs with ropes around his body, barely able to stand on his legs. He was given three days to get better to work or that was it for him. Three days later, Ranger Goad was back at work. Polish prisoners helped him pull out his broken and rotten teeth. Shit sucked but he was alive. Ration packages from the U.S. or Britain were very few and far in between.

Goad worked. His legs had recovered, as had he. A miracle happened on 2 January 1945. While laboring in the bitter winter cold and snow, Goad was working on a rail gang. In the distance he saw a strange-looking convoy coming from the east. Horses, horse-drawn carts, and hand-pushed carts made a convoy of Germans fleeing the advancing Soviet army that laid waste and killed without remorse. Goad checked on the single guard, and when he was hidden by the small shifter engine, he rolled into the snowbank and into a ditch. He made it to the train of wagons.

Ever the Ranger, he had a nose for good things—although he didn't know it yet. But the covered wagon he picked had only one driver and so he climbed into the back where he found nothing but luxury, clothing and food. He ate, put on heavy winter clothing, slept. It got dark and he took whatever he needed for his escape—a sheep-skin coat, blankets, boots, and food. He threw the rucksack on his back as the wagons pulled into a nearby farm complex. He hid out in a barn and slept in the hayloft. He was dead to the world, waking up only because of the noises the Germans made preparing to start their journey. The problem was that it was daylight, and it was risky to climb into another wagon. He did grab food, including a soup, horse meat, ersatz coffee with a ton of sugar, offered by a farmer from a cart. Fortune favored the bold. He heard two older German women struggle to harness the horse and hitch them to the wagon. Goad took a gamble and, using pidgin German and hand signals, he explained he was from France, now displaced and a refugee, and, importantly, that he could help. He hitched the horses and rode with them for a while until a roadblock removed all the men for a work detail to dig tank traps. He joined them and dug until nightfall when the workers occupied empty German houses. Goad went with them. Shortly thereafter, he went to relieve himself and spotted a bicycle. His rucksack on his back, he pedaled to the east—to the Soviets. To the front where German soldiers did not bother him. Food, as usual, ran out.

Six days later, having slept in abandoned places en route, he awakened to sunshine and artillery fire to his front. His problem wasn't the battle; it was, as always, hunger. He located a farm and rode to it. To his joy, he heard clucking and found hens in their nest in the back of the barn, and he took two eggs. He was about to scream for joy, but his would-be scream turned to torment as he felt a sharp pain in his bottom. A bayonet had stabbed him. Turning around, he saw two Russians laughing at him. He recognized a Polish insignia on their collar, the same as some prisoners wore. Polish troops, not Russians. He sat down, put the eggs onto the ground, and raised his hands, shouting "Amerikansky."

He tossed his bicycle into the back of a brand-new American-made truck with U.S.A. insignia on it and they took him to higher ranks. Here the Soviet officer was unsympathetic but understood Goad to be an American escapee. To his question of where he was going, the officer said Moscow, to the embassy there. By foot with a paper in hand, Goad left on his bicycle only to have it stolen a little while later by another soldier. He walked east. He begged for rides on anything that moved, and he saw many displaced nationalities on his voyage. Tons of matériel was shipped to Russia to rebuild its infrastructure. Some spoke English and gave him advice or other information. In frozen Warsaw, Goad earned money by burying the dead. There was a possibility of traveling to Archangel in the north. Instead, he joined two young women on a freight train ride to Minsk, Russia. Once there, he discovered that American POWs were evacuated from Odessa, the port at the Black Sea. From Minsk he joined numerous refugees again on freight trains on their way to Kiev. On the train he helped a woman who had initially thought he wanted to steal her bundle. She accepted his help. Sitting on the floor of the train, he finally broke. Head in his hands and on his knees, he cursed his fate, no doubt in Ranger fashion. The woman he had helped spoke English, having studied it at the University of Kiev in 1937–38, telling him she was going home to her husband.

The woman took Goad to her house in Kiev where her husband was. They all spoke English, and to make money they helped clear the rubble off the streets and the rail yard for four to five days. At the yard, he heard American voices coming from some boxcars. He was about to join them when his newfound friends warned him off. Those were Americans of Russian descent and they'd be going to Moscow for interrogation, not be sent to the United States. His friends helped him get to a train heading to Odessa. They said goodbye at the boxcar, and he rolled away from their lives.

The train finally stopped, and Goad got out and walked to the nearby port in Odessa, in southern Ukraine. He saw a ship flying the Stars and Stripes and the hardcore Ranger cried and sat on the street, bawling his eyes out. Finally, Ranger Private First Class Clarence Goad, one of Alvah Miller's men, stood up and walked to the ship where a port guard promptly stopped him from joining the sailors on board. So close and yet so far. He looked at them, raising his hands in desperation, questioning this obstacle. He walked to her, and she arrested him and took Goad to her superior officer. At the office he was treated poorly and made fun of and told to strip naked. He did, was given an old blanket, and was released under the laughter of the Soviets.

Goad made it up the gangplank with the help of sailors. On board he was showered with coffee, bread, sugar, anything he could want— he passed out instead. He weighed 72 pounds. What had kept him going? "I thought it was my duty." He reenlisted on 20 June 1945 into the airborne where he served in Japan and got out in October 1948.

MAPS

Dieppe, France 363

Arzew, Algeria 364

Sened Station, Tunisia 365

El Guettar, Tunisia 366

Sicily—*Operation Husky* 367

Gela 367

Licata 367

Porto Empedocle 367

Maiori, Italy 368

Winter Line around Venafro & Mignano Gap, Italy 369

Anzio, Italy 370

Cisterna: Original Plan 371

Cisterna March 372

Cisterna: Disposition of Companies 373

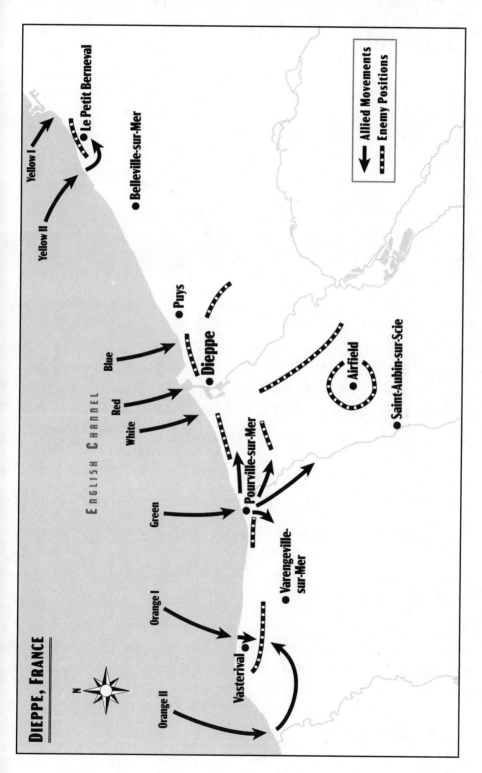

DIEPPE, FRANCE

N

ENGLISH CHANNEL

Yellow I
Yellow II

Le Petit Berneval
Belleville-sur-Mer
Puys
Dieppe
Blue
Red
White
Pourville-sur-Mer
Green
Varengeville-sur-Mer
Orange I
Orange II
Vasterival
Airfield
Saint-Aubin-sur-Scie

Allied Movements
Enemy Positions

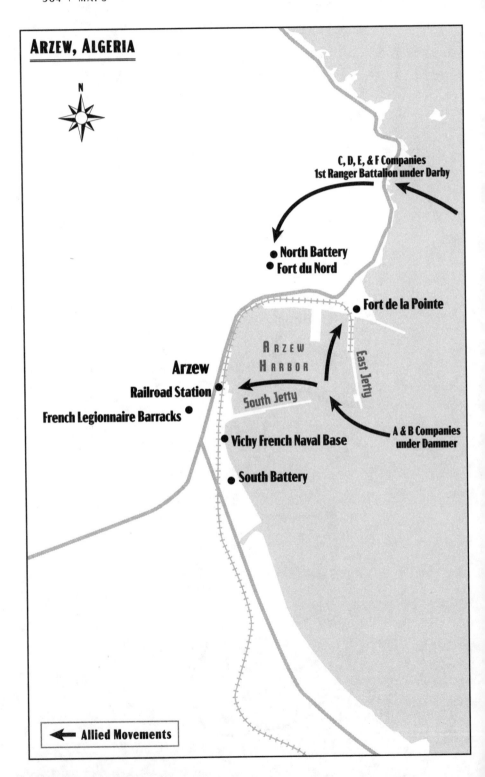

ARZEW, ALGERIA

N

C, D, E, & F Companies
1st Ranger Battalion under Darby

● North Battery
● Fort du Nord

● Fort de la Pointe

ARZEW
HARBOR

East Jetty

Arzew

Railroad Station ●

South Jetty

French Legionnaire Barracks ●

● Vichy French Naval Base

A & B Companies
under Dammer

● South Battery

◄— Allied Movements

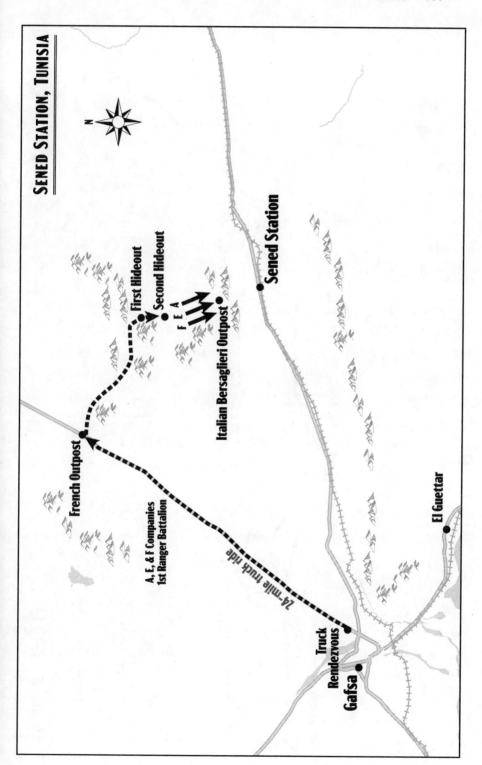

SENED STATION, TUNISIA

N

First Hideout

Second Hideout

Sened Station

F E A

Italian Bersaglieri Outpost

French Outpost

A, E, & F Companies
1st Ranger Battalion

24-mile truck ride

El Guettar

Truck
Rendezvous

Gafsa

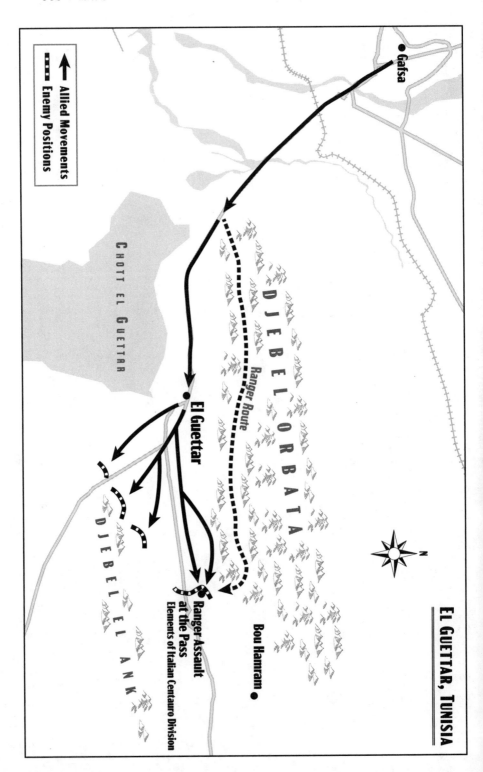

EL GUETTAR, TUNISIA

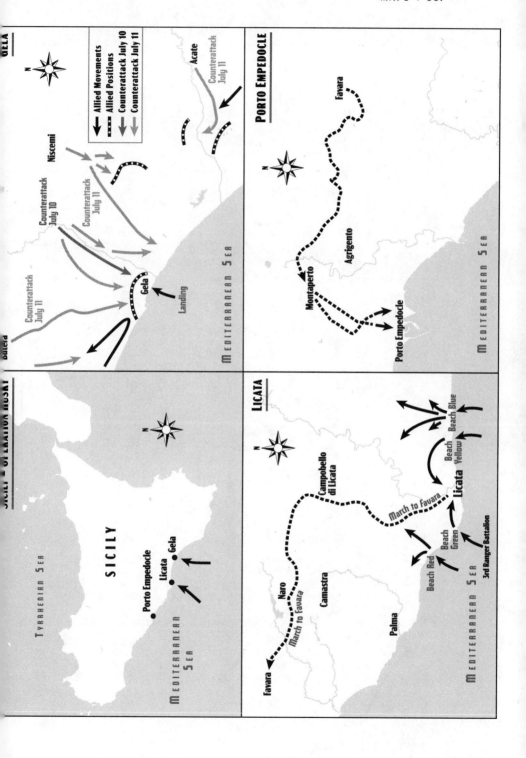

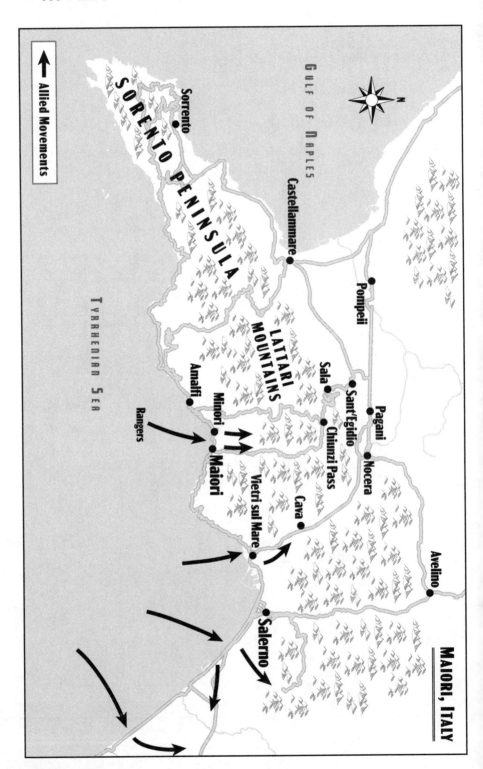

Allied Movements

SORRENTO PENINSULA

Sorrento

GULF OF NAPLES

Castellammare

Pompeii

LATTARI MOUNTAINS

Sala

Amalfi

Sant'Egidio

Pagani

Minori

Chiunzi Pass

Nocera

TYRRHENIAN SEA

Rangers

Maiori

Vietri sul Mare

Cava

Avelino

Salerno

MAIORI, ITALY

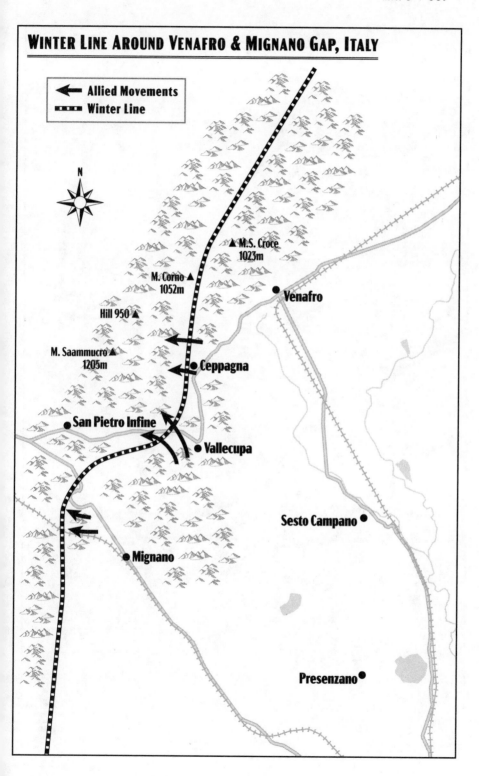

WINTER LINE AROUND VENAFRO & MIGNANO GAP, ITALY

← Allied Movements
▪▪▪▪ Winter Line

N

▲ M.S. Croce
1023m

M. Corno ▲
1052m

● Venafro

Hill 950 ▲

M. Saammucro ▲
1205m

● Ceppagna

● San Pietro Infine

● Vallecupa

Sesto Campano ●

● Mignano

Presenzano ●

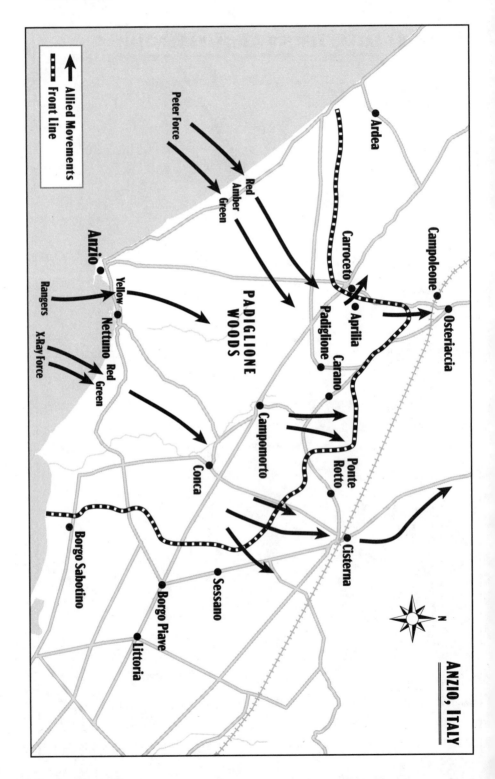

Allied Movements
Front Line

Peter Force

Red
Amber
Green

Ardea

Carroceto

Campoleone

Anzio

Rangers

Yellow

Nettuno

X-Ray Force

Red
Green

PADIGLIONE
WOODS

Padiglione

Aprilia

Carano

Osteriaccia

Campomorto

Ponte
Rotto

Conca

Cisterna

Borgo Sabotino

Sessano

Borgo Piave

Littoria

N

ANZIO, ITALY

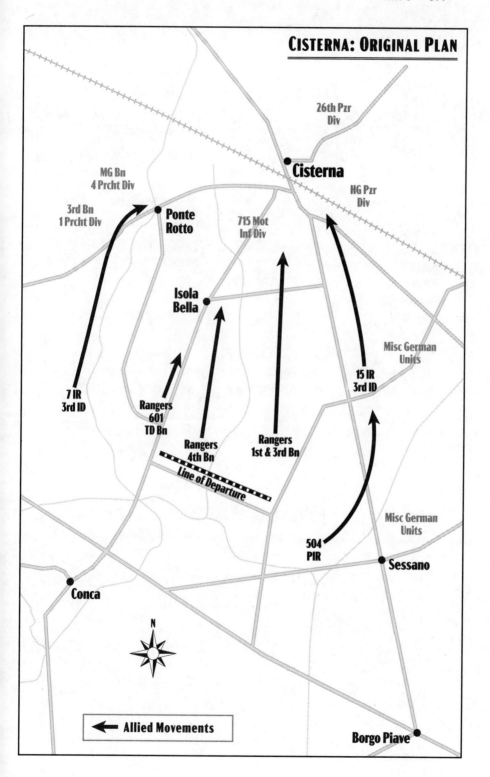

CISTERNA: ORIGINAL PLAN

26th Pzr Div

Cisterna

MG Bn 4 Prcht Div

HG Pzr Div

3rd Bn 1 Prcht Div

Ponte Rotto

715 Mot Inf Div

Isola Bella

Misc German Units

7 IR 3rd ID

15 IR 3rd ID

Rangers 601 TD Bn

Rangers 4th Bn

Rangers 1st & 3rd Bn

Line of Departure

Misc German Units

504 PIR

Sessano

Conca

N

Allied Movements

Borgo Piave

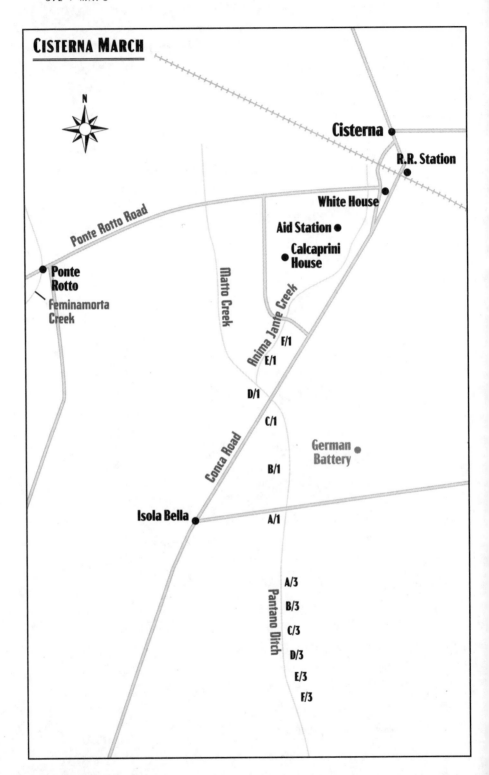

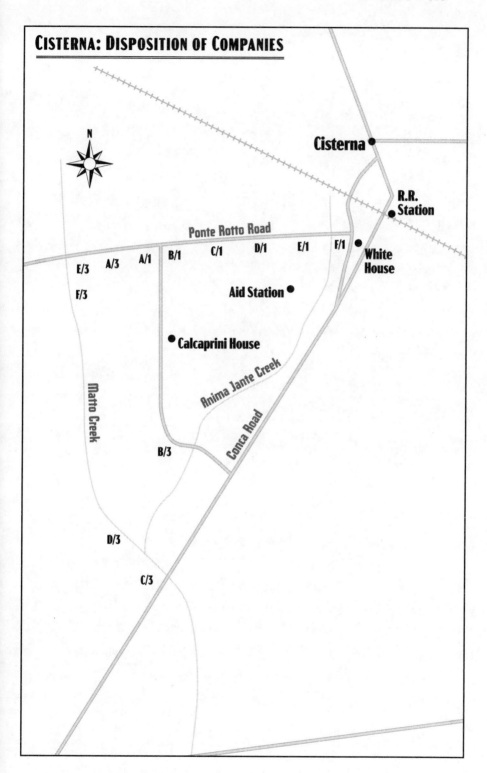

CISTERNA: DISPOSITION OF COMPANIES

SOURCE NOTES

Scan the QR code below to read through the source notes.

ACKNOWLEDGMENTS

The book depended on a number of people. Any and all mistakes are my own.

I have been fortunate to have met some of the men who were Darby Rangers. The interaction started in the late 1980s and ended a decade or so ago with the passing of the Old Timers. There are too many to thank for their confidence in speaking to a fellow Ranger, but special mention must be made. Combat Camera Phil "Snapdragon" Stern opened up his photo archives and spoke candidly about his short time with the men of the First Ranger Battalion. Jim Altieri was a great patriot who provided positive information about the men. He also was a noteworthy author and without his contribution, a lot of detail would have been lost. I inherited some of his possessions when Jim passed, including unpublished books about Darby's Rangers and the 6th Ranger Battalion's actions in the Pacific. Carl Lehmann was outstanding in sending a ton of written material. Gino Mercuriali was a constant source of floppy disks and letters, answering too many questions. Ted Fleser was kind—I still have his signature in a book. Earl Morris and Don Frederick were available when letter writing was still in vogue. Meeting some of them at Ranger reunions was always an interesting experience.

I should thank my agent, Alec Shane of Writers House—why, I don't know; I did all the work—kidding—thanks, Alec. Keith Wallman for his confidence and suggestions to make the book far better. Clara Linhoff and all the good people at Diversion Books—thank you all.

Ranger buddy Rodney LeMay who introduced me to Shirin Murphy, Heritage Officer Carrickfergus Museum, Northern Ireland. Adrian Hack of Lead The Way Tours also in Carrickfergus. The latter two have become great friends and true supporters of Darby's Rangers who willingly share anything Darby Ranger related.

Numerous collections were made available. First and foremost, for any serious work on Rangers, it has to be Ranger Bob Black's amazing collection, which is now housed at Carlisle Barracks. He always supported my efforts to preserve Ranger history, and enthusiastically championed my submission to the Ranger Hall of Fame for Captain Charles Shunstrom (it was rejected). Green Beret Roy Murray Jr. opened up his home and his father's collection without hesitation or demand. Seeing his father's Commando knife with its missing tip, broken in hand-to-hand combat, was eye-opening. Jim DeFelice and Debra Scacciaferro were super kind to make time for lunch and to share their research on Rangers in Dieppe. British author James Holland provided material of his interviews with Sicilians. West Point holds the Henry Perlmutter Collection, which was made available by Susan Lintelmann and Kirsten Cooper, PhD, and the staff at USMA, Archives and Special Collections, New York. I am fortunate to hold Ranger Jim Altieri's collection and my own collected over decades. Vietnam-era Green Beret George Bearpaw spent considerable time discussing his father, Tommy "Chief" Bearpaw of the Cherokee Nation, and provided several images. George is a great man. Vietnam veteran Thomas Lanagan transcribed his uncle's notes, Darby Ranger Thomas Sullivan, in meticulous detail. William Stanton, and his cousin Chris Stanton, provided written records of Darby Ranger John Stanton. William Shunstrom and Ranger Joe Chetwynd collected a mountain of research on Ranger Charles Shunstrom. It is hundreds of pages. Melinda Meade-White also sent hundreds of pages on Ranger Stephen J. Meade and answered many questions. Lisa McCollum, for permission to use Ranger Leilyn Young's diary. Edward Broussard and Camille Cancienne for providing a lot of material, including pictures of Ranger Edward Loustalot.

In Italy, I have to thank my good friend Angelo Munsel. He was instrumental in discussions with locals in Anzio and Cisterna. The book was made far better because of it. Angelo and I first visited the battlefields in 1999. Also, many thanks to Luciano Bucci of the Winterline Venafro Museum for his exceptional tour and his passion for all things Ranger and First Special Service Force, and his friend Franco for the espresso in Venafro. Bucci provided several excellent images because mine were rather poor considering the rain and fog that had hit the area on my visit—Ranger weather. Typical. Patrizio Colantuono—Presidente C.R.D.S.B.A., Museo dello sbarco di Anzio, or the Anzio Beachhead Museum—for his generous time and use of images. He even played a short film about the invasion and gave us a personal tour of the museum and collection. On the battlefield of Cisterna, Angelo not only found the Calcabrini House, but the property owner Augustino Augustini of the battlefield, who as a youth had dug up old boxes of food and hand grenades, which he and his friends began to detonate until the local *carabinieri* arrived. Augustini's father had discovered tanks and vehicles on their field. A warm thank-you to Renzo Mastracci, nephew of Renzo Mastracci, for providing details about Renzo's death in the early hours at Anzio. Thanks to the many Italian civilians who helped in Maiori, Venafro, Rome, and Cisterna.

A special shout-out to Paul Woodadge of WW2TV who provided introductions to several of his remarkable guests—many thanks, Paul. Rangers Mike Hall, Karl Monger, and Jeff Mellinger of the Three Rangers Foundation. The presidents, Brian Halstead of the United States Army Ranger Association and Art Attaway of the 75th Ranger Regiment Association. The great people at Carlisle Barracks—the Army Heritage Center Foundation; Stephen M. Bye; Lisa Newman; Thomas Buffenbarger, B.S.L.; and Justine Melone. A special thank-you for preserving history. Jim Ginther, PhD, supervisory archivist, Eisenhower Presidential Library, Museum, and Boyhood Home. Col (ret.) Edmund Libby, who provided an overlay of the battle of Cisterna. It was extremely useful walking the battlefield in 2024. John Dubuisson, CARL Electronic Resources Librarian, who immediately hunted down and replaced missing maps of the landings at Licata and Gela. Brad St. Croix answered questions on the First Special Service Force. Ranger researcher Julie Foley Belanger provided statistics from her Ranger research. Ranger and Commando author Will Fowler provided insights and referrals. Thanks to Chris McDougal of the Texas Military Forces Museum for being a great guy and sending me a copy of Richard Burrage's memoir, *See Naples and Die!* Paul B. Brown, Archives II Reference Branch, Textual Archives Services Division, National Archives and Records Administration. Melinda M. Adams and Lora Lennertz, University of Arkansas. Joe Crittenden, Secretary of Veterans Administration, and Barbara Foreman, Cherokee Nation. Dr. David Harrisville for German sources, Jeff Leser who provided some Italian sources. Genevieve Maxwell, Senior Reference Librarian, Oscars, Academy of Motion Picture Arts and Sciences. Shannyn Johnson, Canadian War Museum, for 3D images of Dieppe. Richelle Mackenzie, Stanford University, Hoover Library & Archives. Ellie King and Andrew Bolton, The Keep (Archives), East Sussex County Council, U.K., and Steph Georgalakis, New Haven Parish Council, East Sussex, U.K., for sourcing an original map of the raid on Dieppe. Sarah Roberts, Michigan State University Archives & Historical Collections, for going above and beyond on Cadet Alvah Miller. Anna Webb, government information specialist (FOIA/PA analyst), and Christopher Nesbitt, FOIA officer, U.S. Army Special Operations Command. Bree Russell, curator at Warner Bros. Archives, University of Southern California. Oliver Snaith, Archives & Research Collections | Libraries & Collections, King's College London, U.K. Padej Kumlertsakul, The National Archives, Kew, U.K. Megan E. Harris, Veterans History Project, Library of Congress, for answering several questions about their collection. Captain Nicholas A. McCahill, assistant professor of military science, Michigan State University Army ROTC. Suzanne Brady-Dues and Joan Malmrose of the Dickinson Historical Society. If I missed anyone, please accept my deepest apologies.

We know now the world has not been saved for democracy and there can be no war to end all wars. For violence only breeds violence. We know now if a strong nation is not willing to compromise, if a nation is greedy for world power and its leaders lust for new territory—then the road leads to war.

—Don Whitehead

ABOUT THE AUTHOR

MIR BAHMANYAR earned a BA in history from UC Berkeley, enlisted in the 2nd Battalion, 75th Ranger Regiment, and attained an MA in war studies from King's College London. He served on the Board of Directors for the 75th Ranger Regiment Association and was an associate historian of the World War II Ranger Battalions Association. He has been a military technical advisor on such films as *The Good German*, *Black Hawk Down*, and *We Were Soldiers*; a German-language coach; and a producer and writer in Hollywood. He cowrote and produced the award-winning independent historical film *Soldier of God* and has authored numerous books and articles on everything from ancient history to modern war, which have been translated into Arabic, German, Japanese, Polish, and Spanish, and have been featured on several U.S. Army reading lists. Holding dual U.S. and Canadian citizenship, he lives in Toronto.